RETHINKING INTERNATIONAL LAW AND JUSTICE

Law, Ethics and Governance Series

Series Editor: Charles Sampford, Director, Institute for Ethics, Governance and Law, Griffith University, Australia

Recent history has emphasised the potentially devastating effects of governance failures in governments, government agencies, corporations and the institutions of civil society. 'Good governance' is seen as necessary, if not crucial, for economic success and human development. Although the disciplines of law, ethics, politics, economics and management theory can provide insights into the governance of organisations, governance issues can only be dealt with by interdisciplinary studies, combining several (and sometimes all) of those disciplines. This series aims to provide such interdisciplinary studies for students, researchers and relevant practitioners.

Recent titles in this series

International Rule of Law and Professional Ethics
Edited by Vesselin Popovski
ISBN 978-1-4724-2803-5

Responsibility to Protect and Sovereignty
Edited by Charles Sampford and Ramesh Thakur
ISBN 978-1-4094-3782-6

Protection of Refugees and Displaced Persons in the Asia Pacific Region
Edited by Angus Francis and Rowena Maguire
ISBN 978–1–4094–5540–0

Intellectual Liberty
Natural Rights and Intellectual Property
Hugh Breakey
ISBN 978–1–4094–4711–5

Health Workforce Governance
Improved Access, Good Regulatory Practice, Safer Patients
Edited by Stephanie D. Short and Fiona McDonald
ISBN 978–1–4094–2921–0

Fiduciary Duty and the Atmospheric Trust
Edited by Ken Coghill, Charles Sampford and Tim Smith
ISBN 978–1–4094–2232–7

Rethinking International Law and Justice

Edited by

CHARLES SAMPFORD
Griffith University, Australia

SPENCER ZIFCAK
Australian Catholic University, Australia

DERYA AYDIN OKUR
Istanbul Kültür University, Turkey

Routledge
Taylor & Francis Group
LONDON AND NEW YORK

First published 2015 by Ashgate Publishing

Published 2016 by Routledge
2 Park Square, Milton Park, Abingdon, Oxfordshire OX14 4RN
711 Third Avenue, New York, NY 10017, USA

First issued in paperback 2016

Routledge is an imprint of the Taylor & Francis Group, an informa business

British Library Cataloguing in Publication Data
A catalogue record for this book is available from the British Library

The Library of Congress has cataloged the printed edition as follows:
Rethinking international law and justice / by Charles Sampford, Spencer Zifcak and Derya Aydin Okur.
pages cm. – (Law, ethics and governance)
Includes bibliographical references and index.
ISBN 978-1-4724-2668-0 (hardback)
1. International law. I. Sampford, C. J. G. (Charles J. G.) editor. II. Zifcak, Spencer, 1950– editor. III. Aydin Okur, Derya, 1978– editor.
KZ3410.R48 2014
341–dc23

2014016687

ISBN 13: 978-1-138-63797-9 (pbk)
ISBN 13: 978-1-4724-2668-0 (hbk)

Contents

Abbreviations *vii*
List of Contributors *xi*
Acknowledgements *xiii*

1 Rethinking International Law and Justice 1
Spencer Zifcak

PART I: INTERNATIONAL HUMANITARIAN LAW

2 A Right to Fight: The Belligerent's Privilege 23
Steve Nabors

3 Justice and Protection of Civilians in Armed Conflicts through the Enforcement of the International Legal Obligations: The Case of the Gaza Strip 63
Davide Tundo

4 How Effective are National Remedies in Securing International Justice? 81
Selman Karakul

5 Rethinking Justice: Individual Criminal Responsibility, Immunity and Torture 101
Amrita Mukherjee

6 Interpreting the Most-Favoured-Nation Clause in Investment Treaty Arbitration: Interpretation as a Process of Creating an Obligation? 127
Tomoko Ishikawa

PART II: NON-STATE ACTORS IN PROMOTING JUSTICE

7 Accountability of Multinational Corporations for Human Rights and Environmental Abuse: How Far Can Extraterritorial Jurisdiction Go? 151
Angelica Bonfanti

8 The Alien Tort Statute as Access to Justice, Post *Kiobel*: When the International Norm Prohibiting Nonconsensual Human Experimentation is Violated 179
Bethany J. Spielman

9 The Role of NGOs and Accountability of Corporations for Human Right Infringements 193
Genny Ngende

10 Non-State Actors and International Climate Justice under Global Climate Governance 213
Saheed Alabi

11 The Status of Non-State Actors under the International Rule of Law: A Search for Global Justice 233
Mohammad H. Zarei and Azar Safari

PART III: RETHINKING ASPECTS OF INTERNATIONAL JUSTICE

12 The Responsibility to Protect at the United Nations 255
Spencer Zifcak

13 Is Justice the First Virtue of International Institutions? 281
Charles Sampford

14 Is it Justice or Justice(s)? The Concept of Justice in Western and Islamic Natural Law Traditions 303
Ahmet Ulvi Türkbağ

15 General Principles of Law and International Law-Making 313
Gábor Sulyok

Index *333*

Abbreviations

ACOA	American Committee on Africa
ACTUP	AIDS Coalition to Unleash Power
ANC	African National Congress
ASEAN	Association of Southeast Asian Nations
ATS	Alien Tort Statute
AU	Arab Union
AZT	azidothymidine
BIIJ	Brandeis Institute for International Judges
BIT	bilateral investment treaty
BRICS	Brazil, Russia, India, China and South Africa
CAN	Climate Action Network
CCPR	International Covenant on Civil and Political Rights
CDM	Clean Development Mechanism
CEC	Climate Ethics Consensus
CESCR	Committee on Economic, Social and Cultural Rights
CIEL	Center for International Environmental Law
CoE	Council of Europe
CRC	Convention on the Rights of the Child
CSR	corporate social responsibility
DPKO	Department of Peacekeeping Operations
DRC	Democratic Republic of the Congo
ECHR	Convention for the Protection of Human Rights and Fundamental Freedoms (European Convention on Human Rights)
ECJ	European Court of Justice
ECOWAS	Economic Community of West African States
ECtHR	European Court of Human Rights
EPA	Environmental Protection Agency
EU	European Union
FAO	Food and Agriculture Organization
FET	fair and equitable treatment
FIELD	Foundation for International Environmental Law and Development
FoE	Friends of the Earth
GDP	gross domestic product
GIC	Governor in Council
GPW	Third Geneva Convention of 1949
HRL	Human Rights Law
IACHR	Inter-American Commission on Human Rights

ICC	International Criminal Court
ICCPR	International Covenant on Civil and Political Rights
ICESCR	International Covenant on Economic, Social and Cultural Rights
ICISS	International Commission on Intervention and State Sovereignty
ICJ	International Court of Justice
ICRC	International Committee of the Red Cross
ICTFY	International Criminal Tribunal for the Former Yugoslavia
ICTR	International Criminal Tribunal for Rwanda
ICTY	International Criminal Tribunal for Yugoslavia
Idasa	Institute for Democratic Alternatives for South Africa
IGO	intergovernmental organization
IHL	international humanitarian law
ILC	International Law Commission
ILO	International Labour Organization
IPCC	Intergovernmental Panel on Climate Change
IROL	International Rule of Law
KPIA	Kyoto Protocol Implementation Act
MDG	Millennium Development Goals
MFN	most-favoured-nation
MNC	multi-national corporation
MSF	Médecins Sans Frontières
NAM	Non-Aligned Movement
NATO	North Atlantic Treaty Organization
NEPAD	New Partnership for Africa's Development
NGO	non-governmental organization
NIPCC	Nongovernmental International Panel on Climate Change
NSA	non-state actor
OAS	Organization of American States
OECD	Organisation for Economic Cooperation and Development
OED	Oxford English Dictionary
oPt	occupied Palestinian territory
P-5	permanent members of the United Nations Security Council
PCHR	Palestinian Centre for Human Rights of Gaza
PCIJ	Permanent Court of International Justice
POC	Protection of Civilians
R2P	Responsibility to Protect
ROL	Rule of Law
S-5	Singapore, Costa Rica, Lichtenstein, Jordan and Switzerland
SAIRR	South African Institute of Race Relations
SCSL	Special Court for Sierra Leone
SDG	Sustainable Development Goals
SERAP	Socio-Economic Rights and Accountability Project
TAC	Treatment Action Campaign
TRC	Truth and Reconciliation Commission

UDHR	Universal Declaration of Human Rights
UK	United Kingdom
UN	United Nations
UNCAT	United Nations Convention against Torture
UNCTAD	United Nations Conference on Trade and Development
UNDP	United Nations Development Programme
UNEP	United Nations Environment Programme
UNFCCC	United Nations Framework Convention on Climate Change
UNGA	United Nations General Assembly
UNHCR	United Nations High Commissioner for Refugees
UNSC	United Nations Security Council
UNSRSG	United Nations Special Representative of the Secretary-General
US	United States (of America)
VCLT	Vienna Convention of the Law of Treaties
WHO	World Health Organization
WTO	World Trade Organization
WWF	World Wide Fund for Nature

List of Contributors

Saheed Alabi is a tutor in Law, doctoral candidate and Campbell Burn scholar at the University of Strathclyde Law School, Glasgow. His doctoral thesis focuses on the use of climate litigation in reshaping domestic and international responses to climate change. He is a barrister and solicitor of the Supreme Court of Nigeria.

Angelica Bonfanti is a research fellow in International Law and a lecturer in International Investment Law & Dispute Settlement and International Trade Law at the University of Milan.

Tomoko Ishikawa is an assistant professor at the Waseda Institute for Advanced Study in Japan and a qualified Japanese lawyer.

Selman Karakul is an assistant professor of Public Law at Doğuş University, Istanbul. He has worked for the Ministry of Foreign Affairs of Turkey as a human rights expert.

Amrita Mukherjee (Dr) is Lecturer at the School of Law, University of Leeds.

Steve Nabors is a graduate of American University's JD/MA dual-degree programme, where he received a *juris doctor* focused on international human rights, the law of war and national security, and a master's degree in international politics specializing in asymmetric warfare.

Genny Ngende is a masters graduate in International Law with International Relations from the University of Kent. She is a PhD researcher in the Department of International and European Law at Vrije Universiteit Brussel (VUB). She is also a member of the Law and Development Network in Belgium.

Derya Aydin Okur is an assistant professor of International Law and the Head of the Law of the Sea Section at Istanbul Kültür University Law Faculty, Istanbul, Turkey. She is also the founding member and Vice-Principal of the Vocational School of Justice at Istanbul Kültür University.

Azar Safari has a BA in Law from Beheshti University, Tehran and an LLM in Human Rights Law from Allame Tabatabaee University, Tehran. The title of her doctoral thesis is, 'The State's Obligation to Prevent Human Rights Violations by NSAs'. She is a human rights activist.

Charles Sampford is Director, IEGL, The Institute for Ethics, Governance and Law (a joint initiative of the United Nations University, Griffith, Queensland University of Technology, the Australian National University, Center for Asian Integrity in Manila and OP Jindal Global University, Delhi); President, International Institute for Public Ethics; Foundation Dean and Professor of Law and Research Professor in Ethics, Griffith University; Adjunct Professor, QUT and York.

Bethany J. Spielman is Professor of Health Law and Medical Ethics at Southern Illinois University School of Medicine and Law School.

Gábor Sulyok is an associate professor and Vice-Dean for academic affairs at Széchenyi István University, Deák Ferenc Faculty of Law and Political Sciences, Győr, Hungary.

Davide Tundo is a lawyer, member of the bar of Lleida (Spain), currently an international legal consultant within the International Unit of the Palestinian Centre for Human Rights of Gaza (PCHR), Palestine.

Ahmet Ulvi Türkbağ is a professor in and the Head of the Philosophy and Sociology of Law Department at Galatasaray University and a member of the Turkish Philosophical Society.

Mohammad H. Zarei is an assistant professor in the Faculty of Law at Shahid Beheshti University, Tehran, Iran

Spencer Zifcak holds the Allan Myers Chair of Law and is Professor of Law at Australian Catholic University.

Acknowledgements

This research was supported under an Australian Research Council (ARC) Linkage Grant: Building the Rule of Law in International Affairs. The views expressed herein are those of the authors and are not necessarily those of the Australian Research Council.

The editors also wish to acknowledge the support provided by the Center for International Governance Innovation (CIGI), the UN Rule of Law Unit and the United Nations University.

Chapter 1
Rethinking International Law and Justice

Spencer Zifcak

Overview

The past two decades have witnessed a substantial revision in thinking about the nature and scope of international law. The shift is encapsulated in an alteration in thought as to who should be the primary subject of the law. There is now a progressive appreciation in political and legal spheres that the primary concern of international law should be not only with the relations between sovereign states but also and equally with the protection of the individual dignity of the human person.[1] This shift is most evident in the recent prominence given to the idea of human security, its character and advancement. Beneath this change in perspective there lies an awakening moral commitment to the international rule of law and to the incremental achievement of some legitimate form of global justice.[2]

Serious attention to these matters was galvanized in two reports commissioned by the then Secretary-General of the United Nations (UN), Kofi Annan, in 2004. The first report was that of the High-Level Panel on Threats, Challenges and Change.[3] The Panel was asked to address four key issues. First, it dealt with contemporary challenges to international peace and security. Next, it considered possible reforms to the existing international system of collective security in the interests of dealing more effectively with international and intranational conflict and violence. Then

---

1 Kofi Annan, 'Two Concepts of Sovereignty', *Economist*, 18 September 1999.

2 See generally J. Glover, *Humanity: A Moral History of the Twentieth Century* (New Haven, CT: Yale University Press, 2000); J. Goldstein et al., *Legalization and World Politics* (Cambridge, MA: MIT Press, 2001); D. Held, *Global Covenant: The Social Democratic Alternative to the Washington Consensus* (Cambridge: Polity Press, 2004); T. Meron, *The Humanization of International Law* (Boston, MA: Martinus Nijhoff, 2006); A. Peters, 'Humanity as the Alpha and Omega of Sovereignty', *European Journal of International Law* 20, no. 3 (2009); S. Pinker, *The Better Angels of Nature: The Decline of Violence in History and Its Causes* (London: Penguin Books, 2011); R. Teitel, *Humanity's Law* (Oxford: Oxford University Press, 2011); A. Cassese, ed., *Realizing Utopia: The Future of International Law* (Oxford: Oxford University Press, 2012).

3 United Nations, 'High Level Panel on Threats, Challenges and Change, a More Secure World: Our Shared Responsibility', UN Document A/59/565 (2004), para. 30; Kofi Annan, *Larger Freedom: Towards Development, Security and Human Rights for All* (New York: United Nations, 2005).

it turned its attention to the existing functioning of the major organs of the UN. Finally it proposed an extensive programme of reform in their operation.

The Panel began by identifying new and existing threats to international security. In doing so, it engaged in a significant conceptual shift. It did not confine itself to threats of war, civil disorder, terrorism and nuclear weaponry. It cast its net more widely to draw in less evident but no less important causal factors. These included poverty, infectious disease, organized crime, the abuse of human rights, and environmental degradation. In the Panel's view, security, development and human rights were inextricably linked. Each contributed to and was affected by the other. One could no longer therefore consider the problem of international peace and security in isolation. Their protection was critically dependent upon the achievement of economic and social security and international respect for human rights.[4]

Perhaps the most important thread that ran through the Panel's analysis was that, in certain circumstances, the protection of human security might override the prerogatives of state sovereignty. By switching its conceptual frame from one that privileged states' entitlements to another that was concerned with states' responsibilities to underpin and maintain their people's individual and collective security, the Panel sought to situate human security at the centre of global political, legal and social concerns. As its report put the matter,

> What we seek to protect reflects what we value. The Charter of the United Nations seeks to protect all states, not because they are intrinsically good but because they are necessary to achieve the dignity, justice, worth and safety of their citizens. These are the values that should be at the heart of any collective security system for the 21st century, but too often states have failed to protect and promote them. The collective security we seek to build today asserts a shared responsibility on the part of all states and international institutions, and those who lead them, to do just that.[5]

A second report, from the Millennium Project, sought to undergird and supplement the new approach.[6] It proposed a concrete plan of action through which the Millennium Development Goals for the reduction of poverty could be achieved.[7] Under this plan, developing countries would take primary responsibility for strengthening their economic and social performance. For their part, developed countries should

4 See further United Nations Commission on Human Security, *Human Security Now* (New York: Commission on Human Security, 2003).

5 United Nations, 'High Level Panel on Threats, Challenges and Change, a More Secure World: Our Shared Responsibility', UN Document A/59/565, para. 30.

6 UN Millennium Project, *Investing in Development: A Practical Plan to Achieve the Millennium Development Goals* (New York: United Nations, 2005).

7 See further, P. Collier, *The Bottom Billion: Why the Poorest Countries Are Failing and What Can Be Done About It* (Oxford: Oxford University Press, 2007).

increase their development assistance so that the Goals could be attained by 2015. Together the two reports provided the foundations upon which new thinking about the role of law and politics in international affairs might be constructed.[8]

International law has been at the centre of subsequent developments that have promoted this expanded conception of security. Moving to the position that its original concern with state sovereignty should now be balanced by a parallel commitment to the advancement of human security, international law has undergone rapid change substantively and procedurally. Perhaps the two most prominent threads of that change have been, first, a progressive extension of states' legal responsibility to prevent the commission of genocide and crimes against humanity and to protect civilian populations from the ravages of violent conflict. Secondly, there has been a remarkable expansion in international legal mechanisms designed to ascribe individual responsibility for the commission of such crimes and to try to punish them. A desire to limit states' internal sovereignty in the interests of the protection of people's fundamental human rights has been a powerful and unifying force in both of those trends.

A third thread has emerged even more recently. That is, a growing recognition within international law, in particular in international human rights law, of the significant role played by non-state actors in the commission of human rights violations and, consequently, the need for states and international institutions to regulate them. Each of these threads deserves further elaboration. The purpose of this volume is to cast a new and critical eye over prominent aspects of these significant legal innovations.

Each of the threads identified has been driven by its context. The most significant driver has been the change in the nature and extent of global violence.[9] War between states has faded at the same time as wars and violence within them has increased dramatically. States remain significant initiators of violence within borders, but they have been joined there by non-state actors, in particular rebel movements and terrorist organizations. The changing character and intensity of violence, engendered by alterations in its forums and actors, has focused global attention as never before upon the fate of individual civilians in its wake. Violence against citizens has increased exponentially. Out of this, the revivified concern with human security has arisen.

One result has been an expansion in and increasing confluence between international humanitarian law, human rights law and criminal law.[10] Common

8 See further, M. Salomon, *Global Responsibility for Human Rights: World Poverty and the Development of International Law* (Oxford: Oxford University Press, 2007).

9 See M. Kaldor, *New and Old Wars: Organized Violence in a Global Era* (Stanford, CA: Stanford University Press, 1999); M. Leitenberg, *Deaths in Wars and Conflicts in the Twentieth Century* (Ithaca, NY: Cornell University Peace Studies Program, 2003).

10 See R. Provost, *International Human Rights and Humanitarian Law* (Cambridge: Cambridge University Press, 2002); M. Byers, *War Law* (London: Atlantic Books, 2005); D. Wippman and M. Evangelista, *New Wars, New Laws: Applying the Wars of Law in*

Article 3 of the Geneva Conventions, which provides for the humane treatment of non-combatants, has attained new prominence and two Additional Protocols have been added to the Conventions. The protection of civilians has become a core principle of international humanitarian law. Article 51(2) of Additional Protocol 1, for example, prohibits acts or threats of violence the primary purpose of which is to spread terror among the civilian population.[11] This prohibition has also matured into a principle of customary international law. Consequently, it binds all countries, even those who have not ratified the conventions and protocols. Protocol 1 adds that fundamental human rights apply fully in situations of armed conflict. Common Article 3 of the Geneva Conventions extends its protections of civilians to any armed conflict, thus embracing not only interstate conflict but also ethnic and religious civil wars and transnational terror.

The reach of international humanitarian law has again been significantly expanded in the Statutes of the International Criminal Tribunals for Yugoslavia (ICTY) and Rwanda (ICTR).[12] The Tribunals were given the power to prosecute individuals for breaches of the Geneva Conventions, the violations of the laws or customs of war, genocide, and crimes against humanity. The way was opened for persons to be prosecuted for the crimes defined when committed in armed conflict, whether the conflict was international or internal in character, and directed against civilians. The definition of crimes against humanity has been widened from crimes such as murder, extermination, torture and rape to include persecution on political, racial and religious grounds and other similarly inhumane actions.

Subsequent judicial decisions made by the ICTY have further demonstrated the progressive interpenetration of international humanitarian and human rights law. Each of these fields retains its exclusive jurisdictional domains, but in particular in relation to issues relevant to international crimes and criminal proceedings, the lines of demarcation have become more hazy. The ICTY has determined, for example, that crimes against humanity do not require a connection to international armed conflict. It is the occurrence of a widespread and systematic attack on a civilian population that makes the relevant act a crime

---

Twenty First Century Conflicts (Ardsley, NY: Transnational, 2002); O. Ben-Nafatli, ed., *International Humanitarian Law and International Human Rights Law* (Oxford: Oxford University Press, 2011).

11 International Committee of the Red Cross (ICRC), 'Protocol Additional to the Geneva Conventions of 12 August 1949, and Relating to the Protection of Victims of International Armed Conflicts (Protocol I)', 1125 UNTS 3 (Geneva: ICRC, 8 June 1977).

12 T. Meron, 'War Crimes in Yugoslavia and the Development of International Law', *American Journal of International Law* 88(1994); M. Othman, *Accountability for International Humanitarian Law Violations: The Case of Rwanda and East Timor* (Heidelberg: Berlin Springer, 2005); W. Schabas, *Genocide in International Law*, 2nd edn (Cambridge: Cambridge University Press, 2009); D. Scheffer, *All the Missing Souls: A Personal History of the War Crimes Tribunals* (Princeton, NJ: Princeton University Press, 2012).

against humanity as opposed to a war crime.[13] Similarly, the Geneva Conventions have increasingly been interpreted with reference to their implications for the protection of the human person.

In that context, the second remarkable development in international law has been the introduction of new judicial mechanisms and procedures designed to confer individual responsibility for the commission of grave crimes against humanity.[14] Following from the ad hoc criminal tribunals for Yugoslavia and Rwanda, the International Criminal Court was created.[15] Hybrid tribunals such as the Special Court for Sierra Leone and similar bodies in Lebanon and Cambodia have come into being. Truth and Reconciliation Commissions in countries as diverse as South Africa and East Timor have also been initiated as a crucial component in the pursuit of transitional justice.[16] These new judicial and quasi-judicial bodies have stepped into the gaps left initially by the laws of war and their limited application to novel arenas and situations of institutional violence, civil war and terrorist attack. Human rights law and international criminal law have combined to provide new and creative means for the prosecution of offences against humanity in the interests of protecting people and peoples who are vulnerable to grave harm.

Within that framework, a crucially important development has been the expansion of the idea and actuality of universal jurisdiction:[17]

> Today, international law will sometimes … reflect not only substantive agreement as to certain universally condemned behaviour but also procedural agreement that universal jurisdiction exists to prosecute a subset of that behaviour. That subset includes torture, genocide, crimes against humanity and war crimes. The fact that this procedural consensus exists suggests that recognition of universal jurisdiction in respect to a limited set of norms is consistent with principles of international comity.[18]

---

13 Prosecutor v Tadić, Appeals Chamber, International Criminal Tribunal for the former Yugoslavia, Case No. IT-94-1-AR72, 15 July 1999.

14 R. Teitel and R. Howse, 'Crossjudging: Tribunalization in a Fragmented but Interconnected Global Order', *New York University Journal of International Law and Politics* 41 (2009): 959.

15 W. Schabas, *An Introduction to the International Criminal Court*, 4th edn (Cambridge: Cambridge University Press, 2011).

16 P. Hayner, *Unspeakable Truths: Confronting State Terror and Atrocity*, 2nd edn (London: Routledge, 2011).

17 N. Roht-Arriaza, 'Universal Jurisdiction: Steps Forwards, Steps Back', *Leiden Journal of International Law* 17 (2004); Amnesty International, 'Universal Jurisdiction: A Preliminary Survey of Legislation around the World' (2011); M. Langer, 'The Diplomacy of Universal Jurisdiction', *American Journal of International Law* 105(2011); S. Macedo, ed., *Universal Jurisdiction: National Courts and the Prosecution of Serious Crimes under International Law* (Philadelphia, PA: University of Pennsylvania Press, 2011).

18 *Sosa v Alvarez-Machain*, 542 US 692 (Supreme Court of the United States 2004), per Breyer J.

It is, of course, essential that the exercise of universal jurisdiction is confined to only those crimes the international community regards as most grave. But once that prerequisite is met, obstacles to its application such as extraterritoriality necessarily fall away. Consequently it has now been recognized that states may prosecute individuals for the commission of crimes against humanity even though the state in question has no territorial links with the offence or ties of nationality to the alleged offender. The offences are subject to international jurisdiction as a matter of customary international law. Similarly, the obligations upon states derived from customary international law are generally considered as sufficiently powerful as to override any objections to their exercise on the grounds of state immunity. Crimes against humanity now attract universal jurisdiction if two preconditions are met. First, they must be contrary to a peremptory norm of international law. Secondly, they must be so serious, so systematic and so widespread that they can justly be regarded as an attack on the international legal order.[19]

The application of universal jurisdiction is not without its difficulties. An accused person must still be in the territory of the prosecuting authority. Many escape justice by not leaving their own. In many states, governments may still reserve their authority to determine whether alleged crimes will be investigated, prosecuted or tried. Particularly where the accused are senior political or military figures, there will be a natural reluctance in governmental circles to pursue individuals who may still possess substantial political power or influence. An associated difficulty relates to the achievement of an appropriate balance between keeping the peace and prosecuting crime. Potentially successful endeavours to end civil war by political means may be thwarted by the assertive exercise of universal jurisdiction, whether by a home or foreign state, to prosecute those engaged in sensitive negotiations for their perceived criminal activity during the course of the conflict. Nevertheless, particularly under the aegis of international tribunals, universal jurisdiction to try individuals responsible for crimes against humanity has become an established part of the framework of international law.

A third but still fledgling thread in international law's development as a key means of promoting human security has been its recent acknowledgement of novel problems posed by non-state actors. Actors such as armed opposition groups, non-governmental organizations, multilateral governmental bodies and transnational corporations have become prominent players both in the abuse and protection of human rights. The changing nature of violence and conflict has contributed to the emergence of new kinds of insurgency activity, rebel movements and terrorist organizations. Transnational corporations have inflicted or connived in the abuse of human rights. Their activities have consequently become an increasing focus of international concern.[20] An explosion in international treaty making has

---

19 *Regina v Bartle (The Pinochet Case)*, 37 I.L.M. 1302 (UK House of Lords 1998), per Lord Millett.

20 S. Colliver, J. Green and P. Hoffman, 'Holding Human Rights Violators Accountable by Using International Law in US Courts: Advocacy Efforts and Complementary Strategies',

created powerful private and intergovernmental regulatory organizations. Their lack of accountability and failure to incorporate human rights standards into their deliberations presents new challenges for legitimate global governance.[21] More positively, in response to worldwide human rights abuses, international civil society organizations dedicated to their prevention and remedy have also assumed an increasingly important political and legal role. This in turn has seen governments, among others, focus greater attention on their accountability.[22]

International law has yet to cope adequately with abuses of power in which non-state actors engage. The challenge faced by international law is to address the international community's concern to prevent human rights violations committed by non-state actors before their seeming immunity from the law's reach begins to make the existing human rights regime, directed to states, seem secondary. The central strategy here must be to persuade and induce states themselves to set in place the laws required to regulate the conduct of non-state actors in the human rights sphere.

This is a task upon which international organizations, in particular the UN, have already embarked. The UN has begun to draft agreements, pursue policies and encourage practices that may in time alleviate the disturbances that the absence of non-state actors from the conventional domain of international law still generates. For example, under the guidance of the UN's Special Representative of the Secretary-General on the issue of human rights and transnational corporations, the world body has formulated the Guiding Principles on Business and Human Rights.[23] These set down the distinct responsibilities that both states and corporations should assume if the human rights of citizens affected by corporations are to be adequately protected. States are enjoined to take appropriate steps to prevent, investigate, punish and redress human rights abuse by business enterprises through effective policies, legislation and adjudication. They should assume the responsibility for creating an expectation that business enterprises within their territory are expected to respect human rights in every facet of their operations. Equally, the Guidelines insist that transnational corporations should avoid infringing the human rights of others and should address the adverse human rights impacts of their operations. They are also encouraged to prevent or mitigate the adverse human rights impacts that are linked to their operations, even if they have made no contribution to those impacts.

Emory International Law Review 19(2005).

21 R. Grant and R. Keohane, 'Accountability and Abuses of Power in World Politics', *American Political Science Review* 99(2005): 35; R. Keohane, 'The Concept of Accountability in World Politics and the Use of Force', *Michigan Journal of International Law* 24(2003): 1121.

22 See D. Kennedy, *The Dark Sides of Virtue: Reassessing International Humanitarianism* (Princeton, NJ: Princeton University Press, 2004); D. Bell and M. Coicaud, eds, *Ethics in Action: The Ethical Challenges of International Human Rights Non-Governmental Organizations* (Cambridge: Cambridge University Press, 2007).

23 P. Alston, *Non-State Actors and Human Rights* (Oxford: Oxford University Press, 2005); R. Mares, *The UN Guiding Principles on Business and Human Rights: Foundations and Implementation* (Leiden: Martinus Nijhoff Publishers, 2012).

On a more practical level, substantial hope had been invested in the successful legal elaboration of the US Alien Tort Statute. This legislation provides that the district courts of the US shall have original jurisdiction in any civil action by an alien for a tort committed in violation of the law of nations. The definition is wide enough to embrace corporate malfeasance in the commission of human rights violations in countries other than America. US courts have subsequently allowed legal actions to be brought under the ATS for infringements of international law in relation to crimes such as genocide, torture, war crimes and forced disappearances. Regrettably, however, the US Supreme Court has recently narrowed jurisdiction under the ATS by ruling that it cannot be utilized where a corporation commits an alleged human rights violation entirely outside the territory of the US. Further, even where a claim made outside the US touches and concerns US territory, that connection must be sufficiently strong to displace the assumption against extraterritorial application. This brings to an end, at least for the time being, national provision for universal civil jurisdiction parallel to the universal criminal jurisdiction now recognized.

Armed opposition groups and terrorist organizations are another category of non-state actor that presents formidable problems for the international legal order.[24] The extension of international humanitarian and human rights law to intrastate conflicts, for example, renders obsolete the traditional distinction between combatants and civilians.[25] It has become necessary to distinguish between legitimate and illegitimate armed opposition groups, making the distinction between, for example, rebel movements defending populations against state-sponsored violence and terrorist organizations seeking to bring down legitimate state authorities. It is generally accepted that armed opposition groups, such as rebel movements, should respect international humanitarian and international human rights law even when they are not parties to the relevant treaties. That is in part owed to their assumed coverage by international customary law. It is much less clear, however, when any such group reaches the threshold at which humanitarian and human rights obligations may attach to it. The case of terrorist organizations is entirely different as they are highly unlikely ever to acknowledge that the writ of international law may run with respect to any of their causes or actions. Their situation seems best left to regulation by the complex and comprehensive web of international counter-terrorism treaties and their subsequent incorporation into national laws, assuming there are any. That leaves aside, of course, the vexed question of how individuals accused of terrorist activity should be treated upon

24 A. Cassese, 'Should Rebels Be Treated as Criminals? Some Modest Proposals for Rendering Internal Armed Conflicts Less Inhumane', in *Realizing Utopia: The Future of International Law*, ed. A. Cassese (Oxford: Oxford University Press, 2012), Ch. 39; L. Zegveld, *Accountability of Armed Opposition Groups in International Law* (Cambridge: Cambridge University Press, 2002).

25 R. Arneson, 'Just Warfare and Non-Combatant Immunity', *Cornell International Law Journal* 39(2006): 663.

apprehension. Extraordinary rendition and the Guantanamo Bay solution are hardly the answer. In dealing with the problems that non-state actors present, then, there remains a great deal of legal work to be done to ensure that human rights can be made real.

One final development on the boundary of international law should be noted in this survey of its recent transformations. International humanitarian law deals more or less effectively with crimes committed during the conduct of interstate and intrastate conflict. But it has little influence until crimes against humanity have been committed. This raises the question as to how mass atrocities, particularly those committed by governments against their own people, might be prevented and what responsibility, if any, the international community might have, to intervene when such atrocities are realistically in prospect. The UN Charter provides that a state may use force in self-defence in response to actual or imminent attack by another state and defensive force may also be legitimated when approved by the UN Security Council. The Charter is silent, however, with respect to any duty or authority the international community may have to avert or intervene in intrastate conflict to protect civilian populations from the commission of atrocity crimes.

To fill that gap, in 2005 the UN General Assembly unanimously endorsed the new doctrine of 'the responsibility to protect', a more sophisticated and nuanced version of what had previously been known as humanitarian intervention. In accordance with this doctrine, a state has primary responsibility for the protection of its citizens from the commission of mass-atrocity crime. Where, however, a state fails in its exercise of this responsibility, that responsibility shifts to the international community. It may then take action, with the endorsement of the Security Council, to take such measures as are necessary to prevent or intervene to stop the escalation of violence reaching the level of genocide, crimes against humanity, war crimes and ethnic cleansing.

While possessing the general endorsement of the international community as represented in the UN General Assembly, the doctrine is yet to be fully tested and accepted in practice. In 2011, the Security Council referred to the doctrine when authorizing military intervention in Libya to prevent mass slaughter in Benghazi. In response to a request from the government of Mali, in 2013 the Security Council authorized external military intervention to put down attacks by armed Islamic groups that threatened the stability of the country. In radical contrast, however, the Security Council was paralyzed when confronted with the devastating loss of life in Syria as first the government and then armed rebel groups committed war crimes and crimes against humanity in a conflict that had rapidly assumed that form of an intrareligious civil war. There is no doubt that the responsibility to protect represents a significant doctrinal advance in attempting to fashion a solution to the commission of intrastate offences against humanity. How effective and durable it will be in practice remains to be seen.

This brief survey of recent developments in international law suggests that in the past two decades or so it has taken a distinctly humanitarian turn. Partly in response to the changing nature of global conflict and violence and partly in response to the developing conceptual significance of the idea of human security, a more ethically and politically appropriate balance is being forged between the law's original concentration upon regulating the relationship between states and a newer focus on and commitment to the protection of the individual person, people, and their common humanity. That development in turn leads one naturally to consider the relationship between human security and global justice.[26]

In his recent book, *The Idea of Justice*, Amartya Sen draws a contrast between two different approaches to the definition of justice.[27] The first he terms transcendental institutionalism, an approach most closely identified with the paradigmatic political philosopher John Rawls. The purpose of transcendental institutionalism, Sen argues, is to attempt to construct an ideal set of just institutions. That task is to be undertaken in terms of social contract. Sen argues in contrast for an idea of justice founded on public reasoning and on the ranking of reasonable alternatives that can in fact be realized. Put more simply, Sen's social choice approach is one that takes note of social states that actually exist, asks how they are going, and inquires whether the arrangements can in some way be improved. The key in providing an answer to those questions is to focus first and foremost on the avoidance of manifest injustice.

This second approach is more practical and realizable than the first. And it links up well with the concept of human security. A more just society will be one that advances human security, practically defined. A less just set of arrangements will diminish human protection. Global justice, then, may best be conceived as the prevention of global injustice.

In that endeavour, international law has a major role to play. By turning its attention to the practical concern of humanity with the prevention of war, civil conflict and the violation of fundamental rights, that is, to the progressive elimination of manifest injustice, the last two decades have seen the law make incremental, sometimes halting, but nevertheless significant steps towards the achievement of human security. In so doing it has already made a notable contribution to a more just community of nations.

The Book's Contributions

In their different ways, the chapters in this collection each make original and interesting contributions to our understanding of several of the significant developments delineated above. What follows is an outline of that contribution.

---

26 See further T. Nagel, 'The Problem of Global Justice', *Philosophy and Public Affairs* 33, no. 2 (2005): 113; C. Barry and T. Pogge, *Global Institutions and Responsibilities: Achieving Global Justice* (Malden, MA: Blackwell Publishing, 2005); T. Pogge and D. Moellendorf, eds, *Global Justice: Seminal Essays* (St. Paul, MN: Paragon House, 2008).

27 A. Sen, *The Idea of Justice* (Cambridge, MA: Harvard University Press, 2009).

Steve Nabors enters the sphere of international humanitarian law by tracing the history of what has become known as the belligerent's privilege. The privilege constitutes an authorization, in international law, for an individual to engage in combat hostilities. That authorization entitles the participant to immunity from prosecution under domestic law for hostile and destructive actions undertaken in the course of war. It also entitles them to certain guaranteed protections under the Third Geneva Convention if captured and detained as a prisoner of war. The essential condition for the conferral of belligerent's privilege was the notion of 'right authority'. A person had right authority in war if their participation could properly be justified by reference to their cause and status. The cardinal example of belligerent's privilege was that of members of the armed forces engaged in a just war.

The key distinction in this regard was between combatants and non-combatants. Traditionally, non-combatants were not entitled to the privilege. In time, the advent of guerilla warfare, popular rebellion against repressive rule, and the use by the state of irregular militias to suppress liberation movements blurred the distinction substantially. In an illuminating discussion, Nabors tracks historically the position of ever more diverse categories of non-combatant: volunteer corps, auxiliary groups, partisans, indigenous peoples, informal militia and irregular forces, among others. He concludes that, particularly following the adoption of the Geneva Conventions, the idea that unprivileged belligerents' engagement in hostilities automatically constitutes a violation of the laws of war is no longer tenable. New classes of belligerent need to be afforded the privilege where circumstances suggest that their participation possesses an updated and expanded justification of 'right authority'.

Davide Tundo presents a dispassionate yet highly charged assessment of the non-protection of civilians in the case of the 2008 Israeli attack on the Gaza Strip. He begins by reciting the protections for civilians provided for in international humanitarian law. These include the requirement to separate combatants from civilians, to provide proportionate responses to armed attack, and to engage in conflict only when there is the military necessity to do so. Against these protections, he cites the conclusions of the Goldstone Report, which found that Israeli military operations were aimed not just at Gazan rebels but also and critically at the civilian population and supporting infrastructure. The barricading of the Gazan population during the course of the violence, he suggests, amounted to a form of illegal collective punishment.

The Israeli intervention, Tundo argues, constituted a gross injustice. It may have included the commission of crimes against humanity. Yet the international legal and political systems have failed as yet to take meaningful action to provide any remedies or to try any perpetrators of the allegedly severe offences. The Israeli authorities have not undertaken any meaningful inquiry into the actions of their military forces. The International Criminal Court has declined to consider prosecution on jurisdictional grounds. The only option left, Tundo concludes, is the exercise by other states of universal criminal jurisdiction.

As noted previously, there has been a new proliferation of international organizations and tribunals whose purpose is to draw individuals and organizations to account for human rights violations. Another important, potential source of investigation and remedy lies within domestic law. *Selman Karakul* proposes, however, that alterations to the procedural treatment of individual applications to international and regional courts may have the effect of prejudicing the fair hearing and determination of such applications. This is because such applications may be returned to domestic courts for further and final determination; and there, causes and remedies may still be inadequate.

Karakul examines the general rule that, before an application can be heard by an international tribunal, all domestic remedies in relation to an alleged case of human rights abuse must be exhausted. Given the absence of effective protections in domestic law, the number of applications to the European Court of Human Rights, among others, has increased dramatically. That has led to the Court adopting a new procedural expedient to handle the number and complexity of cases that come before it. Where the Court determines that many cases before it appear to constitute a systemic human rights failure, the Court will take one case and deliver a 'pilot judgment'. Having identified the failure, the Court will give clear indications to the government in question as to how the human rights issue may best be resolved within domestic law. The problem, however, is that governments may not favour the recommended actions, may be unwilling to alter their domestic laws, may capitalize on their 'margin of appreciation', and may place procedural obstacles in the way of further review.

Amrita Mukherjee argues that the principles of extraterritorial or universal jurisdiction and immunities from prosecution in relation to individual criminal liability for violations of international crimes have been the subject of recent controversy. The international legal system has developed specialized courts and tribunals, such as the International Criminal Court, to address international criminal responsibility. However, primacy is given in international law to the prosecution of perpetrators under domestic laws and in domestic courts. This chapter examines these principles in relation to rules of customary international law and treaty law, particularly the United Nations Convention against Torture. It explores how these principles have been applied in international and national case law – the subject matter from the context of national courts' jurisdiction to prosecute and punish offences committed extraterritorially by individual officials of other states and the law on immunities that acts as a bar to prosecution. The chapter examines whether, in the light of current problems in international criminal justice, 'the most potent mechanism for overcoming individual impunity for acts of torture is the requirement of international law that at the national level each state must criminalize torture and prosecute perpetrators under its domestic law and its domestic courts.'[28]

28 N. Rodley and M. Pollard, 'Criminalisation of Torture: State Obligations under the United Nations Convention against Torture and Other Cruel, Inhuman or Degrading

Tomoko Ishikawa turns his attention to the international commercial sphere. His concern is with the operation of arbitral bodies examining international investment treaties. In particular he looks at the operation of most-favoured-nation (MFN) clauses within those treaties. The purpose of MFN clauses is to effect greater harmonization of the standards that exist among the many and various investment treaties. The essential question in relation to such clauses is whether a third party investment treaty provides more favourable treatment to a party or parties in dispute than in the treaty pursuant to which the parties have already conducted their negotiations. If so, a party or parties may take advantage of the more favourable treatment in the third party treaty.

Ishikawa's argument is that, in determining this question, arbitral tribunals should found their decisions upon established rules of treaty interpretation rather than policy considerations. Policy considerations should be considered as relevant only in so far as they cast light on the interpretative process. Should policy considerations beyond this limitation become dominant in the interpretation of MFN clauses, the legitimacy of international investment arbitration tribunals may well be undermined.

The next five chapters examine the significance of non-state actors for the development of international law. *Angelica Bonfanti* introduces the subject matter by considering how multinational corporations might be brought to account for actions they take that infringe upon human rights or adversely affect the environment. She observes that a substantial volume of investment by multinational corporations in developing countries originates in developed ones. Of these, the two most significant sources of investment are from corporations domiciled in the United States and Europe. She examines the key international instruments that provide authoritative guidance as to the obligations upon multinational corporations not to infringe upon human rights, namely, the UN Global Compact and the UNSRSG Guiding Principles described above. She points in particular to the Guiding Principle that recommends that states should take steps to ensure the effectiveness of domestic judicial mechanisms when addressing business-related human rights abuse.

Bonfanti then moves to a consideration of the judicial mechanisms present in Europe and the USA. EC Regulations confer jurisdiction on EU member states courts in relation to defendants' domiciled EU territory. This may be extended to defendants outside EU territory if so provided by the domestic law of a member state. In the US, jurisdiction is founded upon the Alien Tort Statute, which provides that district courts have original jurisdiction with respect to torts committed in violation of the law of nations or a treaty to which the United States is a party. In both cases, significant limitations are imposed upon the assumption of civil jurisdiction in cases where MNCs are not incorporated in the country in which proceedings are initiated. Even where there is some connection to the

---

Treatment or Punishment', *European Human Rights Law Review* 2(2006): 116.

home country, complex corporate structures may still frustrate an attempt to hold independent subsidiaries located elsewhere to account for their actions.

The Alien Tort Statute is also the focus of *Bethany J. Spielman*'s contribution. She examines the implications of the 2013 United States Supreme Court decision in *Kiobel v Royal Dutch Petroleum and Shell Transport and Trading Co.* for the exercise by US courts of jurisdiction under the Statute. By way of establishing the significance of the jurisdiction, she introduces her chapter with a brief description of recent uncontrolled human clinical trials of new but as yet unproven pharmaceutical medicines undertaken without proper consent from participants in poor, developing countries.

Spielman then moves to a consideration of the limitations imposed by the Supreme Court on jurisdiction under the Alien Tort Statute. The extraterritoriality bar imposed by the Court, she concludes, will have the effect of depriving damaged victims of non-consensual experimentation of a remedial path that had previously been thought to be open to them. This is because the Statute will no longer be applicable to human rights violations engaged in by foreign corporations in foreign countries. Nor will it apply to companies that do have a connection to the United States if that connection affects the political or commercial interests of the US only indirectly or tenuously.

Genny Negende contends that, through the past two decades, the relationship between developing countries in Africa and the MNCs that invest in them has been radically transformed. Investment by MNCs in developing countries has increased dramatically and to such an extent that it now constitutes the primary form of international aid to these countries' economies. At the same time, the structure, organization and powers of such countries' governments has remained weak. This has produced an asymmetrical relationship of power between governments and MNCs in which increasingly the latter dictate the terms of their involvement often heedless of attempted domestic constraints. The power vacuum this has created between the two, Ngende argues, has recently been filled, at least partially, by the rise of non-governmental human rights organizations.

To make the argument, she explores a number of significant case studies. She traces the role of NGOs in working with the United Nations to weaken the hold of Apartheid. She analyses the role of the Treatment Action Campaign in pressing for substantial reductions in the price of anti-retroviral drugs to combat the widespread and severe health problems provoked by HIV/AIDS. In this case, the South African Government's response was slow, owed in part to AIDS denialism. Threatened legal action by the Treatment Action Campaign achieved substantial price concessions from the pharmaceutical manufacturer, Pfizer, that the government had been unwilling or unable to negotiate. Other pharmaceutical manufacturers soon followed. The South African example, she concludes, can provide a powerful example as to how NGOs in other developing countries can compensate for the weaknesses of government through targeted and tactical legal action.

Saheed Alabi provides a thoughtful and complementary account of the role that non-state actors might play in the achievement of climate justice. He identifies three kinds of non-state actors in the climate field: social advocacy groups, legal rights organizations, and scientific and technical experts. Each of these has a role to play in the achievement of climate justice. Climate justice is understood as the fair treatment and meaningful involvement of all people with respect to the development, implementation and enforcement of international and national environmental laws and policies.

Alabi cites important examples of the role that advocacy organizations have played in the development, negotiation and implementation of international environmental treaties. Legal organizations have also played their part by attempting to draw governments to account for their non-performance of international environmental treaty obligations and parallel domestic legal obligations. In this latter sphere, however, progress has been made difficult by the fact that it has been hard for non-governmental environmental organizations to obtain legal standing in the courts. This is because they are not parties to international climate agreements. The author suggests, therefore, that in future international treaties, for example the successor treaty to the Kyoto Protocol, a provision should be inserted allowing recognized NGOs to bring non-compliance actions to relevant international arbitral and treaty monitoring bodies. Treaties should also provide for appropriate access to information regarding national performance and more favourable opportunities for NGOs to contribute to treaty-related monitoring and implementation.

Mohammad H. Zarei and *Azar Safari* conclude this section with a more general discussion of the status of non-state actors under international law. They observe that non-state actors have come to possess very significant economic, financial, political and institutional power. This is as true of multinational civil society organizations as it is of multinational corporations. However, they lack any semblance of corresponding legal or social responsibility. Since this is so, more concerted efforts are required to draw them to account by subjecting them to the rule of international law.

To assist with determining how this might best be done, the authors contrast formal and substantive conceptions of the rule of law. They do so by considering different perspectives of the legal philosophers Joseph Raz and Ronald Dworkin. Raz argues that the rule of law is animated by two governing ideas. First, people should be ruled by the law and obey it. Secondly, the law should be such that people will be able to be guided by it. This conception of the rule of law is concerned predominantly with the character of law rather than with its content. As Raz puts it, the rule of law is just one of the virtues by which a legal system may be judged. It is not to be confused with parallel virtues such as democracy, justice, equality or human rights. For Ronald Dworkin, in contrast, principle matters as much as legality. He insists that individuals have political rights against the state, in addition to moral rights as against one another. These rights, he argues, must be recognized as essential threads in the rule of law's fabric. It is for this reason that Dworkin's conception is characterized as substantive. While the authors are inclined to favour the formal conception, they conclude by affirming that non-state actors should nevertheless be held to account pursuant to the rule of law for human rights violations.

One of the most hopeful developments in the direction of achieving human security has been the international community's adoption of the doctrine of the *responsibility to protect*. In his chapter, *Spencer Zifcak* traces the development of the doctrine in its first decade through a detailed description and analysis of its consideration by the UN General Assembly. The chapter examines the most important Assembly debates on the subject of responsibility to protect (R2P) with a view to determining to what extent and in what ways the doctrine has been advanced or trimmed as its practical application has been progressively exposed to critical international political scrutiny.

The chapter tracks discussion immediately prior to the UN World Summit in 2005. It follows with a consideration of the debate upon the Secretary-General's first three reports on R2P, which sought both to support and to set limits to the doctrine. Then, it explicates the discussion on R2P that took place following the first coercive intervention under the doctrine's banner, in Libya in 2011. The author concludes that, although the speed with which the international community first embraced R2P was remarkable, many problems have emerged following cases of its practical implementation. The Libyan intervention in particular has had the effect of dividing nations as to its desirability and efficacy. The recent attempt by the government of Brazil to mitigate this disunity with its revised doctrine of the 'responsibility while protecting' seems likely to create just as many problems as it seeks to resolve.

Three final chapters then deal with the complex question of how best to rethink aspects of international justice.

Charles Sampford asks, when Rawls famously declared that justice is the first virtue of institutions, should we say the same thing about international institutions? When Rawls wrote *A Theory of Justice*, theories of strong state sovereignty were at or near their apex. The institutions he then had in mind were internal state institutions. His methodology, imagining individuals who knew nothing about themselves but pretty well everything else, has long been discredited as a source of universal norms. However, it is a good way for those within an existing community to think about the values their institutions should serve – just as Rawls helped to tease out the values that moderate Americans would like to see their governments deliver. As we move to a more globalized world where non-state institutions (international, regional, corporate, NGO and professional) are assuming ever greater prominence and an ever greater role in both governance problems and governance solutions, it is worthwhile considering whether Rawls's dictum should run more widely. In doing so, the chapter revisits the various kinds of justice that might make claim to be the first virtue of institutions as well as the non-justice claims that have been considered (and some might still consider) to outrank justice claims: efficiency, prosperity and survival.

The chapter then examines the same questions for international institutions and other international actors with which they interact. It argues that justice was generally a secondary, frequently inconvenient value and it still has many competitors. If we are to hope that justice could become the first virtue of international institutions, it needs to be a form of justice that reflects the ideals of, and insights into, justice from the world's cultures and the world's peoples – and especially of their experiences of injustice.

Ahmet Ulvi Türkbağ provides a timely perspective on the idea of justice by contrasting Western with Islamic ideas on its nature and content. He takes St Thomas Aquinas and Al-Ghazali as representative thinkers of the two intellectual traditions. Aquinas proposes that natural law, and through it justice, may be derived from two different sources. The first is divine revelation, the second is through reason. Ghazali suggests similarly, that natural law may be revealed through divine grace. Then a process of reason and evaluation takes place to determine the parameters of the natural laws that may be derived from what has been revealed. Given these commonalities of approach, it is no surprise, the author argues, that the content of natural law in both the Western and Islamic traditions is fundamentally similar.

Finally, *Gábor Sulyok* tackles a vexed contemporary issue in debates about the content of international law. The question he poses is whether general principles of law, which constitute a recognized source of international law, are to be derived principally from international law itself or from an aggregation of legal principles common to the domestic law of nations. The author favours the latter view. He argues that domestic principles of law are incorporated as general principles of law by a customary rule of reception. This rule of reception accepts principles of domestic law as general principles if they meet two criteria. They must be generally recognized among nations and they must be suitable for the government of international relations. The requirement of general recognition does not mean that a principle must be present universally. It is sufficient if it is generally recognized in the world's dominant legal systems. The requirement of suitability is met if the principle concerned is capable of effective application to relations between states or between states and their citizens.

Sulyok observes that general principles derived in this way may still be very broad. To become genuinely effective, therefore, they require detailed elaboration by the International Court of Justice and other international judicial organs. Through elaboration and interpretation, for example, the European Court of Justice has determined that general principles of law that have been incorporated into the law of the European Union now include respect for fundamental rights, a prohibition on discrimination, a requirement of judicial independence and control, and a prohibition on retrospective legislation. It is likely that the primary international judicial bodies will arrive at similar conclusions. Elaborated in this way, general principles of law have made, and are likely further to make, a significant contribution to our understanding of the constituent elements of global justice.

Cases

Bosnia and Herzegovina v Serbia and Montenegro, International Court of Justice, February 26, 2007.
Prosecutor v Tadić (Judgment of 15 July 1999), ICTY AC, Case IT-94-1-A.
Regina v Bartle (The Pinochet Case), 37 I.L.M. 1302 (UK House of Lords 1998), per Lord Millett.
Sosa v Alvarez-Machain, 542 US 692 (Supreme Court of the United States 2004), per Breyer J.

Bibliography

Alston, P. *Non-State Actors and Human Rights*. Oxford: Oxford University Press, 2005.
Amnesty International. 'Universal Jurisdiction: A Preliminary Survey of Legislation around the World', 2011.
Annan, Kofi. *Larger Freedom: Towards Development, Security and Human Rights for All*. New York: United Nations, 2005.
———. 'Two Concepts of Sovereignty', *Economist*, 18 September 1999, 49.
Arneson, R. 'Just Warfare and Non-Combatant Immunity', *Cornell International Law Journal* 39(2006): 663.
Barry, C., and T. Pogge. *Global Institutions and Responsibilities: Achieving Global Justice*. Malden, MA: Blackwell Publishing, 2005.
Bell, D., and M. Coicaud, eds. *Ethics in Action: The Ethical Challenges of International Human Rights Non-Governmental Organizations*. Cambridge: Cambridge University Press, 2007.
Ben-Nafatli, O., ed. *International Humanitarian Law and International Human Rights Law*. Oxford: Oxford University Press, 2011.
Byers, M. *War Law*. London: Atlantic Books, 2005.
Cassese, A., ed. *Realizing Utopia: The Future of International Law*. Oxford: Oxford University Press, 2012.
———. 'Should Rebels Be Treated as Criminals? Some Modest Proposals for Rendering Internal Armed Conflicts Less Inhumane'. In *Realizing Utopia: The Future of International Law*, edited by A. Cassese. Oxford: Oxford University Press, 2012.
Collier, P. *The Bottom Billion: Why the Poorest Countries Are Failing and What Can Be Done About It*. Oxford: Oxford University Press, 2007.
Colliver, S., J. Green and P. Hoffman. 'Holding Human Rights Violators Accountable by Using International Law in US Courts: Advocacy Efforts and Complementary Strategies', *Emory International Law Review* 19(2005): 169.
Glover, J. *Humanity: A Moral History of the Twentieth Century*. New Haven, CT: Yale University Press, 2000.

Goldstein, J., M. Kahler, R. Keohane and A. Slaughter. *Legalization and World Politics*. Cambridge, MA: MIT Press, 2001.

Grant, R., and R. Keohane. 'Accountability and Abuses of Power in World Politics', *American Political Science Review* 99(2005): 29.

Hayner, P. *Unspeakable Truths: Confronting State Terror and Atrocity*. 2nd edn. London: Routledge, 2011.

Held, D. *Global Covenant: The Social Democratic Alternative to the Washington Consensus*. Cambridge: Polity Press, 2004.

International Committee of the Red Cross (ICRC). 'Protocol Additional to the Geneva Conventions of 12 August 1949, and Relating to the Protection of Victims of International Armed Conflicts (Protocol I)', 1125 UNTS 3. Geneva: ICRC, 8 June 1977.

Kaldor, M. *New and Old Wars: Organized Violence in a Global Era*. Stanford, CA: Stanford University Press, 1999.

Kennedy, D. *The Dark Sides of Virtue: Reassessing International Humanitarianism*. Princeton, NJ: Princeton University Press, 2004.

Keohane, R. 'The Concept of Accountability in World Politics and the Use of Force', *Michigan Journal of International Law* 24(2003): 1121.

Langer, M. 'The Diplomacy of Universal Jurisdiction', *American Journal of International Law* 105(2011): 1.

Leitenberg, M. *Deaths in Wars and Conflicts in the Twentieth Century*. Ithaca, NY: Cornell University Peace Studies Program, 2003.

Macedo, S., ed. *Universal Jurisdiction: National Courts and the Prosecution of Serious Crimes under International Law*. Philadelphia, PA: University of Pennsylvania Press, 2011.

Mares, R. *The UN Guiding Principles on Business and Human Rights: Foundations and Implementation*. Leiden: Martinus Nijhoff Publishers, 2012.

Meron, T. *The Humanization of International Law*. Boston, MA: Martinus Nijhoff, 2006.

———. 'War Crimes in Yugoslavia and the Development of International Law', *American Journal of International Law* 88(1994): 79.

Nagel, T. 'The Problem of Global Justice', *Philosophy and Public Affairs* 33, no. 2 (2005): 113.

Ogata, Sadako. 'Statement Delivered at the Asian Development Bank Seminar: Inclusion or Exclusion: Social Development Challenges for Asia and Europe', Geneva: United Nations, 27 April 1998.

Othman, M. *Accountability for International Humanitarian Law Violations: The Case of Rwanda and East Timor*. Heidelberg: Berlin Springer, 2005.

Peters, A. 'Humanity as the Alpha and Omega of Sovereignty', *European Journal of International Law* 20, no. 3 (2009): 513

Pinker, S. *The Better Angels of Nature: The Decline of Violence in History and Its Causes*. London: Penguin Books, 2011.

Pogge, T., and D. Moellendorf, eds. *Global Justice: Seminal Essays*. St. Paul, MN: Paragon House, 2008.

Provost, R. *International Human Rights and Humanitarian Law*. Cambridge: Cambridge University Press, 2002.

Rodley, N., and M. Pollard. 'Criminalisation of Torture: State Obligations under the United Nations Convention against Torture and Other Cruel, Inhuman or Degrading Treatment or Punishment', *European Human Rights Law Review* 2(2006): 115.

Roht-Arriaza, N. 'Universal Jurisdiction: Steps Forwards, Steps Back', *Leiden Journal of International Law* 17(2004): 375.

Salomon, M. *Global Responsibility for Human Rights: World Poverty and the Development of International Law*. Oxford: Oxford University Press, 2007.

Schabas, W. *Genocide in International Law*. 2nd edn. Cambridge: Cambridge University Press, 2009.

———. *An Introduction to the International Criminal Court*. 4th edn. Cambridge: Cambridge University Press, 2011.

Scheffer, D. *All the Missing Souls: A Personal History of the War Crimes Tribunals*. Princeton, NJ: Princeton University Press, 2012.

Sen, A. *The Idea of Justice*. Cambridge, MA: Harvard University Press, 2009.

Teitel, R. *Humanity's Law*. Oxford: Oxford University Press, 2011.

Teitel, R., and R. Howse. 'Crossjudging: Tribunalization in a Fragmented but Interconnected Global Order', *New York University Journal of International Law and Politics* 41(2009): 959.

UN Millennium Project. *Investing in Development: A Practical Plan to Achieve the Millennium Development Goals*. New York: United Nations, 2005.

United Nations. 'High Level Panel on Threats, Challenges and Change, a More Secure World: Our Shared Responsibility', UN Document A/59/565, 2004.

United Nations Commission on Human Security. *Human Security Now*. New York: Commission on Human Security, 2003.

Wippman, D., and M. Evangelista. *New Wars, New Laws: Applying the Wars of Law in Twenty First Century Conflicts*. Ardsley, NY: Transnational, 2002.

Zegveld, L. *Accountability of Armed Opposition Groups in International Law*. Cambridge: Cambridge University Press, 2002.

PART I
International Humanitarian Law

Chapter 2
A Right to Fight: The Belligerent's Privilege

Steve Nabors

Throughout history, the belligerent's privilege has served several functions. Initially, the privilege was used to abate the outbreak of war by limiting the number of individuals who could profit from hostilities. Later, the privilege was used as a means of protecting captured and surrendered soldiers from abuses in the hands of their captors. Finally, the privilege was offered as an incentive for combatants to comply with the principle of distinction under the laws of war.

This chapter traces the historical development of the belligerent's privilege and argues that the privilege is not a 'bundle of sticks', but two individual rights that emerged separately and remain separable from each other: the protections of combatant immunity and the right to protected status as a prisoner of war upon surrender or capture. Further, by tracing the evolution of the concepts of privileged and unprivileged belligerency, this chapter argues that *right authority* remains the most critical component of the belligerent's privilege.

The Belligerent's Privilege, Combatant Immunity, and Prisoner of War Status Defined and Distinguished

The belligerent's privilege, also known as the combatant's privilege, is an authorization recognized under international law for an individual to engage in hostilities.[1] Persons authorized to engage in hostilities are privileged belligerents (or privileged combatants) and are entitled to both combatant immunity and the guaranteed protections of prisoner of war status.[2] Combatant immunity shields a privileged belligerent from prosecution under any state's domestic law for the wounding, maiming, death or capture of individuals, as well as the destruction of enemy property so long as these acts are carried out in compliance with the law of

1 Robert Goldman and Brian Tittemore, 'Unprivileged Combatants and the Hostilities in Afghanistan: Their Status and Rights under International Humanitarian and Human Rights Law', *ASIL Task Force on Terrorism Paper* (2002). Online. Available HTTP: http://www.pegc.us/archive/Journals/goldman.pdf (accessed 20 September 2013).

2 Waldemar Solf, 'The Status of Combatants in Non-International Armed Conflicts under Domestic Law and Transnational Practice', *American University Law Review* 33 (1983–84).

war.[3] Privileged belligerents are entitled to the juridical protections of combatant immunity even if they are not captured; therefore a state may not try a privileged belligerent after the cessation of hostilities for violations of its domestic law that resulted from lawful acts of war.[4]

Privileged belligerents are also entitled to the protections guaranteed to prisoners of war under the Third Geneva Convention of 1949 (GPW).[5] These protections are mostly grouped together in the early part of the GPW and include several fundamental guarantees including: humane treatment and protection against acts of violence, intimidation, insults, and public curiosity;[6] respect for persons and their honour;[7] and a prohibition on discrimination based on race, nationality, religious belief or political opinions.[8] In contrast, unprivileged belligerents are only entitled to the minimum protections provided by Common Article 3 of the 1949 Geneva Conventions.[9]

Just War and the *Jus Militare*: From the Middle Ages to Early Modern Europe

The basis for the modern law of war emerged from two legal mechanisms developed during the Middle Ages. The first, Just War Theory, attempted to restrict warfare by narrowing the circumstances under which hostilities could be lawfully initiated. The second, the *jus militare*, sought to limit who could profit from hostilities by requiring noble birth and sovereign authorization in order to reap the spoils of war. This concept of sovereign authorization, known as *right authority*, became the cornerstone of the *jus militare*; and without it, an individual was not entitled to any of the privileges or protections afforded to combatants. As such, *right authority* became the basis for the modern belligerent's privilege.

The 'Privileged' Class

Warfare during the Middle Ages was a jealously guarded profession that revolved around the profit generated during hostilities.[10] Recognizing that war was an

3 Michael Bothe, Karl Partsch and Waldemar Solf, *New Rules for Victims of Armed Conflicts: Commentary on the Two 1977 Protocols Additional to the Geneva Conventions of 1949* (The Hague, Boston, MA, and London: Martinus Nijhoff Publishers, 1982).

4 Solf, 'The Status of Combatants in Non-International Armed Conflicts under Domestic Law and Transnational Practice', 57.

5 Ibid., Commentary, 244.

6 Convention Relative to the Treatment of Prisoners of War, Aug. 12, 1949, art. 13, 6 U.S.T. 3316, 75 U.N.T.S. 135 [hereinafter 'GPW'].

7 Ibid., art. 14.

8 Ibid., art. 16.

9 Ibid., art. 3.

10 '[T]he laws of war, *jus in bello*, were an entirely secular creation developed to suit the needs of a rigidly stratified social order in which the right to bear arms was a jealously

omnipresent force in Middle Age Europe, the Christian Church developed an array of religious, moral, and legal mores to restrict the outbreak of war under a theory called Just War. Just War sought to limit the destructive effects of warfare by restricting when wars could be fought and who could fight in them.[11] Under Christian canons, only wars that aimed to 'restore harmony and redress wrong' could be just and therefore legal.[12] Wars that failed to meet the Just War criteria were deemed 'private wars', 'freebooting', or 'looting' and were categorically prohibited as violations of Christian principles.[13] Just Wars also required 'open avowals' declaring publically that hostilities had commenced.[14] Waging so-called 'private wars' that were neither just, public, nor open not only divested sovereigns

---

guarded privilege.' Michael Howard, 'Constraints on Warfare', in *The Laws of War: Constraints on Warfare in the Western World*, ed. Michael Howard, George J. Andreopoulos, and Mark R. Shulman (New Haven, CT: Yale University Press, 1994), 3. 'War-making [was] a jealous calling, limited to those who follow the profession of arms.' G.I.A.D. Draper, 'Combatant Status: An Historical Perspective', *Military Law and Law of War Review* 11 (1972): 136. The legal restriction on the class of persons who were permitted to engage in hostilities, though, can be traced as far back as Roman law: '*Cicero* tells us, in his *Offices*, that by the Roman fecial law [*jus fetaile*], no person could lawfully engage in battle with the public enemy, without being regularly enrolled and taking the military oath.' Henry Wheaton, *Elements of International Law*, 4th edn (London: Stevens & Sons, 1904), 501.

11 Draper, 'Combatant Status: An Historical Perspective', 136 ('The Church, rather like the I.C.R.C. in our own time, saw that war could not be eliminated, but that various kinds of persuasive religious, moral, and legal forces might restrict its scope and thus the evil that could be wrought.). 'The justification of war, it was pointed out, lay not in the manner in which it was conducted, but in its end; as [Saint] Augustine had written "war is waged that peace may be had."' M.H. Keen, *The Laws of War in the Late Middle Ages* (London: Routlege & Kegan Paul, 1965), 8. According to the jurist Raymond of Pennaforte, five prerequisites had to be met for a Just War: (1) the war must be fought by those authorized to engage in war-making, that is, knights and soldiers; (2) the aim must be to redress some injury either to person or possessions; (3) there must be no alternative way of achieving the aim without recourse to arms; (4) the person levying the war must be moved by a genuine desire for justice and not out of vengeance; and (5) the war must be waged on valid authority – either on authority of Church or of a sovereign prince. See ibid., 66–67. Of these criteria, the first and last requirements are the most significant for the purposes of the modern belligerent's privilege. See also, Mark Evans, 'Moral Theory and the Idea of a Just War', in *Just War Theory: A Reappraisal*, ed. Mark Evans (Edinburgh: Edinburgh University Press, 2005).

12 Keen, *The Laws of War in the Late Middle Ages*, 66; Evans, 'Moral Theory and the Idea of a Just War'; G.I.A.D. Draper, 'The Status of Combatants and the Question of Guerilla Warfare', *British Yearbook of International Law* 45 (1971).

13 Keen, *The Laws of War in the Late Middle Ages*, 99 (explaining that just wars required 'open and formal acts of avowals by the prince for the troops who served him, formal acts to mark the opening of the war, and formal actions on the battlefield or at the start of the siege, to show to all that the Law of Arms had come into operation').

14 Ibid., 70 ('What mattered to [the professional soldier] was that in public war and public war alone he had the right to make himself rich on the spoils of victory').

of the legal right to profit from the war, but also prohibited their knights from making claims over ransoms and plunder.[15]

The rules governing monetary claims made during and after war were coalesced within the *jus militare*.[16] Only those persons whose hereditary occupation was fighting, that is, knights drawn from the nobility, were allowed to enjoy the privileges of the *jus militare*.[17] Under these rules, an individual could petition the court of his lord or the court of his enemy's master to validate a claim.[18] These claims were usually heard by a lord's constable or marshal[19] who had permanent authority to hear matters pertaining to the law of arms and was accessible to any party under the *jus militare*'s jurisdiction.[20] Claims would be dismissed, though, if they stemmed from an unjust war or were made by someone outside of the privileged class.[21] For instance, peasants could not make claims under the *jus militare* for ransom or loot, nor request its protections.[22]

In addition to being a recognized member of the warrior class, a knight also needed *right authority* to reap the spoils of war.[23] Only a sovereign such as a king or duke could grant *right authority*, but the validity of this authorization was dependent on whether or not the war was just.[24] As a result, '[t]he really important question from the [professional] soldier's point of view, was therefore not the justice of the cause, but whether a given lord had a right to levy public war in its pursuit.'[25] The Chivalric concept of honour served as an enforcement mechanism by holding a knight at risk of losing his title for waging war without the authorization of his sovereign, so-called *right authority*, or resorting to treachery or perfidy.[26] Without his title, an individual was excluded from the *jus militare* and thereby prohibited from participating in battle or gaining the spoils of war.[27]

---

15 Robert Stacy, 'Age of Chivalry', in *The Laws of War: Constraints on Warfare in the Western World*, ed. Michael Howard, George J. Andreopoulos, and Mark R. Shulman (New Haven, CT: Yale University Press, 1994), 27–39.

16 Ibid.

17 Keen, *The Laws of War in the Late Middle Ages*.

18 Hence the name 'Courts *Martial*'.

19 Keen, *The Laws of War in the Late Middle Ages*, 27.

20 Ibid., 65.

21 Ibid., 19 (emphasizing that 'a peasant could not claim rights in an enemy prisoner under the law of arms, because it applied only to military persons and therefore only they [knights] could sue for rights under it').

22 Ibid., 85.

23 Ibid.

24 Ibid., 70–71.

25 Ibid., 85.

26 G.I.A.D. Draper, 'The Interaction of Christianity and Chivalry in the Historical Development of the Law of War', *International Review of the Red Cross* 46 (1965); Draper, 'The Status of Combatants and the Question of Guerilla Warfare', 175; Keen, *The Laws of War in the Late Middle Ages*, 20.

27 Draper, 'Combatant Status: An Historical Perspective', 137.

Moreover, by violating the sovereign's monopoly on the use of force, the knight was committing *lèse majesté* and could be put to death.[28]

Of the rights and privileges that could be forfeited, the ransoming of prisoners was by far the most valuable.[29] Ransom was effectively a contract in which a captured knight promised his captor a price in exchange for his life.[30] While the *jus militare* allowed a surrendered knight to request to be ransomed, his captor was under no obligation to provide it.[31] Once a captor did agree to ransom, though, a prisoner became a non-combatant and enjoyed immunity for both himself and his lands.[32] However, only knights could ransom other knights, and if a knight was captured by foot soldiers, archers, engineers, or peasant levies, they were given no quarter.[33] Because commoners could draw no profit from surrendered knights and were not given quarter if captured themselves, they had few compunctions about killing their noble and common prisoners alike.[34]

The 'Unprivileged' Classes

Though the *jus militare* is the basis for modern international humanitarian law, it provided a very limited scope of non-combatant immunity. Churchmen and their belongings, pilgrims, prisoners of war, and heralds were entitled to total immunity by way of their status, but civilians were not.[35] In occupied areas, 'civilians were treated as enemies, and the miseries which they suffered were usually far more

28 Ibid., 92. See also, M.H. Keen, 'Treason Trials under the Law of Arms', *Transactions of the Royal Historical Society* 5th Series 12 (1962), 97 ('[T]he right to take spoil and hold men ransom by the law of arms applied only in "just" or public war, which for legal purposes mean a war authorized by a prince. In other kinds of war, for instance feudal war, such rights were severely limited. Pillaging and taking prisoners in a war other than that of a prince was therefore not only public robbery but also *lèse majesté*, since the commander of the troops in question was arrogating to himself royal power. It was on these grounds that commanders of free companies … were sentenced to death for *lèse majesté*').

29 Keen, *The Laws of War in the Late Middle Ages*, 156 ('Far and away the most valuable gains of war were the ransoms of prisoners').

30 Ibid., 57 (quoting Paris of Pozzo, 9 DE RE MILITARI ¶2, 'When a man surrenders, and his victor accepts him as a prisoner then he makes a contract with him, that he shall be a captive and not killed'). See also, Stacy, 'Age of Chivalry', 37 (describing the contractual relationship as 'the captor's actionable interest in the contract was acquired by the service he performed in saving his captive's life; the prisoner's body, in turn, became the pledge for his ransom').

31 Draper, 'The Status of Combatants and the Question of Guerilla Warfare', 174 (noting that 'such restrictions as existed in relation to sparing prisoners … had no humanitarian qualities. Ransom was lost if a prisoner were not spared').

32 Keen, *The Laws of War in the Late Middle Ages*, 160.

33 Stacy, 'Age of Chivalry', 36.

34 Ibid.

35 Keen, *The Laws of War in the Late Middle Ages*, 189–90. A convincing argument could be made that the heraldic immunity so keenly observed by all participants under the

inhuman than any hardship a soldier might have to face.'[36] Even those entitled to immunity could lose it through prohibited conduct and some categories of immunity were more respected than others.[37]

The *jus militare* also permitted harsh measures in response to rebellions. As Balthazar Ayala later explained, 'disobedience in the part of subjects and rebellion against the prince is treated as a heinous offense and put on par with heresy.'[38] The phrase 'heinous offense' described a capital offence that permitted a sovereign to employ all measures available to put down the rebellion, including enslaving and confiscating the property of his enemies.[39] Those who attempted insurrection not only lacked *right authority*, but were considered a special class of offenders who warranted especially harsh punishment.[40] In the same vein, the *jus militare* did not apply during wars with non-Christians – so called *guerre mortelle* or 'Roman War'.[41] As a result, all those conquered could be slain or enslaved upon capture.[42]

---

jus militare is the foundation for granting civilians accompanying the armed forces in time of war POW status under the modern law of war. See GPW, art. 4(a)(4).

36 Keen, *The Laws of War in the Late Middle Ages*, 191.

37 Among the protected classes, the immunity of heralds was by far the best respected. Ibid., 195.Respect for Church immunity was spotty at best, but did improve over time. Even in cases where Church immunity was respected, members of the clergy could forfeit that immunity if they took up arms. Ibid., 193 ('If he [a clergyman] was proved to have been in arms, then he was treated as the subject of a hostile sovereign'). This seems to be a historical and legal foundation for the 'direct participation in hostilities' mechanism in modern international humanitarian law that identifies the threshold of conduct in which non-combatants lose immunity and become the lawful target of attack. See Protocol I Additional to the Geneva Conventions of 12 August 1949, and Relating to the Protection of Victims of International Armed Conflicts, 51(3) June 8, 1977, 1125 U.N.T.S. 3 [hereinafter 'Additional Protocol I'].

38 Keen, *The Laws of War in the Late Middle Ages*, 44 (quoting Ayala Balthazar, 1 De Jure et Officiis Bellicis et Disciplina Militari 2 (23)).

39 Geoffrey Parker, 'Early Modern Europe', in *The Laws of War: Constraints on Warfare in the Western World*, ed. Michael Howard, George J. Andreopoulos, and Mark R. Shulman (New Haven, CT: Yale University Press, 1994), 40–58.

40 Ibid.

41 Keen, *The Laws of War in the Late Middle Ages*, 4.

42 Ibid. Nonetheless, ransom between Christians and Muslim forces was commonplace, particularly during the Third Crusade, hence why the massacre at Acre was considered such a shock to the conscience of Saladin's forces. See James Reston, *Warriors of God: Richard the Lionheart and Saladin in the Third Crusade* (London: Anchor Books, 2001). Nonetheless, as the Turkish experience with Vlad III (also known as 'Vlad the Impaler' or 'Dracula') shows, wars between Christians and non-Christians could be quite barbaric even into the Modern Era. See Radu R. Florescu and Raymond T. McNally, *Dracula, Prince of Many Faces: His Life and His Times* (Boston, MA: Little, Brown and Company, 1989).

Summation of the Belligerent's Privilege under the Jus Militare

The *jus militare* and Just War Theory laid the foundation for the modern concept of the belligerent's privilege by establishing who was entitled to the privilege and how the privilege immunized combatants.[43] In order to enjoy the privilege, an individual had to meet four requirements:

1. the individual had to belong to the hereditary class of warriors generally known now as knights,[44]
2. the individual needed to possess *right authority* – authorization from his sovereign to engage in hostilities,[45]
3. the individual had to refrain from dishonourable means of warfare, namely perfidy,[46]
4. the individual's sovereign had to be engaged in a 'just war'.[47]

A privileged belligerent was entitled to combatant immunity consisting of three different types of privileges:

1. an ecclesiastical privilege that exempted soldiers belonging to the 'privileged class' of hereditary warriors from the Christian prohibition on waging war and murder,[48]
2. an international privilege that protected knights from the charge of 'brigandage' or 'freebooting' when fighting in enemy territory,[49] and
3. a domestic privilege that immunized a knight from prosecution for *lèse majesté* by his lord or sovereign.[50]

The belligerent's privilege devised under the *jus militare* was an attempt to restrict the outbreak of war by limiting the class of persons and circumstances under which the spoils of war could be reaped, thereby reducing war's profitability. By conditioning the rights and privileges of the *jus militare* on a sovereign's lawful authorization to engage in hostilities, the *jus militare* concreted the connection between *right authority* and the belligerent's privilege. As warfare continued to evolve, though, the interdependent requirements under Just War and the *jus militare* would prove to perpetuate more conflicts than they prevented.

---

43 Draper, 'The Status of Combatants and the Question of Guerilla Warfare', 173.

44 Draper, 'Combatant Status: An Historical Perspective', 136.

45 Keen, *The Laws of War in the Late Middle Ages*, 85.

46 Draper, 'The Interaction of Christianity and Chivalry in the Historical Development of the Law of War', 20 ('For a chivalrous knight, however, perfidy was a disgrace that no act of valor could redeem').

47 Keen, 'Treason Trials under the Law of Arms', 12.

48 *The Laws of War in the Late Middle Ages*, 80–81.

49 Draper, 'Combatant Status: An Historical Perspective', 137.

50 Keen, *The Laws of War in the Late Middle Ages*, 54.

Restructuring of the Privilege: Early Modern Europe to Colonization

The major restructuring of the Christian world during and immediately following the Renaissance significantly altered both the function and purpose of the belligerent's privilege. Spurred by brutal sectarian wars resulting from the breakdown of the Catholic Church's authority, theologians and jurists began to argue for universal application of the laws of war to encourage humanity among Christian belligerents. Simultaneously, the evolution of European warfare antiquated the *jus militare* and gave rise to a more inclusive law of war enforced through reciprocal agreements and reprisals, but inapplicable to newly encountered indigenous populations. As a result, the belligerent's privilege, its requirements, and its immunities evolved in an effort to provide humane treatment to European combatants while also facilitating colonization.

The Emergence of the Dualistic Axiom

Under the Just War Theory of feudal Europe, application of the law regulating the conduct of hostilities, known as the *jus in bello*, depended on compliance with the law governing the right to initiate war or *jus ad bellum*.[51] In other words, the application of the *jus militare* could be denied to a sovereign who initiated an unjust war.[52] The gradual breakdown of the Catholic Church's authority coupled with the advent of centralized, secular monarchies under the Peace of Westphalia gave rise to a period of intense and brutal wars between Christian sects.[53] Because these wars were based upon religious grounds, both sides deemed the other's cause to be heresy in violation of the *jus ad bellum* and consequently refused to observe the protections afforded by *jus in bello*.[54] Recognizing the inherent conundrum created by interdependent requirements, European jurists[55] began to argue that all of Christendom was subject to a common law known as *jus gentium*,

51 Judith Gail Gardam, 'Proportionality and Force in International Law', *American Journal of International Law* 87 (1993): 391, 395.

52 Robert Sloane, 'The Cost of Conflation: Preserving the Dualism of the Jus Ad Bellum and Jus in Bello in the Contemporary Law of War', *Yale Journal of International Law* 34 (2009): 47, 60.

53 James Turner Johnson, *Just War Tradition and the Restraint of War: A Moral and Historical Inquiry* (Princeton, NJ: Princeton University Press, 1981), 172–3.

54 G.I.A.D. Draper, 'The Christian and War', in *Reflections of Law and Armed Conflicts*, ed. Michael Meyer and Hillary McCoubrey (The Hague: Kluwer Law International, 1998). Both rebellion and heresy were considered to be 'heinous offenses' and violations of the *jus ad bellum* that warranted the use of all measures (including enslavement, torture, and murder) to prevail. Parker, 'Early Modern Europe', 44.

55 The term 'European jurists' denotes the combined efforts of several different legal theorists, namely Vitoria, Suarez and Grotius. Though Grotius is considered the originator of international law, his efforts built upon the work of numerous others before him. Attribution for these contributions is beyond the scope of this chapter.

or law of nations, and that this law mandated *temperamenta belli*, or 'moderation in war', under the *jus in bello*.[56] Specifically, moderation urged that warfare should be restricted to those means necessary to prevail over one's enemies, thereby illegitimating the execution of captured or surrendered foes or civilians.[57] Because all Christians were required to observe the *jus in bello* as a subset of the laws of nations, these jurists argued that the *jus in bello* was applicable in all wars among Christian sovereigns and no longer depended upon just cause.[58] This separation of *jus in bello* from *jus ad bellum*, known as the dualistic axiom of the law of war, would permanently alter the belligerent's privilege.[59]

The Effect of Reciprocity on the Belligerent's Privilege

In addition to the efforts of contemporary legal scholars, changes in the belligerent's privilege were also compelled by practical necessities. Whereas warfare in the Middle Ages was oriented toward mounted knights encased in expensive armour, developments in military technology around the fifteenth century began to favour the use of weapons and tactics that required large masses of foot soldiers.[60] Due to the *jus militare*'s intentional efforts to limit the size of the warrior class during the Middle Ages, armies were forced to augment their ranks with commoners in order to fill these units.[61] Though scholars and legal theorists had introduced the dualistic

---

56 Malcolm Shaw, *International Law*, 6th edn (Cambridge: Cambridge University Press, 2008); G.I.A.D. Draper, 'Grotius' Place in the Development of Legal Ideas about War', in *Reflections of Law and Armed Conflicts*, edited by Michael Meyer and Hillary McCoubrey (The Hague: Kluwer Law International, 1998); Arthur Nussbaum, 'The Significance of Roman Law in the History of International Law', *University of Pennsylvania Law Review* 100 (1952): 678, 682. In order to achieve universal implementation of this principle, jurists had to overcome the Church's view that both sides could not be engaged in just war because Divine Will was indivisible. Building from Vittoria's arguments, Grotius argued that law was natural rather than divine and, as a result, was applicable to all Christians regardless of creed. It should be noted, though, that Vitoria originally argued for the extension of natural rights to all humans, particularly indigenous populations in the Western Hemisphere. Johnson, *Just War Tradition and the Restraint of War: A Moral and Historical Inquiry*.

57 Draper, 'The Christian and War', 17; Johnson, *Just War Tradition and the Restraint of War: A Moral and Historical Inquiry*, 201–2.

58 Benedict Kingsbury and Adam Roberts, 'Introduction: Grotian Thought in the Law of Nations', in *Hugo Grotius and International Relations*, ed. Hedley Bull, Benedict Kingsbury, and Adam Roberts (Oxford: Clarendon Press, 1990), 20–21; Johnson, *Just War Tradition and the Restraint of War: A Moral and Historical Inquiry*, 79.

59 G.I.A.D. Draper, 'The Development of International Humanitarian Law', in *International Dimensions of Humanitarian Law* (Geneva/Paris: Henry Dunant Institute/UNESCO, 1988).

60 Johnson, *Just War Tradition and the Restraint of War: A Moral and Historical Inquiry*, 181–83.

61 Ibid., 184.

axiom, the problem still remained that only members of the hereditarily privileged class were protected under the *jus militare* and commoners could still be executed upon capture.[62] In light of the increasingly important role commoners played on the battlefield, European commanders began to recognize the belligerent's privilege in commoners through reciprocal agreements.[63] Because commoners were ignorant of the provisions of the laws of war and breaches were punished through reprisals, members of the hereditary warrior class were installed as officers and expected to use their knowledge of the law of war to prevent common soldiers from committing war crimes.[64] With reciprocity expanding the belligerent's privilege to commoners and replacing honour as the primary means of enforcing compliance with the law of war, the traditional requirement that combatants belong to the hereditary warrior class was rendered obsolete.

Based on the historical inapplicability of Just War Theory to non-Christian 'heathens', European jurists and sovereigns also utilized reciprocity and the 'standard of civilization' to legitimize colonization under the laws of nations.[65] Because the engenderment of the dualistic axiom was based upon the universal applicability of the laws of nations, an argument arose that the laws of nations were applicable to indigenous populations in wars of colonization.[66] In response, European jurists developed a doctrine where the application of the laws of nations was limited to conduct between sovereigns and a nation of people could only be sovereign if they abided by the laws of nations.[67] In other words, the laws of

62 Ibid., 183.

63 Parker, 'Early Modern Europe', 52.

64 Mark Osiel, *The End of Reciprocity* (New York: Cambridge University Press, 2009), 32–33; Johnson, *Just War Tradition and the Restraint of War: A Moral and Historical Inquiry*, 173–74, 185. The simple fact that reciprocity existed as an option by no means mandated its application. Rather, reciprocity depended upon the threat of reprisals to ensure that both sides observed their obligations under the law of war. Kalshoven Frritz, *Belligerent Reprisals*, ed. Christopher Greenswood and Timothy L.H. McCormack, International Humanitarian Law Series (Leiden and Boston, MA: Martinus Nijhoff Publishers, 1971), 2–3. This was particularly true in asymmetric conflicts where illegitimate parties had the most to gain and sovereign monarchs the most to lose. For instance, the Dutch were able to achieve reciprocity with the Spanish despite the Duke of Alva's notorious policies. Alva treated the rebellion in the Low Countries as a war of heresy and employed a strategy of exemplary brutality to stamp it out. Spain's policies abruptly ceased in the autumn of 1573 after the Dutch captured one of Alva's favourite commanders and threatened to hang him unless a reciprocal agreement for humane treatment was established. Alva acquiesced and a formal convention called the 'cuartel general' was signed. Parker, 'Early Modern Europe', 52.

65 Brent Bowden, 'In the Name of Progress and Peace: The "Standard of Civilization" and the Universalizing Project' *Alternatives: Global, Local, Political* 29 no. 1 (2004): 43, 51; Anthonie Anghie, *Imperialism, Sovereignty and the Making of International Law* (Cambridge: Cambridge University Press, 2004).

66 Shaw, *International Law*, 23.

67 Anghie, *Imperialism, Sovereignty and the Making of International Law*, 24. As recently as 1945, the United States still considered meeting the standard of civilization a

nations were reciprocal and European sovereigns would only afford privileges and protections of the laws of nations, specifically the laws of war, if non-European peoples extended them first.[68] This effectively created a dichotomy in international law and the laws of war whereby Europeans would treat each other by one standard and non-Europeans by another, *even if all sides were involved in the same conflict.*[69] This concept of sovereignty is the foundation for separate application of the modern law of war during conflicts between sovereign states (international armed conflict) and conflicts involving a sovereign state and a non-sovereign entity (non-international armed conflict).

Summary of the Developments of the Belligerent's Privilege during Early Modern Europe

Fundamental shifts in Europe's religious and political composition triggered significant changes in the belligerent's privilege in several ways. First, though the *jus militare* had required that a combatant fight for a sovereign engaged in a just war, the establishment of the dualistic axiom rendered this requirement superfluous. Second, the replacement of honour with reciprocity as the primary means of enforcing the law of war archaized the traditional requirement that belligerents belong to the hereditary class of warriors. As a result, the four requirements of the belligerent's privilege under the *jus militare* were reduced to two:

---

fifth express requirement for statehood: 'Fifthly, the inhabitants of the territory must have attained a degree of civilization such as to enable them to observe with respect to the outside world those principles of law which are deemed to govern the members of the international society in their relations with each other.' Charles Cheney Hyde, *International Law Chiefly as Interpreted and Applied by the United States* 2nd edn, 3 vols, vol. 1 (Boston, MA: Little, Brown & Co, 1945), 17. But see, Ian Brownlie, *Principles of Public International Law*, 1st edn (Oxford: Oxford University Press, 1966) (stating that the requirement for a certain degree of civilization 'is usually omitted from enumerations of criteria and is redolent of the period when non-European states were not accorded equal treatment by the European Concert and the United States').

68 Anghie, *Imperialism, Sovereignty and the Making of International Law*, 20–21, 26.

69 For example, during the French and Indian War, British and French forces afforded and respected the laws of war with regard to each other, but applied varying standards of treatment to Native American warriors according to political considerations. Alfred A. Cave, *The French and Indian War*, ed. Linda S. Frey and Marsha L. Frey, Greenwood Guides to Historic Events 1500–1900 (Westport, CT: Greenwood Press, 2004); William Nester, *The First Global War: Britain, France and the Fate of North America 1756–1775* (Westport, CT: Praeger Publishers, 2000). Moreover, both sides expected that any Native Americans in their employ would be mandated to respect the laws of war in encounters with Europeans. Edward Dodge, *Relief Is Greatly Wanted: The Battle of Fort William Henry* (Bowie, MD: Heritage Books, 1998) (regarding the massacre at Ft. William Henry); Fred Anderson, *Crucible of War: The Seven Years' War and the Fate of Empire in British North America* (New York: Vintage Books, 2000), 62–70 (regarding then Col. Washington's involvement in the Jumonville Affair).

1. the individual needed to possess *right authority* granted by a kingdom or state recognized as sovereign under the laws of nations, and
2. the individual had to abide by the laws of war, namely by refraining from perfidious or 'savage/uncivilized' conduct.

Finally, the disintegration of the Church's authority significantly diminished the need for ecclesiastical immunity and the immunity conferred by the belligerent's privilege was effectively reduced to two forms:

1. an international privilege permitting participation in hostilities and allowing for protected status upon capture through reciprocal observation of the laws of war, and
2. a domestic privilege immunizing the individual from any punishment for engaging in hostilities.

The Frustration and Divide in Custom: 1796–1907

At the beginning of the nineteenth century, international custom held that combatants and non-combatants formed two distinct classes during war and that an individual could not obtain the rights and protections of a combatant except by enlisting in the regular army.[70] If an individual who was not a member of a sovereign's armed forces engaged in hostilities and was captured, they were guilty of violating international law and could be summarily executed.[71] The advent of the *levée en masse* forced European states to reconsider this rule and devise a means of distinguishing the lawful irregular combatant from bandits and brigands.[72] As a result, a split in custom occurred in Europe, with one side favouring Prussia's blanket denial of the privilege to irregular combatants and the other side favouring the Belgian/Netherlands view that every inhabitant has a natural right to defend his home and country.[73] To the United States, though, the *levée en masse* was hardly a new development and American application of the laws of war reflected a deeper understanding of the relationship between irregulars and the regular army. This fracture of custom would persist until the first Hague Conference in 1899.

The Problem of Irregular Warfare under the Laws of War

At the dawn of the nineteenth century, efforts to limit war through further development of the *jus ad bellum* had generally been abandoned and war had

70 H.R. Droop, 'The Relations between an Invading Army and the Inhabitants, and the Conditions under which Irregular Combatants are Entitled to the Same Treatment as Regular Troops', *Solicitor's Journal and Reporter* 15 (1870): 22.

71 Ibid.

72 Ibid.

73 Ibid.

become a highly structured confrontation conducted according to the customary *jus in bello*.[74] The right to engage in hostilities was restricted to the armed forces of a state on the belief that doing so would limit the cruelties of war to the narrowest segment of the population possible.[75] In turn, anyone who participated in hostilities without *right authority* violated the laws of war *per se* and could be summarily executed upon capture.[76]

The introduction of self-constituted and untrained guerrilla forces to the battlefield drawn from the civilian population created several significant issues for the law of war. First, guerrilla warfare was highly effective against the linear formations of a state's armed forces in the field.[77] The ability of guerrillas to attack and melt away, as well as surprise enemy units when resting or unprepared for battle created numerous hardships for conventional armies.[78] Second, guerrillas blurred the lines of distinction between civilians and combatants. By the nineteenth century, *temperamenta belli* had developed into theory of non-combatant immunity on the belief that, since civilians posed no threat, destruction of civilians or their property should be strenuously avoided because it had no military necessity.[79] In contrast, combatants openly displayed their status as combatants to their enemies, usually through ornate and decorative uniforms, and were entitled to humane treatment and combatant immunity as a result.[80] Because civilians who engaged in hostilities did not wear uniforms, military units struggled to distinguish them from civilians who had not participated in hostilities thereby contributing to collateral damage.[81] Finally, because civilians were untrained in the law of war, they usually resorted to tactics outside the bounds of 'civilized' warfare.[82] In response, military commanders would often respond with exceptional brutality against the entire civilian population.[83]

74 Stephen C. Neff, *War and the Law of Nations: A General History* (Cambridge: Cambridge University Press, 2005), 186; Yoram Dinstein, *War, Aggression, and Self-Defence*, 3rd edn (Cambridge and New York: Cambridge University Press, 2001), 63.

75 Draper, 'The Status of Combatants and the Question of Guerilla Warfare', 175.

76 Ibid.

77 Ibid.

78 Ibid.

79 W.E. Hall, *A Treatise on International Law*, 4th edn (Buffalo, TX: Kessinger Publishing, 1895), 537; Johnson, *Just War Tradition and the Restraint of War: A Moral and Historical Inquiry*, 212–13; Geoffrey Best, *Humanity in Warfare* (London: Weidenfeld & Nicolson, 1980), 64–65.

80 Draper, 'The Status of Combatants and the Question of Guerilla Warfare', 176; Toni Pfanner, 'Military Uniforms and the Law of War', *International Review of the Red Cross* 86 no. 853 (2004): 93, 98.

81 Gunther Rothenburg, 'The Age of Napoleon', in *The Laws of War: Constraints on Warfare in the Western World* ed. Michael Howard, George J. Andreopoulos, and Mark R. Shulman (New Haven, CT: Yale University Press, 1994), Chapter 6, 82.

82 Ibid.

83 Ibid.

Inconsistency with Irregulars: The European Approach

Europe's troubles with irregular combatants began in earnest on 23 August 1793, when the French Republic decreed the *levée en masse* to respond to the growing threat of war on France's borders.[84] The *levée en masse* was based on the principle that the French Republic could demand military service as a fundamental duty of its citizens.[85] For the first time in history, a state was authorizing *and* obligating all able citizens to take up arms.[86] This completely reversed the long-held custom cemented by the *jus militare* that only a very narrow and clearly defined class of individuals could engage in hostilities.

France would later be on the receiving end of popular resistance beginning in 1808 when Napoleon invaded the Iberian Peninsula and named his brother king of Spain.[87] Within weeks, French forces were combating a nation-wide insurgency comprising two forms of widely dispersed and loosely organized insurgents: guerrillas and Ordenanza.[88] Supplied by the British and operating from remote and inaccessible mountain areas, the guerrillas disrupted French communications and supplies, attacked Iberian collaborators, and preyed on weak or isolated French detachments.[89] In response, the French declared that the guerrillas lacked *right authority*, executed any guerrillas they captured, and burned villages that were considered to be complicit in their activities.[90] Ordenanza, organized military units that did not wear uniforms, also carried out regular operations against the French.[91] While France protested the use of Ordenanza, it did so on the basis that the Ordenanza did not wear uniforms, not for lack of *right authority*.[92] By 1810, reprisals by Spanish guerrillas forced the French into reciprocal recognition of the guerrillas' belligerency and acceptance of the Duke of Wellington's declaration that the Ordenanzas were operating under *right authority*.[93]

Wellington was forced to reverse course, though, when he invaded France and faced a *levée en masse* as an invader rather than a liberator. Despite the fact that the French authorized every national to resist the British, Spanish and

---

84 Alan Forrest, 'La Patrie En Danger: The French Revolution and the First Levée En Masse', in *The People in Arms: Military Myth and National Mobilization since the French Revolution*, ed. Daniel Moran and Arthur Waldron (Cambridge and New York: Cambridge University Press, 2003), Chapter 2, 10.

85 Ibid, 8.

86 Ibid.

87 David Gates, *The Spanish Ulcer: A History of the Peninsular War* (London: George Allen & Unwin, 1986), 11.

88 Ibid., 12.

89 Ibid., 34–35.

90 Charles Oman, *A History of the Peninsula War*, vol. III (Oxford: Clarendon Press, 1908), 489–90.

91 W.E. Hall, *International Law* (Oxford: Clarendon Press, 1908), 452.

92 Ibid.

93 Ibid.

Portuguese armies by any means, Wellington issued a proclamation ordering the inhabitants to take arms openly and join with the French army, or stay peaceably in their homes.[94] If they failed to comply, he threatened to hang them and burn their villages.[95] By making these threats, Wellington aimed to eradicate part-time soldiering by establishing the modern requirement of 'carrying arms openly' for privileged belligerent status.

Prussia, which would later become notorious for its harsh treatment of irregulars, also relied heavily upon mass conscription to repel Napoleon's invasion of Northern Germany. Prussian's *Landwehr* and the *Landsturm* combined elements of both a *levée en masse* and guerrilla warfare.[96] The *Landwehr*, which also included the upper-class *Jäger*, was a general militia based upon compulsory service for men between seventeen and forty.[97] The *Landsturm* was composed of older men between forty and sixty, to be called upon to conduct scorched-earth operations, sabotage, and disrupt enemy lines of communication.[98] While the *Landwehr* were drafted to augment regular units, the *Landsturm* were specifically designed to carry out guerrilla operations.[99] The *Landsturm*'s uniforms reflected this role because their only means of distinction were a cap and belt, but these units were instructed to hide both when hard-pressed in order to avoid capture.[100] Napoleon responded by branding the *Landsturm* brigands and authorizing summary executions.[101]

France accorded similar treatment to Mexican irregulars after invading Mexico in 1861. At first, the French treated all combatants, regardless of tactics or dress, as lawful belligerents.[102] After settling into occupation, though, the French emperor Maximilian declared that all forces opposing him were bandits subject to trial and

---

94 T.E. Holland, *Lectures on International Law*, ed. T.A. and W.L. Walker (London: Sweet & Maxwell, 1933), 350–372, 363.

95 James Spaight, *War Rights on Land* (London: Macmillan, 1911), 37, n. 2.

96 Michael Leggiere, *Napoleon and Berlin: The Franco-Prussian War in North Germany 1813*, Campaigns and Commanders (Norman, OK: University of Oklahoma Press, 2002), x.

97 Daniel Moran, 'The Dilemmas of German Liberalism', in *The People in Arms: Military Myth and National Mobilization since the French Revolution*, ed. Daniel Moran and Arthur Waldron (Cambridge and New York: Cambridge University Press, 2003), Chapter 4, 53.

98 Leggiere, *Napoleon and Berlin: The Franco-Prussian War in North Germany 1813*, 57.

99 Holland, *Lectures on International Law*, 6.

100 Droop, 'The Relations between an Invading Army and the Inhabitants, and the Conditions under Which Irregular Combatants Are Entitled to the Same Treatment as Regular Troops', 122.

101 Ibid.; Francis Lieber, 'Guerilla Parties with Reference to the Laws and Usages of War', in *Lieber's Code and the Laws of War*, ed. Richard Shelly Hartigan (Chicago, IL: Precedent, 1862 [1982]), 35, 15.

102 Jack Dabbs, *The French Army in Mexico, 1861–1867: A Study in Military Government* (The Hague: Mouton, 1963), 50, 119.

execution.[103] During their withdrawal, the French granted insurgents prisoner of war status, but this may have been compelled by reprisals and the desire to prevent flare-ups during the drawdown.[104]

Ironically, French irregulars would endure the same treatment during the Franco-Prussian War. After Prussia invaded in 1870, the French government called the population to arms and established *corps francs* ('free corps') distinct and separate from the national army.[105] The combination of the *corps francs* and local measures of self-defence opened a second phase of the war involving approximately 60,000 irregular soldiers outside of Paris.[106] The Prussians considered the *corps francs* to be unlawful and treacherous, and branded them *francs-tireurs* ('free shooters').[107] They further declared that *francs-tireurs* would be afforded belligerency status only if they were incorporated into formal units that Prussian forces could recognize as combatants.[108] In particular, Prussia required every French prisoner to be listed on an official list of organized military units in order to avoid execution as a brigand.[109] After Prussia occupied Paris, the *francs-tireurs* began small-scale operations to destroy Prussian logistics and instil a sense of fear in Prussian troops.[110] The Prussians responded with summary executions of captured *francs-tireurs* and collective reprisals against supportive civilian populations.[111] Prussia's troubling experiences with the *francs-tireurs* shaped its perspective that irregular combatants had no place on the battlefield, and that unprivileged belligerency in and of itself constituted a violation of the laws of war.[112] Both in 1874 and 1899, Prussia would defend this viewpoint as the correct interpretation of international law.

A Second Approach: Irregulars in North America up to and during the American Civil War

To the United States, the *levée en masse* was hardly a novel concept. The American Revolution had been fought and won through popular resistance, and

103 William Winthrop, *Military Law and Precedents*, ed. Igor I. Kavass and Adolf Sprudzs (New York: William S. Hein & Co., 1979 [1920]), 782–833, 798, n. 62.

104 Dabbs, *The French Army in Mexico, 1861–1867: A Study in Military Government*, 204–05.

105 John Horne, 'Defining the Enemy: War, Law and the Levée En Masse from 1870 to 1945', in *The People in Arms: Military Myth and National Mobilization since the French Revolution*, ed. Daniel Moran and Arthur Waldron (Cambridge and New York: Cambridge University Press, 2003), 100–23.

106 Ibid.

107 Ibid., 109.

108 Ibid.

109 Hall, *International Law*, 541.

110 Walter Laqueur, *Guerilla* (Boston, MA: Little, Brown, 1976), 86.

111 Horne, 'Defining the Enemy: War, Law and the Levée En Masse from 1870 to 1945', 109.

112 Ibid., 86–87.

the American 'Minute Man' could have easily been a forerunner to the *corps francs*.[113] Moreover, compulsory service in local militias was still commonplace in the American South at the outbreak of the Civil War.[114] Further, in the limited wars the United States had fought against Britain and Mexico, the small regular American army depended heavily upon locally raised *ad hoc* units to meet the nation's military requirements.[115] These experiences helped the United States craft a far more nuanced standard for determining who was entitled to the belligerent's privilege than its European counterparts.

The United States began to distinguish its treatment of irregular combatants in 1847 during the Mexican–American War. After capturing Mexico City, General Winfield Scott was faced with the dilemma of adjudicating war crimes committed by Mexican irregulars.[116] In response, Scott established 'councils of war' to try individuals for engaging in hostilities without *right authority* as well as any violations of the laws of the war.[117] Before the end of the war, Scott folded the councils of war into the jurisdiction of general military commissions that were the forerunners to the modern American military commissions.[118] Of course, the United States was also a leader in maintaining the savage/civilized dichotomy in the laws of war as demonstrated by its egregious treatment of Native Americans.

By far the most important American contribution to the treatment of irregular combatants under international law is General Orders 100, also known as the Lieber Code. The Lieber Code is a compilation of the Union Army's obligations and rights during the US Civil War and it advanced four major developments in the law of war.

First, the Code formally recognized that individuals authorized by their state to take up arms are entitled to combatant immunity as an element of their status as POWs.[119] As such, they could not be prosecuted for any legitimate acts of war under the domestic law of a state.

---

113 John Whiteclay Chambers, II, 'American Views of Conscription and the German Nation in Arms in the Franco-Prussian War', in *The People in Arms: Military Myth and National Mobilization since the French Revolution*, ed. Daniel Moran and Arthur Waldron (Cambridge and New York: Cambridge University Press, 2003), 76.

114 Ibid., 79.

115 Ibid.

116 Frederic L. Borch, 'The History of Military Commissions in the U.S. Army: From the Mexican–American War to the War on Terrorism', in *The U.S. Army and Irregular Warfare* (2007), ed. Richard Davis. Online. Available HTTP: http://www.history.army.mil/html/books/irregular_warfare/index.html (accessed 4 February 2014).

117 Winthrop, *Military Law and Precedents*, 833.

118 Ibid.

119 'So soon as a man is armed by a sovereign government and takes the soldier's oath of fidelity he is a belligerent, his killing, wounding, or other warlike acts are no individual crimes or offenses. No belligerent has a right to declare that enemies of a certain class, color, or condition, when properly organized as soldiers, will not be treated by him as public enemies.' Lieber, 'Guerilla Parties with Reference to the Laws and Usages of War',

Second, the Code recognized a sovereign state's right to afford the protections of POW status to unprivileged belligerents without recognizing the legitimacy of their cause or organization.[120] The article that provides for this right, Article 153, may be the Code's most important article for comparative purposes. By directing Union forces to treat Confederates as POWs without granting them combatant immunity, Lieber concreted the connection between combatant immunity and *right authority*. Affirming the requirement of sovereignty, Lieber emphasized that only *legitimate* and *recognized* states can authorize individuals to take part in hostilities.[121] Because only combatants who possess *right authority* are entitled to combatant immunity and secessionist movements are unable to confer *right authority* because they lack sovereignty, members of secession or insurrection movements are not protected by combatant immunity after capture.[122] More importantly, Lieber provided states with the flexibility to offer humane treatment to captured rebels while still refuting the legitimacy of their cause.[123] As demonstrated in the US Civil War, Union forces were able to provide Confederate soldiers 'all the privileges of the prisoner of war' without forfeiting their right to prosecute the Confederates for treason.[124] In doing so, the United States established that combatant immunity and prisoner of war status are separate benefits conferred by the belligerent's privilege.

Third, the Code distinguished between irregulars entitled to POW status and those who are not.[125] In particular, Lieber distinguished between the privileged partisan and the unprivileged guerrilla. Partisans were 'soldiers armed and wearing the uniform of their army, but belonging to a corps which acts detached from the main body for the purpose of making inroads into the territory occupied by the enemy.'[126] They were distinguished by, (a) their authorization to take part in hostilities, (b) being under the command of an accountable leader, (c) forming an integrant part of the regular army, and (d) being paid regularly by a party to the conflict.[127] So long as they wore uniforms and abided by the laws of war, partisans were privileged and entitled to combatant immunity upon capture.[128]

The best example of partisans under Lieber's formulation was Mosby's Raiders, an irregular Confederate unit created by General J.E.B. Stuart that

U.S. Dep't of war General orders no. 100, Instructions for the Government of Armies of the United States in the Field, art. 82 (Apr. 24, 1863) [hereinafter 'Lieber Code'].

120 Ibid., art. 152.

121 Ibid., art. 152.

122 Ibid., art. 154.

123 Ibid., art. 152.

124 Ibid.

125 Ibid., art. 81.

126 Ibid.

127 Lieber Code, 33.

128 Ibid.

operated behind enemy lines in Northern Virginia.[129] An extremely effective cavalry leader, Mosby was able to continuously and repeatedly disrupt Union lines of communication and supply through surprise, subterfuge, and ruses of war.[130] Nonetheless, Mosby, a trained lawyer, ensured that his units complied with international law and took at least one occasion to remind his Union counterpart of his obligations under the same law.[131]

In contrast, 'guerrillas' were any band of armed men carrying out irregular warfare who were not constituted by the government.[132] Generally speaking, guerrillas were disconnected from the main army's movement and were not supplied or paid by any army.[133] Additionally, they were not a permanent unit and could be disbanded and recalled at the whim of their leader.[134] Under the umbrella of guerrillas, Lieber included freebooters, brigands, and prowlers.[135] Upon capture, guerrillas were not entitled to combatant immunity or protection as a prisoner of war, and could be tried for unauthorized engagement in hostilities as well as any violations of domestic law.[136]

Finally, Lieber discussed the rights and duties of a population during invasion and occupation. On the issue of *levée en masse*, Lieber found that international law recognized the right for the people of an invaded state to spontaneously take up arms in defence of their country.[137] Due to the instantaneous nature of a *levée en masse*, members were not required to wear uniforms and were not required to be organized in any particular manner.[138] So long as members of a *levée en masse* refrained from perfidy and only resisted in areas still being contested, they were entitled to the full protections of POW status and combatant immunity.[139] Once an invader effected an occupation, though, any form of resistance was illegitimate and its members could be prosecuted and executed.[140]

---

129 Evan J. Wallach, 'Partisans, Pirates, and Pancho Villa: How Interational and National Law Handled Non-State Fighters in the "Good Old Days" before 1949 and That Approach's Applicability to the "War on Terror"', *Emory International Law Review* 24 (2010): 549, 570.

130 Phillip Sutter, 'The Continuing Role for Belligerent Reprisals', *Journal of Conflict and Security Law* 13 (2008): 93, 97.

131 'Letter from Lieut. Col. John S. Mosby to Maj. Gen. P.H. Sheridan (Nov. 11, 1864)', in *John Singleton Mosby, the Memoirs of Colonel John S. Mosby*, ed. Charles Wells Russell (Boston, MA: Little, Brown and Company, 1917), 302–03.

132 Lieber Code, 33.

133 Ibid.

134 Ibid.

135 Ibid., 34.

136 Ibid.

137 Ibid., 39.

138 Ibid.

139 Ibid.

140 Ibid., 40 (explaining, '[n]or could it be maintained in good faith, or with any respect for sound sense and judgment, that an individual – and armed prowler – (now frequently

In comparing the European and American approaches to irregular combatants, two points are particularly relevant. First, most of the European conflicts dealt with a recognized state invading another recognized state, whereas the American model was based mostly on the South's secession in the Civil War.[141] As such, the irregular combatants that the Europeans faced were generally individuals in conquered states resisting occupation rather than secessionist movements attempting to break away. Second, the American perspective was based upon the myth of the volunteer army. Americans not only recognized the right of citizens to resist invasion, they saw such resistance as a patriotic duty. Because of this, Americans distinguished the *levée en masse* from irregular combatants, established a criteria for determining which irregular combatants were entitled to prisoner of war status, and concreted a state's right to provide humane treatment without recognizing the legitimacy of unprivileged combatancy.

The Brussels Declaration and the Hague Conventions

Growing disparities in the treatment of irregular combatants in the nineteenth century produced the need for a clear international standard. In an effort to define this standard, the Brussels and Hague Conferences were convened to, among other things, coalesce varying customs of treatment into a single customary law. In order to do so, the international community distinguished the use of irregular forces by a state from the spontaneous taking up of arms by the population. In recognizing the right of a population to spontaneously resist an armed invasion through a *levée en masse*, the international community implicitly acknowledged that combatants in an exceptionally defined class of conflicts are universally granted *right authority* by function of international law, rather than by act of a sovereign. This implicit grant constitutes not only an international right of a population to defend its state, it constitutes a re-conflation of the dualistic axiom of the law of war by granting rights in *jus in bello* based on criteria under *jus ad bellum*.

The State of Custom prior to the Brussels Declaration

In 1870, English barrister H.R. Droop gave a lecture to the Juridical Society in London on the topic of the laws of war. After explaining the quickly dissolving barrier between combatants and non-combatants, Droop moved on to explain contemporary standards regarding treatment of irregular combatants. He

---

called a bushwhacker) shall be entitled to the protection of the law of war simply because he says that he has taken up his gun in defense of his country, or because his government or his chief has issued a proclamation by which he calls upon the people to infest the bushes and commit homicides which every civilized nation will consider murders').

141 Or the North's aggression. The author intends no insult or injury to those who prefer their iced tea sweet and their football on Saturdays.

maintained that irregular combatants, whether they were auxiliaries, militia, or volunteer corps, were entitled to prisoner of war status if they met four conditions.

First, '[t]hey must have an authorization from an established government or from some *de facto* substitute for such a Government.'[142] This obligation reflected the customary requirement of *right authority*, while re-emphasizing the Just War doctrine that war could only be fought between sovereigns and not individuals.[143] This standard confirmed that only individuals deputed by sovereigns to fight on their behalf could be considered as carrying out legitimate warfare.[144] Droop added that the treatment of Confederate soldiers and Garibaldi's corps during the unification of Italy indicated that secessionist or unification movements could acquire belligerency status if they functioned as *de facto* governments.[145] This contradicted Lieber's point of view that secessionist movements were not entitled to belligerency status, but could attain POW status under the dictates of humanity rather than law.[146]

Second, '[t]hey must be under the actual control of officers who are recognized by and responsible to the chief military authorities of the state.'[147] This provision extends the military custom established during the Renaissance that a noble officer corps ensure that common ranks abided by the law of war.[148] By placing them under the command of officers answerable to the command of the regular army, irregulars could be prosecuted for any war crimes they committed.[149]

Third, '[t]hey themselves must observe the rules of war.'[150] This complements the second rule while also addressing the fear that irregulars who violated the laws of war would still be entitled to POW status upon capture.[151] Given the major tactical advantages afforded to irregulars during this period of warfare, this was likely an attempt to level the playing field.

142 Droop, 'The Relations between an Invading Army and the Inhabitants, and the Conditions under Which Irregular Combatants Are Entitled to the Same Treatment as Regular Troops', 124.

143 Hall, *International Law*, 538.

144 Droop, 'The Relations between an Invading Army and the Inhabitants, and the Conditions under Which Irregular Combatants Are Entitled to the Same Treatment as Regular Troops', 122.

145 Ibid.

146 Lieber Code, art. 152.

147 Droop, 'The Relations between an Invading Army and the Inhabitants, and the Conditions under Which Irregular Combatants Are Entitled to the Same Treatment as Regular Troops', 124.

148 Johnson, *Just War Tradition and the Restraint of War: A Moral and Historical Inquiry*, 181–83.

149 Droop, 'The Relations between an Invading Army and the Inhabitants, and the Conditions under Which Irregular Combatants Are Entitled to the Same Treatment as Regular Troops', 124.

150 Ibid., 124.

151 Ibid., 125.

Fourth, '[a]ll combatants intended to act singly or in small parties must have a permanent distinctive uniform, but this is not indispensable for troops acting together in large bodies.'[152] The objective of this fourth requirement was to better distinguish between combatants and civilians. In this regard, the obligations under the principle of distinction could be argued to be more exacting on irregulars due to the fact that they operated in small groups and relied upon stealth.[153] In contrast, regular units could be easily distinguished from civilians because of the military character of their activities. This requirement also reflects the difficulties associated with issuing uniforms to armies at the onset of war.[154]

The Codification of Levée en Masse and Irregular Units

At the time of Droop's lecture, clear lines between a *levée en masse* and guerilla resistance had yet to be established. The Brussels Conference, which occurred four years later, attempted to codify these distinctions, as well as the requirements for prisoner of war status into an international agreement.[155] From the onset, the larger states (particularly Russia and Germany) argued for strict separation between combatants and non-combatants, and for persons failing to distinguish themselves to be tried under military law.[156] This position was visible in the early drafts of the Brussels Declaration that required even members of a *levée en masse* to be under a 'general military command.'[157] The Netherlands, Spain, Portugal, and others rejected his approach on the basis that it weakened national defence and detached citizens 'from their duty towards their country.'[158] In the end, the parties recognized the automatic of right of the members of the armed forces to prisoner of war status and dichotomized irregular combatants into (a) militia, volunteer corps, and auxiliary groups forming 'part of the permanent forces of a state' or (b) 'the unorganized population rising in arms spontaneously or otherwise in face of the invader' (*levée en masse*).[159]

Irregular forces: militia, volunteer corps, and auxiliary groups

Irregular units under the Brussels Declaration were closer to the Prussian Landsturm and Landswehr than the French levée en masse. Prior to the Brussels

152 Ibid.

153 Ibid.

154 Ibid.

155 Percy Bordwell, *The Law of War between Belligerents* (Chicago, IL: Callaghan & Co, 1908), 102.

156 Ibid., 104.

157 Hall, *International Law*, 544.

158 Bordwell, *The Law of War between Belligerents*, 105.

159 Hall, *International Law*, 545; 'Project of an International Declaration Concerning the Laws and Customs of War (1873–74)', *British and Foreign State Papers* 65 (27 Aug. 1874): 1005.

Declaration, irregular soldiers were presumed to be war criminals operating without right authority and were shot upon capture unless they could demonstrate right authority through some kind of express authorization from a government.[160] In an effort to regularize unconventional warfare, the Brussels Conference used the belligerent's privilege as an incentive for irregular soldiers to comply with the laws of war.[161] Irregular soldiers would be considered privileged belligerents entitled to combatant immunity and prisoner of war status upon capture if they met four criteria under Article 9.[162]

First, they had to be commanded by a person responsible to his subordinates.[163] This requirement codified the historic practice of installing nobility as officers to ensure that common soldiers complied with the laws and customs of war.[164] This requirement could be satisfied by both regularly and temporarily commissioned officers or by a civilian with sufficient civil authority to compel compliance with the laws of war.[165]

Second, they had to wear a fixed distinctive emblem recognizable at a distance.[166] This requirement served two purposes: (1) to protect the members of the enemy's armed forces 'from treacherous attacks by apparently harmless individuals', and (2) to protect the civilian population from being misidentified as perfidious combatants.[167] This requirement was satisfied if a lone soldier was dressed in a way that his enemy would know he was a combatant and not a civilian.[168] 'Fixed distinctive emblem', therefore, does not require a uniform but merely a 'sign' that is attached externally and cannot be concealed at will.[169] This requirement was complemented by the third requirement that irregular combatants carry their arms openly.

Finally, they were obligated to conduct their operations in accordance with the laws of war.[170] This requirement best demonstrates the use of the belligerent's privilege as a means of inducing irregulars to comply with the laws of war,

---

160 Herbert Fooks, *Prisoners of War* (Federalsburg, MD: The J.W. Stowell Printing Co, 1924), 34.

161 Howard S. Levie, 'Prisoners of War in International Armed Conflict', *U.S. Naval War College International Law Studies* 59 (1978): 46.

162 'Project of an International Declaration Concerning the Laws and Customs of War (1873–74)', art. 9.

163 Levie, 'Prisoners of War in International Armed Conflict', 50.

164 Johnson, *Just War Tradition and the Restraint of War: A Moral and Historical Inquiry*, 172–73, 185.

165 Hall, *International Law*, 546.

166 'Project of an International Declaration Concerning the Laws and Customs of War (1873–74)', art. 9(2)

167 Levie, 'Prisoners of War in International Armed Conflict', 46–47.

168 Fooks, *Prisoners of War*, 35.

169 Spaight, *War Rights on Land*, 57.

170 'Project of an International Declaration Concerning the Laws and Customs of War (1873–74)', art. 9(4).

particularly the principle of distinction, in exchange for protection upon surrender. Implicit in this requirement was the expectation that irregulars would be instructed on the laws of war, especially regarding perfidy, treatment of prisoners, truce and surrender, and the immunity of civilians.[171]

Levée en masse

When discussing the *levée en masse* at the Brussels Conference, two major viewpoints emerged. First, Germany and Russia argued that a member of a *levée en masse* should have to meet the same requirements of combatancy as militia and volunteer corps.[172] In particular, members of a *levée en masse* had to be placed under responsible command to ensure compliance with the laws of war.[173] In opposition, Spain, Belgium, Holland, and Switzerland argued that the right of a population to defend their nation was not only a right, but a sacred duty recognized in the customs of war and no organization was required.[174] Ultimately, the Conference settled on the language contained in Article 10:

> The population of a territory which has not been occupied, who on the approach of the enemy spontaneously take up arms to resist the invading troops without having had time to organize themselves in accordance with Article 9, shall be regarded as belligerents if they respect the laws and customs of war.[175]

In contrast with irregular units, the belligerent's privilege was automatically granted by function of international law to members of a *levée en masse* subject to three major limitations.[176] First, the right of a population to take up arms is limited geographically to that territory which has been invaded, but has not been legally occupied by a foreign army.[177] Once an occupation is legally effected, the population is no longer entitled to resist under the auspices of a *levée en masse*.[178] Second, a *levée en masse* must be a spontaneous response to a foreign invasion.[179] 'Spontaneously' means not only immediately, but under circumstances where a population has not been able to organize themselves under responsible commanders, nor to procure distinctive emblems recognizable at a

171 Fooks, *Prisoners of War*, 38.

172 Spaight, *War Rights on Land*, 48–49; Lester Nurick and Roger W. Barrett, 'Legality of Guerilla Forces under the Laws of War', *American Journal of International Law* 40 (1946): 563, 566.

173 Spaight, *War Rights on Land*, 50.

174 Hall, *International Law*, 544–45.

175 'Project of an International Declaration Concerning the Laws and Customs of War (1873–74)', art. 10.

176 Ibid.

177 Fooks, *Prisoners of War*, 32–33.

178 Levie, 'Prisoners of War in International Armed Conflict', 64.

179 Ibid.

distance.[180] Third, the *levée en masse* still had to abide by the laws and customs of war, and Hague 1907 added the requirement of carrying arms openly.[181] These last two requirements were concessions to larger states that sought to narrow the asymmetric advantages conferred on a *levée en masse* by compelling adherence to the laws of war, specifically the principle of distinction.[182]

Accordingly, the *levée en masse* also has certain implicit attributes. First, 'inhabitants' has no legal definition and is generally understood to mean the civilian population of a territory.[183] While this could open the door for any civilian regardless of citizenship to participate in a *levée en masse*, the historic justification of a *levée en masse* based on a citizen's patriotic duty seems to imply that only the invaded state's citizens are entitled to participate.[184] However, a non-citizen able to demonstrate a convincing tie to the invaded territory could make a plausible argument for inclusion. Second, a *levée en masse* is expected to be a large mass of combatants resisting an invasion and, by nature of this quality, should be inherently distinguishable from the non-combatant civilian population.[185] This expectation is made even more overt by the requirement that its members carry their arms openly. Third, due to its quality as a spontaneous uprising, a *levée en masse* does not require express government authorization.[186]

The Brussels Declaration was not signed into law, but its criteria for POW status was replicated in both Hague Conventions and is the customary basis for the criteria found in the Third Geneva Convention. The Hague Conventions went further and promulgated obligations and responsibilities in time of occupation, the most important of which permitted the occupier to enact laws and regulations to compel the civilian population into peacefulness.[187]

Despite the fact that neither the Brussels Declaration nor the Hague Conventions expressly mention a requirement for *right authority*, it remained 'a fundamental premise implicit in the Hague Regulations; and an individual does not become a lawful combatant merely because he dons a uniform, carries arms openly, and is commanded by a person responsible for his subordinates.'[188]

An even more interesting point on *right authority* is the condition created by the *levée en masse*. Because its members are entitled to the belligerent's privilege even though no sovereign has granted *right authority*, the traditional requirement of *right authority* seems to be absent with a *levée en masse*. In reality, though, a *levée*

---

180 Lassa Oppenheim, *International Law: A Treatise*, vol. 2 (1905), 90.

181 Fooks, *Prisoners of War*, 30.

182 Levie, 'Prisoners of War in International Armed Conflict', 65.

183 Ibid., 64.

184 Spaight, *War Rights on Land*, 48–49.

185 Hall, *International Law*, 546.

186 Ibid., 545–46.

187 'Project of an International Declaration Concerning the Laws and Customs of War (1873–74)', art. 48.

188 Nurick and Barrett, 'Legality of Guerilla Forces under the Laws of War', 267–68.

en masse constitutes one of two exceptional circumstances where *right authority* is automatically conferred by international law in light of an extraordinary cause. In this instance, the international community has recognized that 'the patriotic feeling which impels all the able-bodied men of a nation to take up arms in defence of the national territory if invaded, is not only an imprescriptible right, but also a sacred duty.'[189]

As a result, the international community devised an automatic conferral of *right authority* whenever a population met the legal requirements of a *levée en masse* and granted its members privileged belligerent status.

Nonetheless, the right to defend one's territory was limited to 'civilized' peoples and indigenous populations were still considered outside the ambit of the laws of war. European powers frequently utilized prohibited means and methods in dealing with colonial revolts, and belligerent recognition of indigenous groups in revolt was simply out of the question.[190] While the 1899 Hague Convention produced the famous Martens Clause that laid the foundation for the principle of humanity for all mankind, an argument could be made that the exclusion of indigenous warriors in anti-colonial uprisings had less to do with racism than *right authority*.[191]

As combatants fighting for nations that could not attain sovereignty, indigenous fighters lacked *right authority* and were not protected by the laws of war. Imperial warfare was, after all, a game in which Europeans made the rules.

In review, at the beginning of the twentieth century, the belligerent's privilege was expanded yet again to include two classes of irregular combatants. In order to be entitled to the belligerent's privilege:

1. An individual needed to possess *right authority* granted by a sovereign state in one of three ways:
   - as a member of a sovereign state's armed forces, or
   - as a member of a militia, volunteer corps, or auxiliary unit belonging to a sovereign state while also fulfilling the four requirements enumerated in the Hague Conventions, or
   - as a member of *levée en masse*, and
2. The individual had to abide by the laws of war, namely by refraining from perfidy and espionage.
3. Privileged belligerents were entitled to:
   - an international privilege permitting participation in hostilities and guaranteeing enumerated protections as a prisoner of war upon capture, and

189 Spaight, *War Rights on Land*, 49 (quoting the language adopted by the President of the Brussels Conference, Baron Jomini).

190 Frederic Megret, 'From "Savages" to "Unlawful Combatants": A Postcolonial Look at International Humanitarian Law's "Other"', in *International Law and Its 'Others'*, ed. Anne Orford (Cambridge: Cambridge University Press, 2006), 274.

191 Fooks, *Prisoners of War*, 27 ('The lack of civilization and not the color of captives in the true test as to whether they should be treated as prisoners of war').

– a domestic privilege immunizing the individual from any punishment for engaging in hostilities.

The Belligerent's Privilege under Current Law

Sir Adam Roberts once described the law of war during the period between The Hague Conventions and the Nuremberg Tribunal as 'an account of a failure.'[192] Despite hundreds of years of custom and a half-century's worth of negotiation and treaty formation, World War I degenerated into a no-holds-barred conflict in fewer than six months. While World War II was slightly more constrained between combatants, even more egregious atrocities were purposefully and systematically committed against civilians. Out of these experiences emerged the 1949 Geneva Conventions and their Additional Protocols, a dedicated and devoted effort by the international community to limit the suffering caused by war.

The Geneva Conventions, which were ratified in 1949, consist of four different conventions covering the laws governing hostilities between states or 'international armed conflict'. Additionally, the 1977 Additional Protocols consist of two treaties intended to supplement the 1949 Geneva Conventions. Additional Protocol I supplements the law governing international armed conflicts and Additional Protocol II covers non-international armed conflicts. Under the Geneva Conventions, all persons who engage in hostilities during an international armed conflict fall into one of seven categories. The first five groups are governed by the Third Geneva Convention of 1949 (GPW), which covers the treatment of prisoners of war.[193] The sixth group is recognized in Additional Protocol I. The seventh group consists of unprivileged belligerents.

4(A)(1): Members of the Armed Forces

The first group of combatants entitled to the belligerent's privilege under the Geneva Conventions is 'members of the armed forces' and consists of all military personnel regardless of their branch of service.[194] All members of the armed forces are automatically entitled to the belligerent's privilege, thereby mandating prisoner of war status upon capture.[195] Additionally, by virtue of the belligerent's privilege, members of the armed forces are granted combatant immunity and may

---

192 Adam Roberts, 'Land Warfare: From Hague to Nuremberg', in *The Laws of War: Constraints on Warfare in the Western World*, ed. Michael Howard, George J. Andreopoulos, and Mark R. Shulman (New Haven, CT: Yale University Press, 1994), 110–30, 116.

193 GPW, art. 4.

194 ICRC, *Commentary to the Third Geneva Convention*, ed. Jean Pictet (1960), 51.

195 GPW, art. 4(A)(1); Protocol I Additional to the Geneva Conventions of 12 August 1949, and Relating to the Protection of Victims of International Armed Conflicts, June 8, 1977, 1125 U.N.T.S. 3 [hereinafter 'Additional Protocol I'], art. 43(2).

not be tried for violations of domestic law committed during lawful acts of war.[196] However, if a member of the armed forces is captured in civilian clothing in enemy territory while engaging in espionage or sabotage, he is not entitled to prisoner of war status and may be considered an unprivileged belligerent.[197] Members of the armed forces are not required to wear a fixed distinctive sign or a uniform, but states have an affirmative obligation to ensure that they are always distinguishable from the civilian population.[198] In cases of doubt regarding their status, members of the armed forces should be able to demonstrate *right authority* by producing an identification card and are entitled to have their status reviewed by a competent tribunal.[199] Subsumed into this category, like The Hague Conventions, are militias or volunteer corps, which make up the armed forces of a state.[200] An example of this category would be the United States Army, its reserve components, and National Guard units when called to active duty.

---

196 Ibid., art. 87. Article 87 prohibits a detaining power from trying prisoners of war for crimes that it would not punish its own soldiers for, thereby mandating reciprocal observation of combatant immunity. R.R. Baxter, 'The Privy Council on the Qualifications of Belligerents', *American Journal of International Law* 63 (1969): 290, 294; Levie, 'Prisoners of War in International Armed Conflict', 37. See also, Convention Respecting the Laws and Customs of War on Land, Oct. 18, 1907, 36 Stat. 2277, 205 Consol. T.S. 277, art. 29 [hereinafter 'Hague Convention IV 1907']; Additional Protocol I, art. 46.

197 ICRC, *Commentary to the Third Geneva Convention*, 52 ('The drafters of the 1949 Convention, like those of the Hague Convention, considered that it was unnecessary to specify the sign which members of armed forces should have for purposes of recognition. It is the duty of each State to take steps so that members of its armed forces can be immediately recognized as such and to see to it that they are easily distinguishable from members of the enemy armed forces or from civilians'); W. Hays Parks, 'Special Forces Wear of Non-Standard Uniforms', *Chicago Journal of International Law* 4 (2003): 493, 542 ('The codified law of war for international armed conflict does not prohibit the wearing of a non-standard uniform. It does not prohibit the wearing of civilian clothing so long as military personnel distinguish themselves from the civilian population, and provided there is legitimate military necessity for wearing something other than standard uniform'); but see Pfanner, 'Military Uniforms and the Law of War', 119 ('In the light of this practice, it would be difficult to affirm that soldiers are not obliged to wear a distinctive sign in military operations in addition to carrying their arms openly. On the other hand, it would be contrary to the current practice if overly stringent conditions were to be attached to this criterion of identification solely by uniforms or distinctive signs. Only an examination on a case-by-case basis, taking into account all circumstances, makes it possible to assess whether the principle of distinction between combatants and civilian population was upheld in a particular situation or not').

198 Ibid.; GPW, art. 5.

199 Ibid.

200 W. Hays (Schmitt Parks, ed.,), 'Combatants, in the War in Afghanistan: A Legal Analysis', *U.S. Naval War College International Law Studies* 85 (2009): 268.

4(A)(2): Partisans

Article 4(A)(2) restates the customary provisions first articulated in the Brussels Declaration and, later, the Hague Conventions, but also includes 'organized resistance movements' operating within *and* outside of their own territory. Though only four requirements are expressly listed in the Geneva Conventions, in order to be considered privileged belligerents under 4(A)(2), combatants must actually meet seven requirements.[201] First, because the belligerent's privilege as conferred by the Geneva Conventions is only applicable in international armed conflicts, there must be an international armed conflict.[202] Second, the individual must be a member of an organized resistance movement.[203]

Third, the organized resistance movement to which the individual belongs must demonstrate *right authority* by 'belonging to a party to the conflict.'[204] Though the Hague Conventions required express *right authority*, usually in writing, the Commentary to the Third Geneva Conventions explains that 4(A)(2) only requires a *de facto* relationship.[205] In reviewing this issue, the International Criminal Tribunal for Yugoslavia in *Tadić* dismissed the Commentary as too vague and set a higher threshold. 'In order for irregulars to qualify as lawful combatants, it appears that international rules and State practice therefore require control over them by a Party to an international armed conflict and, by the same token, a relationship of dependence and allegiance of these irregulars *vis-à-vis* that Party to the conflict.'[206] If accepted as precedential, the *Tadić* ruling affirms the customary requirement of *right authority* by requiring evidence of control and dependence prior to recognizing privileged belligerency.

Similarly, the International Court of Justice (ICJ) has impliedly recognized *right authority* by way of its test for attribution and imputation. Under the Draft Articles on State Responsibility, conduct of armed non-state actors can be attributed to a state for the purposes of liability if 'the person or group of persons is in fact acting on the instructions of, or under the direction or control of, that State in carrying out the conduct.'[207] In both the *Nicaragua* case and the *Genocide*

201 Ibid.

202 Ibid., 269.

203 GPW, art. 4(A)(2); Parks, 'Combatants, in the War in Afghanistan: A Legal Analysis', 269; ICRC, *Commentary to the Third Geneva Convention*, 57.

204 ICRC, *Commentary to the Third Geneva Convention*, 57.

205 *Prosecutor v Tadić* (Judgment of 15 July 1999), ICTY AC, Case IT-94-1-A [hereinafter '*Tadić*'] ¶¶ 94–95.

206 Draft Articles on Responsibility of States for Internationally Wrongful Acts, *in Report of the International Law Commission to the General Assembly*, 56 U.N. GAOR Supp. (No. 10) at 59, U.N. Doc. A/56/10 (2001), art. 8. Online. Available HTTP: http://www.un.org/documents/ga/docs/56/a5610.pdf (accessed 3 January 2014).

207 Application of the Convention on the Prevention and Punishment of the Crime of Genocide (*Bosnia and Herzegovina v Serbia and Montenegro*), International Court of Justice, February 26, 2007, ¶¶ 403–406 [hereinafter 'Genocide Case'].

Convention, the ICJ found that a state could be held responsible for the conduct of armed non-state actors if a state gave instructions or provided directions to the armed non-state actors or exercised effective control over their military actions.[208] While the ICJ's standard was intended to determine attribution for international wrongs, the 'instruction, direction or effective control' test syncs with the standard of 'belonging to' articulated in the GPW commentary and confirms *right authority* as a continuing requirement for privileged belligerency.[209]

The remaining four requirements are replicated identically from the Brussels Declaration and the Hague Conventions: (4) being commanded by a person responsible for his subordinates, (5) having a fixed distinctive sign recognizable at a distance,[210] (6) carrying arms openly, and (7) conducting their operations in accordance with the laws and customs of war.[211] If an individual meets all seven requirements, he is entitled to both combatant immunity, and prisoner of war status upon capture.

4(A)(3): Members of the Armed Forces of an Unrecognized Government or Authority

Article 4(A)(3) was based upon the experience of certain units in World War II who continued to fight after their states were conquered and occupied by Germany.[212] As Jean Pictet, former President of the International Committee of the Red Cross, emphasized, 'This provision must be interpreted, in the first place, in light of the actual case which motivated its drafting – that of the forces of General de Gaulle which were under the authority of the Free French National Liberation Committee.'[213] Based on this reading, 4(A)(3) contains three requirements. First, individuals must be members of the regular armed forces of an authority not recognized by an adversary.[214] Second, reflecting the customary qualities of

208 ICRC, *Commentary to the Third Geneva Convention*, 57. Compare with Genocide Case, ¶406. A highly contentious argument could be made that the ICJ's ruling implies that armed non-state actors could be entitled to the belligerent's privilege despite disavowal by their sponsoring state if 'instruction, direction or effective control' is found.

209 However, Article 44(3) of Additional Protocol I recognized that 'there are situations in armed conflicts where, owing to the nature of the hostilities, an armed combatant cannot so distinguish himself', thereby permitting a combatant to hide his fixed distinctive sign and receive prisoner of war status. Nonetheless, he must still carry his arms openly prior to and during each armed attack. Additional Protocol I, art. 44(3). This was a contentious point during the Conference and is a primary reason why the United States has not ratified the treaty.

210 GPW, art. 4(A)(2).

211 Parks, 'Combatants, in the War in Afghanistan: A Legal Analysis', 269.

212 ICRC, *Commentary to the Third Geneva Convention*, 62.

213 Ibid.

214 Ibid. It is doubtful that the Geneva Conventions would require a state to meet the five requirements of statehood sometimes articulated by the United States, but rather the

right authority, that detaining power must be recognized by parties other than the adversary as legitimate or sovereign.[215] Third, the unrecognized authority must consider itself to be a high contracting party to the Geneva Conventions or declare that it accepts the obligations stipulated in the Convention and wishes to apply them.[216] Additionally, this class of combatants is impliedly expected to operate in the same capacity as members of the armed forces under article 4(A)(1) by distinguishing themselves and being under responsible command.[217]

4(A)(6): Levée en Masse

The provision concerning a *levée en masse* is also replicated from the Hague Conventions. The Commentary adds that inhabitants who take up arms need not be surprised by the invasion and inhabitants who have been warned of an invasion may still form a *levée en masse*.[218] A *levée en masse* may only operate until a party can organize its armed forces, at which time the *levée* must be withdraw or be incorporated into the armed forces pursuant to 4(A)(2).[219]

Art. 1(3): Struggles Against Colonial Domination, Alien Occupation, and Racist Regimes

Additional Protocol I added individuals fighting against colonial domination, alien occupation, and racist regimes to the class of combatants entitled to privileged belligerent status.[220] In order to do so, Additional Protocol I established that wars against colonial domination, alien occupation, and racist regimes would be considered international armed conflicts even if both parties were not states parties to the Geneva Conventions.[221] Article 1(4) states:

> The situations referred to in the preceding paragraph include armed conflicts in which peoples are fighting against colonial domination and alien occupation and against racists regimes in the exercise of their right of self-determination, as enshrined in the Charter of the United Nations and the Declaration on Principles of International Law concerning Friendly Relations and Cooperation among States in accordance with the Charter of the United Nations.

---

generally accepted four of a territory, a people, jurisdiction over the territory, and the ability to conduct foreign relations.

215 Ibid.

216 Ibid., 63.

217 Ibid., 67.

218 Ibid.

219 Additional Protocol I, arts 1(4), 96(3).

220 Solf, 'The Status of Combatants in Non-International Armed Conflicts under Domestic Law and Transnational Practice', 46.

221 Ibid.

To effect article 1(4), non-state authorities must comply with article 96(3), which requires a unilateral declaration of intent to abide by Additional Protocol I and the 1949 Geneva Conventions. Once that declaration is made, the non-state authority is considered to be a party to the Additional Protocol with all the same rights and obligations as a states' party, including providing its members with the belligerent's privilege and prisoner of war status upon capture.[222]

Article 1(4) is the second instance in international law where the international community has deemed a cause so sacred or noble that it automatically confers *right authority* by function of international law rather than state sovereignty. Whereas the *levée en masse* was raised to exceptional status based on the belief that a citizen's defence of his homeland was a sacred duty, article 1(4) reflects the international community's belief in the natural and inalienable right to self-determination.[223] Also like the *levée en masse*, article 1(4) constitutes a re-conflation of the dualistic axiom by conditioning rights under the *jus in bello* on the nature of one's cause for going to war.[224] Article 1(4) could also be seen as an effort to reconcile the historically disparate standards of treatment under the laws of war between European and non-European peoples as non-European peoples were the primary benefactors of this provision.

Persons Entitled to Prisoner of War Status without the Belligerent's Privilege

Under the Geneva Conventions, contractors, journalists, and other civilians who accompany the armed forces during times of war are granted prisoner of war status if captured.[225] Similarly, members of the merchant marine and civil defence forces are also entitled to prisoner of war status.[226] While these individuals are automatically entitled to POW status upon capture and are entitled to a status review in situations of doubt, their authorization to accompany the armed forces does not constitute *right authority*.[227] If they engage in hostilities, they not only lose their civilian immunity and become the lawful targets of attack, they also become unprivileged belligerents subject to prosecution under an enemy state's domestic law.[228] Regardless of whether they participate in hostilities, they are always entitled to treatment at least equivalent to that of prisoners of war.

Unprivileged Belligerents

The nature and extent of abuses against human dignity during World War II caused a major shift on the issue of unprivileged belligerents. Prior to World War II,

222 Ibid., 243, 556.
223 Ibid., 48.
224 Ibid., 40.
225 GPW, art. 4(A)(4).
226 Ibid., art. 4(A)(5).
227 ICRC, *Commentary to the Third Geneva Convention*, 65.
228 Ibid.

unprivileged belligerents were considered to be violating the laws of war *per se* and subject to summary execution upon capture. No example better illustrates this point than the case of *Ex Parte Quirin* heard before the United States Supreme Court in 1942.[229] *Quirin* revolved around a group of Nazi saboteurs who had infiltrated the United States in civilian clothing in order to sabotage several targets.[230] After being captured, all but two were executed after being found guilty of violating the law of war in a special military tribunal.[231] The Supreme Court upheld this treatment, finding that Quirin and his compatriots had violated the laws of war by removing their uniforms to further their missions and that this violation sanctioned the death penalty.[232]

The position that engaging in hostilities as an unprivileged belligerent constitutes a violation of the laws of war no longer seems tenable in light of the Geneva Conventions, particularly Common Article 3. In essence, Common Article 3 provides a minimum standard of treatment to all persons captured during any armed conflict. It is applicable during international armed conflicts and non-international armed conflicts, and protects unprivileged belligerents who are denied prisoner of war status. Richard Baxter, author of the seminal work on unprivileged belligerency, has explained that international law no longer proscribed the unauthorized participation in hostilities.[233] Instead, unprivileged belligerents are left unprotected by the laws of war (with the exception of Common Article 3) and may be prosecuted for any violations of domestic law that result from their unprivileged warlike acts.[234]

Summary of the Current Belligerent's Privilege

The addition of new classes of combatants under the Geneva Conventions and the Additional Protocols further expanded the class of combatants entitled to the belligerent's privilege under the laws of war. Under the Geneva Conventions and its Additional Protocols, an individual is entitled to the belligerent's privilege if:

1. He possesses *right authority* granted by a sovereign state in one of three ways:
   i. as a member of a sovereign state's armed forces, or
   ii. as a member of a militia, volunteer corps, or auxiliary unit belonging to a sovereign state while also fulfilling the four requirements enumerated in the Hague Conventions and Geneva Conventions, or

229 317 U.S. 1 (1952).

230 Ibid., 21.

231 Ibid., 23.

232 R.R. Baxter, 'So-Called "Unprivileged Belligerency": Spies, Guerillas, and Saboteurs', *British Yearbook of International Law* 28 (1951): 323, 340.

233 Ibid., 337.

234 Ibid., 338.

   iii. as a member of the armed forces of a pre-existing authority not presently recognized by an adversary, or
2. He possesses *right authority* as conferred by function of international law in one of two ways:
   i. as a member of *levée en masse*, or
   ii. as a member of a non-state authority engaged in an armed conflict against colonial domination, alien occupation, or racist regimes that has complied with its depositing requirements under Additional Protocol I, art. 96(3), and
3. The individual has not removed his uniform to engage in espionage or perfidy. Additionally, the introduction of the Geneva Conventions and the minimum standards of protection provided by their Common Article 3 overrides any argument under custom considering unprivileged belligerency to be a war crime. As a result, privileged belligerents are entitled to:
   i. the international privilege of combatant immunity that shields them from prosecution by a state for any violations of domestic law that result from lawful acts of war, and
   ii. the enumerated protections of prisoner of war status under the Geneva Conventions and their Additional Protocols.

Conclusion

The belligerent's privilege originally distinguished those eligible to engage in hostilities for profit from those who were not. The primary means in which a person was designated as eligible was through the authorization of his lord or sovereign, called *right authority*. Those with *right authority* were eligible to be taken hostage and ransomed, but were not entitled to it. As warfare humanized through reciprocity, sovereigns developed the right to grant prisoner of war status to persons lacking *right authority*. This was most evident during insurrections or civil wars. Though these individuals were entitled to 'all the privileges of the prisoner of war', combatant immunity was not among them; therefore the privileges of prisoners of war do not include combatant immunity. As a result, combatant immunity can be separated from prisoner of war status by a detaining power when dealing with otherwise unprivileged belligerents for the purposes of providing humane treatment.

In light of the sacred nature of certain principles under international law, namely defence of one's country and the right of self-determination, the international community devised an automatic legal mechanism by which persons engaged in conflicts for these purposes would always be considered privileged belligerents. In doing so, the international community re-conflated the dualistic axiom of the *jus in bello* and *jus ad bellum*, but affirmed the role of *right authority* in the belligerent's privilege. As such, *right authority* remains the most fundamental requisite to privileged belligerency status. An individual who engages in hostilities with *right authority* is a privileged belligerent who is shielded from domestic prosecution for lawful acts of war by combatant immunity and is entitled to POW status upon capture. Individuals who engage in hostilities without *right authority* are unprivileged belligerents who are not entitled to POW status upon capture and may be prosecuted under domestic law for their acts of war. Though it has been significantly expanded, the belligerent's privilege remains a narrowly conferred right under international law.

Cases

Bosnia and Herzegovina v Serbia and Montenegro, International Court of Justice, February 26, 2007.

Prosecutor v Tadić (Judgment of 15 July 1999), ICTY AC, Case IT-94-1-A (*Tadić*) ¶¶ 94–95.

References

Anderson, Fred. *Crucible of War: The Seven Years' War and the Fate of Empire in British North America*. New York: Vintage Books, 2000.

Anghie, Anthonie. *Imperialism, Sovereignty and the Making of International Law*. Cambridge: Cambridge University Press, 2004.

Baxter, R.R. 'So-Called "Unprivileged Belligerency": Spies, Guerillas, and Saboteurs'. *British Yearbook of International Law* 28 (1951): 323.

———. 'The Privy Council on the Qualifications of Belligerents'. *American Journal of International Law* 63 (1969): 290.

Best, Geoffrey. *Humanity in Warfare*. London: Weidenfeld & Nicolson, 1980.

Borch, Frederic L. 'The History of Military Commissions in the U.S. Army: From the Mexican–American War to the War on Terrorism'. In *The U.S. Army and Irregular Warfare*, edited by Richard Davis, 2007. At http://www.history.army.mil/html/books/irregular_warfare/index.html (accessed 4 February 2014).

Bordwell, Percy. *The Law of War between Belligerents*. Chicago, IL: Callaghan & Co, 1908.

Bothe, Michael, Karl Partsch, and Waldemar Solf. *New Rules for Victims of Armed Conflicts: Commentary on the Two 1977 Protocols Additional to the Geneva Conventions of 1949*. The Hague, Boston, MA, and London: Martinus Nijhoff Publishers, 1982.

Bowden, Brent. 'In the Name of Progress and Peace: The "Standard of Civilization" and the Universalizing Project'. *Alternatives: Global, Local, Political* 29 no. 1 (2004): 43.

Brownlie, Ian. *Principles of Public International Law*. 1st edn. Oxford: Oxford University Press, 1966.

Cave, Alfred A. *The French and Indian War*, Greenwood Guides to Historic Events 1500–1900, edited by Linda S. Frey and Marsha L. Frey. Westport, CT: Greenwood Press, 2004.

Chambers, John Whiteclay, II. 'American Views of Conscription and the German Nation in Arms in the Franco-Prussian War'. In *The People in Arms: Military Myth and National Mobilization since the French Revolution*, edited by Daniel Moran and Arthur Waldron. Cambridge and New York: Cambridge University Press, 2003.

Dabbs, Jack. *The French Army in Mexico, 1861–1867: A Study in Military Government*. The Hague: Mouton, 1963.

Dinstein, Yoram. *War, Aggression, and Self-Defence*. 3rd edn. Cambridge and New York: Cambridge University Press, 2001.

Dodge, Edward. *Relief Is Greatly Wanted: The Battle of Fort William Henry*. Bowie, MD: Heritage Books, 1998.

Draper, G.I.A.D. 'The Christian and War'. In *Reflections of Law and Armed Conflicts*, edited by Michael Meyer and Hillary McCoubrey. The Hague: Kluwer Law International, 1998.

———. 'Combatant Status: An Historical Perspective'. *Military Law and Law of War Review* 11 (1972): 135.

———. 'The Development of International Humanitarian Law'. In *International Dimensions of Humanitarian Law*. Geneva/Paris: Henry Dunant Institute/ UNESCO, 1988.

———. 'Grotius' Place in the Development of Legal Ideas about War'. In *Reflections of Law and Armed Conflicts*, edited by Michael Meyer and Hillary McCoubrey. The Hague: Kluwer Law International, 1998.

———. 'The Interaction of Christianity and Chivalry in the Historical Development of the Law of War'. *International Review of the Red Cross* 46 (1965): 3–23.

———. 'The Status of Combatants and the Question of Guerilla Warfare'. *British Yearbook of International Law* 45 (1971): 173.

Droop, H.R. 'The Relations between an Invading Army and the Inhabitants, and the Conditions under which Irregular Combatants are Entitled to the Same Treatment as Regular Troops', *Solicitor's Journal and Reporter* 15 (1870): 122.

Evans, Mark. 'Moral Theory and the Idea of a Just War'. In *Just War Theory: A Reappraisal*, edited by Mark Evans. Edinburgh: Edinburgh University Press, 2005.

Florescu, Radu R., and Raymond T. McNally. *Dracula, Prince of Many Faces: His Life and His Times*. Boston, MA: Little, Brown and Company, 1989.

Fooks, Herbert. *Prisoners of War*. Federalsburg, MD: The J.W. Stowell printing co., 1924.

Forrest, Alan. 'La Patrie En Danger: The French Revolution and the First Levée En Masse'. In *The People in Arms: Military Myth and National Mobilization since the French Revolution*, edited by Daniel Moran and Arthur Waldron. Cambridge and New York: Cambridge University Press, 2003.

Frritz, Kalshoven. *Belligerent Reprisals*, International Humanitarian Law Series, edited by Christopher Greenswood and Timothy L.H. McCormack. Leiden and Boston, MA: Martinus Nijhoff Publishers, 1971.

Gardam, Judith Gail. 'Proportionality and Force in International Law'. *American Journal of International Law* 87 (1993): 391.

Gates, David. *The Spanish Ulcer: A History of the Peninsular War*. London: George Allen & Unwin, 1986.

Goldman, Robert, and Brian Tittemore. 'Unprivileged Combatants and the Hostilities in Afghanistan: Their Status and Rights under International Humanitarian and Human Rights Law'. *ASIL Task Force on Terrorism Paper* (2002). At http://www.pegc.us/archive/Journals/goldman.pdf (accessed 20 September 2013).

Hall, W.E. *International Law*. Oxford: Clarendon Press, 1908.

———. *A Treatise on International Law*. 4th edn. Buffalo, TX: Kessinger Publishing, 1895.

Holland, T.E. *Lectures on International Law*, edited by T.A. and W.L. Walker. London: Sweet & Maxwell, 1933.

Horne, John. 'Defining the Enemy: War, Law and the Levée en Masse from 1870 to 1945'. In *The People in Arms: Military Myth and National Mobilization since the French Revolution*, edited by Daniel Moran and Arthur Waldron. Cambridge and New York: Cambridge University Press, 2003.

Howard, Michael. 'Constraints on Warfare'. In *The Laws of War: Constraints on Warfare in the Western World*, edited by Michael Howard, George J. Andreopoulos, and Mark R. Shulman. New Haven, CT: Yale University Press, 1994.

Hyde, Charles Cheney. *International Law Chiefly as Interpreted and Applied by the United States*. 2nd edn, 3 vols, Vol. 1, Boston, MA: Little, Brown & Co, 1945.

ICRC. *Commentary to the Third Geneva Convention*, edited by Jean Pictet, 1960.

Johnson, James Turner. *Just War Tradition and the Restraint of War: A Moral and Historical Inquiry*. Princeton, NJ: Princeton University Press, 1981.

Keen, M.H. *The Laws of War in the Late Middle Ages*. London: Routlege & Kegan Paul, 1965.

———. 'Treason Trials under the Law of Arms'. *Transactions of the Royal Historical Society* 5th Series 12 (1962).

Kingsbury, Benedict, and Adam Roberts. 'Introduction: Grotian Thought in the Law of Nations'. In *Hugo Grotius and International Relations*, edited by Hedley Bull, Benedict Kingsbury, and Adam Roberts. Oxford: Clarendon Press, 1990.

Laqueur, Walter. *Guerilla*. Boston, MA: Little, Brown, 1976.

Leggiere, Michael. *Napoleon and Berlin: The Franco-Prussian War in North Germany 1813*, Campaigns and Commanders. Norman, OK: University of Oklahoma Press, 2002.

'Letter from Lieut. Col. John S. Mosby to Maj. Gen. P.H. Sheridan (Nov. 11, 1864)'. In *John Singleton Mosby, the Memoirs of Colonel John S. Mosby*, edited by Charles Wells Russell. Boston, MA: Little, Brown and Company, 1917.

Levie, Howard S. 'Prisoners of War in International Armed Conflict'. *U.S. Naval War College International Law Studies* 59 (1978): 46.

Lieber, Francis. 'Guerilla Parties with Reference to the Laws and Usages of War'. In *Lieber's Code and the Laws of War*, edited by Richard Shelly Hartigan, 1862 (1982).

Megret, Frederic. 'From "Savages" to "Unlawful Combatants": A Postcolonial Look at International Humanitarian Law's "Other"'. In *International Law and Its 'Others'*, edited by Anne Orford. Cambridge: Cambridge University Press, 2006.

Moran, Daniel. 'The Dilemmas of German Liberalism'. In *The People in Arms: Military Myth and National Mobilization since the French Revolution*, edited by Daniel Moran and Arthur Waldron. Cambridge and New York: Cambridge University Press, 2003.

Neff, Stephen C. *War and the Law of Nations: A General History*. Cambridge: Cambridge University Press, 2005.

Nester, William. *The First Global War: Britain, France and the Fate of North America 1756–1775*. Westport, CT: Praeger Publishers, 2000.

Nurick, Lester, and Roger W. Barrett. 'Legality of Guerilla Forces under the Laws of War'. *American Journal of International Law* 40 (1946): 563.

Nussbaum, Arthur.'The Significance of Roman Law in the History of International Law'. *University of Pennsylvania Law Review* 100 (1952): 678–87.

Oman, Charles. *A History of the Peninsula War*. Vol. III. Oxford: Clarendon Press, 1908.

Oppenheim, Lassa. *International Law: A Treatise*. Vol. 2, 1905.

Osiel, Mark. *The End of Reciprocity*. New York: Cambridge University Press, 2009.

Parker, Geoffrey. 'Early Modern Europe'. In *The Laws of War: Constraints on Warfare in the Western World*, edited by Michael Howard, George J. Andreopoulos, and Mark R. Shulman. New Haven, CT: Yale University Press, 1994.

Parks, W. Hays. 'Special Forces Wear of Non-Standard Uniforms'. *Chicago Journal of International Law* 4 (2003): 493.

Parks, W. Hays (Schmitt, ed.,). 'Combatants, in the War in Afghanistan: A Legal Analysis'. *U.S. Naval War College International Law Studies* 85 (2009): 268

Pfanner, Toni. 'Military Uniforms and the Law of War'. *International Review of the Red Cross* 86 no. 853 (2004): 93.

'Project of an International Declaration Concerning the Laws and Customs of War (1873–74)'. *British and Foreign State Papers* 65 (27 Aug. 1874): 1005.

Reston, James. *Warriors of God: Richard the Lionheart and Saladin in the Third Crusade*. London: Anchor Books, 2001.

Roberts, Adam. 'Land Warfare: From Hague to Nuremberg'. In *The Laws of War: Constraints on Warfare in the Western World*, edited by Michael Howard, George J. Andreopoulos, and Mark R. Shulman. New Haven, CT: Yale University Press, 1994.

Rothenburg, Gunther 'The Age of Napoleon'. In *The Laws of War: Constraints on Warfare in the Western World*, edited by Michael Howard, George J. Andreopoulos, and Mark R. Shulman. New Haven, CT: Yale University Press, 1994.

Shaw, Malcolm. *International Law*. 6th edn. Cambridge: Cambridge University Press, 2008.

Sloane, Robert. 'The Cost of Conflation: Preserving the Dualism of the Jus Ad Bellum and Jus in Bello in the Contemporary Law of War', *Yale Journal of International Law* 34 (2009): 47.

Solf, Waldemar. 'The Status of Combatants in Non-International Armed Conflicts under Domestic Law and Transnational Practice'. *American University Law Review* 33 (1983–84): 53.

Spaight, James. *War Rights on Land*. London: Macmillan, 1911.

Stacy, Robert. 'Age of Chivalry'. In *The Laws of War: Constraints on Warfare in the Western World*, edited by Michael Howard, George J. Andreopoulos, and Mark R. Shulman. New Haven, CT: Yale University Press, 1994.

Sutter, Phillip 'The Continuing Role for Belligerent Reprisals'. *Journal of Conflict and Security Law* 13 (2008): 93.

Wallach, Evan J. 'Partisans, Pirates, and Pancho Villa: How International and National Law Handled Non-State Fighters in the "Good Old Days" before 1949 and That Approach's Applicability to the "War on Terror"'. *Emory International Law Review* 24 (2010): 549.

Wheaton, Henry. *Elements of International Law*. 4th edn. London: Stevens & Sons, 1904.

Winthrop, William. *Military Law and Precedents*, edited by Igor I. Kavass and Adolf Sprudzs: William S. Hein & Co., 1979 (1920).

Chapter 3

Justice and Protection of Civilians in Armed Conflicts through the Enforcement of the International Legal Obligations: The Case of the Gaza Strip

Davide Tundo

In memory of the silent victims of Gaza

Introduction

This chapter engages the issues of justice and protection of civilians in armed conflicts: do the existing legal tools provide civilians with the due protection of the law? More importantly, are they being fully implemented by those mandated to respect and ensure respect for the rights of civilians?

Rethinking justice in international law – notably in humanitarian and human rights law – requires acknowledging the lack of enforcement of the existing legal mechanisms. If implemented fully and in good faith, these will likely contribute to enhancing the protection of human rights and providing justice for civilians in armed conflicts.

In territories such as the Gaza Strip – where the prolonged conflict has inhibited all basic human rights with the complicity of the international community – there is a pressing need to safeguard civilians against the burden of wars. The chronic lack of justice must be reversed and victims be granted the equal protection of the law.

Framing the Issue of Justice and Protection of Civilians in Armed Conflict

The Consolidation and Codification of the Human Rights Discourse

The consolidation of the human rights discourse in the nineteenth century has challenged the monolithic vision whereby subjects of international law were traditionally only sovereign states. The erosion of state sovereignty as the traditional ordering principle in international relations by the increasing development of human rights theories has been evidenced by the work of academics and researchers.[1] Communities, peoples and individuals have been granted rights and faculties that impose concomitant duties on states and limit the latter's arbitrariness, particularly at the domestic level of jurisdiction.

The process of codification of human rights norms by means of multilateral treaties – begun in the aftermath of the Second War World – and the high ratification rate by states clearly point to a new relational model between subjects of international law and evidence the increasing importance of the individuals' legitimacy as international legal subjects *vis-à-vis* traditional state actors.

The Universal Declaration of Human Rights,[2] the International Covenant on Civil and Political Rights (ICCPR)[3] together with its two Optional Protocols, and the International Covenant on Economic, Social and Cultural Rights (ICESCR),[4] adopted by the United Nations (UN), form the so-called 'International Bill of Human Rights'.

A series of other core human rights treaties has contributed to creating the international legal system of human rights protection.[5]

Despite the lack of effective enforcement mechanisms in the human rights treaties, a new legal paradigm has evolved over the past decades.

In effect, the former reflects a legal *vacuum* that is to be addressed in order to enhance the protection of human rights. It further evidences states' unwillingness to give up their sovereignty to an extent they are not yet willing to bear.

However, as recalled above, the widespread adhesion to human rights treaties by states of all political, cultural and geographical areas reflects another element: states are increasingly concerned in avoiding the label of human rights violators.

The 'name and shame game' and the 'moral persuasion', based on the recourse to effective awareness-raising campaigns by influential media and human rights groups – seen as 'moral entrepreneurs'[6] – has clearly achieved its

1 D.P. Forsythe, *Human Rights in International Relations* (New York: Cambridge University Press, 2006); K. Mills, *Human Rights in the Emerging Global Order: A New Sovereignty?* (London: Macmillan Press, 1998).

2 UN General Assembly, 'UN General Assembly, Universal Declaration of Human Rights' (217 A (III), 10 December 1948). Although it is a non-binding UN General Assembly resolution, its influence is unquestionable.

3 'International Covenant on Civil and Political Rights' (United Nations, 16 December 1966). Adopted in 1966 and entered into force in 1976.

4 'International Covenant on Economic, Social and Cultural Rights' (United Nations, 16 December 1966). Adopted in 1966 and entered into force in 1976.

5 For example, at the UN level, United Nations, 'Convention on the Elimination of All Forms of Racial Discrimination (CERD)' (1966); 'Convention on the Elimination of All Forms of Discrimination against Women (CEDAW)' (1979); 'Convention against Torture and Other Cruel, Inhuman or Degrading Treatment or Punishment' (UNTS 1465 851984); 'Convention on the Rights of the Child (CRC)' (1989).

6 R. Price, 'Reversing the Gun Sights: Transnational Civil Society Targets Land Mines', *International Organization* 52, no. 3 (1998): 613–44.

goal: even the most ignominious regimes are sensible to critics of human rights violations and act to reverse or at least improve their bad reputation. This is done not to avoid enforceable sanctions that human rights treaties lack even before serious patterns of human rights violations but rather in response to the political elites' desire of avoiding infamous characterizations. In turn, this can facilitate norm adoption through emulation.

Therefore the once-unfettered freedom of states *vis-à-vis* their citizens, built upon the notion of sovereignty, is nowadays counterbalanced by the spread of the human rights discourse: states are responsible for ensuring human rights to individuals and communities subjected to their jurisdiction.

In this regard, it is worth recalling that the ICCPR, one of the most important human rights treaties, is binding on states parties even beyond the national boundaries. In effect, the so-called 'extraterritoriality' of the ICCPR has been recognized by the Human Rights Committee – which monitors states' implementation – in stating that,

> A State party must respect and ensure the rights laid down in the Covenant within the power or effective control of that State party, even if is not situated within the territory of the State party.[7]

Furthermore, in *Lopez Burgos v Uruguay*,[8] the Human Rights Committee argued that under Article 2.1 of the ICCPR a state party can be held accountable for violations committed by its agents in the territory of another state.

This is a clear recognition of states' increasing responsibilities towards individuals and the latter's consolidating legal subjectivity.

The Protection of Civilians under International Humanitarian Law

While human rights law (HRL) applies at all times, particularly in peace, it remains to observe the relation between individuals and communities' human rights and states' responsibilities in times of armed conflict and military occupation during which the norms of international humanitarian law (IHL), also known as the 'Law of Armed Conflict', come into play.

In other words, it is opportune to review the effectiveness and consistency of the international legal regime as regards the protection of human rights in the event of an armed conflict during which states' interests of, *inter alia*, survival and self-defence are most likely to bypass human rights and violations to go unpunished.

---

7 UN Human Rights Committee, 'Nature of the General Legal Obligation Imposed on States Parties to the Covenant' (General Comment no. 31 CCPR/C/21/Rev.1/Add.13, 26 May 2004).

8 'Lopez Burgos v Uruguay' (Communication no. 52, CCPR/C/OP/1 6 June 1979 (1984)).

Such appraisal will help verify the consistency of the international legal system of protection of human rights – the aim of this chapter – and to this end the Israeli–Palestinian context will serve as a specific case study.

In times of occupation[9] and armed conflict,[10] either international[11] (including wars waged by national liberation movements[12]) or non-international[13] – letting aside the own legality of resorting to war that is to be judged in light of the UN Charter – international law, specifically IHL and HRL, provides for a set of legal rules of mandatory application for states and their agents as well as non-state actors. Such rules are intended to protect people who do not take part in the hostilities.

Furthermore, international criminal law can also help protect human rights, as will be discussed below.

Regulated by the principle of *lex specialis*, these branches of international law, both based upon the values of humanity, apply concurrently as clearly pointed out by the UN International Court of Justice (ICJ).[14]

The main treaties that make up IHL are The Hague Regulations of 1907, considered of customary nature, the four Geneva Conventions of 1949 – ratified by all states – and their two Additional Protocols of 1977, equally regarded as a codification of norms of customary international humanitarian law.[15] The four

9 'Geneva Convention Relative to the Protection of Civilian Persons in Time of War (Fourth Geneva Convention)' (75 UNTS 287, 12 August 1949). Regulated as international armed conflict in light of Article 2 of the IV Geneva Convention of 1949 and defined by Article 42 of the Hague Convention of 1907: 'A territory is considered occupied when it is actually placed under the authority of the hostile army. The occupation extends only to the territory where such authority has been established and can be exercised', 'Hague Convention' (1907), Art. 42

10 'An armed conflict exists whenever there is a resort to armed force between States or protracted armed violence between governmental authorities and organized armed groups or between such groups within a State', *Prosecutor v Dusko Tadic* (Decision on the Defence Motion for Interlocutory Appeal on Jurisdiction), ICTY, Appeals Chamber, IT-94-1, 2 October 1995, §70.

11 International armed conflicts refer to situations in which two or more states engage in armed conflict and are regulated by the four Geneva Conventions of 1949 (with the exception of common Article 3) and their Additional Protocol I.

12 Defined by Article 1.4 of Additional Protocol I to the four Geneva Conventions of 1949 as wars 'against colonial domination and alien occupation and against racist regimes in the exercise of their right of self-determination', 'Geneva Convention Relative to the Protection of Civilian Persons in Time of War (Fourth Geneva Convention)'.

13 Two types of non-international armed conflicts are regulated in treaty-based IHL by common art. 3 to the four Geneva Conventions of 1949 and under their Additional Protocol II. Customary IHL does not distinguish between these two types of non-international armed conflict.

14 *Armed Activities on the Territory of the Congo (Democratic Republic of the Congo v Uganda)* (Judgment), ICJ, 19 December 2005, §216.

15 J.M. Henckaerts and L. Doswald-Beck, *Customary International Humanitarian Law: Rules*, vol. I (New York: Cambridge University Press, 2009); ICRC, *Commentary to*

Geneva Conventions and the Additional Protocols are particularly relevant *vis-à-vis* the protection of civilians.

Although IHL does not ban armed conflicts as such – as it is built on the assumption that wars may occur – still this *corpus* of law aims at ensuring that due protection is afforded by all actors to civilians as well as individuals *hors de combat*. They are 'protected persons' under Article 33 of the IV Geneva Convention and as such entitled to special protection.

In effect, IHL standards regulate the conduct of hostilities by putting restraints in the form of concrete legal obligations binding the belligerent parties such as state agents and individuals taking part in the hostilities. If fully respected, these norms can effectively contribute to eliminating or reducing the suffering of civilians, protecting their human rights to life, health and so on.

In particular, the IHL principles of distinction between civilian and military targets,[16] of precaution[17] in and proportionality of attacks,[18] of military necessity[19] and the restrictions in the use of weapons[20] are intended to spare civilians from the destruction brought about by wars and are of mandatory application without exemptions.

Moreover, as recalled above, the protection afforded by human rights treaties – traditionally operating in peacetime – 'does not cease in case of armed conflict' as authoritatively stated by the ICJ in *The Wall* in specifically addressing the situation in the occupied Palestinian territory (oPt).[21] The following questions need to be addressed at this point. Is the international legal regime of protection of civilians' human rights satisfactory? How well does international law safeguard human rights in times of occupation and armed conflict? Is justice – as a deterrent and a restoring measure – available for civilian victims? Are legal mechanisms being genuinely applied by those mandated to enforce the rule of law?

---

the IV Geneva Convention Relative to the Protection of Civilian Persons in Time of War, ed. J. Pictet (Geneva, 1958).

16 Article 48 (Basic rule), Additional Protocol I to the four Geneva Conventions.

17 Articles 57 (Precautions in attack) and 58 (Precautions against the effects of attacks), Additional Protocol I to the four Geneva Conventions.

18 Article 51 (Protection of the civilian population), Additional Protocol I to the four Geneva Conventions.

19 Article 52 (General protection of civilian objects), Additional Protocol I to the four Geneva Conventions.

20 See, *inter alia*, the 'Convention on the Prohibition of the Use, Stockpiling, Production and Transfer of Anti-Personnel Mines and on Their Destruction' (1997); 'Convention on Certain Conventional Weapons' (1980); 'Geneva Protocol on the Use of Biological and Chemical Weapons' (1925).

21 ICJ, 'Legal Consequences of the Construction of a Wall in the Occupied Palestinian Territory (Advisory Opinion)' (9 July 2004), 106.

Justice and Protection of Civilians' Human Rights in Armed Conflict: The Case of the Gaza Strip

Framing the key topic of the protection of civilians in the Gaza Strip firstly requires recalling the long-standing Israeli belligerent occupation of the oPt that constitutes *per se* a violation of the *erga omnes* human right to self-determination of the Palestinian people.

The Israeli occupation has been characterized by continuous violations of international law that have affected Palestinian civilians' human rights. The lack of accountability has given rise to impunity and paved the way to new violations. In effect, though not discussed in this chapter, so-called 'Operation Protective Edge' – conducted by Israel in the Gaza Strip from 8 July to 26 August 2014 – is indicative of such pernicious trend. Two further events illustrate this violation–impunity cycle.

In the course of Israel's December 2008–January 2009 offensive on the Gaza Strip (so-called 'Operation Cast Lead'), according to the Palestinian Centre for Human Rights of Gaza (PCHR) Israeli military forces and state officials were responsible for the death of about 1,419 Palestinians, 82 per cent of whom were civilians – including 318 children – and the injury of approximately 5,300 – the majority of whom were also civilians.[22]

Moreover, Israeli military forces extensively damaged public and civilian infrastructures such as homes, schools, universities, hospitals and healthcare centres, and mosques.[23]

The magnitude of the destruction together with the actuation of the military and the words of political leaders prior to and during the operation exhibited the criminal intention of wilfully targeting civilians despite their status of 'protected persons'.

As stated in the report of the UN Fact-Finding Mission on the Gaza Conflict (the so-called 'Goldstone Report'), the military operations 'were premised on a deliberated policy of disproportionate force aimed not at the enemy but at the supporting infrastructure [...] in practice, the civilian population [...] with the aim of inflicting a collective punishment'.[24]

It is worth recalling that collective penalties are strictly prohibited under customary IHL in both international and non-international armed conflict.[25]

---

22 PCHR, 'Targeting Civilians: Report on the Israeli Military Offensive against the Gaza Strip (27 December 2008–18 January 2009)' (21 October 2009, 10). Online. Available HTTP: http://www.pchrgaza.org/files/Reports/English/ (accessed 28 August 2012).

23 Ibid.

24 UN Human Rights Council, 'Report of the UN Fact-Finding Mission on the Gaza Conflict' (A/HRC/12/48, 25 September 2009), 1886–934.

25 Henckaerts and Doswald-Beck, *Customary International Humanitarian Law: Rules*, I, Rule 102, 'No one may be convicted of an offence except on the basis of individual criminal responsibility'.

The Mission found evidence pointing to the commission of war crimes[26] and possibly crimes against humanity[27] in the context of 'Operation Cast Lead' and called on Israel and the Palestinian side to undertake investigations in accordance with international law standards into such serious allegations of international crimes.[28] The UN General Assembly endorsed the findings and recommendations of the Mission in December 2009.[29]

The effects of the military operations upon Palestinian civilians have been further exacerbated by Israel's illegal closure policy of the Gaza Strip that was tightened in June 2007 – following Hamas takeover of the Gaza Strip – and has been continuously in place ever since. The closure is in application of an official policy designed by the Israeli Security Cabinet and based on the declaration of the Gaza Strip as 'hostile territory'.[30] Israeli officials have described the closure as 'economic warfare' designed to exert pressure on the civilian population in the hope that this would have weakened the Gaza authorities.

In effect, in the *Al-Bassiouni* case – brought before the Israeli High Court of Justice following a petition by several Israeli and Palestinian NGOs challenging the Israeli government's restrictions in the supply of energy to the Gaza Strip – the State response before the court was:

> Targeting the economy itself is a legitimate means of warfare and a relevant consideration, even when deciding on the transfer of aid consignment [...]. These measures amount to legitimate economic warfare.[31]

---

26 War crimes are typically committed in the context of an armed conflict. Article 8 of the Rome Statute of the International Criminal Court contains a detailed list of acts qualified as war crimes in both international and non-international armed conflicts.

27 Crimes against humanity can be committed in times of peace as well as armed conflict 'as part of either a widespread or systematic attack against a civilian population', in *Prosecutor v Kordic and Cerkez* (Judgment), ICTY, Appeals Chamber, IT- 95-14/2-A, 17 December 2004, §93. A list of crimes against humanity is contained in Article 7 of the Rome Statute of the International Criminal Court.

28 International crimes, such as grave breaches of the four Geneva Conventions and other war crimes, crimes against humanity and torture, are of such graveness that they affect the international community as a whole. For a listing of international crimes see Articles 6, 7 and 8 of the Rome Statute of the International Criminal Court.

29 UN General Assembly, 'Follow-up to the Report of the United Nations Fact-Finding Mission on the Gaza War' (A/RES/64/10, 1 December 2009), 1–7.

30 Israeli Ministry of Foreign Affairs, 'Security Cabinet Declares Gaza Hostile Territory' (19 September 2007). Online. Available HTTP: http://www.mfa.gov.il/MFA/Government/Communiques/2007/.htm (accessed 25 August 2012).

31 State of Israel, 'State Response to HCJ Petition 9132/07 Al-Bassyouni Vs. Prime Minister' (1 November 2007). Online. Available HTTP: http://www.gisha.org/item.asp? (accessed 20 August 2012).

By severely restricting the movement of people and goods in and out of the Gaza Strip, the closure hampered the necessary post-war reconstruction and overall affected the entire spectrum of Palestinian civilians' basic human rights, including life, work, health, housing and culture.[32]

The closure clearly amounts to an unlawful collective punishment of the civilian population and violates Israel's specific obligations to ensure the well-being of civilians as an Occupying Power. This conclusion has been endorsed, *inter alia*, by the International Committee of the Red Cross[33] and the UN Special Rapporteur on the oPt.[34]

The Obligation to Enforce International Law, Including International Justice Mechanisms, to Ensure Justice and Protect Human Rights in the Gaza Strip

The Applicable Legal Framework

International law provides a set of standards that, if applied fully and in good faith, enables the international community – including UN member states – to safeguard civilians in times of occupation and armed conflict and further ensures coherence of the international legal regime of protection of human rights.

Enforcement of international law – including international criminal law – is key in this regard.

In other words, the rule of law and in particular the enforcement of the law is essential to protect human rights during armed conflicts. To be relevant, international law – particularly international criminal law – must be enforced. The commission of international crimes entails international legal responsibility at both criminal and civil level.

The prosecution of the responsible individuals is decisive in protecting civilians in so far as holding the former to account will serve as deterrence and discourage the future commission of such serious violations of law. The true meaning of justice is to provide civilian victims with the full and equal protection of the law.

Furthermore, prosecuting international crimes is not merely a faculty but it reflects a treaty (Articles 1–146, IV Geneva Convention) and customary

32 For an in-depth analysis see PCHR, 'The Illegal Closure of the Gaza Strip: Collective Punishment of the Civilian Population' (December 2010). Online. Available HTTP: http://www.pchrgaza.org/files/2010/.pdf (accessed 30 August 2012).

33 ICRC, 'Gaza Closure: Not Another Year' (14 June 2010). Online. Available HTTP: http://www.icrc.org/eng/resources/documents/.htm (accessed 28 February 2012).

34 UN Human Rights Council, 'Report of the UN Special Rapporteur on the Situation of Human Rights in the Palestinian Territories Occupied since 1967' (A/HRC/13/53/ Rev 1, 7 June 2010); 'Report of the UN Special Rapporteur on the Situation of Human Rights in the Palestinian Territories Occupied since 1967' (A/HRC/16/72, 10 January 2011).

international law[35] obligation on all states to respect and ensure respect for IHL in all circumstances and to search for and prosecute suspected war criminals before national courts, irrespective of the traditional links with the crime (nationality or territory), in application of the principle of universal jurisdiction, as will be discussed below.

Likewise, the *jus cogens* nature of the crimes against humanity – confirmed by the International Criminal Tribunal for the Ex-Yugoslavia (ICTY)[36] – imposes an obligation to investigate and prosecute such crimes at the international level under customary international law.[37]

Investigations into possible violations committed during armed conflict must:

1. be independent and impartial;[38]
2. address all individuals having potential legal responsibilities, including senior military and civilian personnel;[39]
3. look into the overall policy behind the military operation;[40]
4. be able to identify and lead to the prosecution of all those bearing responsibilities.[41]

If responsible for a violation of international law, a state incurs the concomitant civil responsibility to the benefit of the victims since under treaty[42] and customary IHL 'a State responsible for violations of international humanitarian law is required

35 Henckaerts and Doswald-Beck, *Customary International Humanitarian Law: Rules*, I, Rule 158, 'States must investigate war crimes allegedly committed by their nationals or armed forces, or on their territory, and, if appropriate, prosecute the suspects. They must also investigate other war crimes over which they have jurisdiction and, if appropriate, prosecute the suspects'.

36 *Prosecutor v Dusko Tadic* (Judgment), ICTY, Trial Chamber, 7 May 1997, IT-94-1-t, §618–623.

37 M.C. Bassiouni, 'International Crimes: Jus Cogens and Obligatio Erga Omnes', *Law and Contemporary Problems* 59, no. 4 (1996): 63–74.

38 *Findlay v the United Kingdom*, European Court of Human Rights, 25 February 1997, Application no. 22107/93, §73; *Bati v Turkey*, 3 September 2004, Application no. 33097/96, 57834/00, §135.

39 Articles 25 (Individual criminal responsibility) and 27 (Irrelevance of official capacity), Rome Statute of the International Criminal Court.

40 *Ergi v Turkey*, European Court of Human Rights, 28 July 1998, Application no. 23818/94, §84.

41 *Hugh Jordan v the United Kingdom*, European Court of Human Rights, 4 August 2001, Application no. 24746/94, §107; *McCann and Others v the United Kingdom*, 27 September 1995, Application no. 18984/91.

42 Article 91 (Responsibility) Additional Protocol I to the four Geneva Conventions: 'A Party to the conflict which violates the provisions of the Conventions or of this Protocol shall, if the case demands, be liable to pay compensation. It shall be responsible for all acts committed by persons forming part of its armed forces'.

to make full reparation for the loss or injury caused'.[43] Moreover, Article 148 of the IV Geneva Convention states that,

> No High Contracting Party shall be allowed to absolve itself or any other High Contracting Party of any liability incurred by itself or any other High Contracting Party in respect of breaches referred to in the preceding Article.

Equally, 'adequate, effective and prompt reparation' for victims, and therefore the latter's right to access justice, is provided for under HRL,[44] including the ICCPR that is – according to the ICJ in *The Wall*[45]– *binding on Israel in its dealings with the Palestinian population of the oPt.*[46]

Moreover, the ICJ in *The Wall* had also specifically confirmed Israel's obligation 'to make reparation for the damage caused to all the natural or legal persons concerned' in relation to the illegal construction of the annexation wall in occupied West Bank.[47]

The Israeli Legal System and the Denial of Justice and Protection of the Law for Palestinian Civilians of the Gaza Strip

Despite such clear legal framework, the situation in the oPt, particularly in the Gaza Strip, is one of complete disregard for civilians' human rights and of total impunity.

As recalled above, the UN General Assembly called on Israel to investigate into the allegations of serious violations of IHL and HRL presented in – but not limited to – the 'Goldstone Report'.

The UN Human Rights Council mandated a Committee of Independent Experts to assess the state of national investigations into these allegations.

The Committee documented Israel's unwillingness to duly investigate and, whenever appropriate, hold its nationals to account for international criminal charges against Palestinian civilians in the context of 'Operation Cast Lead'.

---

43 Henckaerts and Doswald-Beck, *Customary International Humanitarian Law: Rules*, I, Rule 150.

44 UN General Assembly, 'The Basic Principles and Guidelines on the Right to a Remedy and Reparation for Victims of Gross Violations of International Human Rights Law and Serious Violations of International Humanitarian Law' (A/RES/60/147, 16 December 2005).

45 ICJ, 'Legal Consequences of the Construction of a Wall in the Occupied Palestinian Territory (Advisory Opinion)', 106–11.

46 ICCPR, Article 2.3 (a). The Human Rights Committee further noted that, 'Without reparations to individuals whose Covenants rights have been violated, the obligation to provide an effective remedy […] is not discharged', ICCPR, 'Nature of the General Legal Obligation Imposed on States Parties to the Covenant', 16.

47 ICJ, 'Legal Consequences of the Construction of a Wall in the Occupied Palestinian Territory (Advisory Opinion)', 152.

Upon conclusion of its work, the Committee stated,

> There is no indication that Israel has opened investigations into the actions of those who designed, planned, ordered and oversaw Operation Cast Lead.[48]

Despite the huge number and the seriousness of the criminal allegations – including possible commission of war crimes – only three cases led to the conviction of Israeli soldiers, as follows:

> 1. for the theft of a credit card, a soldier has served seven and a half months in prison;
> 2. in relation to the use of a nine-year-old boy as a human shield, two soldiers were given a three-month suspended sentence on charges of 'inappropriate behaviour' and 'overstepping authority';
> 3. in relation to the shooting of a group of unarmed civilians carrying white flags, resulting in the killing of two women, one soldier was convicted for 'misuse of firearm', rather than wilful killing, and only spent 45 days in prison.[49]

As a result of the inherently flawed Israeli investigative and judicial system, these convictions and the lenient sanctions as pronounced failed to fit the seriousness of the crimes.

In other instances, given the paucity of information provided by the Israeli authorities, it is believed that the legal qualification of the facts under scrutiny had been systematically downgraded resulting at most in disciplinary infractions.[50]

This situation denotes the consolidated climate of impunity that shields Israeli suspected war criminals – at all levels and grades – within the Israeli investigative and judicial system.[51]

Moreover, Palestinians wishing to pursue civil compensation cases before Israeli courts are currently faced with discriminatory burdens – particularly of monetary

48 UN Human Rights Council, 'Report of the UN Committee of Independent Experts in International Humanitarian and Human Rights Law Established Pursuant to Council Resolution 13/9' (A/HRC/16/24, 18 March 2011), 79.

49 PCHR, 'An Illusion of Justice: An Update of Genuinely Unwilling' (March 2013). Online. Available HTTP: http://www.pchrgaza.org/files/2013/.pdf (accessed 25 April 2013), 15.

50 Ibid., 13.

51 This conclusion is reached in 'Genuinely Unwilling: An Update. The Failure of Israel's Investigative and Judicial System to Comply with the Requirements of International Law, with Particular Regard to the Crimes Committed During the Offensive on the Gaza Strip' (27 December 2008–18 January 2009)' (August 2010). Online. Available HTTP: http://www.pchrgaza.org/files/2010/.pdf (accessed 28 August 2012).

nature such as court guarantees – which inhibit any meaningful justice and reparation for violations perpetrated by the Israeli military forces in the Gaza Strip.[52]

As recognized by the UN Fact-Finding Mission on the Gaza Conflict, considered in combination with other human rights violations committed in the context of Israel's illegal closure of the Gaza Strip, this may constitute the crime against humanity of persecution.[53]

International Legal Mechanisms and the Obligation to Ensure Justice to Palestinians

The International Criminal Court

All of the above reinforces the need to resort to mechanisms of international justice to protect Palestinians' human rights in compliance with the international community's specific legal obligations to punish international crimes.

In effect, should domestic systems fail – which they indisputably have in Israel and the oPt – international justice must be enforced and activated as subsidiary recourse.

To this end, the creation of the International Criminal Court (ICC) as a complementary judicial authority to national criminal jurisdictions was intended to bypass the latter's recurrent failure in persecuting international crimes at the domestic level. Moreover, the ICC could be an appropriate venue for victims to advance reparation claims.[54]

In response to the suspected commission of war crimes and possible crimes against humanity in the context of the Israeli 'Operation Cast Lead', on 22 January 2009 the Palestinian National Authority lodged a declaration to the Registrar of the ICC accepting the jurisdiction of the Court with respect to acts committed on the territory of Palestine since 1 July 2002, date of entry into force of the Rome Statute. The Court represented the most appropriate forum to pursue accountability in light of the inability and unwillingness of all interested parties. This also constituted one of the key recommendations of the UN Fact-Finding Mission on the Gaza Conflict.[55]

However, on 3 April 2012 and so after more than three years, the Office of the Prosecutor of the ICC decided not to open an investigation in the situation of Palestine on the grounds that it was not authorized by the Statute of Rome (instituting the ICC) 'to make the legal determination whether Palestine qualifies

---

52 'Penalizing the Victim' (April 2013). Online. Available HTTP: http://www.pchrgaza.org/files/2013/.pdf (accessed 25 April 2013).

53 UN Human Rights Council, 'Report of the UN Fact-Finding Mission on the Gaza Conflict', 1733.

54 ICC, 'Rome Statute of the International Criminal Court' (2187 UNTS 3 adopted 17 July 1998, entered into force 1 July 2002). Article 75 (Reparations to victims) of the Rome Statute of the International Criminal Court.

55 UN Human Rights Council, 'Report of the UN Fact-Finding Mission on the Gaza Conflict', 1968 (c), 69 (c) (e).

as a State for the purpose of acceding to the Rome Statute and thereby enabling the exercise of jurisdiction by the Court under article 12(1)'.[56]

This pronouncement is questionable as 'the Office of the Prosecutor, rather than unilaterally deciding on the admissibility of such investigations [...] without referring the question to the Pre-Trial Chamber [...] should have immediately referred the question to the Assembly of the States Parties'.[57] As a result, this late pronouncement has barred civilian victims from obtaining justice before the ICC and left the issue to the political arena at the UN where political calculations matter more than the interests of justice and the victims' rights to protection.

The ICC could exercise its jurisdiction over Palestine should the UN Security – acting under Chapter VII of the UN Charter – decide to refer the situation in Palestine to the Office of the Prosecutor, either *motu proprio* or so requested by the UN General Assembly. This outcome, although grounded in Article 13 (b) of the Statute of Rome and in line with the recommendations of the Goldstone Report[58] and its Follow-up before the UN Human Rights Council,[59] has not been reached due to political expediency at the UN.

However, an important event could finally allow Palestinian victims to gain access to the ICC. Following an overwhelming majority of votes within the UN General Assembly resulting in the admission of Palestine as a non-member observer state in the UN on 29 September 2012, the Palestinian leadership could now sign and ratify the Rome Statute instituting the ICC and lodge again the above-mentioned declaration accepting the jurisdiction of the Court.

In turn, this would allow the Office of the Prosecutor to initiate investigations *motu proprio* into acts contrary to the Statute committed in the territory of Palestine from 1 July 2002 and request the Pre-Trial Chamber of the Court to make the judicial determinations of the matter.

However, at the time of writing, regrettably the Palestinian leadership has not yet taken such steps. It is believed that this is the result of political pressure heavily exerted by those countries who were satisfied with admitting Palestine in the UN but much less, including of course those countries who were contrary (i.e. the United States), with having Palestinian victims gaining access to the ICC.

---

56 ICC, 'Situation in Palestine', *Communication of the Office of the Prosecutor of the ICC* (3 April 2012). Online. Available HTTP: http://www.icc-cpi.int/.pdf (accessed 13 September 2012).

57 PCHR, 'A Dark Day for International Justice: ICC Office of the Prosecutor Decides Not to Open Investigations into Situation of Palestine' (4 April 2012). Online. Available HTTP: http://www.pchrgaza.org/portal/en/index.php? (accessed 30 August 2012).

58 UN Human Rights Council, 'Report of the UN Fact-Finding Mission on the Gaza Conflict', 1969 (c) (e).

59 'Follow-up to the Report of the UN Fact-Finding Mission on the Gaza Conflict' (A/HRC/RES/16/32, 13 April 2011), 8.

The principle of universal jurisdiction

The current unavailability of the ICC should not be an insurmountable obstacle to the aspirations of justice for Gaza civilian victims. In effect, international justice could be activated through the principle of states' universal jurisdiction.

It is constructed on the *fictio iuris* that international crimes are offences of such seriousness to affect the international community as a whole and therefore, should the competent state (for one of the traditional links to the crime) be unable or unwilling to investigate and hold responsible individuals to account, third states are empowered to exercise jurisdiction in compliance with treaty-based (Articles 1–146 of the IV Geneva Convention) and customary IHL.[60]

Universal jurisdiction is of paramount importance to ensure full and effective protection of human rights in armed conflicts and coherence of the overall international legal system of human rights protection.

For Palestinian civilian victims, this principle has so far proven to be the only mechanism available to pursue justice and accountability 'in the context of increasing unwillingness on the part of Israel to open criminal investigations that comply with international standards and establish judicial accountability over its military actions in the Occupied Palestinian Territory'.[61]

Regrettably, the exercise of the principle of universal jurisdiction has been obstructed within the national legal system of certain countries such as Spain[62] and the United Kingdom,[63] where criminal charges against Israeli high-rank officials – not only related to Operation Cast Lead – were brought and due process initiated based on the existing legislation that had such principle incorporated.

However, as a result of political calculations, amendments to such legislations were passed resulting in the restriction of the scope of universal jurisdiction at the expenses of Palestinian victims' right to justice.

In the Netherlands, political expediency is equally believed to have influenced the Court's decision to deny a torture complaint brought under Article 6 and 7 of the UN Convention against Torture (CAT) by a Palestinian victim against the former head of the Israeli General Security Services (Shin Bet).[64]

---

60 See Henckaerts and Doswald-Beck, *Customary International Humanitarian Law: Rules*, I, Rule 158.

61 UN Human Rights Council, 'Report of the UN Fact-Finding Mission on the Gaza Conflict', 1857.

62 PCHR, 'PCHR and Spanish Civil Society Organize Conferences in Madrid in Defense of Universal Jurisdiction Press-Release' (21 June 2009); 'PCHR Will Appeal to Supreme Court against Spanish Appeals Court's Decision Press-Release' (30 June 2009). Online. Available HTTP: http://www.pchrgaza.org/portal/ (both accessed 28 August 2012).

63 'U.K. Changes Universal Jurisdiction Law to Provide Safe-Haven to Suspected Israeli War Criminals Press-Release' (19 September 2011). Online. Available HTTP: http://www.pchrgaza.org/portal/ (accessed 30 August 2012).

64 'Justice Denied: Dutch Court Denies Appeal Petition in Ayalon Torture Case Press-Release' (30 October 2009). Online. Available HTTP: http://www.pchrgaza.org/portal/ (accessed 28 August 2012).

This outcome, inconsistent with states' international legal obligations, has shielded Israeli war criminals from justice, allowed impunity in the oPt, and set the conditions for future violations of Palestinian civilians. Again, Operation 'Protective Edge' is indicative in this regard.

Political expediency must not prevail over human rights. Whether at the UN, at a regional level, or within their national jurisdiction, states are bound by specific legal obligations, including the prosecution of international crimes and the enforcement of the rule of law.

If international justice is absent and accountability unattainable, civilian victims will be continuously exposed to the burden of war and their human rights infringed.

If the very role of justice is to protect victims, it must be fully implemented.

Rethinking justice in international law firstly requires acknowledging the lack of or the unequal enforcement of existing legal mechanisms and remedies, such as the principle of universal jurisdiction and the ICC.

The advancement of human rights theories – which has been able to erode the traditional state-centric approach in international relations – must be coherently supported by all relevant actors and duty-bearers, including when conflicts with *raison d'État* may arise.

The international legal regime of human rights protection will never be credible and consistent should impunity continue to be allowed in the oPt and other world scenarios alike.

Cases

Armed Activities on the Territory of the Congo (Democratic Republic of the Congo v. Uganda) (Judgment), ICJ, 19 December 2005.

Bati v Turkey, 3 September 2004, Application no. 33097/96, 57834/00.

Ergi v Turkey, European Court of Human Rights, 28 July 1998, Application no. 23818/94.

Findlay v the United Kingdom, European Court of Human Rights, 25 February 1997, Application no. 22107/93.

Hugh Jordan v the United Kingdom, European Court of Human Rights, 4 August 2001, Application no. 24746/94.

Lopez Burgos v Uruguay (Communication no. 52, CCPR/C/OP/1 6 June 1979 (1984)).

McCann and Others v the United Kingdom, 27 September 1995, Application no. 18984/91.

Prosecutor v Dusko Tadic (Judgment), ICTY, Trial Chamber, 7 May 1997, IT-94-1-t.

Prosecutor v Kordic and Cerkez (Judgment), ICTY, Appeals Chamber, IT-95-14/2-A, 17 December 2004.

Bibliography

Bassiouni, M.C. 'International Crimes: Jus Cogens and Obligatio Erga Omnes'. *Law and Contemporary Problems* 59, no. 4 (1996): 63–74.

'Convention on Certain Conventional Weapons'. 1980.

'Convention on the Prohibition of the Use, Stockpiling, Production and Transfer of Anti-Personnel Mines and on Their Destruction'. 1997.

Forsythe, D.P. *Human Rights in International Relations*. New York: Cambridge University Press, 2006.

'Geneva Protocol on the Use of Biological and Chemical Weapons'. 1925.

'Hague Convention'. 1907.

Henckaerts, J.M., and L. Doswald-Beck. *Customary International Humanitarian Law: Rules*. Vol. I, New York: Cambridge University Press, 2009.

ICC. 'Rome Statute of the International Criminal Court'. 2187 UNTS 3, adopted 17 July 1998, entered into force 1 July 2002.

———. 'Situation in Palestine'. *Communication of the Office of the Prosecutor of the ICC* (3 April 2012). At http://www.icc-cpi.int/.pdf (accessed 13 September 2012).

ICCPR. 'Nature of the General Legal Obligation Imposed on States Parties to the Covenant'.

ICJ. 'Legal Consequences of the Construction of a Wall in the Occupied Palestinian Territory (Advisory Opinion)'. 9 July 2004.

ICRC. *Commentary to the IV Geneva Convention Relative to the Protection of Civilian Persons in Time of War*, edited by J. Pictet. Geneva, 1958.

———. 'Gaza Closure: Not Another Year' (14 June 2010). At http://www.icrc.org/eng/resources/documents/.htm (accessed 28 February 2012).

———. 'Geneva Convention Relative to the Protection of Civilian Persons in Time of War (Fourth Geneva Convention)': 75 UNTS 287, 12 August 1949.

Israeli Ministry of Foreign Affairs. 'Security Cabinet Declares Gaza Hostile Territory' (19 September 2007). At http://www.mfa.gov.il/MFA/Government/Communiques/2007/.htm (accessed 25 August 2012).

Mills, K. *Human Rights in the Emerging Global Order: A New Sovereignty?* London: Macmillan Press, 1998.

PCHR. 'A Dark Day for International Justice: ICC Office of the Prosecutor Decides Not to Open Investigations into Situation of Palestine' (4 April 2012). At http://www.pchrgaza.org/portal/en/index.php? (accessed 30 August 2012).

———. 'Genuinely Unwilling: An Update. The Failure of Israel's Investigative and Judicial System to Comply with the Requirements of International Law, with Particular Regard to the Crimes Committed During the Offensive on the Gaza Strip (27 December 2008–18 January 2009)' (August 2010). At http://www.pchrgaza.org/files/2010/.pdf (accessed 28 August 2012).

———. 'The Illegal Closure of the Gaza Strip: Collective Punishment of the Civilian Population' (December 2010). At http://www.pchrgaza.org/files/2010/.pdf (accessed 30 August 2012).

———. 'An Illusion of Justice: An Update of Genuinely Unwilling' (March 2013). At http://www.pchrgaza.org/files/2013/.pdf (accessed 25 April 2013).
———. 'Justice Denied: Dutch Court Denies Appeal Petition in Ayalon Torture Case Press-Release' (30 October 2009). At http://www.pchrgaza.org/portal/ (accessed 28 August 2012).
———. 'PCHR and Spanish Civil Society Organize Conferences in Madrid in Defense of Universal Jurisdiction Press-Release' (21 June 2009).
———. 'PCHR Will Appeal to Supreme Court against Spanish Appeals Court's Decision Press-Release' (30 June 2009).
———. 'Penalizing the Victim' (April 2013). At http://www.pchrgaza.org/files/2013/.pdf (accessed 25 April 2013).
———. 'Targeting Civilians: Report on the Israeli Military Offensive against the Gaza Strip (27 December 2008–18 January 2009)' (21 October 2009). At http://www.pchrgaza.org/files/Reports/English/ (accessed 28 August 2012).
———. 'U.K. Changes Universal Jurisdiction Law to Provide Safe-Haven to Suspected Israeli War Criminals Press-Release' (19 September 2011). At http://www.pchrgaza.org/portal/ (accessed 30 August 2012).
Price, R. 'Reversing the Gun Sights: Transnational Civil Society Targets Land Mines'. *International Organization* 52, no. 3 (1998): 613–44.
State of Israel. 'State Response to HCJ Petition 9132/07 Al-Bassyouni Vs. Prime Minister' (1 November 2007). At http://www.gisha.org/item.asp? (accessed 20 August 2012).
UN General Assembly. 'The Basic Principles and Guidelines on the Right to a Remedy and Reparation for Victims of Gross Violations of International Human Rights Law and Serious Violations of International Humanitarian Law'. A/RES/60/147, 16 December 2005.
———. 'Follow-up to the Report of the United Nations Fact-Finding Mission on the Gaza War', §1–7: A/RES/64/10, 1 December 2009.
———. 'International Covenant on Civil and Political Rights'. United Nations, 16 December 1966.
———. 'International Covenant on Economic, Social and Cultural Rights'. United Nations, 16 December 1966.
———. 'UN General Assembly, Universal Declaration of Human Rights'. 217 A (III), 10 December 1948.
UN Human Rights Committee. 'Lopez Burgos Vs. Uruguay'. Communication no. 52, CCPR/C/OP/1 6 June 1979 (1984).
———. 'Nature of the General Legal Obligation Imposed on States Parties to the Covenant'. General Comment no. 31 CCPR/C/21/Rev.1/Add.13, 26 May 2004.
UN Human Rights Council. 'Follow-up to the Report of the UN Fact-Finding Mission on the Gaza Conflict'. §8: A/HRC/RES/16/32, 13 April 2011.
———. 'Report of the UN Committee of Independent Experts in International Humanitarian and Human Rights Law Established Pursuant to Council Resolution 13/9'. §79: A/HRC/16/24, 18 March 2011.

———. 'Report of the UN Fact-Finding Mission on the Gaza Conflict'. §1733, §1886–934: A/HRC/12/48, 25 September 2009.
———. 'Report of the UN Special Rapporteur on the Situation of Human Rights in the Palestinian Territories Occupied since 1967'. A/HRC/13/53/ Rev 1, 7 June 2010.
———. 'Report of the UN Special Rapporteur on the Situation of Human Rights in the Palestinian Territories Occupied since 1967'. A/HRC/16/72, 10 January 2011.
United Nations. 'Convention against Torture and Other Cruel, Inhuman or Degrading Treatment or Punishment'. UNTS 1465 85, 1984.
———. 'Convention on the Elimination of All Forms of Discrimination against Women (CEDAW)', 1979.
———. 'Convention on the Elimination of All Forms of Racial Discrimination (CERD)', 1966.
———. 'Convention on the Rights of the Child (CRC)', 1989.

Chapter 4
How Effective are National Remedies in Securing International Justice?

Selman Karakul

Introduction

The modest idea of human rights 'that limits admissible domestic law of societies in good standing in a reasonably just Society of Peoples'[1] is perceived to play a significant role in securing international justice. Hopefully, it is still a common understanding that, 'by making the respect for and the observance of human rights and fundamental freedoms an effective part of the international legal system, the law will assist in ensuring an essential condition of the security of nations'.[2] At least rhetorically, the relationship between human rights and international justice has become more evident in the last few years especially through the activities of international and regional organisations.

The constituent documents of international and regional organisations give special emphasis to common values such as peace, cooperation, justice and respect for human rights and fundamental freedoms. As indicated in article 1, paragraph 3 of the Charter of the United Nations (UN), one of the purposes of the organisation is 'to achieve international co-operation in solving international problems of an economic, social, cultural, or humanitarian character, and in promoting and encouraging respect for human rights and for fundamental freedoms for all without distinction as to race, sex, language, or religion.'[3] Article 1, paragraph b of the Statute of the Council of Europe (CoE) states that the aim of the organisation shall be pursued by discussion of questions of common concern and by agreements and common action *inter alia* in the maintenance and further realisation of human rights and fundamental freedoms. To this extent, a great number of treaties were adopted under the auspices of these organisations.

Some writers and activists focus on the failures and shortcomings of intergovernmental organisations while others glorify them in an extravagant

---

1 John Rawls, *The Law of Peoples: With the Idea of Public Reason Revisited*, 4th edn (Cambridge, MA: Harvard University Press, 2000), 80.

2 Hersch Lauterpacht, *International Law: Disputes, War and Neutrality*, ed. Sir Elihu Lauterpacht, vol. 5, Collected Papers (Cambridge: Cambridge University Press, 2004), 86.

3 United Nations, 'United Nations Charter' (1945). Online. Available HTTP: http://www.un.org/en/sc/repertoire/principles.shtml (accessed 24 February 2014).

manner. With a neutral point of view, both failures and success stories can be found in the relatively short history of international and regional organisations. To give an example, the establishment and functioning of international courts and tribunals by the UN to try those responsible for war crimes or violations of international humanitarian law should be regarded as a favourable outcome, despite the fact that the organisation had failed to take any preventive measures to avoid such violations. During the 1990s, the efforts of the CoE in assisting the countries of central and eastern Europe to carry out democratic reforms and expand their borders to include the rest of the continent were no doubt successful; but the full observance and implementation of human rights and fundamental freedoms in the member countries has a long way to go.

Prior to the adoption of international human rights treaties by intergovernmental organisations, most of the states had already recognised fundamental rights and freedoms in their constitutions or other legal instruments. It was, and still is, the responsibility of each member state to prevent human rights violations within their jurisdiction.[4] International and regional human rights treaties urge member states to ensure to all individuals within their territory and subject to their jurisdiction the rights recognised in the relevant treaties. In this context, the states parties are obliged to introduce an effective national human rights protection system. They can opt for establishing legislative, administrative or judicial institutions to secure convention rights and freedoms at a national level. In other words, it is to be presumed *prima facie* that the states parties to human rights treaties are in a better position to redress the grievance of the applicants under domestic law.

Among other provisions, article 2 paragraph 3 (a) of the International Covenant on Civil and Political Rights (CCPR or the Covenant) requires each state party to ensure that any person whose rights or freedoms as herein recognised are violated shall have an effective remedy, notwithstanding that the violation has been committed by persons acting in an official capacity. The Human Rights Committee stated in its General Comment No. 31 [80] adopted on 29 March 2004 concerning 'The Nature of the General Legal Obligation Imposed on States Parties to the Covenant' that,

> 15. Article 2, paragraph 3, requires that in addition to effective protection of Covenant rights States Parties must ensure that individuals also have accessible and effective remedies to vindicate those rights. Such remedies should be appropriately adapted so as to take account of the special vulnerability of certain categories of person, including in particular children. The Committee attaches importance to States Parties' establishing appropriate judicial and administrative mechanisms for addressing claims of rights violations under domestic law. The Committee notes that the enjoyment of the rights recognized under the Covenant can be effectively assured by the judiciary in many different ways, including direct applicability of the Covenant, application of comparable constitutional

4 Bertrand G. Ramcharan, *Preventive Human Rights Strategies* (New York: Routledge, 2010), 59.

> or other provisions of law, or the interpretive effect of the Covenant in the application of national law. Administrative mechanisms are particularly required to give effect to the general obligation to investigate allegations of violations promptly, thoroughly and effectively through independent and impartial bodies. National human rights institutions, endowed with appropriate powers, can contribute to this end. A failure by a State Party to investigate allegations of violations could in and of itself give rise to a separate breach of the Covenant. Cessation of an ongoing violation is an essential element of the right to an effective remedy (…).[5]

Article 13 of the Convention for the Protection of Human Rights and Fundamental Freedoms (ECHR or the Convention) imposes a similar obligation on member states to provide an effective domestic remedy for the victims of human rights violations before a national authority notwithstanding that the violation has been committed by persons acting in an official capacity. The European Court of Human Rights (ECtHR or the Court) notes in the *Kudła v Poland* judgment of 26 October 2000 that, '[t]he object of Article 13, as emerges from the *travaux préparatoires*, is to provide a means whereby individuals can obtain relief at national level for violations of their Convention rights before having to set in motion the international machinery of complaint before the Court.'[6]

It is a general and well-established requirement of admissibility in international human rights law that all available domestic remedies must be exhausted before lodging a complaint with the human rights protection mechanisms envisaged in the international or regional human rights treaties. As indicated by the ECtHR in the *Akdivar v Turkey* judgment of 16 September 1996,

> States are dispensed from answering before an international body for their acts before they have had an opportunity to put matters right through their own legal system. The rule is based on the assumption, reflected in Article 13 of the Convention (art. 13) – with which it has close affinity –, that there is an effective remedy available in respect of the alleged breach in the domestic system whether or not the provisions of the Convention are incorporated in national law (...).[7]

The ECtHR clarifies the purpose of the rule as follows: 'The rationale for the exhaustion rule is to afford the national authorities, primarily the courts, the

5 UN Human Rights Committee (HRC), 'General Comment No. 31 [80], the Nature of the General Legal Obligation Imposed on States Parties to the Covenant', 26 May 2004, CCPR/C/21/Rev.1/Add.13 (2004).

6 *Kudła v Poland*, App No 30210/96, Grand Chamber, Judgment of ECtHR, 26 October 2000, para 152.

7 *Akdivar v Turkey*, App No 21893/93, Grand Chamber, Judgment of ECtHR, 16 September 1996, para 65.

opportunity to prevent or put right the alleged violations of the Convention. It is based on the assumption, reflected in Article 13, that the domestic legal order will provide an effective remedy for violations of Convention rights. This is an important aspect of the subsidiary character of the Convention machinery: see among many authorities *Selmouni v France* [GC], no. 25803/94, ECtHR 1999-V, § 74; *Kudła v Poland* [GC], no. 30210/96, ECHR 2000-XI, § 152; *Andrášik and Others v Slovakia* (dec.), nos. 57984/00 et al., ECtHR 2002-IX.'[8]

Despite these obligations under international and regional human rights instruments, the number of individual complaints received by the treaty bodies has increased significantly. The exponential growth in the number of applications brought before the monitoring mechanisms of the existing treaties urged international and regional organisations to take measures to cope with the new situation. Within this framework, international and regional organisations have focused on organisational and operational restructuring of monitoring systems in order to ensure the effectiveness of human rights enshrined in those treaties.

Both international and regional organisations have adopted several decisions encouraging the protection and promotion of human rights at a national level in order to decrease their workload. They reminded member states of their obligations and urged them to fulfil their commitments under the international agreements. Accordingly, the member states were requested to ascertain the existence of domestic remedies for anyone with an arguable complaint of a violation of the human rights treaties, and to assert that these remedies are effective, in that they can result in a decision on the merits of the complaint and adequate redress for any violation found.[9]

Similar measures were also taken by the UN for improving the protection of human rights at the national level. According to the 'Basic Principles and Guidelines on the Right to a Remedy and Reparation for Victims of Gross Violations of International Human Rights Law and Serious Violations of International Humanitarian Law' adopted and proclaimed by the General Assembly of the UN on 16 December 2005 (resolution 60/147), the scope of the obligation to respect, ensure respect for and implement international human rights law and international humanitarian law as provided for under the respective bodies of law, included, *inter alia*, the duty to:

> (*a*) Take appropriate legislative and administrative and other appropriate measures to prevent violations;

---

8 European Court of Human Rights, 'Key Case Law Issues: Exhaustion of Domestic Remedies' (28 April 2006). Online. Available HTTP: http://www.echr.coe.int (accessed 1 September 2012).

9 Council of Europe Committee of Ministers, 'Recommendation Rec (2004) 6 of the Committee of Ministers to Member States on the Improvement of Domestic Remedies' (Council of Europe, 12 May 2004). Online. Available HTTP: https://wcd.coe.int/ViewDoc.jsp?id=743317 (accessed 1 September 2012).

> (*b*) Investigate violations effectively, promptly, thoroughly and impartially and, where appropriate, take action against those allegedly responsible in accordance with domestic and international law;
> (*c*) Provide those who claim to be victims of a human rights or humanitarian law violation with equal and effective access to justice, (…), irrespective of who may ultimately be the bearer of responsibility for the violation; and
> (*d*) Provide effective remedies to victims, including reparation, (…).[10]

Despite the fact that the national remedies are supposed to offer the most appropriate way to deal with human rights violations in a given country, almost all of the applications lodged with the international and regional human rights mechanisms result from the lack of an effective domestic remedy to address the violations in question.

The abundance of similar complaints from a particular state indicates a systemic problem resulting from the legislation or the application of existing legislation. The monitoring bodies should point out structural or general deficiencies in national law or practice and the effectiveness of the existing domestic remedies. Nevertheless, encouraging respondent states to set up effective remedies to avoid repetitive cases is of a political nature that should be placed on the agenda of decision-making bodies of the international and regional organisations. Decision-making bodies should apply necessary measures in order to prevent the recurrence of similar violations in the future.

Once an allegation is submitted to judicial human rights protection mechanisms of international or regional organisations, a reasonable expectation exists that the application will be handled according to the procedures set out in the convention. Where the judicial authority establishes that there has been a violation of the relevant convention by the responding state, it shall, if necessary, afford just satisfaction to the injured party. Nevertheless, particularly due to the unexpected increase in the number of applications lodged with the ECtHR following a major revision of the Convention system by Protocol No. 11 to the Convention that came into force on 1 November 1998 and the membership of new democracies to the CoE in the early 1990s, the Convention organs regrettably endorsed a fresh approach to overcoming the significant increase in the number of applications.

In search of increasing the effectiveness of the Convention system, following the entry into force of Protocol No. 14 to the Convention on 1 June 2010, in line with the reports and observations of the CoE institutions, the plenary ECtHR amended, *inter alia*, Rule 61 of the Rules of Court. Rule 61 sets out a pilot

10 UN General Assembly, 'Basic Principles and Guidelines on the Right to a Remedy and Reparation for Victims of Gross Violations of International Human Rights Law and Serious Violations of International Humanitarian Law: Resolution / Adopted by the General Assembly', A/RES/60/147 (21 March 2006).

judgment procedure that was already applied by the Court on 22 June 2004, the date of Grand Chamber judgment in the case of *Broniowski v Poland.*[11]

Rule 61 of the Rules of Court can be construed in such a way as to enable the Court to address chronic human rights situations in responding states by requiring states to establish effective domestic remedies, which are supposed to be under the authority of the decision-making body of the CoE that is the Committee of Ministers. With a teleological approach, one might say that, if the Court contributes to the introduction of new domestic remedies in the respondent states, it would be a positive step anyhow. Nonetheless, it ought to be taken into consideration that the newly amended rules shall be applicable to all pending applications that may affect the applicants without their consent.

This chapter intends to argue that the domestic legal remedies are neither available nor effective in protecting human rights in various member states of the international organisations. Therefore, it is asserted that the very idea of international justice would be undermined if the international organisations return the mandate to the member states by suggesting that human rights could only be effectively protected at the domestic level. The chapter is organised in three parts. The first part deals with the internal application of human rights norms, particularly the CCPR and ECHR, in member states. The second part explores the new measures taken by the ECHR organs to improve domestic implementation of human rights. The third part analyses the performance of newly established domestic remedies.

Internal Application of Human Rights Norms

Inspired by the principles of liberalism, most of the written constitutions contained provisions of some sort dealing with human rights, before the adoption of international human rights instruments.[12] In the subsequent period, both horizontal and vertical influences and pressures were effective in drafting new constitutions. The adoption of liberal constitutions as a consequence of the influence and pressures exerted by powerful countries in the liberal constitutional tradition is suggested to be 'horizontal'. On the other hand, the spread of liberal constitutions

11 *Broniowski v Poland,* App No 31443/96, Grand Chamber, Judgment of ECtHR, 22 June 2004.

12 Sartori argues that a constitution without a declaration of rights still is a constitution; whereas a constitution whose core and centrepiece is not within a frame of government is not a constitution – though he endorse the idea that in vital matters some redundancy does not hurt, and under the impetus of the various French declarations of the rights of men and citizens, bill of rights have usefully won their way into nineteenth- and twentieth-century constitutions. See, Giovanni Sartori, *Comparative Constitutional Engineering: An Inquiry into Structures, Incentives and Outcomes*, 2nd edn (New York: New York University Press, 1997), 196.

under the influence and pressure of international law and institutions above the state is considered as 'vertical'. In this context, it should be pointed out that both horizontal and vertical influences and pressures were intertwined in a way that the states, exerting a horizontal influence, were also the creators and members of the international system wielding pressure from above.[13]

Whatever the motives of states in adopting liberal constitutions guaranteeing fundamental rights and freedoms, it has become a legal obligation for governments to protect and promote international human rights in their jurisdiction. For the application and status of international human rights instruments in the domestic legal system, the classical debate of monism and dualism is still valid in many aspects. In monist countries, international and domestic legal orders constitute a single system, while in dualist countries each domestic legal system rests self-contained, separate from others and from the international system. However, there is no pure application of monism or dualism in a given country since these systems are closely linked and both systems can be jointly used by the national authorities in different situations.[14] Following the ratification of a human rights treaty, it is the obligation of state parties to secure everyone within their jurisdiction the rights and freedoms defined in the treaty. To this extent, the contracting parties may employ different methods for implementing treaty obligations at the domestic level.

Article 2 paragraph 2 of the CCPR calls for state parties 'to adopt such laws or other measures as may be necessary to give effect to the rights recognized in the present Covenant' where not already provided for by existing legislative or other measures. However, the literal interpretation of Article 2 suggests that the Covenant rights could not be claimed before domestic courts *per se* without any domestic incorporating measure. That is, by rejecting a proposal during the drafting process, the provisions of the Covenant should not become effective as domestic law. A direct application of the Covenant was, at least, not ruled out by the drafters.[15]

In its General Comment No. 3 (1981) on implementation of the Covenant at the national level (Art. 2), the Human Rights Committee noted that,

> (...) article 2 of the Covenant generally leaves it to the States parties concerned to choose their method of implementation in their territories within the framework set out in that article. It recognizes, in particular, that the implementation does not depend solely on constitutional or legislative enactments, which in themselves

13 Henry J. Steiner and Philip Alston, *International Human Rights in Context: Law, Politics, Morals*, 2nd edn (Oxford: Oxford University Press, 2000), 988.

14 Dinah Shelton, 'Introduction', in *International Law and Domestic Legal Systems*, ed. Dinah Shelton (Oxford: Oxford University Press, 2011), 2–3.

15 Anja Seibert-Fohr, 'Domestic Implementation of the International Covenant on Civil and Political Rights Pursuant to Its Article 2 Para. 2', in *Max Planck Yearbook of United Nations Law*, ed. J.A. Frowein and R. Wolfrum (The Hague: Kluwer Law International, 2001), 424.

> are often not per se sufficient. The Committee considers it necessary to draw the attention of States parties to the fact that the obligation under the Covenant is not confined to the respect of human rights, but that States parties have also undertaken to ensure the enjoyment of these rights to all individuals under their jurisdiction. This aspect calls for specific activities by the States parties to enable individuals to enjoy their rights. This is obvious in a number of articles (…), but in principle this undertaking relates to all rights set forth in the Covenant (...).[16]

In a subsequent General Comment No. 31 [80] on the nature of the general legal obligation imposed on states parties to the Covenant dated 26 May 2001, the Human Rights Committee stated that,

> (...) Article 2 allows a State Party to pursue this in accordance with its own domestic constitutional structure and accordingly does not require that the Covenant be directly applicable in the courts, by incorporation of the Covenant into national law. The Committee takes the view, however, that Covenant guarantees may receive enhanced protection in those States where the Covenant is automatically or through specific incorporation part of the domestic legal order. The Committee invites those States Parties in which the Covenant does not form part of the domestic legal order to consider incorporation of the Covenant to render it part of domestic law to facilitate full realization of Covenant rights as required by article 2 (...).[17]

In its General Comment No. 9 (1998) on the domestic application of the Covenant, the Committee on Economic, Social and Cultural Rights took it one step further, stating that,

> (...) while the Covenant does not formally oblige States to incorporate its provisions in domestic law, such an approach is desirable. Direct incorporation avoids problems that might arise in the translation of treaty obligations into national law, and provides a basis for the direct invocation of the Covenant rights by individuals in national courts. For these reasons, the Committee strongly encourages formal adoption or incorporation of the Covenant in national law (...).[18]

As can be inferred from the general comments, Article 2 of the Covenant has been gradually interpreted as requiring states parties to incorporate it into

16 'General Comment No. 03: Implementation at the National Level (Art. 2) CCPR'.

17 UN Human Rights Committee (HRC), 'General Comment No. 31 [80], the Nature of the General Legal Obligation Imposed on States Parties to the Covenant', 26 May 2004, CCPR/C/21/Rev.1/Add.13.

18 UN Committee on Economic Social and Cultural Rights (CESCR), 'General Comment No. 9: The Domestic Application of the Covenant', 3 December 1998, E/C.12/1998/24 (1998).

national legislation so as to ensure better implementation of the Covenant. For CoE member states, there are several ways in which international treaties are recognised in domestic legal systems. Through transformation, the international rules are addressed to the contracting states that, in turn, use them as a basis for the establishment of a corresponding set of rules for public authorities, individuals, or other legal entities considered to be subjects under domestic law.[19] Under the second method, the constitutions of some states allow the automatic incorporation of a treaty that has been duly approved by the legislature and subsequently concluded.[20] In some countries, international treaties have a higher legal status than ordinary legislation. The third method is similar to the preceding one in that it allows legislative authorisation to ratify a treaty, although its force in domestic law is secured by (a governmental decree or) a special act of parliament.[21]

The legal status of the ECHR in state parties has evolved along with the role of the ECtHR gradually after the 1970s and especially in the 1990s when the judiciaries of the various states recognised the significance of the Convention, giving it a more robust status in domestic law. In the 1990s, more dualist states passed specific legislation giving the Convention domestic force and recognised direct applicability of the Convention by the national authorities. According to one observation, in some respects, the remarkable shift since the 1970s is the ultimate marker of the evolution of the Convention's status generally.[22]

Vested with the mandate of ensuring the observance of the engagements undertaken by the states parties in the Convention, the ECtHR clarified the obligations of the contracting parties in several instances. In the *Ireland v the United Kingdom* judgment of 18 January 1978, the Court held in paragraph 239 as follows,

> (…) Unlike international treaties of the classic kind, the Convention comprises more than mere reciprocal engagements between contracting States. It creates, over and above a network of mutual, bilateral undertakings, objective obligations which, in the words of the Preamble, benefit from a 'collective enforcement'. By virtue of Article 24 (art. 24) [this concerned inter-state cases, at the time], the Convention allows Contracting States to require the observance of those obligations without having to justify an interest deriving, for example, from the fact that a measure they complain of has prejudiced one of their own nationals.

19 For instance, the United Kingdom, Ireland and the Scandinavian countries. See, Andrew Z. Drzemczewski, *European Human Rights Convention in Domestic Law* (Oxford: Oxford University Press, 1997), 36.

20 For instance, France, the Netherlands, Austria, Luxembourg and Switzerland. Ibid., 36–37.

21 For instance, Germany, Italy and Turkey. Ibid., 37.

22 Ed Bates, *The Evolution of the European Convention on Human Rights: From Its Inception to the Creation of a Permanent Court of Human Rights* (Oxford: Oxford University Press, 2010), 162–63.

> By substituting the words 'shall secure' for the words 'undertake to secure' in the text of Article 1 (art. 1), the drafters of the Convention also intended to make it clear that the rights and freedoms set out in Section I would be directly secured to anyone within the jurisdiction of the Contracting States (document H (61) 4, pp. 664, 703, 733 and 927). That intention finds a particularly faithful reflection in those instances where the Convention has been incorporated into domestic law (…).[23]

Although the Court acknowledges that the Convention rights and freedoms would be directly secured to anyone within the jurisdiction of the contracting states where the Convention has been incorporated into domestic law, it consistently reiterated that, 'Article 13 does not go so far as to require incorporation of the Convention or a particular form of remedy, Contracting States being afforded a margin of appreciation in conforming with their obligations under this provision'.[24] Nevertheless, the European Commission on Human Rights had departed from the Court, stating that, 'to hold that Art 13 imposed an obligation on States to provide a remedy in respect of legislation would effectively oblige them to incorporate it into domestic law with superior status to other law, whereas the Court has held that neither Art 13 nor the Convention in general imposes such an obligation.'[25]

In Recommendation (2004) 6 of 12 May 2004, the Committee of Ministers of the CoE observed that the Convention had become an integral part of the domestic legal order of all states parties. In practice, the impact of legal status and incorporation of the Convention rights into domestic law is significant but not decisive in ensuring effective implementation of the Convention at the domestic level. The first reason for that is that fundamental rights were already recognised in existing national laws of the member states prior to the adoption of the international or regional human rights treaties. Nonetheless, it was the treaty organs rather than the national authorities who revealed serious violations of human rights in member states and significant progress was achieved through the supervision of the execution of the judgments of the ECtHR by the Committee of Ministers. Past experience suggests that the national authorities need international encouragement for ensuring adequate protection of human rights at the domestic level. In exceptional cases where the human rights and fundamental freedoms are better protected under the laws (and practice) of any contracting party, obviously national legislation shall prevail in accordance with Article 53 of the Convention. Second, the incorporation of the Convention into domestic legislation shall not be conceived in an abstract manner. The national authorities of the member

23 *Ireland v United Kingdom*, App No 5310/71, Judgment of ECtHR 1, 18 January 1978.

24 *Smith and Grady v the United Kingdom*, App Nos 33985/96 and 33986/96, Judgment of ECtHR, 27 September 1999, para 135.

25 *Lithgow and Others v the United Kingdom*, App Nos 9006/80 et al., Report of the Commission, 7 March 1984.

states should align with the established case-law of the ECtHR. However, it presents a problem that the national courts are not very eager to set aside national jurisprudence and give priority to the decisions of the ECtHR. To make it worse, in a number of cases, national courts misinterpreted the case-law of the ECtHR so as to provide legal grounds for resolving disputes and claims.[26]

New Measures to Improve Domestic Implementation of Human Rights

As indicated in the preamble of the Protocol No. 14 to the ECHR, the continuing increase in the workload of treaty bodies urged international and regional organisations to take the necessary measures in order to maintain and improve the efficiency of the control system for the long term. The most dramatic increase was observed in the caseload of the ECtHR, which led experts to conclude that the Court was the victim of its own success. To this end, a set of measures has been introduced by the CoE institutions. First and foremost, the Protocol No. 14 to the ECHR amending the control system of the Convention was adopted in 2004.[27] Furthermore, the Committee of Ministers of the CoE adopted several recommendations and resolutions with a view to guaranteeing the effectiveness of the ECHR.[28] In the Resolution Res 2004 (3) adopted by the Committee of Ministers on 12 May 2004, bearing in mind the Court's own submission on this matter, the Committee of Ministers invited the Court,

> I. as far as possible, to identify, in its judgments finding a violation of the Convention, what it considers to be an underlying systemic problem and the source of this problem, in particular when it is likely to give rise to numerous applications, so as to assist States in finding the appropriate solution and the Committee of Ministers in supervising the execution of judgments;

---

26 For example, in a number of cases concerning the retrial applications of political parties (*United Communist Party of Turkey and others v Turkey, Yazar, Karataş, Aksoy and the People's Labour Party (HEP) v Turkey* and *Freedom and Democracy Party (ÖZDEP) v Turkey* cases) dissolved in breach of the ECHR, the Turkish Constitutional Court held that the violations of the freedom of assembly and association established by the ECHR were not related to the material evidence before the Constitutional Court but rather concerned with the assessment of the evidence, which led the Constitutional Court to decline the requests of the applicants. Surprisingly, in its Resolution CM/ResDH(2007)100 in June 2007, the Committee of Ministers of the CoE had decided to close the examination of these cases prior to the delivery of the decisions of the Constitutional Court in June 2008.

27 Entry into force 1 June 2010 – Protocol No 14 *bis* entered into force on 1 October 2009 and ceased to be in force on the date of entry into force of Protocol No 14.

28 Directorate General of Human Rights, *Guaranteeing the Effectiveness of the European Convention on Human Rights: Collected Texts* (Strasbourg: Council of Europe, 2004).

> II. to specially notify any judgment containing indications of the existence of a systemic problem and of the source of this problem not only to the State concerned and to the Committee of Ministers, but also to the Parliamentary Assembly, to the Secretary General of the Council of Europe and to the Council of Europe Commissioner for Human Rights, and to highlight such judgments in an appropriate manner in the database of the Court.[29]

Following the adoption of the above-mentioned legal documents, the Court adopted a similar position to that of the CoE institutions in order to cope with the ever-increasing caseload. The general approach of the Court has been to emphasise the importance of domestic legal remedies and encourage responding states to set up effective domestic remedies and to find solutions to already-pending cases. To this extent, the Court 'has developed a new procedure known as the pilot-judgment procedure, as a means of dealing with large groups of identical cases that derive from the same underlying problem. The Court has for some time had pending before it a great many of these cases, referred to as repetitive cases. They represent a significant proportion of the Court's workload and therefore contribute to the congestion in the Court's processes.'[30] As stipulated in the information note issued by the Registrar of the Court,

> (...) 2. The way in which the procedure operates is that when the Court receives a significant number of applications deriving from the same root cause, it may decide to select one or more of them for priority treatment. In dealing with the selected case or cases, it will seek to achieve a solution that extends beyond the particular case or cases so as to cover all similar cases raising the same issue. The resulting judgment will be a pilot judgment.
>
> 3. In this judgment the Court will aim:
>
> – to determine whether there has been a violation of the Convention in the particular case;
> – to identify the dysfunction under national law that is at the root of the violation;
> – to give clear indications to the Government as to how it can eliminate this dysfunction;
> – to bring about the creation of a domestic remedy capable of dealing with similar cases (including those already pending before the Court awaiting the pilot judgment), or at least to bring about the settlement of all such cases pending before the Court.

---

29 Council of Europe Committee of Ministers, 'Resolution Res(2004)3 of the Committee of Ministers on Judgments Revealing an Underlying Systemic Problem' (adopted by the Committee of Ministers on 12 May 2004, at its 114th Session) (2004).

30 European Court of Human Rights, *The Pilot-Judgment Procedure: Information Note Issued by the Registrar* (Strasbourg: European Court of Human Rights, 2009).

> 4. The pilot judgment is therefore intended to help the national authorities to eliminate the systemic or structural problem highlighted by the Court as giving rise to repetitive cases. In doing this it also assists the Committee of Ministers in its role of ensuring that each judgment of the Court is properly executed by the respondent State. (…).[31]

Along with the other CoE institutions, the Court tried to revitalise the domestic remedies in the respondent states experiencing systemic or structural human rights problems. Serious problems exist because of the lack of effective remedies under domestic law for the victims of human rights violations. While Article 35 paragraph 1 of the ECHR states that the Court may only deal with a matter after all domestic remedies have been exhausted, an applicant is only required to pursue remedies that are 'available', 'effective' and 'sufficient'.[32]

For a remedy to be available, the applicant must be able to initiate the proceedings directly (without being reliant upon a public body or official). The unavailability of legal aid may affect the accessibility of a remedy, depending upon the applicant's financial resources, complexity of the remedy and necessity of legal representation in domestic proceedings. The existence of the remedies in question must be sufficiently certain not only in theory but also in practice. A remedy will be effective and sufficient if it provides redress for the applicant in respect of the alleged Convention violation. This includes not only judicial remedies, but also any administrative domestic remedy that may provide redress in the circumstances of the particular case. The length of domestic proceedings will be a factor in the consideration of their effectiveness. In principle, a remedy should be immediately available to every aggrieved person, particularly in cases of alleged maltreatment. If there are a number of possible domestic remedies, an applicant will not be required to have exhausted them all, or even to have utilised more than one if nothing further could be achieved. Clearly, failure by the authorities to investigate serious allegations is likely to obviate the need for the victims to take up additional potential avenues of redress.[33]

As for pending claims before the ECHR, whether they were processed and allocated to a judicial formation or not, the applicants who have done their best to exhaust all domestic remedies available and to submit a well-prepared application within a period of six months from the date on which the final national decision was taken can be (and were) subjected to this new procedure, which is adopted after the date of their application.

Another brand new procedure developed by the ECtHR, especially for the handling of repetitive cases, is a unilateral declaration that is set out under new Rule 62A of the Rules of Court to come into force in September 2012. As to

31 Ibid.

32 Philip Leach, *Taking a Case to the European Court of Human Rights*, 3rd edn (Oxford: Oxford University Press, 2011), 128.

33 Ibid., 129–33.

the new procedure reviewed by the Court to ensure clarity and consistency in its practice, in a case 'where a friendly settlement procedure has been unsuccessful, the respondent Government may make a declaration acknowledging the violation of the [Convention] and undertaking to provide the applicant with redress.' In an information note, the Court listed the non-exhaustive criteria that must be satisfied by the unilateral declaration as follows:

- Existence of sufficiently well-established case-law in the matter raised by the application.
- Clear acknowledgment of a violation of the Convention in respect of the applicant – with an explicit indication of the nature of the violation.
- Adequate redress, in line with the Court's case-law on just satisfaction.
- Where appropriate undertakings of a general nature (amendment of legislation or administrative practice, introduction of new policy, etc.).
- Respect for human rights: the unilateral declaration must provide a sufficient basis for the Court to find that respect for human rights does not require the continued examination of the application.[34]

Despite the fact that the new Rule 62A of the Rules of Court came into force in September 2012, it is reported by the Court that 692 applications were dealt with on the basis of a unilateral declaration in 2011 compared with 30 in 2007. The disadvantage of this procedure on the part of the applicants is that,

> [t]he Committee of Ministers is not empowered to supervise the fulfilment of undertakings in a unilateral declaration as endorsed by the Court in a decision. In the event of failure by a government to take the individual measures granted, the applicant may request that his or her application be restored to the Court's list. The decision will not, in itself and in principle, have the effect of preventing the applicant from pursuing any remedy that may be available at domestic level.[35]

The Performance of Newly Established Domestic Remedies

Prior to the discovery of the pilot judgment procedure, the Court adopted a similar procedure in several applications[36] particularly in relation to the cases of excessive length of proceedings against Italy. Italian Parliament passed Law 89 on 2001 known

34 European Court of Human Rights, *Unilateral Declarations: Policy and Practice* (Strasbourg: Council of Europe, 2012). Online. Available HTTP: http://www.echr.coe.int (accessed 1 September 2012).

35 Ibid.

36 Leach et al. address the question in a three-tier system, i.e. the first tier comprising 'full' pilot judgments, the second tier 'quasi-pilot' judgments, and the third tier other judgments addressing systemic issues. See, Philip Leach et al., *Responding to Systemic*

as the Pinto Act, in order to set up an effective domestic remedy allowing any party to criminal, civil, administrative and even tax proceedings to complain of a breach of the 'reasonable time' requirement and obtain financial compensation from a domestic court. In an initial test case (*Brusco*), the ECtHR noted the existence of the Law 89, of its own motion (contrary to its usual practice concerning objections to admissibility) and made use of it 'retroactively' to reject the application on the grounds of failure to exhaust domestic remedies. Those who refused to apply to the domestic courts had their cases thrown out by the ECtHR. A very large number of the applicants requested the Court to suspend consideration of the application pending the outcome of the domestic proceedings. Since the applicants were not content with the outcome of the domestic proceedings, they reactivated their application in Strasbourg.[37] It was criticised that the Pinto Act has not solved any problems, yet it has increased both the caseload of the already-suffering Courts of Appeal and the state budget deficit in Italy. The Pinto Act was an expensive and useless placebo that attempted to hide the problem rather than seek a remedy.[38]

The first case in which the Court delivered a 'pilot judgment' is *Broniowski v Poland* (application no. 31443/96). The case concerned Poland's failure to implement the applicant's entitlement to compensatory property; the applicant's family had been repatriated from the 'territories beyond the Bug River' in the aftermath of the Second World War and had to abandon its property. According to the Polish Government, the anticipated total number of people entitled to such property is nearly 80,000. In its Grand Chamber decision of 22 June 2004, the Court held that there had been a violation of the applicant's right to property and that the violation had originated in a systemic problem connected with the malfunctioning of Polish legislation and practice caused by the failure to set up an effective mechanism to implement the 'right to credit' of Bug River claimants. Through appropriate legal measures and administrative practices, Poland was to secure the implementation of the property right in question in respect of the remaining claimants or provide them with equivalent redress in lieu. On 6 July 2004, the Court decided that all similar applications – including future applications – should be adjourned pending the outcome of the leading case and the adoption of the measures to be taken at national level.[39] Following the Court's adjournment of

---

Human Rights Violations: An Analysis of 'Pilot Judgments' of the European Court of Human Rights and Their Impact at National Level (Antwerp: Intersentia, 2010), 15–27.

37 Francesco Crisafulli, 'The Italian Experience', in *Reforming the European Convention on Human Rights: A Work in Progress*, prepared by the Steering Committee for Human Rights (CDDH) (Strasbourg: Council of Europe Publishing, 2009), 105–06.

38 Marco Fabri, 'The Italian Maze towards Trials within Reasonable Time', in *The Right to Trial within a Reasonable Time and Short-Term Reform of the European Court of Human Rights*, round table organised by the Slovenian chairmanship of the Committee of Ministers of the Council of Europe (Strasbourg: Council of Europe Publishing, 2009), 17–18.

39 Directorate of Commnunications European Court of Human Rights, *Press Release Issued by the Registrar: 'Bug River' Cases Adjourned* (Strasbourg: Council of Europe,

similar applications, Poland passed a new law in July 2005 providing for financial compensation for properties abandoned beyond the Bug River. The Court, finding that the new law and the compensation scheme were effective in practice, struck out in 2007 and 2008 more than 200 similar applications that had been adjourned.[40]

The Act for the Bug River claimants introduced a ceiling of 20 per cent of the original property's current value on compensation recoverable by the applicants. The persons who were not satisfied with this solution brought proceedings to Strasbourg but got no relief. This was followed by 246 strike out-decisions in 2008. The Court held that the procedures under the July 2005 Act had provided the Bug River claimants with relief at the domestic level, which made its further examination of similar applications no longer justified.[41]

After the *Broniowski* judgment and the conclusion of similar cases of Bug River claimants, the Court applied pilot judgment procedure in various cases containing different complaints. For instance, following the *Ananyev and Others v Russia* judgment of 10 January 2012, which included findings of violations of Articles 3 and 13 covering structural problems of inadequate conditions of detention, the Court requested Russian authorities to produce, in cooperation with the Committee of Ministers, preventive and compensatory measures in respect of the allegations of violations of Article 3. Fortunately, the Court has not decided to adjourn the examination of similar applications, in view of the fundamental nature of the right not to be treated inhumanly or degradingly, as part of the follow-up arrangements of the *Ananyev* judgment. Nonetheless, in *Torreggiani and Others v Italy* judgment of 8 January 2013, the Court ruled that the examination of applications dealing solely with overcrowding in Italian prisons would be adjourned for one year from the date on which the judgment becomes final, pending the adoption by the domestic authorities of measures at the national level.[42]

Most of the subsequent pilot judgments are related to excessive length of proceedings and prolonged non-enforcement of court decisions under Article 6 and lack of domestic remedy for those grievances under Article 13 of the Convention.[43] Newly created domestic remedies upon the request of the ECtHR mainly focus on compensating the losses of the applicants rather than addressing

---

31 August 2004). Online. Available HTTP: https://wcd.coe.int/ViewDoc (accessed 1 September 2012).

40 European Court of Human Rights, 'Pilot Judgments: Origins of the Pilot Judgment Procedure', *Fact Sheet*, October 2013. Online. Available HTTP: http://www.echr.coe.int (accessed 15 November 2013).

41 Helen Keller, Magdalena Forowicz, and Lorenz Engi, *Friendly Settlements before the European Court of Human Rights: Theory and Practice* (Oxford: Oxford University Press, 2010), 73.

42 See n 40. For the summary of pilot judgments delivered as of 28 August 2012 see Dominik Haider, *The Pilot Judgment Procedure of the European Court of Human Rights* (Leiden: Martinus Nijhoff Publishers, 2013), 299–311.

43 See for instance, *Ümmühan Kaplan v Turkey*, App No 24240/07, Judgment of ECtHR, 20 March 2012.

the structural problems of member states. Therefore, similar violations are likely to reoccur after the quick disposal of the pending cases.[44] It should be emphasised that up to now the pilot judgment procedure has not met with any success other than shaking the confidence of the applicants in the effective protection and implementation of human rights.

Conclusion

With a view to ensuring the effectiveness of the Convention system in the short- and medium term, the CoE and the Court take measures that are more convenient for respondent states than for applicants. What is more dramatic is that the ECtHR is developing new procedures for reducing the backlog of applications to the detriment of the applicants, which could not be anticipated at the time of their original application.

In general, the rules of procedure are supposed to contribute to securing justice and therefore the amended rules apply retroactively to all pending applications unless otherwise provided by law. However, the amended rules of procedure shall not infringe the vested rights of the parties in pending cases. Nevertheless, this is not the case in terms of repetitive applications in which the applicants could not reasonably expect that their grievances would be classified as such and referred to newly established domestic remedies. Perhaps the Court realised that it had gone too far and decided to act in judicial self-restraint, which is not an appropriate method for the promotion of fundamental rights and freedoms.

As applied by the ECtHR, adjourning the examination of similar applications and encouraging responding states to set up a new domestic remedy to declare the pending applications inadmissible is somehow changing the rules during the game. This attitude may lead to discrediting the international and regional organisations in the eyes of the citizens of the member states.

The nation states are given a second (maybe third) chance to improve the observance of international human rights standards in some sense to realise international justice. Although it is sincerely hoped that the states can achieve the objectives by their own actions, reasonable doubt still exists that international human rights standards will be met and thus that the very idea of international justice will be preserved.

44 According to Haider, the Court should continue the examination of applications stemming from a particular systemic problem after the delivery of the pilot judgment. However, it may proceed to striking pending applications out of its list once a domestic remedy has been installed. Haider, *The Pilot Judgment Procedure of the European Court of Human Rights*, 295.

Cases

Akdivar v Turkey, App No 21893/93, Grand Chamber, Judgment of ECtHR, 16 September 1996.

Ananyev and Others v Russia, App Nos 42525/07 and 60800/08, Chamber, Judgment of ECtHR, 10 January 2012.

Andrášik and Others v Slovakia, App Nos 57984/00 et al., Chamber, Decision of ECtHR, 22 October 2002.

Broniowski v Poland, App No 31443/96, Grand Chamber, Judgment of ECtHR, 22 June 2004.

Freedom and Democracy Party (ÖZDEP) v Turkey, App No 23885/94, Grand Chamber, Judgment of ECtHR, 8 December 1999.

Ireland v United Kingdom, App No 5310/71, Court (Plenary), Judgment of ECtHR, 18 January 1978.

Kudła v Poland, App No 30210/96, Grand Chamber, Judgment of ECtHR 2000, 26 October 2000.

Lithgow and Others v the United Kingdom, App Nos 9006/80 et al., Report of the Commission, 7 March 1984.

Selmouni v France, App No 25803/94, Grand Chamber, Judgment of ECtHR, 28 July 1999.

Smith and Grady v the United Kingdom, App Nos 33985/96 and 33986/96, Chamber, Judgment of ECtHR, 27 September 1999.

Torreggiani and Others v Italy, App Nos 43517/09 et al., Chamber, Judgment of ECtHR, 8 January 2013.

Ümmühan Kaplan v Turkey, App No 24240/07, Chamber, Judgment of ECtHR, 20 March 2012.

United Communist Party of Turkey and Others v Turkey, App No 19392/92, Grand Chamber, Judgment of ECtHR, 30 January 1998.

Yazar, Karataş, Aksoy and the People's Labour Party (HEP) v Turkey, App Nos 22723/93, 22724/93 and 22725/93, Chamber, Judgment of ECtHR, 9 April 2002.

Bibliography

Bates, Ed. *The Evolution of the European Convention on Human Rights: From Its Inception to the Creation of a Permanent Court of Human Rights*. Oxford: Oxford University Press, 2010.

Council of Europe Committee of Ministers. 'Recommendation Rec (2004) 6 of the Committee of Ministers to Member States on the Improvement of Domestic Remedies'. Council of Europe, 12 May 2004. At https://wcd.coe.int/ViewDoc.jsp?id=743317 (accessed 1 September 2012).

———. 'Resolution Res(2004)3 of the Committee of Ministers on Judgments Revealing an Underlying Systemic Problem (Adopted by the Committee of Ministers on 12 May 2004, at its 114th Session)'. 2004.

Crisafulli, Francesco. 'The Italian Experience'. In *Reforming the European Convention on Human Rights: A Work in Progress*, prepared by the Steering Committee for Human Rights (CDDH). Strasbourg: Council of Europe Publishing, 2009.

Directorate General of Human Rights. *Guaranteeing the Effectiveness of the European Convention on Human Rights: Collected Texts*. Strasbourg: Council of Europe, 2004.

Directorate of Commnunications European Court of Human Rights. *Press Release Issued by the Registrar: 'Bug River' Cases Adjourned.* Strasbourg: Council of Europe, 31 August 2004. At https://wcd.coe.int/ViewDoc (accessed 1 September 2012).

Drzemczewski, Andrew Z. *European Human Rights Convention in Domestic Law*. Oxford: Oxford University Press, 1997.

European Court of Human Rights. 'Key Case Law Issues: Exhaustion of Domestic Remedies'. 28 April 2006. At http://www.echr.coe.int (accessed 1 September 2012).

———. *The Pilot-Judgment Procedure: Information Note Issued by the Registrar*. Strasbourg: European Court of Human Rights, 2009.

———. 'Pilot Judgments: Origins of the Pilot Judgment Procedure'. *Fact Sheet*, October 2013. At http://www.echr.coe.int (accessed 15 November 2013).

———. *Unilateral Declarations: Policy and Practice*. Strasbourg: Council of Europe, 2012. At http://www.echr.coe.int (accessed 1 September 2012).

Fabri, Marco. 'The Italian Maze towards Trials within Reasonable Time'. In *The Right to Trial within a Reasonable Time and Short-Term Reform of the European Court of Human Rights*, round table organised by the Slovenian chairmanship of the Committee of Ministers of the Council of Europe. Strasbourg: Council of Europe Publishing, 2009.

Haider, Dominik. *The Pilot Judgment Procedure of the European Court of Human Rights*. Leiden: Martinus Nijhoff Publishers, 2013.

Keller, Helen, Magdalena Forowicz, and Lorenz Engi. *Friendly Settlements before the European Court of Human Rights: Theory and Practice*. Oxford: Oxford University Press, 2010.

Lauterpacht, Hersch. *International Law: Disputes, War and Neutrality*. Collected Papers edited by Sir Elihu Lauterpacht. Vol. 5, Cambridge: Cambridge University Press, 2004.

Leach, Philip. *Taking a Case to the European Court of Human Rights*. 3rd edn. Oxford: Oxford University Press, 2011.

Leach, Philip, Helen Hardman, Svetlana Stephenson, and Brad K. Blitz. *Responding to Systemic Human Rights Violations: An Analysis of 'Pilot Judgments' of the European Court of Human Rights and Their Impact at National Level*. Antwerp: Intersentia, 2010.

Office of the High Commisoner for Human Rights. 'General Comment No. 03: Implementation at the National Level (Art. 2) CCPR'. 29 July 1981.

Ramcharan, Bertrand G. *Preventive Human Rights Strategies*. New York: Routledge, 2010.

Rawls, John. *The Law of Peoples: With the Idea of Public Reason Revisited*. 4th edn. Cambridge, MA: Harvard University Press, 2000.

Sartori, Giovanni. *Comparative Constitutional Engineering: An Inquiry into Structures, Incentives and Outcomes*. 2nd edn. New York: New York University Press, 1997.

Seibert-Fohr, Anja. 'Domestic Implementation of the International Covenant on Civil and Political Rights Pursuant to Its Article 2 Para. 2'. In *Max Planck Yearbook of United Nations Law*, edited by J.A. Frowein and R. Wolfrum. The Hague: Kluwer Law International, 2001.

Shelton, Dinah. 'Introduction'. In *International Law and Domestic Legal Systems*, edited by Dinah Shelton. Oxford: Oxford University Press, 2011.

Steiner, Henry J., and Philip Alston. *International Human Rights in Context: Law, Politics, Morals*. 2nd edn. Oxford: Oxford University Press, 2000.

UN Committee on Economic Social and Cultural Rights (CESCR). 'General Comment No. 9: The Domestic Application of the Covenant'. E/C.12/1998/24 (1998). 3 December 1998.

UN General Assembly. 'Basic Principles and Guidelines on the Right to a Remedy and Reparation for Victims of Gross Violations of International Human Rights Law and Serious Violations of International Humanitarian Law: Resolution / Adopted by the General Assembly'. A/RES/60/147. 21 March 2006.

UN Human Rights Committee (HRC). 'General Comment No. 31 [80], the Nature of the General Legal Obligation Imposed on States Parties to the Covenant'. . CCPR/C/21/Rev.1/Add.13. 26 May 2004.

United Nations. 'United Nations Charter'. 1945. At http://www.un.org/en/sc/repertoire/principles.shtml (accessed 24 February 2014).

Chapter 5
Rethinking Justice: Individual Criminal Responsibility, Immunity and Torture

Amrita Mukherjee[1]

Introduction

This chapter explores the rules of individual criminal liability and immunities – between the concept of fairness in holding individuals who have acted as State organs to account for breaches of international crimes and applying procedural laws that have been accepted in the practice of national courts. It examines these concepts by primarily using the example of the prohibition of torture in international law, which has been the subject matter of significant cases in international and national courts. Universal jurisdiction and the rules that relate to different categories of immunities are explored and lastly, the operation and jurisdiction of the international criminal legal system is assessed in light of questions of complementarity and conflict. International criminal justice, which relates also to the jurisdiction of forum courts – in other words, foreign courts, is seen to be developing a role in combating impunity at the national level.

The prohibition of torture is protected under customary international law, and accorded special status as a rule of *jus cogens*,[2] as well as acknowledged as fulfilling the requirements of the principle of universal jurisdiction. A *jus cogens* norm does not allow for derogation and may only be modified by a subsequent norm having that same character. Prohibitions of aggression, genocide, crimes against humanity and torture are some of the norms accepted as *jus cogens*. Despite recent efforts to undermine the scope of the prohibition of torture in the 'war against terror', it is quite clear that international law and many national systems seek to ensure that those who perpetrate torture are subject to prosecution and punishment. The purpose is to require that individual criminal responsibility and justice prevail and that legal and administrative barriers that support impunity are set aside.

Perhaps the most problematic legal barrier in this regard is the law that relates to immunities of individuals acting on behalf of the State, which operate to shield

1 I would like to thank Professor Gerard McCormack and Professor Anna Lawson for their helpful comments on this chapter.

2 See United Nations, 'Vienna Convention on the Law of Treaties', in *Treaty Series* (Geneva: United Nations, 1969), 331, Article 53, 8ILM, entered in force, 27 January 1980.

public officials from prosecution. The status of the official concerned (*ratione personae* or status immunity) and whether the subject matter concerns conduct performed in their official capacity (*ratione materiae* or functional immunity) may have the effect of acting as a bar from prosecution. It is important to examine the principles upon which immunities rely, particularly in light of the way that immunities conflict with individual criminal responsibility. If the former acts as a bar to prosecution, impunity will prevail and would seem to allow for violations of the prohibition of torture.

As has been stated, 'the very purpose of international criminal law is to attribute responsibility to individuals, including state officials, and to defeat the defence of official capacity or act of state'.[3] The integral role of courts in deciding whether or not to apply immunity as a procedural bar or allow for individual criminal liability has become more resonant but, as we shall see, resulted in an inconsistent line of case law on the subject. Given that individual criminal responsibility for acts of torture has become a central issue of concern recently, and the numbers of States using torture in covert operations and seemingly in a systematic way has increased, international legal experts need to be clear over what they consider to be illegal State practice and not allow for torturers to remain hidden and not held accountable for their crimes. This chapter develops the argument that acts of torture cannot be considered as 'official acts' and therefore should be excluded from *ratione materiae*, as private conduct should be attributable to individuals and not the State. Rather, in relation to avoiding affecting good relations between States, and sovereign equality, attribution to the State would be avoided and instead the senior official would be held accountable.

The emphasis here is on examining case law – how international and national courts have approached this issue – and also on exploring the writings of publicists in the area and the clash of fundamental norms that raise questions as to the contemporary understanding and practice of justice in State and individual criminal responsibility in relation to acts of torture. The focus on domestic courts and their role in deliberating on international justice when faced with allegations of torture conducted by foreign State agents helps to reassess thinking on accountability since the famous 1999 *Pinochet No.3*[4] judgment of the UK House of Lords. The role of international courts such as the International Criminal Court is also considered in light of its jurisdiction and treatment of the subject of immunities.

---

3 D. Akande and S. Shah, 'Immunities of State Officials, International Crimes and Foreign Domestic Courts', *European Journal of International Law* 24, no. 4 (2010): 840.

4 *R v Bow Street Magistrates ex parte Pinochet Ugarte (Amnesty International Intervening) No. 3* [2000] AC 147 (HL) 266. The case is hereinafter referred to as *Pinochet No.3*.

Torture and Universal Jurisdiction

The Rome Statute of the International Criminal Court[5] states that genocide, crimes against humanity, war crimes and aggression are 'the most serious crimes of concern to the international community as a whole'. The significance of the prohibition of torture, which is also considered as a crime against humanity, is that it forms an absolute prohibition and an integral core of international human rights and humanitarian norms, constituting a rule in *jus cogens*. Apart from its place in customary international law, treaty law also provides protections. Despite this special legal status in international law it is also apparent that the violations of the prohibition occur with regularity in many places.

As the United Nations Convention against Torture[6] (UNCAT, the Convention) is primarily concerned with violations carried out by State officials, the most significant international treaty against torture has as one of its purposes, to hold those in positions of power in government to account. Given that incumbent office holders are often shielded from prosecution in foreign States, the Convention has incorporated a system of 'quasi universal jurisdiction' into its provisions. Universal jurisdiction is the principle that every State has jurisdiction to try particular offences. This requires for the competent authorities in foreign ('forum') governments, in circumstances where the alleged perpetrator is present in their territory, to conduct preliminary investigations into the allegations of torture and subsequently to take into custody and apply other legal measures to ensure his or her presence. Following these proceedings and if the investigations warrant, the obligation under the Convention is either to bring criminal proceedings against the alleged perpetrator, or to extradite him or her to where criminal proceedings will be brought.

In light of these obligations the role of domestic courts in responding to allegations of torture, becomes pivotal and also controversial. It is apparent that foreign domestic courts may be important forums for addressing violations by State officials who have otherwise avoided the trial and enforcement of international and national obligations whether in customary international law, treaty obligations or domestic law. This is a separate system from that of the Rome Statute of the International Criminal Court, which was established in 2001 to ensure that, in relation to State parties, all persons who are responsible for serious crimes of international concern whether or not they remain incumbent may not act with impunity. The subject matter here focuses on the law relating to the jurisdiction over and immunities of former State officials who have retired from their posts but have escaped prosecution by their domestic systems. The question is, whom may domestic courts try, and moreover, should domestic courts subject any foreign State agents to criminal prosecution?

5 ICC, 'Rome Statute of the International Criminal Court' (2187 UNTS 3, adopted 17 July 1998), entered into force 1 July 2002.

6 United Nations, 'Convention against Torture and Other Cruel, Inhuman or Degrading Treatment or Punishment' (UNTS 1465 851984), entered into force 26 June 1987.

UNCAT has then in its 30 years provided a framework of obligations for State Parties to apply to their legal and administrative systems that builds upon the general prohibition of torture. During this period, the Convention system has been developed by the adoption of an Optional Protocol[7] on preventative measures and also, through the work of national and international courts, clarified the obligations under the Convention in relation to universal jurisdiction. Important provisions in the Convention relate to the obligations of States to ensure that all violations of the prohibition are punished in domestic criminal law. Amnesties and immunities are not provided for by the Convention, even when granted for transitional justice purposes, for example to avoid prosecutions so that truth and reconciliation proceedings may be established.

Further, the Convention explicitly establishes a system of universal jurisdiction – under Articles 5 to 9 of the Convention. According to Article 7 UNCAT,

> The State Party in the territory under whose jurisdiction a person alleged to have committed any offence referred to in article 4 is found, shall in the cases contemplated in article 5, if it does not extradite him, submit the case to its competent authorities for the purpose of prosecution.

As has been noted, 'the strongest obligation to avoid a safe haven for perpetrators of torture by bringing them to justice before their domestic courts applies to the forum State'[8] and this obligation applies even if there is no connecting factor to the suspected torturer – in other words, the Convention applies universal jurisdiction for those States that are parties to the Convention. By imposing this obligation on all States but particularly forum States, the effect is extra-territorial. The suspect may be a national of, or have carried out the alleged criminal activities, in a State outside the Convention system. This obligation applies even if the person in question is undergoing medical treatment or professional training in the forum State.[9]

This, the *aut dedere aut judicare* principle, was discussed in a recent case before the ICJ – in the *Questions relating to the Obligation to Prosecute or Extradite (Belgium v Senegal)*[10] – and the obligations under UNCAT were reconfirmed. Here, the Court ruled that Senegal 'must, without further delay, submit the case of Mr Hissène Habré to its competent authorities for the purpose of prosecution, if it does not extradite him' after many years of residing in Senegal without standing trial for human rights violations that had occurred during his term of office. Here the Court stated that, '[e]xtradition and prosecution are alternative ways to combat impunity in accordance with Art. 7, para. 1 [of the Convention against Torture and

7 Optional Protocol to the Convention against Torture and Other Cruel, Inhuman or Degrading Treatment or Punishment, 2375 UNTS 237, entered into force 22 June 2006.

8 M. Nowak and E. McArthur, *The United Nations Convention against Torture: A Commentary* (Oxford: Oxford University Press, 2008), 345.

9 See ibid.

10 Judgment of 20 July 2012.

Other Cruel, Inhuman or Degrading Treatment or Punishment of 1984]'[11] and that parties to the UNCAT have 'a common interest to ensure, in view of their shared values, that acts of torture are prevented and that, if they occur, their authors do not enjoy impunity.'[12] The Court reiterated that the object and purpose of the Convention are 'to make more effective the struggle against torture by avoiding impunity for the perpetrators of such acts.'[13]

In the UK, a specific offence against the official use of torture can be found in the Criminal Justice Act 1988. Section 134 of the Act has the effect of making all torture, wherever committed, criminal in the jurisdiction of the UK. However, it was not until July 2005, with the prosecution and sentencing of a former Afghan warlord, Faryadi Zardad, by the Attorney-General, that the section was applied. Zardad was convicted of charges relating to torture of victims including foreign nationals. This case has been considered a breakthrough – the first time that a foreign national has been tried on charges relating to foreign torture of victims who were also foreign nationals.

Another 'test case' currently under consideration by the Central Criminal Court, is that of a Nepali Army officer, Colonel Kumar Lama, arrested on 3 January 2013 in the UK under Section 134 (1) 1988 Criminal Justice Act. Lama is subject to allegations of inflicting torture when acting in an official capacity as the head of the Gorusinghe Army Barracks between 15 April and 1 May 2005 and 15 April and 31 October 2005. He was arrested in London while on leave from serving as a UN peacekeeper in South Sudan.

In Nepal, the criminal justice system has been criticised as it has allowed for impunity of those involved in torture, sexual violence and enforced disappearances,[14] and the government has promoted officials and security force members suspected of involvement in human rights abuses.[15] Further, a Presidential Ordinance passed in March 2013 to establish the transitional justice mechanism – a Truth and Reconciliation Commission to investigate human rights violations during the 1996–2006 conflict – allows for amnesties, limitations on criminal prosecution, and a 35-day limit for filing cases. According to international human rights law, States may not grant amnesty for gross violations of human rights and any such provision shall be subject to the State's overall responsibility to fulfil victims' rights to truth, justice and reparations. However, the Supreme Court of Nepal ruled on 2 January 2014 that these provisions contravene fundamental rights guaranteed

---

11 Ibid., para 50.

12 Ibid., para 68.

13 Ibid., para 74.

14 See Office of the High Commissioner for Human Rights, 'Media Centre'. Online. Available HTTP: http://www.ohchr.org/EN/NewsEvents/Pages/Media (accessed 5 January 2014).

15 See Human Rights Watch, 'Human Rights in Nepal' (2014). Online. Available HTTP: http://www.hrw.org/asia/nepal (accessed 5 January 2014).

by the Constitution of Nepal,[16] its justice system and international law. Given that the Nepali justice system is, eight years after the alleged violations, unable to subject to prosecution such alleged perpetrators denotes implied impunity and therefore grounds for the application of universal jurisdiction.

One of the barriers to successful trial and punishment of perpetrators is the rules and application of principles of immunity that relate to criminal law processes in other States.

Immunity

A plea of immunity prevents an individual from being subjected to criminal proceedings in another State. It relates to a procedural rule whose application by courts results in the bar from prosecution of the alleged crime, even when the official in question has allegedly committed international 'universal' crimes. This chapter considers cases and principles that have distinguished certain criteria in relation to questions of jurisdiction and immunity that have sought to address opposing notions of international justice. In relation to the prohibition of torture, as noted, also protected under customary international law, the requirements of the principles of universal jurisdiction, *jus cogens* status, and international human rights treaties pull in the opposite direction, requiring that individual criminal responsibility and justice prevail as impunity is set aside.

The purposes of State immunity relate to understandings of fairness and impartiality and include conferring orderly allocation and exercise of jurisdiction, respecting sovereign equality of States, and permitting effective performance of the functions of persons who act on behalf of States. It finds its rationale in the equality of sovereign States and the doctrine of non-interference in the internal affairs of other States. As such, its rationale is premised on Westphalian understandings of doctrines such as sovereignty.[17] However, immunity seems often at odds with new understandings of human rights violations and remedies, the presumption against immunity, and the requirements of accountability. In relation to *jus cogens* it is clear that torture holds a higher status than immunity in the hierarchy of the norms. *Jus cogens* norms are those that the international community considers to represent fundamental norms, from which no derogation is permitted.

The principle of State immunity in international law has been reconfirmed as a prominent rule in customary international law. Recent decisions of international and national courts and the writings of many publicists have indicated that, rather than receding in prominence in light of questions of conflict, and being superseded by other competing and evolving norms, the need to protect incumbent foreign officials from the civil jurisdiction of national courts remains the predominant rule.

16 Since the 'Interim Constitution of Nepal 2063' (15 January 2007), Part 3.

17 L. McGregor, 'Torture and State Immunity: Deflecting Impunity, Distorting Sovereignty', *European Journal of International Law* 18, no. 5 (2007): 905.

This rule remains even in light of the Rome Statute of the International Criminal Court[18] and international criminal law. However, the issue of the jurisdiction of national courts to prosecute and punish offences committed extraterritorially by officials of other States has remained an unsettled domain particularly when they are faced with questions on the rule of immunities. This uncertainty has led to much discussion, while arguing against inconsistency in understanding and application of the principles, relates to an area of international law that is very much in transition. As stated recently, 'As for official acts, there is some State practice on setting aside immunity for acts constituting international crimes, though the scope of the immunity in such circumstances is still uncertain'.[19]

Some have argued that, in relation to acts of torture, immunities should not apply as such acts cannot be considered as official acts and therefore should be excluded from *ratione materiae*, as private conduct should be attributable to individuals and not the State.[20] This approach would have the effect of holding officials accountable and absolving the State of international responsibility as the crime of torture would no longer be attributable to the State itself. Instead, individuals would be held accountable.[21]

The hope that a universal international criminal court would address the gross violations of human rights of leaders of governments (and indeed those of non-State officials) has been, to some extent, disappointed, as support for the Court is not currently universal[22] and many States have called into question the Court's legitimacy given its current focus on African States. However, until the International Criminal Court is able to effectively address these questions, the important place that foreign national courts may play in combating impunity should be acknowledged and also developed. At the same time, where an individual may be seemingly absolved of responsibility at a domestic court, he or she may still be liable at the international level. It appears at the moment that allegations

18 'Statute of the International Criminal Tribunal for the Former Yugoslavia' (UNSC Res 827 (25 May 1993) UN Doc S/RES/8271993), art 7(2); ICC, 'Rome Statute of the International Criminal Court', Article 27; 'London Agreement for the International Military Tribunal at Nuremberg' (82 UNTS 279), entered into force 8 August 1945, Article 7; 'Statute of the International Criminal Tribunal for Rwanda' (UNSC Res 955 (8 November 1994) UN Doc S/RES/9551994), art 6(2).

19 See H. Fox and P. Webb, *The Law of State Immunity*, 3rd edn (Oxford: Oxford University Press, 2013), 550.

20 See *Prosecutor v. Blaškić* (Objection to the Issue of Subpeona duces Tecum) IT-95-14-AR 108 (1997), 110 ILR (1997) 607, at 707, and *Jones v. Saudia Arabia* [2006] UKHL 26 at para 68.

21 ILC Articles on the Responsibility of State for Internationally Wrongful Acts (2001), Article 58 Individual Responsibility: 'These articles are without prejudice to any question of the individual responsibility under International law of any person acting on behalf of a State'.

22 There are currently 122 State parties to the Statute, and of the Permanent Members of the Security Council only France and the United Kingdom are parties to the Statute.

of inequality are well founded but are related to States' reluctance to enter into voluntary arrangements under treaty. Nonetheless, despite these political pressures on the system, international and national courts are required to apply and interpret the law in cases that have produced interesting and controversial results.

The rules governing immunity from prosecution of State agents are part of customary international law[23] and also, to some extent, in relation to diplomatic staff, in the Vienna Convention on Diplomatic Relations,[24] and are categorised as forming principles of immunity either *ratione materiae* or *ratione personae.* They represent principles of customary international law as they '[remain] largely uncodified at the international level'.[25] However, domestic legislation such as the UK State Immunity Act 1978[26] exists to transpose the obligations in the Vienna Convention on Diplomatic Relations into applicable law. In addition, soft law exists that informs State practice on immunities such as the Institut de Droit International resolution concerning *Immunities from Jurisdiction.*[27] The following sub-sections consider the differences in the scope and effects of these principles, in light of sources on the subject matter.

Immunity ratione personae

Firstly, immunity *ratione personae* relates to the particular status of an official, and covers only those who hold especially high-ranking positions. According to the Arrest Warrant case, this immunity covers 'the head of State, head of government and minister for foreign affairs'.[28] Although more limited in scope in relation to the officials that are covered than *ratione materiae*, it covers all acts and attaches to the individual for as long as the status endures. After the official leaves office, he or she may be prosecuted for any international crimes perpetrated while in or before office.

---

23 *Case Concerning the Arrest Warrant of 11 April 2000*, 2002 I.C.J Reports, paras 58–59

24 United Nations, 'Vienna Convention on Diplomatic Relations', in *UN Treaties Series* (United Nations, 18 April 1961), entered into force 22 June 2006, 24841.

25 C. Wickremasinghe, 'Immunities Enjoyed by Officials of States and International Organisations', in *International Law*, ed. M. Evans (Oxford: Oxford University Press, 2010), 392.

26 State Immunity Act 1978 (Commencement) Order 1978, No.1572 (C.44).

27 Institut de droit international, 'Immunities from Jurisdiction and Execution of Heads of State and of Governments in International Law' (adopted at Session of Vancouver August 2001).

28 *Case Concerning the Arrest Warrant of 11 April 2000 (Democratic Republic of the Congo v Belgium)* ICJ Rep 14 February 2002, 3, 21–22.

It covers both official and private acts,[29] including those prior to taking up office,[30] and the official enjoys full personal inviolability from criminal jurisdiction.[31] It is clear that a Head of State generally enjoys such immunity, as evidenced in the case law[32] and in national legislation,[33] which place the position of a foreign Head of State on par with that of a head of a diplomatic mission. This immunity has also been extended to cover Ministers for Foreign Affairs in the Arrest Warrant case.[34] Although there are objections to the position,[35] it is well established that personal immunities remain absolute even in cases of alleged commission of international crimes, unless the mandate of the International Criminal Court is furthered in respects of the parties. This has been confirmed by the International Court of Justice (ICJ) in the Arrest Warrant case[36] and in cases before national courts.[37]

One instance where the immunity of an incumbent Head of State was not upheld was due to the fact that the United States government did not recognise the

---

29 *Pinochet No.3* (HL) 201–202 (Lord Browne-Wilkinson); *Case Concerning the Arrest Warrant of 11 April 2000 (Democratic Republic of the Congo v Belgium)* (Judgment) [2002] ICJ Rep 3 [55]; ILC, 'Report of the International Law Commission on the Work of its Forty-Third Session' (UN Doc A/CN.4/SER.A/1991/Add.l (Part 2), (29 April–19 July 1991)), 22; Antonio Cassese, *International Criminal Law*, 2nd edn (Oxford: Oxford University Press, 2008), 304.

30 *Case Concerning the Arrest Warrant of 11 April 2000 (Democratic Republic of the Congo v Belgium)* (Judgment) [2002] ICJ Rep 3 [55]; ILC, 'Immunity of State Officials from Foreign Criminal Jurisdiction, Memorandum by the Secretariat' (UN Doc A/CN.4/596, 31 March 2008), para 137.

31 *Case Concerning the Arrest Warrant of 11 April 2000 (Democratic Republic of the Congo v Belgium)* (Judgment) [2002] ICJ Rep 3 [54]; *Case Concerning Certain Questions of Mutual Assistance in Criminal Matters (Djibouti v France)* (Judgment) [2008] ICJ Rep 177 [170].

32 See for example *Case Concerning Certain Questions of Mutual Assistance in Criminal Matters (Djibouti v France)* (Judgment) [2008] ICJ Rep 177 [170].

33 See for example *State Immunity Act (UK)*, s 20.

34 *Case Concerning the Arrest Warrant of 11 April 2000 (Democratic Republic of the Congo v Belgium)* (Judgment) [2002] ICJ Rep 3.

35 See for example *Case Concerning the Arrest Warrant of 11 April 2000 (Democratic Republic of the Congo v Belgium)* (Judgment) [2002] ICJ Rep 3, Dissenting Opinion of Judge Al-Khasawneh, para 7.

36 *Case Concerning the Arrest Warrant of 11 April 2000 (Democratic Republic of the Congo v Belgium)* (Judgment) [2002] ICJ Rep 3 [58].

37 See for examples *Gaddafi* (France, Court of Appeal of Paris (Chambre d'accusation) (2001) 125 ILR 490, 508; *Pinochet No.3* (HL) 266 (Lord Saville); 269 (Lord Millet); *Fidel Castro* case (Spain: Audencia Nacional, 1999), cited in Antonio Cassese, 'When May Senior State Officials Be Tried for International Crimes? Some Comments on the Congo V Belgium Case', *European Journal of International Law* 13, no. 4 (2002): 853, n 21. *Re Sharon and Yaron* (Belgium, Court of Cassation) (2003) 127 ILR 110, 124; *Tatchell v Mugabe* (2004) 136 ILR 572.

official involved as the Head of State of Panama.[38] The resolutions of the Institute of International Law also reflect the position that this immunity is not denied for international crimes.[39] Most commentators have also taken this view,[40] and it has been borne out in actual State practice. For example, the serving defence minister of Israel was assured of immunity by the British government despite his alleged involvement in crimes against humanity.[41] In 2002, the United States government filed a statement asserting that Jiang Zemin, who was President of China at the time, should be accorded State immunity in proceedings against him for allegations of torture and genocide.

In cases before international criminal tribunals and courts, it is generally accepted that immunity cannot apply. This was the position taken by the ICJ in the Arrest Warrant case, where it was stated that the immunity of incumbent officials would not apply in the case of international criminal courts with jurisdiction over the matter.[42] The statutes of the relevant international criminal courts provide that the official capacity of a person cannot exempt him from criminal responsibility.[43] Therefore, the relevant question here is whether the immunity of officials of States

---

38 *United States v Noriega* (United States District Court, Southern District of Florida) (1992) 99 ILR 143, 161.

39 Institute of International Law, '13th Commission Immunities from Jurisdiction and Execution of Heads of State and of Government in International Law (Rapporteur: Mr Joe Verhoeven)' (Vancouver Session 2001); '3rd Commission, 'Resolution on the Immunity from Jurisdiction of the State and of Persons Who Act on Behalf of the State in Case of International Crimes (Rapporteur: Lady Fox)' (Napoli Session 2009), Art III(1).

40 R.A. Kolodkin, 'Second Report on Immunity of State Officials from Foreign Criminal Jurisdiction' (UN Doc A/CN.4/631, 10 June 2010), para 55. For examples, see Paola Gaeta, 'Does President Al Bashir Enjoy Immunity from Arrest?', *Journal of International Criminal Justice* 7 no. 2 (2009): 315, 317–318; Akande and Shah, 'Immunities of State Officials, International Crimes and Foreign Domestic Courts', 815; Cassese, 'When May Senior State Officials Be Tried for International Crimes? Some Comments on the Congo V Belgium Case', 865; Hazel Fox, *The Law of State Immunity*, 2nd edn (Oxford: Oxford University Press, 2008), 694; Wickremasinghe, 'Immunities Enjoyed by Officials of States and International Organisations', 401.

41 Chris McGreal, 'Sharon's Ally Safe from Arrest in Britain', *The Guardian*, 11 February 2004.

42 *Case Concerning the Arrest Warrant of 11 April 2000 (Democratic Republic of the Congo v Belgium)* (Judgment) [2002] ICJ Rep 3 [61].

43 'London Agreement for the International Military Tribunal at Nuremberg'; ICC, 'Rome Statute of the International Criminal Court', art 7; UN Security Council, 'Statute of the International Criminal Tribunal for Rwanda (as Last Amended on 13 October 2006)' (UNSC Res 955 UN Doc S/RES/955 8 November 1994), art 6(2); 'Report of the Secretary-General on the Establishment of a Special Court for Sierra Leone (Statute of the Special Court for Sierra Leone)' (S/2000/9154 October 2000), art 6(2); 'Statute of the International Criminal Tribunal for the Former Yugoslavia', art 7(2).

not party to the statute of a particular international criminal court subsists,[44] and that matter is not a conflict between the legal regime of immunity and the principle of individual criminal responsibility as such.

Immunity ratione materiae

The other principle relates to immunity by virtue of subject matter, or 'functional immunity', and attaches to official acts committed as part of one's duties while in office. It is granted on the basis that the individual involved carried out the criminalised conduct on behalf of the State and thus attaches to the act of the official. This immunity enjoys a wider ambit than *ratione personae* as it covers any person exercising official functions. Also, as this immunity attaches to subject matter, it continues to apply once the official has left office. However, officials may be tried for acts carried out in a private capacity as there is recognition of the difference between conduct that engages the State as an organisation and that of the autonomy of persons acting in their own capacity. This then begs the question, in relation to violations of the prohibition of torture that may have been perpetrated in the name of the State, to what extent may functional immunity protect officials? There are convincing arguments to suggest that such acts cannot be solely attributed to the State; although they may seem to constitute an ostensible exercise of State authority, they must attach to the official.[45] It is this form of immunity that is often cited as not applying to international crimes following the Pinochet case.[46]

Pinochet No.3 is undoubtedly a key authority on immunities of State organs. One interpretation of the judgment is that it has the effect of restricting *ratione materiae* in that it may be overturned where the prohibition of torture has been violated. The majority of the Appellate Committee of the House of Lords decided that a former Head of State did not enjoy subsisting immunity *ratione materiae* in relation to the crime of torture under UNCAT. Despite Lord Browne-Wilkinson's assertion that it was 'no concern of your Lordships … to achieve the best justice',[47] the judgment stands out as one of the most significant cases to undermine impunity for former Heads of State.

The reasons for the inapplicability of immunity given by the six judges in the majority differ. Some of the Lords relied on the idea that torture cannot be

---

44 For the view that immunity is not a bar to prosecution even for officials of States not party to the relevant statute see Gaeta, 'Does President Al Bashir Enjoy Immunity from Arrest?', 315. For an opposing view, see Dapo Akande, 'International Law Immunities and the International Criminal Court', *The American Journal of International Law* 98, no. 3 (2004): 407.

45 Rosanne van Alebeek, 'National Courts: International Crimes and the Functional Immunity of State Officials', *Netherlands International Law Review* 59, no. 01 (2012): 5–41.

46 *Pinochet No.3* (HL) 203.

47 Ibid., 190 (Lord Browne-Wilkinson).

considered an official act[48] or an official function of a Head of State,[49] while others relied on the fact that the extra-territorial jurisdiction established by UNCAT over acts of torture would be inconsistent with a grant of immunity.[50]

General Pinochet was a former Head of State for Chile who pleaded immunity following an extradition request from Spain to stand trials for allegations of torture and other crimes. It was held by six votes to one that immunity *ratione materiae* from the State Immunity Act did not extend to Pinochet,[51] although each judge used different reasoning to come to this conclusion, with Lord Goff dissenting. In doing so, the court formulated a rule that would come to be argued as a 'customary rule that removes functional immunity'.[52] The following paragraphs explore the different approaches taken by the Law Lords.

Lord Browne-Wilkinson based his judgment largely upon the obligations imposed by UNCAT, to which the UK, Spain and Chile were all parties. The fact that 'torture' within the meaning of the Convention can only be committed by 'a public official or other person acting in an official capacity' influenced his decision,[53] as that '[a] torture regime giving rise to immunity *ratione materiae*, would [produce] bizarre results', essentially rendering the Convention void as no public officials could be prosecuted using the instrument.[54] Browne-Wilkinson did not entirely dismiss the possibility of a *jus cogens* norm removing functional immunity, but he raised 'doubts whether, before the coming into force of the Torture Convention, the existence of the international crime of torture as *jus cogens* was enough to justify the conclusion' that immunities do not apply.[55] If individual criminal responsibility is to prevail over national law, apart from under treaty obligations, a customary rule lifting immunities needs to crystallise. On the other hand, the decision has been criticised for taking the role of national courts applying international law too far, 'presented … as the enforcement of an implied treaty term whereby the norm of immunity was overridden by necessary implication given the prohibition on torture and the establishment of universal jurisdiction over it'.[56]

Lord Millet, Lord Hope and Lord Hutton came to the conclusion that individual responsibility for serious crimes in international law, such as torture, cannot be opposed by reliance upon immunity. They distinguished between the purpose

48 Ibid., 278–279 (Lord Millet).

49 Ibid., 262–263 (Lord Hutton); 292 (Lord Phillips).

50 Ibid., 266–267 (Lord Saville); 205 (Lord Browne-Wilkinson).

51 *State Immunity Act (UK)*, (Commencement) Order 1978, No. 572 (C.44).

52 Cassese, 'When May Senior State Officials Be Tried for International Crimes? Some Comments on the Congo V Belgium Case', 870.

53 *Pinochet No.3*, Lord Browne-Wilkinson.

54 Ibid.

55 Ibid.

56 A. Roberts, 'Comparative International Law? The Role of Courts in International Law', *International and Comparative Law Quarterly* 60, no. 1 (2011): 71.

of immunities and crimes of international law, stressing their inviolable nature.[57] For Lord Millet, it was not logical that immunity was available in respect of *jus cogens* norms, and also that the purpose of immunity was for the benefit of States rather than individuals. In addition, it was argued that their purpose was to provide immunity for States rather than the individual. Therefore, in relation to the conflict between a strict application of immunities and individual criminal responsibility, the removal of immunity as a bar to prosecution would be necessary on the basis of fairness and 'privatis[ing] commission of international crimes to make them prosecutable'.[58] Due to the 'notoriety and odium to which the position [of State organ] exposes', public opinion has grown in favour of the position that it is fair that State organs should be held accountable for breaches of international crimes due to the gravity of those offences.[59]

The conclusion of the House of Lords was that Pinochet was not entitled to immunities, instead being individually liable. The majority judgment revolves around the interpretation of UNCAT as providing for quasi-universal jurisdiction. It was advanced that Article 5(1) UNCAT imposes an obligation on States to prosecute international crimes, therefore jurisdiction to decide this case was universal (to those States party to the Convention). Lord Millet went further and took the view that 'universal jurisdiction existed well before the Torture Convention over crimes committed in violation of *jus cogens*'.[60] The *Eichmann* case was used as authority for this understanding. In this case, the State of Israel had prosecuted a former Nazi leader for war crimes committed before Israel became a State on the basis of universal jurisdiction and the passive personality principle.[61] Bianchi expresses doubts over the extent to which Lord Millet's account can be taken as an authority, but the judgment certainly goes some way to assert universal jurisdiction over international crimes where a Convention exists to the protection of these norms.[62] In addition, Article 5(1) of the Torture Convention replicates the principle of '*aut dedere aut punire*';[63] this relates to Article 17 of the Rome Statute of the International Criminal Court, which obliges States to prosecute before the ICC will gain jurisdiction.[64]

---

57 Wickremasinghe, 'Immunities Enjoyed by Officials of States and International Organisations', 403.

58 Fox, *The Law of State Immunity*, 696.

59 Ibid., 667.

60 A. Bianchi, 'Immunity Versus Human Rights: The Pinochet Case', *European Journal of International Law* 10, no. 2 (1999): 246.

61 *Attorney General of Israel v Eichmann* (29 May 1962) 36 ILR, 277–342.

62 Bianchi, 'Immunity Versus Human Rights: The Pinochet Case', 246.

63 See *Pinochet No.3* (HL) per Lord Browne-Wilkinson at 200. Meaning 'extradite or punish'.

64 Article 17, Rome Statute of the International Criminal Court, UN Doc A/CONF 183/9 (17 July 1998). Statute entered into force 1 July 2002 after 60 ratifications.

It is advocated by Cassese that a 'customary rule that removes functional immunity' has emerged.[65] One must be careful to maintain a distinction between the immunities here: Wickremashinghe stresses that *ratione personae* remains 'in the absence of waiver by the sending state, an absolute bar to the criminal jurisdiction of national courts'.[66] At the least, *Pinochet* represents authority in English law of a rule lifting immunities,[67] although it can be argued that this is a precarious authority due to the criticism generated of each judgment.[68]

For this to crystallise into customary law, some evidence of State practice accepting *Pinochet* as law is required.[69] Cassese cites as general practice, case law following *Pinochet* from both national[70] and international forums.[71] *Nicaragua v United States* states that, 'instances of state conduct inconsistent with a given rule should generally have been treated as breaches of that rule, not as indications of a new rule'.[72] If we read this case with *Arrest Warrant*, it becomes apparent that no customary rule yet exists that lifts functional immunities.[73]

The Arrest Warrant case is representative of the second view of immunities,[74] notably that there is no 'exception to immunity in proceedings brought before a national court other than for acts performed in a private capacity',[75] reaffirming that a conflict between immunity and individual criminal responsibility does exist. The case was decided at the International Court of Justice, which as an interim court between national courts and the ICC does not apply individual criminal liability. The court was asked to examine matters of immunity both *ratione personae* and *ratione materiae*, concluding that Ministers for Foreign Affairs '[enjoy] full immunity from

---

65 Cassese, 'When May Senior State Officials Be Tried for International Crimes? Some Comments on the Congo V Belgium Case', 870.

66 Wickremasinghe, 'Immunities Enjoyed by Officials of States and International Organisations', 401.

67 Ibid.

68 See Ingrid Wuerth, 'Pinochet's Legacy Reassessed', *American Journal of International Law* 106, no. 4 (2012): 731–768.

69 United Nations, 'Statute of the International Court of Justice' (adopted 18 April 1946), Article 38 (1)(b).

70 Cassese, 'When May Senior State Officials Be Tried for International Crimes? Some Comments on the Congo V Belgium Case', 870. See: Attorney General of Israel v *Eichmann* (29 May 1962) 36 ILR, 277–342; *Federation Nationale des Deportes et Internes Resistants et Patriotes v. Barbie*, 78 ILR 125.

71 *Advisory Opinion Concerning Reservations to the Convention on the Prevention and Punishment of the Crime of Genocide*, International Court of Justice (ICJ), 28 May 1951.

72 *Nicaragua v United States*, ICJ Reports (1986) 14.

73 *Questions relating to the Obligation to Prosecute or Extradite* (*Belgium v Senegal*), Judgment, I.C.J. Reports 2012, 422.

74 Ibid.

75 Fox and Webb, *The Law of State Immunity*, 551.

criminal jurisdiction and inviolability'.[76] Unsurprisingly for this contested area of law, any further conclusions are difficult to draw and have been criticised.

Here the Court stated that immunity would not be a bar to prosecution where the official is no longer in office, 'in respect of acts committed prior or subsequent to his or her period of office, as well as in respect of acts committed during that period of office in a *private* capacity'.[77] This could be interpreted to mean that immunity *ratione materiae* continues to exist after cessation of an official post for acts that were committed by the individual in an official capacity. If interpreted narrowly, this could mean that there is no exception to this immunity in the case of international crimes.[78] These statements are, however, *obiter dictum*, and there is also no guidance as to what might constitute private or public acts.[79] Three judges in their joint separate opinion expressed the view that immunity cannot exempt an official from individual criminal liability in the light of the growing awareness in international law of the importance of combating impunity for serious international crimes[80] – yet this did not automatically imply that immunity would be inapplicable where impunity would result.[81] These judges tried to resolve the conflict between immunity and impunity by stating that 'serious international crimes cannot be regarded as official acts because they are neither normal State functions nor functions that a State alone can perform' and that whether an act was a public act of the State could not be determined by asking whether the reasons for the act were State related.[82]

The court concluded that immunity *ratione materiae* applied in respect of former State organs – 'unless the State which a former Minister of Foreign Affairs has represented gives its consent, the courts of a foreign State cannot hold such person accountable for international crimes allegedly committed in an official capacity during his or her period of office'.[83] The majority decision failed to properly apply a rule of customary law that exists to lift immunities in *Arrest*

76 *Belgium v Senegal*, Judgment at 54.

77 *Case Concerning the Arrest Warrant of 11 April 2000 (Democratic Republic of the Congo v Belgium)* (Judgment) [2002] ICJ Rep 3 [61] (emphasis added).

78 See Jan Wouters, 'The Judgment of the International Court of Justice in the Arrest Warrant Case: Some Critical Remarks', *Leiden Journal of International Law* 16 (2003): 253–67.

79 Philippe Sands, 'International Law Transformed? From Pinochet to Congo…?', *Leiden Journal of International Law* 16, no. 1 (2003): 50.

80 *Case Concerning the Arrest Warrant of 11 April 2000 (Democratic Republic of the Congo v Belgium)* (Judgment) [2002] ICJ Rep 3, Joint Separate Opinion of Judges Higgins, Koojimans and Buergenthal, para 74.

81 Ibid., para 79.

82 Ibid., para 85.

83 Paola Gaeta, 'Ratione Materiae Immunities of Former Heads of State and International Crimes: The Hissene Habre Case', *Journal of International Criminal Justice* 1, no. 1 (2003): 189.

Warrant[84] but instead succeeded in fuelling further the conflict between individual criminal liability and immunities.

Following this, the recent cases such as *Al-Adsani* decided, in direct contrast to *Pinochet No.3*,[85] 'that even *jus cogens* norms, such as the prohibition against torture, must be construed as existing in harmony with other recognised principles'.[86] Therefore, where *Arrest Warrant* failed to deal with the rule lifting immunities,[87] perhaps because of its complexity, this case directly dismissed the Court's reasoning in *Pinochet No.3*,[88] thus casting serious doubt on the existence of such a rule.[89] The majority then distinguished this case by reasoning that the case concerned the immunity from criminal jurisdiction of an individual, and did not apply to the immunity from civil suit of a State.[90] This was followed by *Jurisdictional Immunities of the State (Germany v Italy, Greece Intervening)*,[91] where the ICJ held that Italy had violated customary international law rules on State immunity by allowing civil claims based on violations of international humanitarian law by the German Reich during the Second World War to be brought against Germany. There could be no exception to State immunity despite serious violations of international human rights and international humanitarian law.[92] Also, the *jus cogens* status did not affect the judgment – there was no conflict between a substantive rule prohibiting certain conduct that has the status of *jus cogens* and the procedural rule establishing State immunity.[93] Further, the European Court of Human Rights in the very recent case of *Jones and Others v United Kingdom*[94] decided that, 'since an act cannot be carried out by a State itself but only by individuals acting on the State's behalf, where immunity can be invoked by the State, then the starting point must be that immunity ratione materiae applied to the acts of [torture committed] by State officials'.[95]

It is submitted here that a better approach towards interpretation is that taken by the dissenting judges in *Al-Adsani* – that it does not matter for the purpose of the overriding action of a peremptory norm whether the proceedings are civil or criminal.[96] However, the majority decisions seem to view State immunity as

---

84 *Belgium v Senegal*, Judgment.

85 Human Rights Watch, 'Human Rights in Nepal'.

86 Office of the High Commissioner for Human Rights, 'Media Centre', 171.

87 *Belgium v Senegal*, Judgment.

88 Human Rights Watch, 'Human Rights in Nepal'.

89 *Al-Adsani v United Kingdom* (2001) 34 EHRR 273 [65].

90 Ibid.

91 Judgment, ICJ Reports 2012.

92 Ibid., para 91.

93 Ibid., para 93.

94 Application nos. 34356/06 and 40528/06, 14 January 2014.

95 Ibid., para 202.

96 *Al-Adsani v United Kingdom* (2001) 34 EHRR 273, Dissenting Opinion of Judges Rozakis and Caflisch Joined by Judges Wildhaber, Costa, Cabral Barreto and Vajic, para 4.

merely a 'procedural bar' and not a 'substantive right',[97] thus considering that immunity is not in conflict with the substantive norm of *jus cogens*.[98]

By failing to address the issue of jurisdiction, the *Arrest Warrant* judgment presents an incomplete consideration of immunity. However, the Separate Opinion of Judges Higgins, Koojimans and Buergenthal provides an important reference point as it expands on issues that the main judgment failed to address in sufficient detail.[99] It was stated that, 'if there is no jurisdiction *en principe*, then the question of an immunity from a jurisdiction which would otherwise exist simply does not arise', as State organs cannot be brought before a court.[100]

The application of the principle of universal jurisdiction over international crimes (apart from that relating to piracy) relies heavily on the judgments of the jurisprudence of *Pinochet No.3*[101] and *Eichmann.*[102] It remains difficult to draw any conclusions beyond these cases. However, in *Pinochet No.3,* it was argued by Lord Millet that, 'when the Geneva Conventions and customary international law conferred universal jurisdiction in respect of those crimes, it cannot be supposed that immunity *ratione materiae* was left intact'.[103] This supports the argument that to do otherwise would be to render the conferment of such jurisdiction practically meaningless. It can be concluded that if universal jurisdiction is lacking then the conflict between individual criminal responsibility and immunity becomes greater and possibly insurmountable as it would prove impossible to call State organs to account.

International Criminal Courts and Tribunals

These immunities, which largely operate in national domestic courts, are subject to interference at international level, where individual criminal liability prevails. Serving Heads of States and other officials may be rendered susceptible to the jurisdiction of international tribunals. This process began with the Nuremburg Tribunal, when the bar of official capacity as a defence was set aside in relation to the Nuremburg and Tokyo Trials, and has been furthered more recently by the Rome Statute of the International Criminal Court, which states that immunities will not limit the court's jurisdiction. This is intrinsically related to individual criminal

97 *Al-Adsani v United Kingdom* (2001) 34 EHRR 273 [48].

98 See Rebecca Zaman, 'Playing the Ace? Jus Cogens Crimes and Functional Immunity in National Courts', *Australian International Law Journal* 17(2010): 62.

99 *Case Concerning the Arrest Warrant of 11 April 2000 (Democratic Republic of the Congo v Belgium)*, ICJ Rep 14 February 2002, Joint Separate Opinion.

100 Ibid., 64.

101 Human Rights Watch, 'Human Rights in Nepal'.

102 *Attorney General of Israel v Eichmann* (29 May 1962) 36 ILR, 277–342.

103 Akande and Shah, 'Immunities of State Officials, International Crimes and Foreign Domestic Courts', 844.

liability, set out in Article 25 of the Rome Statute: 'A person who commits a crime ... shall be individually responsible and liable'. This conflict, between allowing for immunities to prevail at domestic level while developing norms that further individual criminal responsibility at the international level, is creating dichotomies in international law.

This non-equivalence of immunity to impunity is a crucial theme in the conflict between immunity and individual criminal liability. However, as discussed above, State organs may still be called to account at international level, as 'immunity [only] constitutes a procedural bar to the jurisdiction of a court; it does not waive or excuse an accused's potential liability', as was discussed in the Arrest Warrant case. The possibility of prosecution at the level of international courts is possible due to Article 27 of the Rome Statute's bar on immunity at the ICC and among other international tribunals. This provision removes the conflict between individual responsibility and immunity, at least at the international level.

The *ad hoc* International Criminal Tribunals of Rwanda (ICTR) and the Former Yugoslavia (ICTY) are not bound by the laws on immunities – they are free to exclude them on the basis that they derive their powers from a United Nations Security Council resolution under Chapter VII of the Charter and so are able to overcome their immunities from it. Although immunities might still apply at national level, as the conflict may remain unresolved or at a transitional stage, it will be possible to prosecute at international level as individual criminal responsibility applies. Article 27 of the Rome Statute and the statutes of the *ad hoc* tribunals allow (incumbent and former) Heads of State and members of governments to be subject to jurisdiction, remove the bar of prosecution provided by the law on immunities before international tribunals and courts.

The Charles Taylor case decided that the Special Court for Sierra Leone (SCSL) was a tribunal of international character, thereby holding the plea of immunity inapplicable.[104] Charles Taylor, a former President of Liberia, was found guilty of aiding and abetting the execution of war crimes, providing a contemporary understanding of how individual criminal liability can be effective in bringing State organs to justice.[105] *The Prosecutor v Thomas Lubanga Dyilo*[106] was the first case decided by the ICC, which convicted Thomas Lubanga for committing the war crimes of enlisting and conscripting children and using them in hostilities. It is, therefore, the constitutive document, whether in the form of a treaty or Security Council resolution, that establishes these international courts and tribunals and that distinguishes them from foreign criminal jurisdiction in being able to assert individual criminal responsibility.

104 See Decision on Immunity from Jurisdiction, *Prosecutor v Charles Ghankay Taylor* (SCSL-2003-01-I), Appeals Chamber, 31 May 2004.

105 See *Prosecutor v Charles Ghankay Taylor* (SCSL-03-01-T), Trial Chamber II, 18 May 2012.

106 (ICC-01/04-01/06-2842), Trial Chamber I, 14 March 2012.

The case concerning Omar Al Bashir considered whether Sudan, although not a party to the Rome Statute of the ICC, could invoke immunity as a defence.[107] Jurisdiction is derived from the UN Charter under Chapter VII. Security Council Resolution 1593 (2005)[108] referred the situation in Sudan to the ICC. In its proceedings, the Court maintained that, in relation to crimes contravening Article 7 and 8 of the Rome Statute, 'there are reasonable grounds to believe that Omar Al Bashir is criminally responsible under article 25(3)(a) of the Statute as an indirect perpetrator, or as an indirect co-perpetrator, for war crimes and crimes against humanity and thus his arrest appears to be necessary under article 58(1)(b) of the *Rome Statute*'.[109] This case demonstrates the Court's willingness to apply individual criminal responsibility. However, despite the Arrest Warrant case, Al Bashir has avoided arrest and remains in power as President of Sudan. Sudan, Chad, Kenya and Djibouti have so far failed to arrest him despite being parties to the ICC. Stephen argues that this is representative of a conflict between what international criminal law should be, based on individual criminal responsibility and the mechanisms to achieve this; that is, the removal of immunities.[110] McGregor makes the valid point that 'the distinction between laws of procedure and substance attempts to justify the provision of immunity by basing itself on the false premise that a "different method of settlement" exists on the international place', and that accordingly it 'is used to deflect acknowledgement and examination of the impunity which often results by granting immunity to a foreign state.'[111] It is argued that 'the victim ... very rarely enjoys an effective – or, indeed, any – alternative forum in which to seek and obtain his or her right to a remedy and reparation'.[112] Consequently conflict between immunity and individual criminal responsibility is heightened and the latter severely undermined.

The Rome Statute acknowledges a conflict and seeks to bring perpetrators to account for grave breaches to international criminal justice. Article 17 of

107 *The Prosecutor v Omar Hassan Ahmad Al Bashir*, First Warrant of Arrest for Omar Hassan Ahmad Al Bashir (ICC-02/05-01/09-1), Pre-Trial Chamber I, 4 March 2009, 3. See also Second Warrant of Arrest (ICC-02/05-01/09-95), Pre-Trial Chamber I, 12 July 2010, 4.

108 Adopted by the Security Council at its 5158th meeting, on 31 March 2005. The Security Council determined that the situation in Sudan continues to constitute a threat to international peace and security and decided to refer the situation in Darfur since 1 July 2002 to the Prosecutor of the International Criminal Court and requiring all other parties to the conflict in Darfur to cooperate fully with the Court.

109 *The Prosecutor v Omar Hassan Ahmad Al Bashir*, First Warrant of Arrest for Omar Hassan Ahmad Al Bashir (ICC-02/05-01/09-1), Pre-Trial Chamber I, 4 March 2009, 3. See also Second Warrant of Arrest (ICC-02/05-01/09-95), Pre-Trial Chamber I, 12 July 2010, 4.

110 Christopher Stephen, 'International Criminal Law: Wielding the Sword of Universal Criminal Justice', *International and Comparative Law Quarterly* 61, no. 1 (2012): 88.

111 McGregor, 'Torture and State Immunity: Deflecting Impunity, Distorting Sovereignty', 906.

112 Ibid., 905.

the Rome Statute of the ICC concerns complementarity – that 'the Court may assume jurisdiction only when national legal systems are unable or unwilling to exercise jurisdiction', so placing primacy on national legal systems to address violations. However, given that in many States prosecutions do not occur and this is often because of the operation of immunities, it is necessary that the ICC use its jurisdiction to ensure that State agents come under individual criminal responsibility where national law is incapable of holding them to account. It has been argued that these Courts and tribunals aim to '[provide] exemplary justice in special circumstances (i.e. persons in leadership positions)'.[113]

The conflict between individual criminal responsibility and immunities will continue where immunities law is at variance 'with the current pattern of international criminality and does not meet the demands of international criminal justice'.[114] While individual responsibility was developed before the coming prior to the Rome Statute of the ICC, it is only recently that linkage between individual criminal liability and immunities has been made. Fox has argued that, given the development of international crimes,

> international law should equally permit national courts to exercise jurisdiction and disregard immunity where the defendant ... had committed a breach of established rules of international law of fundamental importance.[115]

This understanding is in line with *Pinochet No.3* in arguing that individual criminal responsibility should prevail where *jus cogens* norms have been violated in the interest of fairness. Given the outcome of the Arrest Warrant case, this theory cannot be said to be definitive; therefore, a conflict remains between fairness and a strict application of the law.

Conclusion

Individual criminal responsibility applies at the international criminal level due to the constitutive documents that created such courts and tribunals as the ICC and the ICTY and ICTR. At this level, movement towards greater accountability of State organs can be observed; the prospective liability of Omar Al Bashir as Head of State of a country not party to the ICC is evidence of this trend. However, it

113 P. Benvenuti, 'Complementarity of the International Criminal Court to National Criminal Jurisdictions', in *Essays on the Rome Statute of the International Criminal Court*, ed. F. Lattanzi and W. Schabas (Ripa di Fagnano Alto: Il Sirente, 1999), 22.

114 Cassese, 'When May Senior State Officials Be Tried for International Crimes? Some Comments on the Congo V Belgium Case', 853.

115 H. Fox, 'International Law and Restraints on the Exercise of Jurisdiction by National Courts of States', in *International Law*, ed. M.D. Evans (Oxford: Oxford University Press, 2010), 342.

is at the national level where the conflict is the greatest. The case law concerning the right of a foreign national court to prosecute State organs is in disarray and is 'undergoing rapid change'.[116]

International treaties law such as the UN Convention against Torture and the Rome Statute impose obligations on States to prosecute grave violations that occur on their territory. However, it is apparent that judicial enforcement through domestic courts where the violation or international crime has occurred is considered the primary means of furthering international criminal justice, as expounded in Article 17 of the Rome Statute on complementarity. However, in circumstances, as described at the beginning of this chapter, where it is not possible to conduct such a trial, it may be that the next best option – the forum of foreign domestic courts – may be tenable.

This chapter has been concerned with the extent to which foreign national courts strictly apply immunities as a bar to prosecution of officials for alleged violations of the prohibition of torture, in criminal proceedings. The principles of universal jurisdiction, *jus cogens*, the rules of customary international law in relation to the prohibition of torture as well as the specific obligations under the Convention against Torture, are rules that relate to substance and present opposing objects and purposes from those that underline rules on immunities. International law remains unsettled in this area, as the judgments of the international and national leading cases present contrasting approaches to immunity. National courts are presented with a dilemma – whether to allow for the procedural bar of immunity to prevail or to allow for criminal proceedings for substantive human rights violations and therefore counter impunity.

The focus of the problem is narrowed here to the prohibition of torture and the holding to account of individuals for the violation of this prohibition, which holds a special position in international law. The conflicts in law and principle between universal jurisdiction and the customary nature of the prohibition of torture as well as the UN treaty system on the subject, are at direct odds with the customary rules that relate to immunities that shield States and their agents from prosecution and enforcement actions. The layer provided by the ICC and other international courts and tribunals adds to the multifaceted nature of the debate.

The conflict will remain unsettled while national courts are bound to apply immunity *ratione personae* and *materiae*, as these rules, based on sovereign equality and comity, preclude the possibility of calling State organs to account under individual criminal responsibility at national courts. These principles of immunity arose out of fairness and the right of equality States relating to the understanding that no one State may claim jurisdiction over another State. As they exist in order to prevent the obstruction of international communication and good relations, they ought to be attributed to the State, rather than to the individual. It naturally follows then that individual criminal liability should exist. While the

116 Ibid.

hypothesis 'immunity is not impunity' is 'indisputably sound',[117] the act of bringing a dispute concerning a State organ to the ICC may prove procedurally difficult. It is more likely that, with a greater number of avenues or alternatives for furthering prosecution, for instance by foreign courts, accountability of individuals may be more easily or readily pursued.

International human rights and criminal justice require to be governed by standards of fairness. International courts argue, 'it would be a travesty of law and a betrayal of the universal need for justice, should the concept of state sovereignty be allowed to be raised successfully against human rights'.[118] The matter of fairness is a conflict between the developing trend of individual criminal responsibility and the strict application of rules at national level and raises issues at the heart of State-centric international law – how to combat impunity and how to further international criminal justice.

Cases

Advisory Opinion Concerning Reservations to the Convention on the Prevention and Punishment of the Crime of Genocide, International Court of Justice (ICJ), 28 May 1951.

Al-Adsani v United Kingdom (2001) 34 EHRR.

Attorney General of Israel v Eichmann (29 May 1962) 36 ILR.

Case Concerning Certain Questions of Mutual Assistance in Criminal Matters (Djibouti v France) (Judgment) [2008] ICJ Rep 177.

Case Concerning the Arrest Warrant of 11 April 2000 (Democratic Republic of the Congo v Belgium) (Judgment) [2002] ICJ Rep 3.

Federation Nationale des Deportes et Internes Resistants et Patriotes v Barbie, 78 ILR 125.

Gaddafi (France, Court of Appeal of Paris (Chambre d'accusation)) (2001) 125 ILR 490, 508.

Jones v Saudia Arabia [2006] UKHL 26.

Nicaragua v United States, ICJ Reports (1986) 14.

Prosecutor v Blaškić (Objection to the Issue of Subpeona duces Tecum), IT-95-14-AR 108 (1997), 110 ILR (1997) 607.

Prosecutor v Charles Ghankay Taylor (SCSL-03-01-T), Trial Chamber II, 18 May 2012.

Prosecutor v Charles Ghankay Taylor (SCSL-2003-01-I), Appeals Chamber, 31 May 2004.

117 Cassese, 'When May Senior State Officials Be Tried for International Crimes? Some Comments on the Congo V Belgium Case', 867.

118 ICTY, Appeals Chamber, *Tadić (Interlocutory Appeal)*, judgment of 2 October 1995, at 32, para 58.

Questions relating to the Obligation to Prosecute or Extradite (Belgium v. Senegal) (Judgment) [2012] ICJ Rep 422.

R v Bow Street Magistrates ex parte Pinochet Ugarte (Amnesty International Intervening) (No. 3) [2000] AC 147 (HL).

Re Sharon and Yaron (Belgium, Court of Cassation) (2003) 127 ILR 110.

Tatchell v Mugabe (2004) 136 ILR 572.

The Prosecutor v Omar Hassan Ahmad Al Bashir, First Warrant of Arrest for Omar Hassan Ahmad Al Bashir (ICC-02/05-01/09-1) (ICC-02/05-01/09-95).

United States v Noriega (United States District Court, Southern District of Florida) (1992) 99 ILR 143.

Bibliography

Akande, D., and S. Shah. 'Immunities of State Officials, International Crimes and Foreign Domestic Courts'. *European Journal of International Law* 24, no. 4 (2010): 815–52.

Akande, Dapo. 'International Law Immunities and the International Criminal Court'. *The American Journal of International Law* 98, no. 3 (2004): 407–33.

Benvenuti, P. 'Complementarity of the International Criminal Court to National Criminal Jurisdictions'. In *Essays on the Rome Statute of the International Criminal Court*, edited by F. Lattanzi and W. Schabas, 21–50. Ripa di Fagnano Alto: Il Sirente, 1999.

Bianchi, A. 'Immunity Versus Human Rights: The Pinochet Case'. *European Journal of International Law* 10, no. 2 (1999): 237–77.

Cassese, Antonio. *International Criminal Law*. 2nd edn. Oxford: Oxford University Press, 2008.

———. 'When May Senior State Officials Be Tried for International Crimes? Some Comments on the Congo V Belgium Case'. *European Journal of International Law* 13, no. 4 (2002): 853–75.

Fox, H. 'International Law and Restraints on the Exercise of Jurisdiction by National Courts of States'. In *International Law*, edited by M.D. Evans, 340–79. Oxford: Oxford University Press, 2010.

———, and P. Webb. *The Law of State Immunity*. 3rd edn. Oxford: Oxford University Press, 2013.

Fox, Hazel. *The Law of State Immunity*. 2nd edn. Oxford: Oxford University Press, 2008.

Gaeta, Paola. 'Ratione Materiae Immunities of Former Heads of State and International Crimes: The Hissene Habre Case'. *Journal of International Criminal Justice* 1, no. 1 (2003): 186–96.

———. 'Does President Al Bashir Enjoy Immunity from Arrest?' *Journal of International Criminal Justice* 7, no. 2 (2009): 315–32.

Human Rights Watch. 'Human Rights in Nepal' (2014). At http://www.hrw.org/asia/nepal (accessed 5 January 2014).

ICC. ‘Rome Statute of the International Criminal Court’. 2187 UNTS 3, adopted 17 July 1998, entered into force 1 July 2002.

ILC. ‘Immunity of State Officials from Foreign Criminal Jurisdiction, Memorandum by the Secretariat’. UN Doc A/CN.4/596, 31 March 2008.

———. ‘Report of the International Law Commission on the Work of Its Forty-Third Session’. UN Doc A/CN.4/SER.A/1991/Add.l (Part 2), 29 April–19 July 1991.

Institut de droit international. ‘Immunities from Jurisdiction and Execution of Heads of State and of Governments in International Law’. Adopted at Session of Vancouver, August 2001.

Institute of International Law. ‘3rd Commission, “Resolution on the Immunity from Jurisdiction of the State and of Persons Who Act on Behalf of the State in Case of International Crimes” (Rapporteur: Lady Fox)’. Napoli Session, 2009.

———. ‘13th Commission Immunities from Jurisdiction and Execution of Heads of State and of Government in International Law (Rapporteur: Mr Joe Verhoeven)’. Vancouver Session, 2001.

‘Interim Constitution of Nepal 2063’. 15 January 2007.

Kolodkin, R.A. ‘Second Report on Immunity of State Officials from Foreign Criminal Jurisdiction’. UN Doc A/CN.4/631, 10 June 2010.

‘London Agreement for the International Military Tribunal at Nuremberg’. 82 UNTS 279 (entered into force, 8 August 1945).

McGreal, Chris. ‘Sharon’s Ally Safe from Arrest in Britain’. *The Guardian*, 11 February 2004.

McGregor, L. ‘Torture and State Immunity: Deflecting Impunity, Distorting Sovereignty’. *European Journal of International Law* 18, no. 5 (2007): 903–19.

Nowak, M., and E. McArthur. *The United Nations Convention against Torture: A Commentary*. Oxford: Oxford University Press, 2008.

Office of the High Commissioner for Human Rights. ‘Media Centre.’ http://www.ohchr.org/EN/NewsEvents/Pages/Media. At http://www.ohchr.org/EN/NewsEvents/Pages/Media (accessed 5 January 2014)

Roberts, A. ‘Comparative International Law? The Role of Courts in International Law’. *International and Comparative Law Quarterly* 60, no. 1 (2011): 57–92.

Sands, Philippe. ‘International Law Transformed? From Pinochet to Congo…?’ *Leiden Journal of International Law* 16, no. 1 (2003): 37–53.

State Immunity Act (UK).

‘Statute of the International Criminal Tribunal for Rwanda’. UNSC Res 955 (8 November 1994) UN Doc S/RES/955, 1994.

‘Statute of the International Criminal Tribunal for the Former Yugoslavia’. UNSC Res 827 (25 May 1993) UN Doc S/RES/827, 1993.

Stephen, Christopher. ‘International Criminal Law: Wielding the Sword of Universal Criminal Justice’. *International and Comparative Law Quarterly* 61, no. 1 (2012): 55–89.

UN Security Council. 'Report of the Secretary-General on the Establishment of a Special Court for Sierra Leone (Statute of the Special Court for Sierra Leone)'. S/2000/915, 4 October 2000.

———. 'Statute of the International Criminal Tribunal for Rwanda (as Last Amended on 13 October 2006)'. UNSC Res 955 UN Doc S/RES/955, 8 November 1994.

United Nations. 'Convention against Torture and Other Cruel, Inhuman or Degrading Treatment or Punishment'. UNTS 1465 85, 1984.

———. 'Statute of the International Court of Justice'. Adopted 18 April 1946.

———. 'Vienna Convention on Diplomatic Relations'. In *UN Treaties Series*, 95. Geneva: United Nations, 18 April 1961.

———. 'Vienna Convention on the Law of Treaties'. In *Treaty Series*, 331. Geneva: United Nations 1969.

van Alebeek, Rosanne. 'National Courts. International Crimes and the Functional Immunity of State Officials'. *Netherlands International Law Review* 59, no. 01 (2012): 5–41.

Wickremasinghe, C. 'Immunities Enjoyed by Officials of States and International Organisations'. In *International Law*, edited by M. Evans, 380–410. Oxford: Oxford University Press, 2010.

Wouters, Jan. 'The Judgment of the International Court of Justice in the Arrest Warrant Case: Some Critical Remarks'. *Leiden Journal of International Law* 16 (2003): 253–67.

Wuerth, Ingrid. 'Pinochet's Legacy Reassessed'. *American Journal of International Law* 106, no. 4 (2012): 731–68.

Zaman, Rebecca. 'Playing the Ace? Jus Cogens Crimes and Functional Immunity in National Courts'. *Australian International Law Journal* 17 (2010): 53–87.

Chapter 6

Interpreting the Most-Favoured-Nation Clause in Investment Treaty Arbitration: Interpretation as a Process of Creating an Obligation?

Tomoko Ishikawa

Introduction

In the practice of investment treaty arbitration, it has long been considered that the standard of fair and equitable treatment (FET) is 'wide enough to eclipse all other duties towards investors'.[1] However, while the FET remains the most commonly invoked standard of protection in investment treaty arbitrations,[2] recent tribunals have given most-favoured-nation (MFN) clauses a function even the FET obligation cannot fulfil, and an increasing number of investors have started to rely on these clauses.

An MFN clause typically prescribes the obligation of a Contracting Party to accord to investors of the other Contracting Party ('Other Contracting Party Investors') and their investments treatment that is no less favourable than the treatment it accords in like circumstances to investors of a non-Contracting Party ('Third-Party Investors') and their investments. An obvious function of an MFN clause is to prohibit both *de jure* and *de facto* discrimination among foreign investors by the host state in adopting and applying domestic regulatory measures. Yet it has another function that is more controversial. It is the 'effective imposition', through an MFN clause in the basic treaty,[3] of an obligation on a Contracting Party to accord Other Contracting Party Investors and their investments the 'more favourable' treatment provided in international agreements between the former Contracting Party and a non-Contracting Party ('third-party treaties').

1 V. Lowe, 'Regulation or Expropriation?', *Current Legal Problems* 55 (2002): 454.

2 Yannaca-Small observes that FET is 'present in almost every single claim brought by foreign investors against host States': K. Yannaca-Small, 'Fair and Equitable Treatment Standard: Recent Developments', in *Standards of Investment Protection*, ed. A. Reinisch (Oxford: Oxford University Press, 2008), 111.

3 For the purpose of this chapter, the term 'the basic treaty' refers to a treaty between a Contracting Party and the other Contracting Party that contains an MFN clause.

The controversy over the latter function of an MFN clause has, however, largely been confined to the issue of the applicability of the clause to jurisdictional questions. Where the dispute settlement provision of the basic treaty does not allow an investor to file its claim before international arbitration, the investor invokes the MFN clause in the treaty, seeking to rely on more generous dispute settlement provisions in third-party treaties. The question of whether MFN clauses may be used to overcome jurisdictional defects in the basic treaty has been one of the most controversial issues in the jurisprudence of investment arbitration tribunals.[4]

By contrast, the applicability of an MFN clause to substantive obligations has been regarded as much less problematic. Scholars have observed that such applicability is a generally agreed position.[5] In cases such as *MTD v Chile*,[6] *Rumeli Telekom v Kazakhstan*,[7] *Bayindir v Pakistan*,[8] *White Industries v India*,[9] *EDFI v Argentina*[10] and

4 Recent investment arbitration cases in which tribunals expressed divergent views on this issue include: *Hochtief v Argentina* (ICSID Case No. ARB/07/31, Decision on Jurisdiction, 24 Oct. 2011); *Daimler Financial Services v Argentina* (ICSID Case No. ARB/05/1, Award, 22 Aug. 2012); *Teinver, Transportes de Cercanías and Autobuses Urbanos del Sur v Argentina* (ICSID Case No. ARB/09/1, Decision on Jurisdiction, 21 Dec. 2012, arbitrator Hossain dissenting); *Kılıç İnşaat İthalat İhracat Sanayi ve Ticaret Anonim Şirketi v Turkmenistan* (ICSID Case No. ARB/10/1, Award, 2 Jul. 2013); *Garanti Koza LLP v Turkmenistan* (ICSID Case No. ARB/11/20, Decision on the Objection to Jurisdiction for Lack of Consent, 3 Jul. 2013).

5 J.W. Salacuse, *The Law of Investment Treaties* (Oxford: Oxford University Press, 2010), 253: 'While it is generally agreed that an appropriately drafted MFN clause will import into an investment treaty substantive protective standards, controversy exists as to whether the clause also extends to procedural rights, particularly those relating to dispute settlement in other treaties.' See also, J.R. Weeramantry, *Treaty Interpretation in Investment Arbitration* (Oxford: Oxford University Press, 2012), 177: 'A generally accepted position is that once arbitral jurisdiction has been established in relation to a claim, an MFN clause gives covered home state investors and investments the benefit of more favourable substantive protections contained in other investment treaties'; S. Vesel, 'Clearing a Path through a Tangled Jurisprudence: Most-Favored-Nation Clauses and Dispute Settlement Provisions in Bilateral Investment Treaties', *Yale Journal of International Law* 32 no. 1 (2007): 125, 163: 'the application of the MFN principle to substantive provisions has never been seen as problematic'.

6 *MTD Equity Sdn. Bhd. and MTD Chile S.A. v Republic of Chile*, ICSID Case No. ARB/01/7, Award, 25 May 2004.

7 *Rumeli Telekom A.S. and Telsim Mobil Telekomunikasyon Hizmetleri A.S. v Kazakhstan*, ICSID Case No. ARB/05/16, Award, 29 Jul. 2008.

8 *Bayindir Insaat Turizm Ticaret Ve Sanayi A.S. v Pakistan*, ICSID Case No. ARB/03/29, Award, 27 Aug. 2009.

9 *White Industries Australia Limited v India* (UNCITRAL), Final Award, 30 Nov. 2011.

10 *EDF International S.A., SAUR International S.A. and León Participaciones Argentinas S.A. v Argentina*, ICSID Case No. ARB/03/23, Award, 11 Jun. 2012.

Arif v Moldova,[11] investors were allowed to rely on the 'more favourable' standard of treatment provided in third-party treaties through the applicable MFN clauses. In *AAPL v Sri Lanka*[12] and *Pope & Talbot v Canada*,[13] the tribunals also accepted the general applicability of an MFN clause to substantive obligations.

The tribunal in *White Industries v India* distinguished between substantive obligations and procedural rights in the application of MFN clauses to support its conclusion that the MFN clause is applicable to the former:

> [T]he concern … to this effect [that an MFN clause fundamentally subverts the carefully negotiated balance of the BIT] is confined to the use of an MFN clause to obtain the benefit of a dispute resolution clause in another treaty. However, that is not the situation in the present case, which is qualitatively different. Here, White is not seeking to put in issue the dispute resolution provisions of the BIT, but is instead availing itself of the right to rely on more favourable substantive provisions in the third-party treaty. This does not 'subvert' the negotiated balance of the BIT. Instead, it achieves exactly the result which the parties intended by the incorporation in the BIT of an MFN clause.[14]

Analyses based on this substantive/procedural 'dichotomy' are also found in *Bayindir v Pakistan*[15] and *EDFI v Argentina*.[16]

However, the statement of the *White Industries v India* tribunal (quoted above) does not explain what distinguishes substantive provisions from dispute resolution clauses in the application of an MFN clause. Nor does it explain why the application of an MFN clause to substantive provisions does not 'subvert the negotiated balance of the BIT'. It should also be noted that this dichotomous approach is not universally accepted by tribunals. For example, in *Austrian Airlines v Slovakia*,

---

11 *Mr. Franck Charles Arif v Moldova* (ICSID Case No. ARB/11/23, Award, 8 Apr. 2013). It should be noted, however, that in this case (according to the tribunal) both parties 'agreed that an MFN clause applies to substantive obligations' (para. 396), as a result of which the issue was whether the umbrella clause was procedural or substantive in nature (para. 143). The tribunal concluded the latter on the grounds that '[a] breach of specific undertakings covered by an "umbrella" clause will give rise to a substantive breach of the BIT' (para. 395). See also *ATA v Jordan*, in which the tribunal stated (in a footnote) that the MFN clause applied to the provisions on the FET obligations (*ATA Construction, Industrial and Trading Company v Jordan*, ICSID Case No. ARB/08/2, Award, 18 May 2010, para. 125 (footnote 16)).

12 *Asian Agricultural Products Ltd. v Sri Lanka*, ICSID Case No. ARB/87/3, Final Award, 27 Jun. 1990.

13 *Pope & Talbot Inc. v Canada* (UNCITRAL) Award on the Merits of Phase 2, 10 Apr. 2001.

14 *White Industries v India* (n 9) paras. 11.2.2–11.2.4.

15 *Bayindir v Pakistan* (n 8) para. 159.

16 *EDFI v Argentina* (n 10) para. 936.

the tribunal did not distinguish between 'substantive guarantees' and 'procedural protections' in considering the scope of application of an MFN clause.[17]

This chapter challenges the widely accepted position that an MFN clause, unless accompanied by explicit reservations and exceptions, generally allows the 'incorporation' of more favourable substantive provisions in third-party treaties. The structure of this chapter is as follows. Section I provides a detailed analysis of the effect of invoking an MFN clause to impose obligations under third-party treaties for more favourable treatment. It is argued that the oft-used term 'incorporation' (that is, of more favourable provisions via an MFN clause) is a misnomer because an MFN clause is not designed to introduce or create new rights/obligations in the basic treaty. Rather, we should ask *under what conditions* the failure of the host state to accord such treatment to the investor constitutes a breach of *the MFN obligation in the basic treaty*. Based on this proposition, Section I concludes by identifying the conditions for the operation of an MFN clause in this context. Of these conditions, the most controversial is the applicability of an MFN clause in the basic treaty to the subject matter of the claimed treatment in the third-party treaty. Section II examines this condition as a matter of the boundaries of an MFN obligation. It is argued that there are cases where the interpretation of an MFN clause in light of the rules of treaty interpretation reveals implicit boundaries on the scope of application of the clause. The underlying theory is that the interpretation of an MFN clause should be guided by established rules of treaty interpretation, rather than policy considerations regarding the function of 'MFN obligations in general'.

I. Construction and Effect of an MFN Clause

Grounds for Claim

In considering the construction and effect of an MFN clause, it must first be emphasised that, where an investor invokes the MFN clause in the basic treaty asserting that the host state did not accord it the more favourable treatment under third-party treaties, the ground for that investor's assertion is the state's breach of the MFN clause. In other words, the investor may not claim a breach of the provision in the third-party treaty that provides such more favourable treatment by the host state. This is made clear in the following statement of the International Court of Justice (ICJ) in the Anglo-Iranian Oil case:

17 *Austrian Airlines v Slovakia* (UNCITRAL) Award, 9 Oct. 2009, para. 124: '[a]s a general matter, the Tribunal observes that it sees no conceptual reason why an MFN clause should be limited to substantive guarantees and rule out procedural protections, the latter being a means to enforce the former.'

> A third-party treaty, independent of and isolated from the basic treaty, cannot produce any legal effect as between the United Kingdom [the beneficiary State] and Iran [the granting State]: it is *res inter alios acta.*[18]

The International Law Commission (ILC),[19] in its report on the MFN clause, observes that,

> The solution adopted by the Court is in accordance with the rules of the law of treaties relating to the effect of treaties on States not parties to a particular treaty. The view that the third-party treaty (the treaty by which the granting State extends favours to a third State) is the origin of the rights of the beneficiary State (a State not party to the third-party treaty) runs counter to the rule embodied in article 36, paragraph 1, of the Vienna Convention.[20]

In the investment treaty regime, however, the oft-used expression that more favourable treatment provided in the third-party treaty is 'incorporated' via the MFN clause appears to have caused confusion to tribunals.[21] For example, in the recent *EDFI v Argentina* case, the tribunal concluded that the MFN clause in the basic treaty (Argentina–France BIT) 'permits Claimants to incorporate the "umbrella clauses" from' third-party treaties (Argentina–Germany BIT and Argentina–Luxemburg BIT), and concluded, *inter alia*, the following:

> Respondent has breached its obligations to (i) respect specific commitments undertaken in connection with Claimants' investment and (ii) afford Claimants Fair and Equitable Treatment with respect to their investment.[22]

---

18 *Anglo-Iranian Oil Co. (UK v. Iran)* (Preliminary objection), Judgment of 22 Jul. 1952 ([1952] ICJ Reports 109).

19 Given 'the authoritative status of the members of the Commission as individual jurists, the fact that collectively they represent many nationalities, and the close connection of their work with the international political realities of the day', the work of the ILC is (although not legally binding) 'itself an authoritative influence on the development of the law and a cogent material source of law': R. Jennings and A. Watts, eds, *Oppenheim's International Law, Vol. 1, Peace, Introduction and Part 1*, 9th edn (Harlow: Longman, 1992), 50.

20 United Nations, *International Law Commission Yearbook*, vol. I (New York: United Nations, 1978), vol. I, 8, 26.

21 Vesel aptly states that, 'The purpose of an MFN clause is not to incorporate by reference any specific provision of any other treaty. Rather, "the intention of the most-favoured-nation clauses was to establish and to maintain at all times fundamental equality without discrimination among all of the countries concerned"': (citing Rights of Nationals of the United States of America in Morocco (U.S. v Fr.), [1952] ICJ Reports 176, 192): Vesel, 'Clearing a Path through a Tangled Jurisprudence: Most-Favored-Nation Clauses and Dispute Settlement Provisions in Bilateral Investment Treaties', n 5, 178.

22 *EDFI v Argentina* (n 10) Disposition of the case (305).

That the tribunal did not even mention the MFN clause of the applicable Argentina–France BIT[23] is unfortunate. Argentina could not have breached the 'umbrella clauses' in the third-party treaties because the basic treaty did not impose an obligation on Argentina to comply with those clauses. The effect of applying the MFN clause to the umbrella clauses is not to create the umbrella clauses in the basic treaty or to transplant them from the third-party treaties into the basic treaty.[24] Rather, the effect is that the failure of Argentina to observe the obligation to respect specific commitments undertaken in connection with the claimants as provided in the third-party treaties constitutes a breach of the MFN obligation in the basic treaty.

In sum, the host state's failure to accord the standard of treatment prescribed in third-party treaties gives rise to the responsibility of the state under the basic treaty only where such failure is considered a breach of the MFN clause in the basic treaty. Therefore, the question to be asked is when and how such failure, if proven, constitutes a breach of the MFN clause in the basic treaty. This closely relates to the conditions under which an MFN clause may operate, which is examined in the following subsection.

Conditions for the MFN Operation

When an investor invokes an MFN clause claiming that it is entitled to more favourable treatment provided in a third-party treaty, its first hurdle is to demonstrate that the MFN clause applies to the subject matter of the treatment under the third-party treaty. The applicability of an MFN clause is examined in detail below.

Assuming that this condition is met, the question to follow is whether the Other Contracting Party Investor is entitled to claim the purported treatment even if Third-Party Investors have yet to actually exercise their right to that treatment. This concerns the question of when rights and obligations arise under an MFN clause. Draft Article 20(1) of the ILC Report on the MFN makes it clear that such rights arise 'at the moment when the relevant treatment is extended by the granting State to a third State or to persons or things in the same relationship with that third State'.[25] This means that, in the investment treaty context, Other Contracting Party Investors may claim entitlement to the more favourable treatment at the moment when the third-party treaty takes effect, insofar as other conditions are met.

---

23 The tribunal had concluded that, 'Claimants' claims may be decided solely on the basis of the Argentina–France BIT' (para. 887).

24 *Hochtief AG v Argentina* (n 4) para. 81: 'The MFN clause is not a *renvoi* to a range of totally distinct sources and systems of rights and duties: it is a principle applicable to the exercise of rights and duties that are actually secured by the BIT in which the MFN clause is found'.

25 ILC Report on the MFN Clause (n 20) 52.

Another hurdle for the asserting investor is to demonstrate that the treatment provided in the third-party treaty is actually more favourable than that in the basic treaty. In this context, the term providing allegedly more favourable treatment may not be isolated from its context. This has two implications: the 'beneficial' provisions must be treated as a whole; and exceptions to, conditions on or limitations on the provisions are not severable from each other. Allowing 'provision-by-provision treaty shopping' results in the creation of a treatment more favourable than any treatment intended to be accorded to anyone, which is not the function of an MFN clause.[26]

In sum, the investor invoking the MFN clause has to prove that the following conditions are met:

a. the MFN clause in the basic treaty is applicable to the subject matter of the claimed treatment in the third-party treaty (this will be examined in Section II);
b. the basic treaty is in force;
c. the third-party treaty is in force;[27] and
d. the treatment provided in the third-party treaty, as a whole and in the context of the treaty, is more favourable than that in the basic treaty.

II. Boundaries of an MFN Obligation

This section addresses the first – threshold – condition for the operation of an MFN clause, that is, that the clause in the basic treaty is applicable to the subject matter of the claimed treatment in the third-party treaty. With this respect, two categories of limitations should be recognised. The first comprises explicit exceptions to, reservations on and other limitations on an MFN clause prescribed in the basic treaty.[28] The second consists of implicit limitations of an MFN clause. Of these, the first category of limitations has largely been accepted by investment arbitration tribunals.[29] This section focuses on the second category of limitations, which has been less widely recognised by tribunals.

---

26 See, *ICS Inspection and Control Services v Argentina* (UNCITRAL) PCA Case No. 2010–9, Award on Jurisdiction, 10 Feb. 2012 para. 320; Vesel, 'Clearing a Path through a Tangled Jurisprudence: Most-Favored-Nation Clauses and Dispute Settlement Provisions in Bilateral Investment Treaties', n 5, 168.

27 See, *Anglo-Iranian Oil* (n 18) 110.

28 These consist of the following types of exceptions and reservations: (i) the so-called 'MFN exceptions'; (ii) general exceptions of the basic treaty; (iii) limitations on the scope of the MFN clause; and (iv) limitations on the scope of the basic treaty.

29 For the MFN exceptions, see *ADF Group v US*, ICSID Case No. ARB (AF)/00/1, Award, 9 Jan. 2003, para. 196. For general exceptions of the basic treaty, see *CMS Gas Transmission Company v Argentina*, ICSID Case No. ARB/01/8, Award, 12 May 2005, para. 377. For limitations on the scope of the MFN clause, see *Sergei Paushok, CJSC Golden*

Implicit Limitations: The Ejusdem Generis *Rule*

As noted in the Introduction, absent explicit exceptions to, or limitations on, the MFN clause or the basic treaty, investment arbitration tribunals generally accept the application of MFN clauses to substantive protection standards. On the other hand, outside the context of investment treaty arbitration, it is well established that MFN clauses are subject to implicit limitations derived from the *ejusdem generis* rule.[30] The *ejusdem generis* rule is explained in the following ways:

> [The MFN clause] can only attract matters belonging to the same category of subject as that to which the clause itself relates.[31]

or

> [T]he clause can only operate in regard to the subject-matter which the two States had in mind when they inserted the clause in their treaty.[32]

Therefore, when examining the applicability of an MFN clause to a particular case, a central question is whether or not the relevant provision in the third-party treaty may be considered *ejusdem generis* covered by the clause. It should be emphasised here that there is no rule that all matters concerning substantive

---

East Company and CJSC Vostokneftegaz Company v Mongolia, Award on Jurisdiction and Liability, 28 Apr. 2011 (UNCITRAL), before 28 Apr. 2011 (in this case, the relevant MFN clause provided that the MFN treatment was accorded only with respect to the fair and equitable treatment (paras. 570, 609)). Lastly, for the limitations on the scope of the basic treaty, see: *Técnicas Medioambientales Tecmed, S.A. v Mexico*, ICSID Case No. ARB (AF)/00/2, Award, 29 May 2003, para. 69; and *Société Générale in respect of DR Energy Holdings and Empresa Distribuidora de Electricidad del Este v Dominican Republic*, LCIA Case No. UN 7927, Award on Preliminary Objections to Jurisdiction, 19 Sep. 2008, para. 41; *Les Laboratoires Servier, S.A.A., Biofarma, S.A.S., Arts et Techniques du Progres S.A.S. v Poland* (UNCITRAL), Award, 14 Feb. 2012, para. 519; *Metal-Tech Ltd. v Uzbekistan*, ICSID Case No. ARB/10/3, Award, 4 Oct. 2013, paras. 145–146; *Rafat Ali Rizvi v Indonesia*, ICSID Case No. ARB/11/13, Award on Jurisdiction, 16 Jul. 2013, para. 220. It should be noted that the *Tecmed* tribunal rejected the application of the MFN clause on other grounds than the limitations on the scope of the basic treaty. For a criticism of this approach, see Vesel, 'Clearing a Path through a Tangled Jurisprudence: Most-Favored-Nation Clauses and Dispute Settlement Provisions in Bilateral Investment Treaties', n 5, 162–64.

30 For example, ILC Report on the MFN Clause (n 20) 30 ('No writer would deny the validity of the ejusdem generis rule which, for the purposes of the most-favoured-nation clause, derives from its very nature'). See also, *Renta 4 S.V.S.A et al v Russia*, SCC No. 24/2007, Award on Preliminary Objections, 20 Mar. 2009, para. 100; *Hochtief AG v Argentina* (n 4) para. 77; *Garanti Koza v Turkmenistan* (n 4) para. 54.

31 *Ambatielos (Greece v UK)* 12 RIAA 119 (1956), at 107.

32 Sir Arthur Watts, ed., *The International Law Commission 1949–1998*, vol. III (Oxford: Oxford University Press, 1999), 1821.

protection of investors/investments automatically fall into 'the subject-matter which the two States had in mind when they inserted the [MFN] clause in their treaty'. The *ejusdem generis* rule equally applies to matters concerning substantive protection of investors/investments, and therefore tribunals facing the issue of the applicability of an MFN clause in this context need to examine whether or not such matters fall in the same category of subject to which the clause relates. This sets the implicit boundaries of the scope of an MFN clause. Even the *White Industries* tribunal, which suggested the general applicability of an MFN clause to substantive provisions (see Introduction), appears to have accepted the existence of implicit boundaries of an MFN clause when it cited Schill's argument that '[t]he sole relevant factor is whether MFN treatment applies or whether it is subject to an explicit or implicit exception'.[33]

How to determine ejusdem generis*: rules of treaty interpretation*

Given that the *ejusdem generis* rule applies to matters concerning substantive protection of investors/investments, the question to follow is *how* the application of *ejusdem generis* rule should be approached. In this regard, there are views that stress the function of an MFN clause to harmonise the standards of treatment of investments/investors. Schill argues that MFN clauses 'disable States from entering into bilateral *quid pro quo* bargains that extend preferential treatment to certain States and exclude it with respect to others' and therefore may 'serve as a basis for multilateralizing bilateral investment relations'.[34] He further argues that the approaches that stress the bilateral or *quid pro quo* bargain elements in international investment relations are associated with 'restrictive approaches to the interpretation of MFN clauses', while expansive approaches to the interpretation of MFN clauses lend support to stronger tendencies of multilateralism.[35] With respect, however, a tribunal's task is not to reflect its view on the multilateralism/bilateralism of the investment treaty regime in interpreting the MFN clause but to interpret the given treaty in accordance with established rules of treaty interpretation. While it is undeniable that an MFN clause has the function of harmonising the standards among various investment treaties, such policy considerations are relevant only to the extent that they support the application of the rules of interpretation. Moreover, the argument that MFN clauses 'disable States from entering into bilateral quid pro quo bargains' does not reflect the fact that investment treaties are the products of negotiations between Contracting Parties. A state strategically selects target countries with which it negotiates investment treaties, considering, for example,

33 *White Industries v India* (n 9) para. 11.2.8 (citing Stephan W. Schill, 'Multilateralizing Investment Treaties through Most-Favored-Nation Clauses', *Berkeley Journal of International Law* 27 no. 2 (2009): 496, 524). In this case, however, the tribunal concluded that there was no 'read-in' exception to the MFN clause (para. 11.2.9).

34 'Multilateralizing Investment Treaties through Most-Favored-Nation Clauses' (ibid.), 502–04.

35 Ibid., 505.

the scale of presence of its own investors in the country, or the potential value of the market in that country. Once a state enters into negotiations with the other state, the state then has to strike a delicate balance among conflicting interests in internal policy considerations in deciding what to offer to the other party. Also, the proposals made by a state in the process of negotiation always reflect the proposals offered by the other state. The majority of the tribunal in *Daimler Financial Services* emphasised the character of a bilateral investment treaty (BIT) as a product of negotiations:

> In considering its interpretation, it is essential to recall that BITs are reciprocal bilateral treaties negotiated between two sovereign State parties. The general purpose of BITs is of course primarily to protect and promote foreign investment; but it is to do so within the framework acceptable to both of the State parties.[36]

The *ICS Inspection* tribunal emphasised that policy considerations should not substitute for treaty rules of interpretation:

> The Tribunal cannot therefore create exceptions to treaty rules [of interpretation] where these are merely based upon an assessment of the wisdom of the policy in question, having no basis in either the treaty text or in any supplementary interpretive source, however desirable such policy considerations might be seen to be in the abstract.[37]

Therefore, tribunals, when assessing the scope of application of the MFN clause at issue, should base their analysis on established rules of treaty interpretation, rather than on policy considerations concerning the function of 'an MFN clause'. As to what constitute 'established rules of treaty interpretation', it is widely accepted by international courts and tribunals that customary rules of treaty interpretation are embodied in Article 31 of the Vienna Convention on the Law of Treaties (VCLT).[38] Reliance on Article 31 VCLT is also common in investment treaty arbitration.[39] In addition, there are other interpretative rules that are not specifically mentioned in the VCLT but are widely accepted by international courts and tribunals, including the principles of effective interpretation, contemporaneous interpretation and evolutive interpretation.

36 *Daimler Financial Services v Argentina* (n 4) para. 161.

37 *ICS Inspection v Argentina* (n 26) para. 267.

38 For example, *Pulp Mills* (merits) (20 Apr. 2010) para. 65; *Genocide Convention* (26 Feb. 2007) para. 160; *US-Carbon Steel Flat (AB)* WT/DS213/AB/R (2002) para. 61. See also, I. Sinclair, *The Vienna Convention on the Law of Treaties*, 2nd edn (Manchester: Manchester University Press, 1984), 153.

39 See, Weeramantry, *Treaty Interpretation in Investment Arbitration*, n 5, 61.

Purpose of Treaty Interpretation

It has been demonstrated that the determination of what is *ejusdem generis* covered by an MFN clause should be made through the application of rules of treaty interpretation. This subsection addresses the process of the application of such rules. It should be borne in mind that the primary task of treaty interpretation is to reveal the common intention of the parties.[40] For bilateral agreements between states like BITs, consent to a treaty is still the only legitimate basis of obligation of states, and the parties' intention is the basis of such consent.[41]

In this context, the intention of the parties may be classified into two: the intention *as expressed in the text of the treaty*[42] (an 'objectified' intention), and the intention inferred from the surrounding circumstances of the treaty such as the negotiating or drafting history.[43] In treaty interpretation, the objectified intention should be adopted. The ILC Commentary for the draft articles of the VCLT clearly adopted the objectified intention by stating that,

> [T]he text must be presumed to be an authentic expression of the intention of the parties ... in consequence, the starting point of interpretation is the elucidation of the meaning of the text, not an investigation *ab initio* into the intention of the parties.[44]

In the investment treaty arbitration context, Professor Schreuer expressed his support for objectified intention in the proceedings of the *Wintershall* case in which he acted as an expert witness for the claimant. He stated that,

> If you look at Article 31 and Article 32 of the Vienna Convention, you will see that the intention of the parties is never mentioned there, and for good reasons

40 H. Lauterpacht, 'Codification and Development of International Law', *American Journal of International Law* 49 (1955): 27; Declaration of Judge Higgins in *Kasikili/Sedudu Island (Botswana/Namibia)* [1999] ICJ Reports 4 para. 4.

41 M. Koskenniemi, *From Apology to Utopia: The Structure of International Legal Argument (Reissue with a New Epilogue)* (Cambridge: Cambridge University Press, 2005), 337: '[t]he subjective theory seems necessary to preserve the treaty's legitimacy'; *Daimler Financial Services v Argentina* (n 4) para. 168: 'all international treaties ... are essentially expressions of the contracting states' consent to be bound by particular legal norms'.

42 Separate Opinion of Judge Fitzmaurice in *Golder v UK* (Judgment of 21 Feb. 1975), 57 ILR 200, 293–4.

43 Van Alstine points out that a strict positivist view (that treaties solely reflect a 'contract' between sovereign nations) 'has lead an inflated view of both the subjective intent of "the parties" and the degree of appropriate deference to the views of the Executive Branch in interpretive inquiries': Michael P. Van Alstine, 'Dynamic Treaty Interpretation', *University of Pennsylvania Law Review* 146 no. 3 (1998): 687, 691.

44 United Nations, *International Law Commission Yearbook*, vol. II (New York: United Nations, 1966), 220, para. 11.

> … the intention is relevant to the extent that it finds expression in the text of a Treaty, but not beyond.[45]

The notion of objectified intention is supported in Article 31(1) VCLT, which provides that,

> 1. A treaty shall be interpreted in good faith in accordance with the ordinary meaning to be given to the terms of the treaty in their context and in the light of its object and purpose.

It is also clear from Article 31(1) that the ordinary meaning of the text is the starting point in ascertaining the common intention of the parties expressed in the text of a treaty. This, however, does not mean that the textual approach always supersedes other rules of interpretation. Article 31 does not provide for any hierarchy of the rules of interpretation. Also, the ILC Commentary took the approach that treaty interpretation is a combination of various rules of interpretation (the 'crucible' approach):

> [B]y heading the article 'General rule of interpretation' in the singular [not 'General rules' in the plural] and by underlining the connexion between paragraphs 1 and 2 and again between paragraph 3 and the two previous paragraphs, it intended to indicate that the application of the means of interpretation in the article would be a single combined operation. All the various elements, as they were present in any given case, would be thrown into the crucible, and their interaction would give the legally relevant interpretation.

There is no reason to depart from this principle in interpreting an MFN clause. The tribunal's task is to ascertain the common intention of the parties expressed in the text of the MFN clause and the basic treaty, by applying rules of treaty interpretation in a combined manner (the crucible approach).

The Principle of Effective Interpretation

This subsection addresses the specific question of how such interpretative rules may inform the interpretation of an MFN clause. It is argued that, for the purpose of determining the scope of the application of the clause, the principle of effective interpretation is particularly useful. Although not explicitly stated in the VCLT, this principle is an established canon of interpretation,[46] as may be inferred from

45 *Wintershall Aktiengesellschaft v Argentina*, ICSID Case No. ARB/04/14, Award, 5 Oct. 2008, para. 86.

46 Sinclair, *The Vienna Convention on the Law of Treaties*, n 38, 118.

a number of decisions of international courts and tribunals, including the ICJ,[47] international arbitral tribunal,[48] and the WTO adjudicatory bodies.[49] In investment treaty arbitration, the *ad hoc* Annulment Committee in *Klockner v Cameroon* recognised this principle as a customary principle of interpretation.[50]

As stated above, this principle is particularly useful in determining the scope of an MFN clause. When an investor invokes an MFN clause in the basic treaty in order to rely on a more favourable treatment provided in the third-party treaty, at first glance there are two potentially inconsistent provisions in the basic treaty. One is the MFN clause under which a Contracting Party commits to accord MFN treatment to the Other Contracting Party Investors and their investments. The other is the provision under which a Contracting Party commits to accord treatment less favourable than that accorded under the third-party treaty. The principle of effective interpretation operates in such a situation. Hersch Lauterpacht identifies several situations where this principle may be applicable. They include, in particular, (a) where the treaty actually registers the absence of any common intention, and (b) where the treaty contains inconsistent provisions. The MFN issue noted above falls squarely within the latter case.[51]

The principle of effective interpretation has different propositions, which are not mutually exclusive. The most classic version of the principle is that an interpreter must give meaning and effect to the term being interpreted, which derives from the Latin maxim *ut res magis valeat quam pereat*, 'interpretation should seek to save clauses of a treaty which were threatened with loss of effect

47 For example, *Interpretation of Peace Treaties (Second Phase)* Advisory Opinion [1950] ICJ Reports 221, 229; *Libya/Chad Territorial Dispute* [1994] ICJ Reports 21, para. 47; *Corfu Channel* (merits) [1949] ICJ Reports 4, 24; Dissenting opinion of Judge Fitzmaurice in *Legal Consequences for States of the Continued Presence of South Africa in Namibia (South West Africa) notwithstanding Security Council Resolution 276 Advisory Opinion* [1971] ICJ Reports 16 (para. 30); *Ambatielos* (preliminary objection) [1952] ICJ Reports 28, 45.

48 In *Iron Rhine Arbitration*, the tribunal recognised the principle as a well-established interpretative principle that is not set out in VCLT: *Iron Rhine Arbitration (Belgium v The Netherlands)*, Award of 24 May 2005, para. 49.

49 Since the explicit recognition of the principle of effective interpretation as one of 'the general rule[s] of interpretation' by the Appellate Body in *US-Gasoline (AB)* WT/DS2/AB/R (1996) (at 17), the principle has been affirmed by WTO panels and the Appellate Body in a number of cases. For example, *EC-Sugar* (panel) WT/DS283/R (2004) para. 7.151. See also, WTO, *WTO Analytical Index: Guide to WTO Law and Practice*, 2nd edn (Cambridge: Cambridge University Press, 2007), 1118–19.

50 *Klockner v Cameroon* (decision on annulment) ICSID Case No. ARB/81/2 (1983) para. 62.

51 H. Lauterpacht, 'Restrictive Interpretation and the Principle of Effectiveness in the Interpretation of Treaties', *British Yearbook of International Law* 26 (1949): 48, 76–81.

through interpretation'.[52] In the ILC Commentary on draft articles of the VCLT, the principle in this sense was explained as follows:

> When a treaty is open to two interpretations one of which does and the other does not enable the treaty to have appropriate effects, good faith and the objects and purposes of the treaty demand that the former interpretation should be adopted.[53]

The principle of effective interpretation is also understood in connection with the object and purpose of a treaty.[54] Emphasis on the object and purpose of the treaty is found in the cases that adopted the broad interpretation of MFN clauses.[55] Yet it should be noted that the object and purpose is understood within the framework of the treaty. The majority of the tribunal in *Daimler Financial Services* stated that,

> The general purpose of BITs is of course primarily to protect and promote foreign investment; but it is to do so within the framework acceptable to both of the State parties. These two aspects must always be held in tension. They are the yin and yang of bilateral investment treaties and cannot be separated without doing violence to the will of the states that conclude such treaties.[56]

In addition to these rather 'conventional' functions, there is another version of the principle of effective interpretation. The WTO Appellate Body and panels have recognised this version of the principle that requires an interpreter to give meaning and effect to all the terms of the treaty, and 'read all applicable provisions of a treaty in a way that gives meaning to *all of them, harmoniously*'.[57] In *Anglo-Iranian Oil*, the ICJ stated that it may be said that this version of the principle[58] should 'in general be applied when interpreting the text of a treaty'.[59]

52 United Nations, *International Law Commission Yearbook*, vol. I (New York: United Nations, 1966), 289, para. 90.

53 United Nations, *International Law Commission Yearbook*, vol. II (New York, 1966): 219, para. 6.

54 In the process of drafting the VCLT, it was argued that the principle of effective interpretation is implicit in the requirement of good faith in the sense that, '[a]n interpretation given in good faith and taking account of the objects and purposes of a treaty would always necessarily seek to give a meaning to the text': *International Law Commission Yearbook*, vol. I (New York: United Nations, 1964), 290, para. 106.

55 For example, *Emilio Agustín Maffezini v Spain*, ICSID Case No. ARB/97/7, Decision on Jurisdiction, 25 Jan. 2000, para. 56; *Siemens A.G. v Argentina*, ICSID Case No. ARB/02/8, Decision on Jurisdiction, 3 Aug. 2004; *Camuzzi International v Argentina*, ICSID Case No. ARB/03/2, Decision on Jurisdiction, 11 May 2005, para. 81.

56 *Daimler Financial Services v Argentina* (n 4) para. 161.

57 *Korea-Dairy (AB)* WT/DS98/AB/R (1999) paras. 20–21 (emphasis added); *US-Underwear (AB)* WT/DS24/AB/R (1997) 16.

58 That is, 'a legal text should be interpreted in such a way that a reason and a meaning can be attributed to every word in the text' (*Anglo-Iranian Oil* (n 18) 105).

59 Ibid. It should be noted, however, that the Court did not apply the principle (which was invoked by the UK) to the case on the grounds, *inter alia*, that 'the text of the Iranian

In light of this version of the principle of effective interpretation, therefore, an MFN clause may not be interpreted so as to deprive other provisions in the basic treaty of meaning and effect. This may occur in a case where a substantive obligation provided in the basic treaty is accompanied by specific reservations by a Contracting Party that are absent in the third-party treaty, and the basic treaty is chronologically subsequent to the third-party treaty. In treaty negotiations, exceptions and reservations are typically requested by a Contracting Party, in order to keep consistency between the treaty and its (existing and future) regulatory needs, and in instances where the Contracting Party decided not to offer the commitment to the other Contracting Party as a result of a *quid pro quo* bargaining. In this respect, Vesel aptly observes that, in BIT negotiations,

> If the parties were on equal footing, we might expect a given BIT to closely resemble a compilation of the less favorable of the two states' policies on each specific matter.[60]

If a Contracting Party had undertaken a certain obligation in the third-party treaty, it is unlikely that there is the issue of consistency between the obligation and domestic regulatory measures. Therefore, if the Contracting Party does not offer the same commitment to the other Contracting Party by attaching reservations to the obligation, it is assumed that the choice is deliberate; the Contracting Party decided not to offer to the other Contracting Party the same commitment as that offered to a third country, and the other Contracting Party accepted it. Allowing the MFN clause to rely on the more favourable treatment provided in the third-party treaty means that the MFN clause may always trump such reservations or exceptions, thereby rendering them effectively meaningless. Conversely, even if the MFN clause is found not to apply to such obligations, the MFN clause does not lose its effect – it still operates to eliminate discrimination between investors as long as specific reservations are not made.

The *Impregilo v Argentina* tribunal, while concluding that the relevant MFN was applicable to the dispute settlement rules,[61] suggested that the chronological relationship between the basic treaty and the third-party treaty may be relevant in determining the scope of application of an MFN clause:

Declaration is not a treaty text resulting from negotiations between two or more States' (ibid.).

60 Vesel, 'Clearing a Path through a Tangled Jurisprudence: Most-Favored-Nation Clauses and Dispute Settlement Provisions in Bilateral Investment Treaties', n 5, 140.

61 *Impregilo v Argentina*, ICSID Case No. ARB/07/17, Award, 21 Jun. 2011, paras. 95–109 (arbitrator Stern dissenting). In the annulment decision, the annulment committee concluded that the majority's approach did not constitute a manifest excess of powers (Decision of the ad hoc Committee on the Application for Annulment, 24 Jan. 2014, paras. 140–141).

> [T]he Argentine Republic has pointed out, *inter alia*, that Argentina has included in several of its BITs, even those concluded after the Argentina–US BIT, a clause about domestic proceedings and an 18-month waiting period. This could be seen as an indication that Argentina did not intend these clauses to be replaced, via MFN clauses in the same BITs, by the rules of the Argentina-US BIT as being more favorable to the investor. However, the argument becomes less persuasive in the present case, because the Italy–Argentina BIT (signed on 22 May 1990) preceded the Argentina–US BIT (signed on 14 November 1991).[62]

The same considerations apply to the situation where the basic treaty does not have a particular obligation that had been provided in the third-party treaty predating the basic treaty. Again, it is assumed that the inconsistency between such an obligation and domestic regulatory measures is not at issue because such an obligation had already been committed. The silence in the basic treaty is in itself the manifestation of the fact that it was a deliberate choice of the Contracting Parties not to make such commitment to each other. Due to the reciprocal nature of the treaty, it is quite normal for a Contracting Party that had undertaken a particular obligation *vis-à-vis* a third state not to offer the same commitment to the other state where the latter does not ask for it or does not make a quid pro quo offer. Vesel argues that,

> Each provision of a BIT is, in essence, a concession on the part of the host state that benefits the investor. Thus while it is true that the purpose of the concessions contained in a BIT is to promote and protect investment, it is equally true that the contracting parties pursue other purposes by not making other concessions. The silences of a BIT may thus be pregnant with matters that are of great import to the host state and which are therefore deliberately excluded from the BIT.[63]

The principle of effective interpretation also informs the interpretation of the MFN clause in the case of an 'absence of commitment'. It is argued that the principle of effective interpretation requires an interpreter to take into account 'external materials'[64] in interpreting treaty provisions. This function of effective interpretation is explained by Lauterpacht in the following terms. He suggests that one of the judicial functions when faced with a gap, an obscurity, an absurdity or a frustrated purpose is to attempt to 'fill the lacunae by reference to the intentions of

62 Ibid., para. 102. See also, T. Cole, 'The Boundaries of Most Favored Nation Treatment in International Investment Law', *Michigan Journal of International Law* 33 no. 3 (2012): 537, 576. Contra: *Bayindir v Pakistan* (n 8) para. 160: 'In and of itself that chronology does not appear to preclude the importation of an FET obligation from another BIT concluded by the Respondent'.

63 Vesel, 'Clearing a Path through a Tangled Jurisprudence: Most-Favored-Nation Clauses and Dispute Settlement Provisions in Bilateral Investment Treaties', n 5, 143.

64 Here the term 'materials' refers to various elements that may affect interpretation, including norms, values, circumstances and concerns.

the parties in the wider context of the agreement as a whole and the circumstances accompanying its adoption, to the needs of the community, and to the requirement of good faith'.[65]

In light of the third-party treaty that had provided for a particular obligation before the basic treaty, the fact that the basic treaty does not contain that obligation strongly indicates that the Contracting Parties did not intend to allow the MFN clause to circumvent such exclusion.

These are examples where, in light of the principle of effective interpretation, the common intention of the Contracting Parties expressed in the text of the MFN clause is understood to exclude certain issues from the scope of 'the subject-matter which the two States had in mind when they inserted the clause in their treaty', that is, *ejusdem generis*.

To be sure, the application of the principle of effective interpretation is only one factor in the combined operation of various interpretative rules (see subsection above). Also, the determination of the objectified intention of the parties on what is *ejusdem generis* covered by the MFN clause requires a treaty-by-treaty analysis, taking into account the text, background and circumstances surrounding the treaty. Other factors to be considered include, for example, the response of the respondent to the claimant's invocation of the MFN clause in the arbitration proceedings.[66] The nature of the allegedly 'less favourable' part, for example, whether or not it concerns the scope of the obligation, may also be relevant. For example, an interpretative statement attached to the FET clause (as in *Pope & Talbot v Canada*) may well be circumvented by an MFN clause. This is because the scope of an FET obligation was the same between the basic treaty and the third-party treaty; therefore, it may well be argued that the FET provision in the third-party treaty is 'the subject-matter which the two States had in mind when they inserted the (MFN) clause in their treaty', regardless of any difference in the interpretative note. In this context, the recent *Accession Mezzanine v Hungary* case is suggestive. In this case, the dispute settlement clause in the UK–Hungary BIT limited the scope of tribunals' jurisdiction over disputes arising under the expropriation provision. The claimant invoked the MFN clause in the same treaty in order to bring to bear customary international law on the minimum standards of treatment of foreign investors and on expropriation.[67] While rejecting the expansion of its jurisdiction by virtue of the MFN clause,[68] the tribunal allowed

65 Lauterpacht, 'Codification and Development of International Law', n 40, 74.

66 For example, in cases such as *MTD v Chile* and *Rumeli Telekom v Kazakhstan*, the respondents did not argue against the claimants' reliance on more favourable provisions in the third-party treaties.

67 *Accession Mezzanine Capital L.P. and Danubius Kereskedöház Vagyonkezelö Zrt. v Hungary*, ICSID Case No. ARB/12/3, Decision on Respondent's Objection under Arbitration Rule 41(5), 16 Jan. 2013, para. 37.

68 Ibid., para. 73: 'MFN clauses are not and should not be interpreted or applied to create new causes of action beyond those to which consent to arbitrate has been given by

the claimant to rely on the MFN clause 'only insofar as such provisions relate to expropriation'.[69] In this case, Article 11 of the UK–Hungary BIT provides that, if 'international law existing at present or established hereafter between the Contracting Parties' provides for a more favourable treatment than is provided for by the BIT, such international law prevails over the BIT. Also, the relationship between the expropriation provision in the BIT and the customary international law on expropriation is aptly described by the tribunal as follows: 'it may not be possible to consider the scope and content of the term 'expropriation' in the BIT without considering customary and general principles of international law, as well as any other sources of international law in this area'.[70] Under such circumstances, contracting parties may well have considered that the expropriation provision in the BIT and the customary international law on expropriation were in 'the same category of subject to which the (MFN) clause itself relates'.[71]

However, these factors were absent in cases such as *Bayindir v Pakistan*, *White Industries v India* and *EDFI v Argentina*. Also in the *Bayindir* and *EDFI* cases the basic BITs postdated the relevant third-party BITs. The purpose of this chapter has not been to criticise the conclusions reached by these tribunals in cases that dealt with MFN issues or second-guess the rationale for the conclusions. It is argued, however, that these tribunals should have approached the MFN issue as a matter of treaty interpretation, rather than relying solely on the substantive/procedural dichotomy. A detailed examination of the process of interpreting the MFN clause at issue, taking into account interpretative rules such as the principle of effective interpretation, would have led to a more nuanced analysis on the boundaries of the MFN clauses.

Conclusion

This chapter has examined the ability of an MFN clause to allow recourse to more favourable treatment provided under third-party treaties and its implicit boundaries. It has demonstrated that, even where MFN clauses are invoked in relation to substantive obligations, a case that has been considered less controversial than its application to dispute settlement provisions, the *ejusdem generis* rule would apply. In other words, even in such a case, the question of the applicability of the MFN clause requires a case-by-case examination. In applying the *ejusdem generis* rule, investment arbitration tribunals should clearly recognise that the interpretation of the relevant MFN clause must be based on the established rules of treaty interpretation, not on policy considerations regarding the function of MFN clauses. Policy-oriented interpretation, which appears to underlie the approach that adopts

the Parties'.

69 Ibid., para. 74.

70 Ibid., para. 67.

71 *Ambatielos (Greece v UK)* (n 31) at 107.

the simple substantive/procedural dichotomy, risks disrespecting the will of the Contracting Parties and deviating thereby from the duties of investment tribunals. Tribunals dealing with the MFN issue should always bear in mind that the task of treaty interpretation is to ascertain the common intention of the parties expressed in the text of the treaty, which is possible only through a detailed examination and application of interpretative rules.

Cases

Accession Mezzanine Capital L.P. and Danubius Kereskedöház Vagyonkezelö Zrt. v Hungary, ICSID Case No. ARB/12/3, Decision on Respondent's Objection under Arbitration Rule 41(5), 16 Jan. 2013.

ADF Group v US, ICSID Case No. ARB (AF)/00/1, Award, 9 Jan. 2003.

Ambatielos (Greece v UK) 12 RIAA 119 (1956).

Anglo-Iranian Oil Co. (UK v Iran) (Preliminary objection), Judgment of 22 Jul. 1952, [1952] ICJ Reports 89.

Application of the Convention on the Prevention and Punishment of the Crime of Genocide (Bosnia and Herzegovina v Serbia and Montenegro), Judgment, [2007] ICJ Reports 43 ('*Genocide Convention*').

Asian Agricultural Products Ltd. v Sri Lanka, ICSID Case No. ARB/87/3, Final Award, 27 Jun. 1990.

ATA Construction, Industrial and Trading Company v Jordan, ICSID Case No. ARB/08/2, Award, 18 May 2010.

Austrian Airlines v Slovakia (UNCITRAL) Award, 9 Oct. 2009.

Bayindir Insaat Turizm Ticaret Ve Sanayi A.S. v Pakistan, ICSID Case No. ARB/03/29, Award, 27 Aug. 2009.

Camuzzi International v Argentina, ICSID Case No. ARB/03/2, Decision on Jurisdiction, 11 May 2005.

CMS Gas Transmission Company v Argentina, ICSID Case No. ARB/01/8, Award, 12 May 2005.

Corfu Channel (United Kingdom v Albania), Judgment, Merits, [1949] ICJ Reports 4.

Daimler Financial Services v Argentina, ICSID Case No. ARB/05/1, Award, 22 Aug. 2012.

EDF International S.A., SAUR International S.A. and León Participaciones Argentinas S.A. v Argentina, ICSID Case No. ARB/03/23, Award, 11 Jun. 2012.

Emilio Agustín Maffezini v Spain, ICSID Case No. ARB/97/7, Decision on Jurisdiction, 25 Jan. 2000.

Garanti Koza LLP v Turkmenistan, ICSID Case No. ARB/11/20, Decision on the Objection to Jurisdiction for Lack of Consent, 3 Jul. 2013.

Golder v UK (Judgment of 21 Feb. 1975), 57 ILR 200.

Hochtief AG v Argentina, ICSID Case No. ARB/07/31, Decision on Jurisdiction, 24 Oct. 2011.

ICS Inspection and Control Services v Argentina (UNCITRAL) PCA Case No. 2010–9, Award on Jurisdiction, 10 Feb. 2012.
Impregilo v Argentina, ICSID Case No. ARB/07/17, Award, 21 Jun. 2011.
Interpretation of Peace Treaties with Bulgaria, Hungary and Romania (Second Phase) Advisory Opinion [1950] ICJ Reports 221.
Iron Rhine Arbitration (Belgium v The Netherlands), Award, 24 May 2005.
Joseph Charles Lemire v Ukraine, ICSID Case No. ARB/06/18, Award, 28 Mar. 2011.
Kasikili/Sedudu Island (Botswana/Namibia), Judgment, [1999] ICJ Reports 4.
Kılıç İnşaat İthalat İhracat Sanayi ve Ticaret Anonim Şirketi v Turkmenistan, ICSID Case No. ARB/10/1, Award, 2 Jul. 2013.
Klöckner Industrie-Anlagen GmbH and others v. United Republic of Cameroon and other, ICSID Case No. ARB/81/2, Decision of the first *Ad Hoc* Committee of 3 May 1985, 2 ICSID Rep. 95 (1994).
Korea – Definitive Safeguard Measure on Imports of Certain Dairy Products – Report of the Appellate Body (14 Dec. 1999), WT/DS98/AB/R ('*Korea-Dairy (AB)*').
Les Laboratoires Servier, S.A.A., Biofarma, S.A.S., Arts et Techniques du Progres S.A.S. v Poland (UNCITRAL) Award, 14 Feb. 2012.
Legal Consequences for States of the Continued Presence of South Africa in Namibia (South West Africa) notwithstanding Security Council Resolution 276 Advisory Opinion [1971] ICJ Reports 16.
Libya/Chad Territorial Dispute [1994] ICJ Reports 21.
Metal-Tech Ltd. v Uzbekistan, ICSID Case No. ARB/10/3, Award, 4 Oct. 2013.
Mr. Franck Charles Arif v Moldova, ICSID Case No. ARB/11/23, Award, 8 Apr. 2013.
MTD Equity Sdn. Bhd. and MTD Chile S.A. v Republic of Chile, ICSID Case No. ARB/01/7, Award, 25 May 2004.
Pope & Talbot Inc. v Canada (UNCITRAL) Award on the Merits of Phase 2, 10 Apr. 2001.
Pulp Mills on the River Uruguay (Argentina v Uruguay), Judgment, [2010] ICJ Reports 14 ('*Pulp Mills*').
Rafat Ali Rizvi v Indonesia, ICSID Case No. ARB/11/13, Award on Jurisdiction, 16 Jul. 2013.
Renta 4 S.V.S.A et al v Russia, SCC No. 24/2007, Award on Preliminary Objections, 20 Mar. 2009.
Rumeli Telekom A.S. and Telsim Mobil Telekomunikasyon Hizmetleri A.S. v Kazakhstan, ICSID Case No. ARB/05/16, Award, 29 Jul. 2008.
Sergei Paushok, CJSC Golden East Company and CJSC Vostokneftegaz Company v Mongolia, Award on Jurisdiction and Liability, 28 Apr. 2011.
Siemens v Argentina, ICSID Case No. ARB/02/8, Decision on Jurisdiction, 3 Aug. 2004.
Société Générale In respect of DR Energy Holdings and Empresa Distribuidora de Electricidad del Este v Dominican Republic, LCIA Case No. UN 7927.

Técnicas Medioambientales Tecmed, S.A. v Mexico, ICSID Case No. ARB (AF)/00/2, Award, 29 May 2003.

Teinver, Transportes de Cercanías and Autobuses Urbanos del Sur v Argentina, ICSID Case No. ARB/09/1, Decision on Jurisdiction, 21 Dec. 2012.

US – Countervailing Duties on Certain Corrosion-Resistant Carbon Steel Flat Products from Germany – Report of the Appellate Bfody (28 Nov. 2002) WT/DS213/AB/R ('*US-Carbon Steel Flat (AB)*').

US – Standards for Reformulated and Conventional Gasoline – Report of the Appellate Body (29 April 1996) WT/DS2/AB/R ('*US-Gasoline (AB)*').

US – Restrictions on Imports of Cotton and Man-made Fibre Underwear – Report of the Appellate Body (10 Feb. 1997) WT/DS24/AB/R ('*US-Underwear (AB)*').

White Industries Australia Limited v India (UNCITRAL), Final Award, 30 Nov. 2011.

Wintershall Aktiengesellschaft v Argentina, ICSID Case No. ARB/04/14, Award, 5 Oct. 2008.

Bibliography

Cole, T. 'The Boundaries of Most Favored Nation Treatment in International Investment Law'. *Michigan Journal of International Law* 33 no. 3 (2012): 537–86.

Jennings, R., and A. Watts, eds. *Oppenheim's International Law, Vol. 1, Peace, Introduction and Part 1*. 9th edn. Harlow: Longman, 1992.

Koskenniemi, M. *From Apology to Utopia. The Structure of International Legal Argument (Reissue with a New Epilogue)*. Cambridge: Cambridge University Press, 2005.

Lauterpacht, H. 'Codification and Development of International Law'. *American Journal of International Law* 49 (1955): 16–43.

———, 'Restrictive Interpretation and the Principle of Effectiveness in the Interpretation of Treaties'. *British Yearbook of International Law* 26 (1949): 48, 76–81.

Lowe, V. 'Regulation or Expropriation?' *Current Legal Problems* 55 (2002): 447–66.

Salacuse, J.W. *The Law of Investment Treaties*. Oxford: Oxford University Press, 2010.

Schill, Stephan W. 'Multilateralizing Investment Treaties through Most-Favored-Nation Clauses'. *Berkeley Journal of International Law* 27 no. 2 (2009): 496–569.

Sinclair, I. *The Vienna Convention on the Law of Treaties*. 2nd edn. Manchester: Manchester University Press, 1984.

United Nations. *International Law Commission Yearbook*. Vol. I, New York: United Nations, 1964.

———. *International Law Commission Yearbook.* Vol. I, New York: United Nations, 1966.

———. *International Law Commission Yearbook.* Vol. II, New York: United Nations, 1966.

———. *International Law Commission Yearbook.* Vol. I, New York: United Nations, 1978.

Van Alstine, Michael P. 'Dynamic Treaty Interpretation'. *University of Pennsylvania Law Review* 146 no. 3 (1998): 687–793.

Vesel, S. 'Clearing a Path through a Tangled Jurisprudence: Most-Favored-Nation Clauses and Dispute Settlement Provisions in Bilateral Investment Treaties'. *Yale Journal of International Law* 32, no. 1 (2007): 125–90.

Watts, Sir Arthur, ed. *The International Law Commission 1949–1998*. Vol. III. Oxford: Oxford University Press, 1999.

Weeramantry, J.R. *Treaty Interpretation in Investment Arbitration*. Oxford: Oxford University Press, 2012.

WTO. *WTO Analytical Index: Guide to WTO Law and Practice*. 2nd edn. Cambridge: Cambridge University Press, 2007.

Yannaca-Small, K. 'Fair and Equitable Treatment Standard: Recent Developments'. In *Standards of Investment Protection*, edited by A. Reinisch. Oxford: Oxford University Press, 2008.

PART II
Non-State Actors in Promoting Justice

Chapter 7

Accountability of Multinational Corporations for Human Rights and Environmental Abuse: How Far Can Extraterritorial Jurisdiction Go?

Angelica Bonfanti

1. Introduction

Multinational corporations (MNCs) are inherently transnational economic entities: their supply chain and their business are transnational, as is the impact of their activities on development and human rights and environmental protection. Pursuant to the United Nations Conference on Trade and Development (UNCTAD), more than 80,000 MNCs operate all around the world. Their subsidiaries number more than 800,000.[1] The great majority of them originate from the European Union (EU), the US, and Japan; only 20 per cent are incorporated, through their parent companies, in other countries. While in the 1990s, 95 per cent of foreign investment outflow was from developed- to developed countries, in 2010, 46 per cent was from developed- to developing countries, meaning that foreign investment outflow has progressively been addressed from the developed countries to the developing ones where MNCs' subsidiary companies are incorporated.

When dealing with MNCs, the legal implications of their complex structure must be kept in mind. According to the definition provided by the 1977 Declaration of the Institut de Droit International, they are '[e]nterprises which consist of a decision-making centre located in one country and of operating centres, with or without legal personality, situated in one or more other countries'.[2] Likewise,

1 UNCTAD, 'World Investment Report: Transnational Corporations and the Internalization of R&D' (New York and Geneva: United Nations, 2005); 'World Investment Report: Transnational Corporations. Extractive Industries and Development' (New York and Geneva: United Nations, 2007); 'World Investment Report: Transnational Corporations, and the Infrastructure Challenge' (New York and Geneva: United Nations, 2008); 'World Investment Report: Transnational Corporations, Agricultural Production and Development' (New York and Geneva: United Nations, 2009).

2 Institut de Droit International, 'Multinational Enterprises (Second Commission, Rapporteur: Mr Berthold Goldman)', The Institute of International Law. Online.

pursuant to the 2012 OECD Guidelines on Multinational Enterprises, MNCs are 'companies or other entities established in more than one country and so linked that they may co-ordinate their operations in various ways. While one or more of these entities may be able to exercise a significant influence over the activities of others, their degree of autonomy within the enterprise may vary widely from one multinational enterprise to another'.[3]

It could be expected that, given the complex structure of MNCs, the global dimension of their business, and the transnational nature of their activities, international law should establish the legal framework to engage their accountability when they commit human rights and environmental abuses. However, this conclusion is only partially true. Indeed, if on the one hand international law has progressively evolved to the point of addressing the regulation of MNCs' activities, at least through soft-law instruments, on the other hand it does not provide for the possibility of victims of corporate abuse to file claims directly against MNCs before an international tribunal. Conversely, lawsuits can be lodged exclusively with national courts, with the risk of unsatisfactory outcomes because of the obstacles and the hurdles victims face and the inherently territorial limits by which domestic civil jurisdiction is generally constrained.

This chapter aims to explore MNCs' accountability for human rights and environmental abuse. It first examines the international law instruments providing for corporate accountability (§ 2). Assuming that international law does not yet provide victims with satisfactory remedies against corporate human rights and environmental abuses and pursuing the objective of assessing whether domestic civil remedies are more effective, it then overviews the case-law developed by the EU Member States' and the US courts (§ 3); third, convinced that the obstacles to access to home State courts should be removed, it examines the titles founding domestic civil jurisdiction, highlights their limits, and specifically tackles the controversial issue of extraterritorial jurisdiction (§§ 4 and 5); finally, it focuses on the prospects of the future case-law (§ 6).

2. Corporate Accountability under International Law

Starting from the 1970s, several international legal instruments providing for corporate accountability have been adopted: the OECD Guidelines for Multinational

Available HTTP: http://www.idi-iil.org/idiE/resolutionsE/1977_oslo_02_en.pdf (accessed 12 September 2013).

3 OECD, *OECD Guidelines for Multinational Enterprises* (OECD, 21 June 1976 (21 May 2011)), Concepts and Principles, para. 3. Hereinafter 'OECD Guidelines'.

Enterprises, the ILO Tripartite Declaration,[4] the UN Global Compact,[5] the UN Norms,[6] and the UNSRSG Guiding Principles.[7]

Standards of conduct established by the individual legal instruments have different scopes of subjective and objective application. While the ILO Tripartite Declaration, the UN Norms, and the Global Compact have a universal scope, the OECD Guidelines have just a regional one. As to their content, while the ILO Tripartite Declaration deals only with social rights protection, the other instruments have a broader scope of application, which generally refers to the whole areas affected by the conduct of MNCs. Among these areas are the environment, human and social rights protection, and the fight against corruption.

As far as environmental protection is concerned, the OECD Guidelines call upon MNCs 'within the framework of laws, regulations and administrative practices in the countries in which they operate, and in consideration of relevant international agreements, principles, objectives, and standards' to 'take due account of the need to protect the environment, public health and safety, and generally to conduct their activities in a manner contributing to the wider goal of sustainable development'.[8] To this aim, MNCs should establish and maintain a system of environmental management,[9] and assess and address the foreseeable environmental, health, and safety-related impacts of their activities,[10] while applying a precautionary approach.[11]

The latter version of the OECD Guidelines explicitly calls upon MNCs to protect human rights. 'Within the framework of internationally recognized human rights, the international human rights obligations of the countries in which they

---

4 ILO, 'ILO Tripartite Declaration of Principles Concerning Multinational Enterprises and Social Policy' (16 November 1977), no. 6. Hereinafter 'ILO Tripartite Declaration'.

5 United Nations, 'UN Global Compact'. Online. Available: HTTP: http://www.unglobalcompact.org/docs/ (accessed 5 March 2014).

6 UN Sub-Commission for the Promotion and Protection of Human Rights, 'Norms on the Responsibilities of Transnational Corporations and Other Business Enterprises with Regard to Human Rights' (UN Doc. E/CN.4/Sub.2/2003/12/Rev.2, 26 August 2003). Hereinafter 'UN Norms'.

7 UN Human Rights Council, 'Report of the Special Representative of the Secretary-General on the Issue of Human Rights and Transnational Corporations and Other Business Enterprises, John Ruggie: Guiding Principles on Business and Human Rights: Implementing the United Nations "Protect, Respect and Remedy" Framework Guiding Principles'. (9 April 2010, A/HRC/14/27). Hereinafter 'UNSRSG Guiding Principles'.

8 OECD, *OECD Guidelines for Multinational Enterprises*, Chapter VI. See, Elisa Morgera, 'An Environmental Outlook on the Oecd Guidelines for Multinational Enterprises: Comparative Advantage, Legitimacy, and Outstanding Questions in the Lead up to the 2006 Review', *Georgetown International Environmental Law Review* 18, no. 4 (2006): 751 ff.

9 OECD, *OECD Guidelines for Multinational Enterprises*, Chapter IV, para. 1.

10 Ibid., para. 3.

11 Ibid., para. 4.

operate as well as relevant domestic laws and regulations', Chapter IV recommends MNCs to respect human rights, to avoid causing or contributing to their violation, and to seek ways to prevent or mitigate adverse human rights impacts, through the carrying out of 'human rights due diligence as appropriate to their size, the nature and context of operations and the severity of the risks'.[12]

A similar approach is followed by the UNSRSG Guiding Principles. While the first pillar provides for the State duty to protect human rights and the third one for victims' access to remedy, the second focuses on corporate responsibility to respect human rights. Convinced that 'business enterprises can have an impact on virtually the entire spectrum of internationally recognized human rights',[13] the UNSRSG Guiding Principles call upon MNCs to address adverse human rights impacts, taking adequate measures for their prevention, mitigation, and, where appropriate, remediation.

As far as labour rights are concerned, the ILO Tripartite Declaration covers them. The standards provided therein inspire Chapter IV of the OECD Guidelines, the UN Norms, and Principles nos. 2–6 of the UN Global Compact. More specifically, all these instruments call upon MNCs to comply with the core labour standards listed by the 1998 ILO Declaration on Fundamental Principles and Rights at Work, i.e. freedom of association and the right to collective bargaining, the elimination of all forms of forced and compulsory labour, the effective abolition of child labour, and the elimination of discrimination. Taking into account the transnational reach of MNCs' activities, these instruments recommend that they 'observe standards of employment and industrial relations not less favourable than those observed by comparable employers in the host country'[14] and 'employ local personnel and provide training with a view to improving skill levels'.[15] Moreover, MNCs 'should provide the best possible wages, benefits and conditions of work, within the framework of government policies … at least adequate to satisfy the basic needs of workers and their families'.[16]

Finally, an important role is attributed to the fight against corruption. For instance, the tenth principle of the UN Global Compact, added in 2004, calls upon

12 Ibid., para. 5.

13 UN Human Rights Council, 'Report of the Special Representative of the Secretary-General on the Issue of Human Rights and Transnational Corporations and Other Business Enterprises, John Ruggie: Guiding Principles on Business and Human Rights: Implementing the United Nations "Protect, Respect and Remedy" Framework Guiding Principles', no. 12, Commentary. See, R. Mares, ed., *The UN Guiding Principles on Business and Human Rights: Foundations and Implementation* (Leiden: Nijhoff, 2012).

14 OECD, *OECD Guidelines for Multinational Enterprises*, Chapter IV, para. 4.

15 Ibid., para. 5.

16 ILO, 'ILO Tripartite Declaration of Principles Concerning Multinational Enterprises and Social Policy', para. 34. See H. Günter, 'The International Labour Office Declaration of Multinational Enterprises and the International Code of Conduct Movement', *Loyola of Los Angeles International and Comparative Law Review* 4, no. 1 (1981): 1 ff.

MNCs to avoid bribery, extortion and other forms of corruption, and to develop policies and concrete programmes to address corruption.[17] Likewise, the UN Norms[18] and the OECD Guidelines deal with the topic.[19]

Although all these legal instruments fill with details principles that are already established as binding at the international law level and address MNCs with recommendations that they are called to respect when operating abroad, it cannot be denied that their effects are still limited in practice. Indeed, their non-binding legal status and the lack of an adjudicatory body competent to supervise their application make their respect, when national law does not provide for it, voluntary and exclusively dependent on the corporations' goodwill. Taking these loopholes into consideration, this chapter focuses on the domestic approach to corporate accountability and on victims' access to justice before domestic courts, especially in the US and the EU Member States, where most MNCs are incorporated.

In so doing this chapter takes into account the recommendations provided by the third pillar of the UNSRSG Guiding Principles, according to which, 'States should take appropriate steps to ensure the effectiveness of domestic judicial mechanisms when addressing business-related human rights abuses, including considering ways to reduce legal, practical and other relevant barriers that could lead to a denial of access to remedy.'[20] In order to achieve this objective, States should eliminate barriers that prevent legitimate cases from being brought before their courts. Among the main areas of interest, the UNSRSG identifies: the attribution of legal responsibility among members of a corporate group; the protection of certain groups, such as indigenous peoples and migrants; the reduction of the costs connected to bringing claims, class actions, and other collective action procedures; the investigation of individual and business involvement in human rights-related crimes; the guarantee of judges' independence and opposition to corruption; the

17 United Nations, 'UN Global Compact', Principle no. 9; A. Shemberg, 'New Global Standards for Business and Human Rights', *Business Law International* 13, no. 1 (2012): 27 ff.; William H. Meyer and Boyka Stefanova, 'Human Rights, the UN Global Compact and Global Governance', *Cornell International Law Journal* 34 (2001): 501 ff.

18 UN Sub-Commission for the Promotion and Protection of Human Rights, 'Norms on the Responsibilities of Transnational Corporations and Other Business Enterprises with Regard to Human Rights', no. 10. See Larry Catá Backer, 'Multinational Corporations, Transnational Law: The United Nations' Norms on the Responsibilities of Transnational Corporations as a Harbinger of Corporate Social Responsibility in International Law', *Columbia Human Rights Law Review* 37, no. 2 (2006): 287 ff.; D. Weissbrodt and M. Kruger, 'Norms on the Responsibility of Transnational Corporations and Other Business Enterprises with Regard to Human Rights', *American Journal of International Law* 97, no. 4 (2003): 901 ff.

19 OECD, *OECD Guidelines for Multinational Enterprises*, Chapter VI.

20 UN Human Rights Council, 'Report of the Special Representative of the Secretary-General on the Issue of Human Rights and Transnational Corporations and Other Business Enterprises, John Ruggie: Guiding Principles on Business and Human Rights: Implementing the United Nations "Protect, Respect and Remedy" Framework Guiding Principles', no. 26.

avoidance of denial of justice in the host State; and the removal of obstacles to accessing home State courts.[21]

In light of these recommendations, this chapter looks at the EU and the US legal frameworks and their recent updates, convinced that the removal of the obstacles to access to home State courts should be implemented through the provision at domestic level of adequate heads of jurisdiction, including titles founding extraterritorial jurisdiction in cases characterized by extraterritorial reach and human rights and environmental concerns.

3. MNCs before the US and the EU Domestic Courts

During recent decades a number of lawsuits alleging the violation of human rights and environmental standards by MNCs operating abroad have been filed with the US and the EU Member States' courts. As regards the US case-law, federal courts found their jurisdiction on the Alien Tort Statute (ATS), which provides, 'The district courts shall have original jurisdiction of any civil action by an alien for a tort only, committed in violation of the law of nations or a treaty of the United States'.[22] Among the best-known cases, it is worth recalling: *Doe v Unocal*, which concerns the allegation of forced labour and slavery in Myanmar (settled in 2010);[23] *Presbyterian Church v Talisman Energy*, with the corporation accused of crimes against humanity in Sudan in complicity with the local army;[24] *In Re South African Apartheid*, concerning the complicity of the corporate defendants in the apartheid regime in South Africa;[25] and *Doe v Chevron Texaco*, regarding the massive environmental damage in Ecuador and Peru.[26] In this last case, the dispute led to the adoption by the Ecuador civil courts of an order to pay compensation

21 Ibid., Commentary.

22 Alien Tort Statute, U.S.C. § 1350. Hereinafter 'ATS'. On the federal case-law based on the ATS see: M. Koebele, *Corporate Responsibility under the Alien Tort Statute* (Leiden: Nijhoff, 2009). See also: A. Bonfanti, *Imprese multinazionali, diritti umani e ambiente. Profili di diritto internazionale pubblico e privato* (Milano: Giuffrè Editore, 2012), 311 ff.

23 United States Court of Appeals, Ninth Circuit, *Doe v Unocal*, 395 F.3d 932, 18 September 2002.

24 United States District Court, Southern District of New York, *The Presbyterian Church of Sudan et al. v Talisman Energy, Inc. and the Republic of Sudan*, 244 F.Supp.2d 289, 19 March 2003; United States Court of Appeals, Second Circuit, *The Presbyterian Church of Sudan et al. v Talisman Energy, Inc. and the Republic of Sudan*, 582 F.3d 244, 2 October 2009.

25 United States District Court, Southern District of New York, *In Re South African Apartheid Litigation*, 346 F.Supp.2d 538, S.D.N.Y., 2004, 29 November 2004; United States Court of Appeals, Second Circuit, *Khulumani v Barclay National Bank Ltd et al.*, 05-2141-cv, 05-2326-cv, 12 October 2007.

26 United States District Court, N.D. California, *Doe v Texaco, Inc.*, F.Supp.2d, 2006 WL 2053504, N.D. Cal., 2006, 21 July 2006.

amounting to USD 18 billion.[27] Other well-known cases involve Union Carbide and cross the jurisdictions of the United States and India, addressing the ecologic disaster in Bhopal, Madhya Pradesh (India) in 1984, which caused 500 deaths and some 25,000 individuals to suffer damage to their health.[28] The case was settled by agreement, with compensation amounting to USD 470 million.[29] Later, in 2011, seven managers of Union Carbide India were convicted by the Indian criminal courts.[30] Several disputes were also filed against Royal Dutch Shell for their conduct in Ogoniland (Niger Delta, Nigeria). Among them, it is worth mentioning two cases. The first is *Wiwa v Royal Dutch Shell*, an action brought by the family of Ken Saro-Wiwa, leader of the Movement for the Survival of the Ogoni People (MOSOP), with the allegation of complicity in human rights abuses against the Ogoni people, including summary execution, crimes against humanity, torture, inhumane treatment, arbitrary arrest, wrongful death, and assault and battery.[31] The dispute was settled out of court in 2009. The second case involved the allegation of analogous facts in *Kiobel v Royal Dutch*, which will be dealt with below.

Shell and Royal Dutch are also defendants in disputes currently pending before the Dutch civil courts. The civil court in The Hague recently adopted its decision in a case filed by Milieudefensie and four farmers from the villages of Goi, Ikot Ada Udo, and Oruma against Shell's international headquarters located in the Netherlands – Royal Dutch Shell – and Shell's Nigerian subsidiary,[32] concluding for the latter's civil responsibility in one case of oil pollution in the Niger Delta and ordering it to pay damages.[33] The English courts also have solved a number

27 *Corte Provincial de Justicia de Sucumbios, Sala Unica de la Corte Provincial de Justicia de Sucumbios*, Juicio No. 2011-0106, 3 January 2012. Online. Available HTTP: http://www.redibec.org/pdf/sentencia_TEXACO2.pdf (accessed 8 July 2014).

28 United States District Court, Southern District of New York, *In re Union Carbide Corp. Gas Plant Disaster at Bhopal, India in December, 1984*, 634 F.Supp. 842, S.D.N.Y., 1986, 12 May 1986. See T. Scovazzi, 'Industrial Accidents and the Veil of Transnational Corporations', in *International Responsibility for Environmental Harm*, ed. F. Francioni and T. Scovazzi (London/Dordrecht/Boston: Graham & Trotman, 1991), 395 ff.

29 See Amnesty International, 'Clouds of Injustice. Bophal Disaster 20 Years On' (29 November 2004). Online. Available HTTP: www.amnesty.org (accessed 12 September 2013), citing Civil Appeal Nos. 3187–89, *Union Carbide Corporation v Union of India*, Supreme Court of India.

30 T. Scovazzi, 'La sentenza penale sulla catastrofe di Bhopal', *Rivista Giuridica dell'Ambiente* 26 (2011): 553.

31 United States District Court for the Southern District of New York, *Ken Wiwa et al. v Royal Dutch Petroleum Company and Shell Transport and Trading Company plc.*, F.Supp.2d, 2002 WL 319887 S.D.N.Y., 28 February 2002.

32 District Court of The Hague, *Oguru, Elfanga, Vereniging Milieudefensie v Shell Petroleum N.V and The Shell Transport and Trading Company Limited*, C/09/330891 / HA ZA 09-0579 and C/09/365498 HA ZA 10-1677, 30 January 2013.

33 See also Court of The Hague, Civil Law Section, *Plaintiff 1, Plaintiff 2, Vereniging Milieudefensie, v Royal Dutch Shell Plc, Shell Petroleum Development Company Of Nigeria*

of cases concerning the corporate civil responsibility for human rights violations put in place overseas by English MNCs. Among them are disputes concerning the violations of the right to health of several workers employed at the South African and Namibian premises of the English parent corporations Thor Chemicals, Cape PLC, and RTZ,[34] as well as the lawsuit brought by 32 indigenous Peruvians against a company incorporated in England accused of having aided and abetted their torture and mistreatment by the Peruvian police.[35] Also well known is the *Trafigura* case, with 30,000 plaintiffs from Côte d'Ivoire alleging the responsibility of the London office of Trafigura, a Dutch international petroleum trader, for having chartered the ship Probo Koala that was accused of having unloaded a toxic waste shipment at Abidjan.[36]

While the US courts base their jurisdiction on the ATS, the EU Member States' domestic courts found it on the titles established by EC Regulation No 44/2001,[37] as recently recasted within EU Regulation No 1215/2012.[38] It is worth noting that the disputes solved by the US and the EU courts share a crucial point. Human

---

Ltd., 330891 / HA ZA 09-579, Judgment in motion contesting jurisdiction, 30 December 2009.

34 House of Lords, *Lubbe v Cape PLC*, [2000] WL 976033, 20 July 2000; House of Lords, *Connelly v RTZ Corporation Plc*, [1997] 3 WLR 373, 24 July 1997; Court of Appeal of England and Wales, *Ngcobo v Thor Chemicals Holdings Ltd.*, 1995 WL 1082070, 9 October 1995; Court of Appeal of England and Wales, *Sithole and Others v Thor Chemical Holdings Ltd.*, 1999 WL 477489, 3 February 1999. See R. Meeran, 'Tort Litigation against Multinational Corporations for Violation of Human Rights: An Overview of the Position Outside the United States', *City University of Hong Kong Law Review* 3, no. 1 (2011): 1 ff.; Halina Ward, 'Securing Transnational Corporate Accountability through National Courts: Implications and Policy Options', *Hastings International and Comparative Law Review* 24, no. 3 (2001): 451 ff.; C.G.J. Morse, 'Not in the Public Interest? Lubbe V. Cape PLC', *Texas International Law Journal* 37, no. 3 (2002): 541 ff.; P. Muchlinski, 'Corporations in International Litigation: Problems of Jurisdiction and the United Kingdom Asbestos Cases', *International and Comparative Law Quarterly* 50, no. 1 (2001): 1 ff. On the European case law see also L.F.H. Enneking, 'Crossing the Atlantic? The Political and Legal Feasibility of European Foreign Direct Liability Cases', *George Washington International Law Review* 40, no. 4 (2009): 904 ff.; Jan Wouters and Cedric Ryngaert, 'Litigation for Overseas Corporate Human Rights Abuses in the European Union: The Challenge for Jurisdiction', *George Washington International Law Review* 40, no. 4 (2009): 939 ff.

35 High Court of Justice Queen's Bench Division, *Mario Alberto Tabra Guerrero v Monterrico Metals PLC, Rio Blanco Copper SA*, 2009 WL 3171890, 16 October 2009.

36 C.O. García-Castrillón, 'International Litigation Trends in Environmental Liability: A European Union–United States Comparative Perspective', *Journal of Private International Law* 7, no. 3 (2011): 551 ff.

37 Council Regulation (EC) No 44/2001 of 22 December 2000 on jurisdiction and the recognition and enforcement of judgments in civil and commercial matters, 16 January 2001. Hereinafter 'Regulation No 44/2001'.

38 Regulation (EU) No 1215/2012 of the European Parliament and of the Council of 12 December 2012 on jurisdiction and the recognition and enforcement of judgments

rights and environmental abuses committed by MNCs overseas are characterized by their extraterritorial reach, the legal effect of which negatively affects and dramatically exacerbates the claimants' burden of proof. Moreover, disputes involving MNCs as defendants are often characterized by the complexity of piercing their corporate veil, i.e. reconciling the MNC's legal structure, formally composed of a cluster of multiple independent legal entities connected through the principle of limited responsibility, with its economic unity, under the sole direction of the parent corporation. As in similar cases lawsuits are filed against legal entities composed of parent and subsidiary companies incorporated within the territory of different States, the identification of the civil court competent to adjudicate the arising whole dispute is particularly complex. In light of these premises, the author submits that home state courts' civil extraterritorial jurisdiction can be a useful, if not necessary, tool to ensure victims an adequate access to justice in cases involving MNCs as defendants. This chapter aims to examine whether and to what extent the domestic legal orders of the countries where most MNCs originate, the US and the EU, provide for it.

4. Civil Jurisdiction Pursuant to the EU Legal Framework

The attribution of jurisdiction in civil and commercial matters at EU level is governed by EC Regulation No 44/2001 and its recasted version, EU Regulation No 1215/2012, which will be applicable to legal proceedings instituted from 10 January 2015.[39] The latter is the outcome of the recasting process that originated in April 2009.[40] Pursuant to both Regulations, civil jurisdiction is attributed to the EU Member States' courts in disputes involving defendants domiciled in EU territory,[41] while defendants domiciled outside the EU can be brought before the EU courts if it is so provided under the domestic law of the single Member States.[42]

According to the European Commission's Proposal presented in December 2010, 'in order to promote the interests of claimants and defendants and promote the proper administration of justice within the Union, the circumstance that the defendant is domiciled in a third State should [have] no longer entail[ed] the non-application of certain Union rules on jurisdiction, and there should [have] no

---

in civil and commercial matters (recast), 20 December 2012. Hereinafter 'Regulation No 1215/2012'.

39 Regulation No 1215/2012, art. 66(1).

40 Commission of the European Communities, 'Green Paper on the Review of Council Regulation (EC) No 44/2001 on Jurisdiction and the Recognition and Enforcement of Judgments in Civil and Commercial Matters' (Brussels: Commission of the European Communities, 21 April 2009).

41 Regulation No 44/2001, art. 2(1); Regulation No 1215/2012, art 4(1).

42 Regulation No 44/2001, art. 4(1); Regulation No 1215/2012, art. 6(1).

longer be[en] any referral to national law'.[43] In the same vein, the Commission's Proposal deleted article 4(1) of Regulation No 44/2001, according to which, 'If the defendant is not domiciled in a Member State, the jurisdiction of the courts of each Member State shall [...] be determined by the law of that Member State', including the 'exorbitant' criteria listed in Annex I to the Regulation and dealt with below.

Further, considering that 'access to justice in the EU is overall unsatisfactory in disputes involving defendants from outside the EU',[44] the Commission's Proposal aimed at introducing two main amendments. First, it provided for the extension of the scope of application of the rules on special jurisdiction to disputes involving third-States-domiciled defendants. Second, it added two harmonized titles of jurisdiction, the first establishing that non-EU defendants could be sued at the place where their moveable assets were located ('subsidiary jurisdiction'), and the second consisting of a *forum necessitatis*. Pursuant to the latter, the courts of a Member State should have exercised their jurisdiction only if no other forum guaranteeing the right to a fair trial was available and the dispute had a sufficient connection with the Member State concerned. Through its exceptional character, *forum necessitatis* pursued the aim of guaranteeing the right to a fair trial.

The outcomes of the recasting might have dramatically impacted the basic principles founding the personal scope of civil jurisdiction at EU level. However, such amendments were not endorsed by the European Parliament,[45] which,

---

43 European Commission, 'Proposal for a Regulation of the European Parliament and of the Council on Jurisdiction and the Recognition and Enforcement of Judgments in Civil and Commercial Matters' (Brussels: European Commission, 14 December 2010). Hereinafter 'Commission's Proposal'. See A. Bonfanti, 'Diritti umani e imprese multinazionali dinanzi ai giudici europei: sulla revisione del Regolamento (CE) N. 44/2001', *Rivista di diritto internazionale privato e processuale* 47 no. 3 (2011): 697 ff.; N. Boschiero, 'Il funzionamento del Regolamento Bruxelles I nell'ordinamento internazionale: note sulle modifiche contenute nella Proposta di rifusione del 2011', *Diritto del commercio internazionale* 26 (2012): 253 ff.; Lorna Gillies, 'Creation of Subsidiary Jurisdiction Rules in the Recast of Brussels I: Back to the Drawing Board?', *Journal of Private International Law* 8, no. 3 (2012): 489 ff.; F. Pocar, I. Viarengo, and F.C. Villata, eds, *Recasting Brussels I* (Padova: CEDAM, 2012).

44 European Commission, 'Proposal for a Regulation of the European Parliament and of the Council on Jurisdiction and the Recognition and Enforcement of Judgments in Civil and Commercial Matters', 3.

45 According to the Parliament, 'Although the Commission retains its monopoly power of initiative post-Lisbon, it cannot simply ignore the sentiments of the democratically-elected Parliament, which took the view that it would be premature to take this step without wide-ranging consultations and political debate': European Parliament Committee on Legal Affairs, 'Draft Report on the Proposal for a Regulation of the European Parliament and of the Council on Jurisdiction and the Recognition and Enforcement of Judgments in Civil and Commercial Matters (Recast)', (Brussels: European Parliament, 28 June 2011), 2010/0383(COD), (COM2010/0747 – C7-433/2010 – 10/0383 COD).

jointly with the Council, proceeded to modify the Commission's Proposal to the point of deleting all of the amendments[46] and adopting EU Regulation No 1215/2012.

Under both Regulations No. 44/2001 and 1215/2012, EU courts are allowed to exercise only a limited extraterritorial jurisdiction. Indeed, both identify the defendant's domicile as the basic condition for their applicability and as the general criterion of jurisdiction, leaving Member States free to apply the so-called domestic 'exorbitant criteria' in cases involving defendants not domiciled in the EU.[47] 'Exorbitant criteria' consist of titles of jurisdiction providing the domestic courts with the power to adjudicate disputes less strictly connected with the national territory than the criteria set forth by the Regulations.

Therefore, given these premises, actions against corporations accused of committing human rights and environmental abuses outside the EU territory can be lodged with Member States' courts only in two cases: either under arts. 4 and 63 of Regulation No 1215/2012, corresponding to arts. 2 and 60 of Regulation No 44/2001, when they are domiciled, through their incorporation, in an EU Member State; or, if they do not originate from an EU Member State, on the basis of the domestic exorbitant criteria applicable under art. 6(1) of the former and 4(1) of the latter. Examples of exorbitant titles are those established by English, Finnish, Maltese, Slovak, and Polish law, providing their civil courts with jurisdiction when the defendant is present in the national territory,[48] as well as those provided under the law of Austria, the Czech Republic, Denmark, the UK, Estonia, Finland, Germany, Lithuania, Poland, Sweden, Latvia, Slovenia, and Slovakia, attributing the jurisdiction to the domestic courts when certain defendants' assets are located therein,[49] or those established under the law of Cyprus, Poland, and Portugal,

46 Council of the European Union, 'Proposal for a Regulation of the European Parliament and of the Council on Jurisdiction and the Recognition and Enforcement of Judgments in Civil and Commercial Matters (Recast) – First Reading – General Approach, 10609/12' (Brussels: Council of the European Union, 1 June 2012), ADD1, JUSTCIV 209, CODEC 1975.

47 Art. 6(1) Regulation No 1215/2012; art. 4(1) Regulation No 44/2001.

48 Arnaud Nuyts, 'Study on Residual Jurisdiction (Review of the Member States' Rules Concerning the "Residual Jurisdiction" of Their Courts in Civil and Commercial Matters Pursuant to the Brussels I and II Regulations)' (Brussels: European Commission, 3 September 2007), 58 ff. Hereinafter 'Study on Residual Jurisdiction'. In the UK a foreign corporation is deemed present within the jurisdiction if it has an establishment there, regardless of whether the claim relates to it; conversely, courts in the Netherlands exercise jurisdiction only on claims connected to the foreign corporation's branch present on the Dutch territory. Similar restrictions apply in France, Italy, Latvia, Lithuania, Luxembourg, Romania, Slovakia, Slovenia, Spain, and Sweden. See: International Law Association, 'International Civil Litigation and the Interest of the Public', paper presented at the Sofia Conference, Pisa, 18–25 October 2012, 1–8 at 7.

49 Nuyts, 'Study on Residual Jurisdiction (Review of the Member States' Rules Concerning the 'Residual Jurisdiction' of Their Courts in Civil and Commercial Matters

founding the courts' jurisdiction when certain defendants' activities are present therein.[50] Besides, according to the rules on jurisdiction in tort disputes, the laws of 23 Member States provide that courts can be seized when the tort occurs in the territory of the State, to be intended as the place where either the damage or the event giving rise to the damage occurred, or both.[51] Moreover, claims against multiple defendants domiciled outside the EU can be consolidated before the courts of all the Member States, except for Denmark, Finland, Germany, Greece, Malta, Poland, and Sweden, provided that a connection between the claims exists.[52] In accordance with the domestic law of Austria, Belgium, Denmark, Finland, France, Germany, Greece, Italy, Luxembourg, the Netherlands, Poland, Portugal, Romania, Spain, and Sweden, victims of crimes are permitted to seek monetary compensation in civil actions within criminal proceedings based on universal jurisdiction.[53] Claims can also be lodged in ten Member States (Austria, Belgium, Estonia, the Netherlands, Portugal, Romania, France, Germany, Luxembourg, and Poland) on the basis of *forum necessitatis*.[54] These countries generally condition its application upon two separate requirements. First, claimants must demonstrate that some kind of obstacle prevents them from obtaining justice abroad[55] or that factual obstacles to effectively enforcing the rights abroad occur.[56] Second, claimants must prove that some connection exists with the *forum*. Contacts may be relevant depending on the circumstances: for instance, it might be relevant that the claimant is domiciled or habitually resident in the forum State,[57] that he/she is

Pursuant to the Brussels I and II Regulations)', 58 ff.

50 Ibid., 34.

51 International Law Association, 'International Civil Litigation and the Interest of the Public', 11.

52 Nuyts, 'Study on Residual Jurisdiction (Review of the Member States' Rules Concerning the "Residual Jurisdiction" of Their Courts in Civil and Commercial Matters Pursuant to the Brussels I and II Regulations)', 51–53.

53 Supreme Court of the United States, Kiobel, Brief of the European Commission on Behalf of the European Union as amicus curiae in support of either party, 13 June 2012, p. 18.

54 Nuyts, 'Study on Residual Jurisdiction (Review of the Member States' Rules Concerning the "Residual Jurisdiction" of Their Courts in Civil and Commercial Matters Pursuant to the Brussels I and II Regulations)', 64.

55 This means either that foreign courts lack jurisdiction to hear the claim (this is provided under Polish law), that they have already rejected it for lack of jurisdiction (as established under Romanian law), or that it is 'unreasonable' (as provided under Belgian law) or 'unacceptable' (Austrian law) to bring proceedings abroad. See ibid., 65.

56 For instance, this happens when claimants would be subject to major threats if placing foot on the foreign soil, where the foreign country is affected by war, flooding or other disasters (this is provided by French law), or the cost of bringing proceedings abroad would be 'out of proportion' (as established under Belgian law). See ibid., 66.

57 This is provided under Austrian law: ibid.

a citizen of that State, or that assets belonging to him/her are located there.[58] There is only one country where such condition is not required – the Netherlands.[59]

With this overall picture in mind, as a concluding and general remark it can be noted that under the EU Regulations overseas corporate human rights and environmental abuses can be adjudicated by EU courts in two cases: either when they are ascribed to companies incorporated within the EU, or, in cases of non-EU incorporated defendants, when it is so provided under one of the above-mentioned exorbitant criteria. The latter titles of jurisdiction can found a limited extraterritorial jurisdiction.

5. Civil Jurisdiction under the ATS: The US Supreme Court's Opinion in *Kiobel*

Under the EU Regulations extraterritorial civil jurisdiction is limited. Likewise the interpretation released by the US Supreme Court in its Opinion adopted on 17 April 2013 in *Kiobel v. Royal Dutch Petroleum Co.* ('the Opinion')[60] dramatically

58 Ibid. This is provided by Belgian and French law.

59 According to Dutch law, the impossibility of bringing the claims outside, because of either the lack of competent forum abroad or the occurrence of natural disasters or wars, is the source of a kind of universal jurisdiction. However, in the event that it is merely 'unacceptable' to require the claimant to have his/her claims adjudicated by foreign courts (for instance, because he/she cannot expect to receive a fair trial due to discriminatory legal and societal practices and rules), the courts can assume civil jurisdiction only provided that the claims are sufficiently connected to the Dutch legal order. Dutch Code of Civil Procedure, art 9(b), (c). See Supreme Court of the United States, Kiobel, Brief of Professor Alex-Geert Castermans (Leiden University), Professor Cees Van Dam (Utrecht University), Dr Nicola Jägers (Tilburg University), and Professor Menno Kamminga (Maastricht University) as amici curiae in support of petitioners, 13 June 2012, 22–23.

60 Supreme Court of the United States, *Esther Kiobel, Individually and on Behalf of Her Late Husband, Dr. Barinem Kiobel, et al., Petitioners v Royal Dutch Petroleum Co. et al.*, No. 10–1491, 17 April 2013. Hereinafter 'Supreme Court of the United States, Kiobel'. On this case see R.P. Alford, 'Human Rights After Kiobel: Choice of Law and the Human Rights After Kiobel: Choice of Law and the Rise of Transnational Tort Litigation', *Emory Law Journal* 63 (2014): 1089 ff.; W.C. Cash, 'Sosa's Silence: Kiobel and the Fallacy of the Supreme Court's Limitation on Alien Tort Liability', *Denver Journal of International Law and Policy* 41, no. 1 (2012–13): 101 ff.; J.M. Stanisz, 'The Expansion of Limited Liability Protection in the Corporate Form: The Aftermath of Kiobel v. Royal Dutch Petroleum Co.', *Brooklyn Journal of Corporate, Financial and Commercial Law* 5, no. 2 (2011): 573; M. Theophila, '"Moral Monsters" under the Bed: Holding Corporations Accountable for Violations of the Alien Tort Statute after Kiobel V. Royal Dutch Petroleum Co.', *Fordham Law Review* 79, no. 6 (2011): 2862 ff.; N. Erb and O. Pell, 'Kiobel's New Focus on Extraterritoriality under the Alien Tort Statute Could Put Resolution of the Corporate Liability Issues Indefinitely out of Reach', *Georgetown Journal of International Law* 43, no. 4 (2012): 1073 ff. On the Opinion, see A. Bonfanti, 'Kiobel: No Extraterritorial Jurisdiction under the Alien Tort Statute. Which Forum for Disputes on Overseas Corporate

reduces the extraterritorial reach of the US federal courts under the ATS. Pursuant to the latter, 'The district courts shall have original jurisdiction of any civil action by an alien for a tort only, committed in violation of the law of nations or a treaty of the United States'.[61]

The case was brought by Nigerian plaintiffs – who in the 1990s lived in the Niger Delta area of Ogoniland and before filing the complaint had been granted political asylum and had started residing in the US – against Royal Dutch Petroleum Company and Shell Transport and Trading Company. The latter were holding companies incorporated in the Netherlands and UK respectively. Their joint subsidiary, Shell Petroleum Development Company of Nigeria, Ltd (SPDC), incorporated in Nigeria, was engaged in oil exploration and production in Ogoniland. The defendants were present in the US through an Investment Relations Office established in New York City and their shares were traded on the New York Stock Exchange.. According to the plaintiffs, the defendants had violated the law of nations by aiding and abetting the Nigerian Government in committing extrajudicial killings, crimes against humanity, torture and cruel treatment, arbitrary arrest and detention, violations of the rights to life, liberty, security, and association, forced exile, and property destruction. The District Court confirmed its jurisdiction on the plaintiffs' allegations of crimes against humanity, torture, and arbitrary arrest and detention.[62]

After having the Second Circuit dismissed the entire complaint on the ground that the law of nations does not recognize corporate liability,[63] the US Supreme Court granted certiorari to consider the question. In so doing, it directed the parties to file supplemental briefs addressing the additional issue, 'Whether and under what circumstances the [ATS] allows courts to recognize a cause of action for violations of the law of nations occurring within the territory of a sovereign other than the

Human Rights Violations?', *Diritti umani e diritto internazionale* 7, no. 2 (2013): 379 ff.; N. Boschiero, 'Corporate Responsibility in Transnational Human Rights Cases: The U.S. Supreme Court Decision in Kiobel v. Royal Dutch Petroleum', *Rivista di diritto internazionale privato e processuale* 49, no. 2 (2013): 249 ff.; C.A. Bradley, 'Supreme Court Holds That Alien Tort Statute Does Not Apply to Conduct in Foreign Countries', *ASIL Insights* 17, no. 12 (18 April 2013). Online. Available HTTP: http://www.asil.org/insights/volume/17/issue/12/supreme-court-holds-alien-tort-statute-does-not-apply-conduct-foreign (accessed 12 September 2013); D. Cassel, 'Suing Americans for Human Rights Torts Overseas: The Supreme Court Leaves the Door Open', *Notre Dame Law Review 89*, (2014): 1773 ff.

61 Alien Tort Statute, U.S.C. § 1350.

62 United States District Court, Southern District of New York, *Esther Kiobel et al. v Royal Dutch Petroleum Co., Shell Transport and Trading Company Plc.*, 456 F.Supp.2d 457 (2006), 29 September 2006.

63 United States Court of Appeals for the Second Circuit, *Esther Kiobel et al. v Royal Dutch Petroleum Co., Shell Transport and Trading Company PLC.*, 06-4800-cv, 06-4876-cv, 17 September 2010.

United States'.[64] The Opinion exclusively focuses on this latter discussion point. Confirming the decision on appeal, it concludes, 'all the relevant conduct took place outside the United States. And even where the claims touch and concern the territory of the United States, they must do so with sufficient force to displace the presumption against extraterritorial application. Corporations are often present in many countries, and it would reach too far to say that mere corporate presence suffices'.[65]

Therefore, as a matter of fact, the Opinion denies that the ATS provides the US federal courts with jurisdiction in the so-called 'foreign-cubed cases', i.e. the cases brought by foreign plaintiffs complaining against foreign defendants for international law violations committed abroad. In so doing, the Opinion overturns some of the best-known past cases, such as *Filartiga*[66] *and Marcos*,[67] and even *Sosa*.[68] In the *Filartiga* case, neither the plaintiffs nor the defendants were American nationals, and the actions underlying the lawsuit had taken place abroad, but the defendant had 'resided in the United States for more than nine months' before being sued, while in *Marcos*, a month before being sued, the defendant, 'his family [...] and others loyal to [him] fled to Hawaii', where the case was heard. In both cases the jurisdiction was deemed proper because the alleged conduct violated a well-established international law norm. Conversely, in *Sosa*, the jurisdiction was rejected exclusively because the plaintiff's claim for arbitrary arrest and detention failed to state a violation of the law of nations with the requisite 'definite content and acceptance among civilized nations'. The power of the federal court to adjudicate a foreign-cubed case was not under discussion.

Comparable conditions occurred in *Kiobel*. The plaintiffs were Nigerian citizens, granted political asylum and residing in the US at the time of filing the suit. Even though the defendant companies were incorporated in the Netherlands and the UK, their office in New York City was considered as a sufficient tie with the US territory under the personal jurisdiction doctrine. Conversely, their joint Nigerian subsidiary was dismissed from the case, with the minimum contacts with the US not having been proven.[69] As in *Filartiga* and *Marcos*, according to

64 Supreme Court of the United States, *Kiobel, Esther, et al. v Royal Dutch Petroleum, et al.*, No. 10-1491, Order in pending case, 5 March 2012.

65 Supreme Court of the United States, Kiobel, Opinion, p. 14.

66 United States Court of Appeals for the Second Circuit, *Filartiga v Pena-Irala*, 630 F.2d 876 (2d Cir. 1980), 30 June 1980.

67 United States Court of Appeals for the Ninth Circuit, *In re Estate of Ferdinand Marcos*, 25 F.3d 1467 (9th Cir.1994), 16 June 1994.

68 Supreme Court of the United States, *Jose Francisco Sosa v. Humberto Alvarez-Machain et al.*, 542 U.S. 692 (2004), 29 June 2004. Supreme Court of the United States, Kiobel, Justice Breyer concurring, p. 9; Supreme Court of the United States, Kiobel, Supplemental Brief of Amici Curiae. International Law Scholars in Support of Petitioners, 13 June 2012, 10. Hereinafter 'Supreme Court of the United States, Kiobel, Brief of Amici Curiae. International Law Scholars in Support of Petitioners'.

69 I. Mooreville, 'Kiobel Insta-Symposium: Questions of Personal Jurisdiction Lurk beneath the Surface', *Opinio Juris* (19 April 2013). Online. Available HTTP: opiniojuris.

the District Court for the Southern District of New York, three of the plaintiffs' allegations concerned violations of the law of nations complying with the *Sosa* standard, i.e. crimes against humanity, torture, and arbitrary arrest and detention. Likewise, the actions underlying the lawsuit had taken place abroad.

Given these premises, a number of problematic issues arise from the Opinion. As highlighted by Justice Alito, the formulation according to which 'when the claims touch and concern the territory of the United States, they must do so with sufficient force to displace the presumption against extraterritorial application', leaves much unanswered.[70] More specifically, in Justice Breyer's view, § 403 of the Restatement of the Law Third may legitimize the exercise of jurisdiction when 'the defendant's conduct substantially and adversely affects an important American national interest, and that includes a distinct interest in preventing the United States from becoming a safe harbor (free of civil as well as criminal liability) for a torturer or other common enemy of mankind'.[71] The interest of the US in not being a safe harbour for the violators of the most fundamental human rights and in granting access to justice to victims of human rights abuses could have led the Supreme Court to conclude that the claims touch and concern the territory of the US with sufficient force to displace the presumption against extraterritorial application. This conclusion is far clearer if one recalls that, at least before *Kiobel*, the ATS was generally considered to provide federal courts with universal civil jurisdiction.

Universal jurisdiction is ruled under § 404 of the Restatement of the Law Third, pursuant to which, 'A State has jurisdiction to define and prescribe punishment for certain offences recognized by the community of nations as of universal concern, such as piracy, slave trade, attacks or hijacking of aircraft, genocide, war crimes, and perhaps certain acts of terrorism, even when none of the basis of jurisdiction indicated in § 402 is present'. As to the status of universal jurisdiction, the Comment to the Restatement recognizes that the subjection of the offences listed in § 404 to universal jurisdiction is a matter of customary law; however, it adds that treaties can extend universal jurisdiction to additional offences. As to the means through which universal jurisdiction is exercised at domestic level, even if it is generally implemented in the form of criminal law, under international law the application of non-criminal law, such as tort law, is not precluded.[72]

The ATS might be considered – or might have been considered, before *Kiobel* – as an example of domestic provision for universal civil jurisdiction, as it aims at providing civil remedies to the foreign victims of torts arising from the violation of only those international law provisions the application of which is universally condemned. In the author's view, this characterization is today uncertain. The

---

org (accessed 8 July 2014).

70 Supreme Court of the United States, Kiobel, Justice Alito concurring, 1.

71 Supreme Court of the United States, Kiobel, Justice Breyer concurring, 7.

72 Restatement of the Law Third, § 404, Comment. American Law Institute, Restatement of the Law Third, The Foreign Relations Law of the United States, v 1, 14 May 1986.

possibility to continue to consider it as providing for universal jurisdiction after *Kiobel* must be tested against the Court's representation, according to which 'there is no indication that the ATS was passed to make the United States a uniquely hospitable forum for the enforcement of international norms'.[73] This conclusion contravenes the previous federal case law, according to which the US interest in vindicating international human rights violations was even a factor militating in favour of *forum non conveniens* rejection when 'requiring plaintiffs to seek justice in the courts of an allegedly genocidal regime bent on their extermination would be a grotesque miscarriage of justice, and the case law concerning comity precludes such a result'.[74]

It must be added that, regardless that 'in the thirty-two years since *Filartiga* was announced, not a single court has questioned the relevance of the transitory tort doctrine in analyzing the reach of the ATS' in founding the federal courts' personal jurisdiction,[75] the Supreme Court in *Kiobel* concluded that 'the doctrine is inapposite here'.[76] In so doing, the Court made a distinction between cases falling within the ATS's scope of application and those that, even if personal jurisdiction is proven, nonetheless cannot be adjudicated by federal courts on that basis. The distinction lies in the plaintiffs' place of incorporation and in the localization of the relevant conduct: 'The question here is not whether petitioners have stated a proper claim under the ATS, but whether a claim may reach conduct occurring in the territory of a foreign sovereign'.[77] As in *Kiobel* all the relevant conduct took place in the area of the Niger Delta and the plaintiffs were incorporated in the UK and the Netherlands, 'even if the New York office were a sufficient basis for asserting general jurisdiction [...] it would be farfetched to believe, based solely upon the defendants' minimal and indirect American presence, that this legal action helps to vindicate a distinct American interest, such as in not providing a safe harbor for an "enemy of all mankind"'.[78] Therefore, in *Kiobel* and presumably in the future comparable cases, 'the parties and relevant conduct lack sufficient ties to the United States for the ATS to provide jurisdiction'.[79]

73 Supreme Court of the United States, Kiobel, Opinion, p. 12.

74 United States District Court, Southern District of New York, *The Presbyterian Church of Sudan et al. v Talisman Energy, Inc. and the Republic of Sudan*, 19 March 2003.

75 Supreme Court of the United States, Kiobel, Brief of Amici Curiae. International Law Scholars, p. 17.

76 Supreme Court of the United States, Kiobel, Syllabus, p. 2.

77 Supreme Court of the United States, Kiobel, Opinion, p. 4.

78 Supreme Court of the United States, Kiobel, Justice Breyer concurring, 14.

79 Ibid., 2.

6. The US Supreme Court's Opinion in *Daimler*

The US Supreme Court confirmed and strengthened the conclusions reached in *Kiobel* in its Opinion in *Daimler AG v. Bauman et al*, adopted on 14 Janaury 2014.[80] The case was lodged by 22 residents of Argentina against DaimlerChrysler (hereinafter Daimler), a German public stock company, alleging that the Daimler's Argentinean subsidiary, Mercedes Benz Argentina (hereinafter MB), collaborated with the security forces during the 'dirty war' to kidnap, torture, detain and kill certain MB workers, among them plaintiffs or persons closely related to them. Pursuant to the plaintiffs, personal jurisdiction over Daimler was based on the contacts with California of the Daimler's US subsidiary (MBUSA), a company incorporated in Delaware with its principal place of business in New Jersey.[81]

Following the restrictive interpretation developed in *Kiobel*, the Court denied that Daimler could be amenable to suit in California under the ATS for conducts put in place outside the United States by mean of a foreign subsidiary. As a matter of fact, according to the Court, neither the subsidiary could be considered as satisfying the agency theory – preliminary to engaging Daimler's civil responsibility – nor its contacts with the US territory were sufficient to identify it as 'at home' within the United States. Thus, the general jurisdiction criterion was not fulfilled and federal jurisdiction could not be established under the ATS.

With regard to the latter issue, the Court followed a very narrow approach. As already well established, general jurisdiction can be exercised when a foreign corporation's 'continuous corporate operations within a state [are] so substantial and of such a nature as to justify suit against it on causes of action arising from dealings entirely distinct from those activities'.[82] Pursuant to the Opinion, this situation occurs when the corporation's place of incorporation and its principal place of business are located in the territory of the *forum*; conversely, the criterion is not satisfied when a corporation merely 'engages in a substantial, continuous, and systematic course of business'.[83] Considered that neither Daimler nor MBUSA is incorporated in California, nor does either entity have its principal place of

80 Supreme Court of the United States, Daimler AG v. Bauman et al.,No. 11–965, 14 January 2014. Hereinafter 'Supreme Court of the United States, Daimler'.

81 On *Daimler* see: K. Anderson, 'Legally Distinct Corporate Entities and Agency Theory in Bauman v. Daimler AG and Kiobel', *Opinio Juris*. Online. Available HTTP http://opiniojuris.org/2013/10/19/legally-distinct-corporate-entities-agency-theory-bauman-v-daimler-ag-kiobel/ (accessed 25 July 2014); W. Baude, 'Opinion Recap: a Stricter View of General Jurisdiction', *SCOTUSblog* (15 January 2014). Online. Available HTTP: http://www.scotusblog.com/2014/01/opinion-recap-a-stricter-view-of-general-jurisdiction/ (accessed 25 July 2014); L. Denniston, 'Argument recap: Trying to salvage a lost cause', *SCOTUSblog*. Online. Available HTTP: http://www.scotusblog.com/2013/10/argument-recap-trying-to-salvage-a-lost-cause/ (accessed 25 July 2014).

82 Supreme Court of the United States, Daimler, 8.

83 Ibid., 18-19.

business there, the title of general jurisdiction is not fulfilled. Moreover, in the Court's view, the transnational context of the dispute supports this conclusion.[84]

The restrictive approach followed by the Court adds significant details to the conclusions reached in *Kiobel* and is likely to have a limiting effect on the application of the ATS in disputes involving multinational corporations as defendants. As correctly affirmed by Justice Sotomayor, concurring in the judgment,

> the Court acknowledges that Mercedes-Benz USA, LLC (MBUSA), Daimler's wholly owned subsidiary, has considerable contacts with California. It has multiple facilities in the State, including a regional headquarters. Each year, it distributes in California tens of thousands of cars, the sale of which generated billions of dollars in the year this suit was brought. And it provides service and sales support to customers throughout the State. Daimler has conceded that California courts may exercise general jurisdiction over MBUSA on the basis of these contacts, and the Court assumes that MBUSA's contacts may be attributed to Daimler for the purpose of deciding whether Daimler is also subject to general jurisdiction.

Nonetheless, the Court holds that all these factors are not sufficient to permit the exercise of general jurisdiction over Daimler, not because 'the contacts with California are too few, but because its contacts with other forums are too many'.[85].

By stating that Daimler's contacts must be viewed in the context of its extensive 'nationwide and worldwide'[86] operations, the Court allows multinational corporations to be considered as 'too big for general jurisdiction'.[87] In fact, instead of focusing 'on the magnitude of the defendant's in-state contacts',[88] and so following the principles of due process and reciprocal fairness – according to which 'when a corporation chooses to invoke the benefits and protections of a State in which it operates, the State acquires the authority to subject the company to suit in its courts'[89] – under this newly developed rule 'in order for a foreign defendant to be subject to general jurisdiction, it must not only possess continuous and systematic contacts with a forum State, but those contacts must also surpass some unspecified level when viewed in comparison to the company's "nationwide and worldwide" activities'.[90] This approach is likely to narrow the reach of the US jurisdiction over disputes involving multinational corporations, which are always

---

84 Ibid., 20–21.

85 Supreme Court of the United States, Daimler, Justice Sotomayor concurring in judgment, 1.

86 Ibid.

87 Ibid., 2.

88 Ibid., 8.

89 Ibid., 10.

90 Ibid., 13.

closely linked with multiple States, and shift 'the risk of loss from multinational corporations to the individuals harmed by their actions'.[91]

7. Overseas Corporate Abuses: Prospects on Future Case Law

Some concluding remarks can be drawn upon the restrictive position assumed by the Supreme Court as to the applicability of extraterritorial jurisdiction under the ATS and the corresponding legal framework at EU level.

First, as regards the ATS's restrictive interpretation, it is worth noting that it does not automatically lead to the rejection of the federal courts' jurisdiction in all cases concerning corporate human rights and environmental violations. As stated by Justice Kennedy in *Kiobel*, 'other cases may arise with allegations of serious violations of international law principles protecting persons, cases covered neither by the TVPA nor by the reasoning and holding of today's case'.[92] It can be questioned whether and to what extent these cases consist of the so called 'foreign-squared' cases, i.e. disputes involving either US national defendants and overseas conducts or foreign defendants and conducts partially put in place within the US territory[93]. Depending on the prevailing interpretation, the jurisdiction over disputes on overseas corporate human rights and environmental violations might result in being attributed alternatively either to the US courts or to the courts of another State tied with the dispute, or to none of them, or to both of them. Since 'extraterritorial jurisdiction depends on the flexible approach to sovereignty', and regardless that 'the United States increasingly has appeared to interpret intrusions on national sovereignty as a threat to democracy', while the EU members have considered it 'as necessary for safeguarding democracy',[94] it is submitted that conflicts of jurisdiction might still arise in the future between the US and EU domestic courts.

---

91 Ibid, 18.

92 Supreme Court of the United States, Kiobel, Justice Kennedy concurring, 1.

93 See R. Alford, 'Kiobel Insta-Symposium: Interpreting "Touch and Concern"', *Opinio Juris* (19 April 2013). Online. Available HTTP: http://opiniojuris.org/2013/04/19/kiobel-insta-symposium-interpreting-touch-and-concern/ (accessed 21 April 2013); Donald Childress, 'A Brave New World of Transnational Human Rights Litigation', SCOTUSblog, 2012. Online. Available HTTP: http://www.scotusblog.com/2012/07/online-kiobel-symposium-a-brave-new-world-of-transnational-human-rights-litigation/ (accessed 21 August 2012); A. Metlisky, 'What's Left of the Alien Tort Statute', *SCOTUSblog* (18 April 2013). Online. Available HTTP: http://www.scotusblog.com/2013/04/commentary-whats-left-of-the-alien-tort-statute/ (accessed 20 April 2013); M. Lederman, 'Kiobel Insta-Symposium: What Remains of the Ats', *Opinio Juris* (18 April 2013). Online. Available HTTP: http://opiniojuris.org/ (accessed 20 April 2013).

94 J.A. Kirshner, 'Why is the U.S. Abdicating the Policing of Multinational Corporations to Europe?: Extraterritoriality, Sovereignty, and the Alien Tort Statute', *Berkeley Journal of International Law* 30, no. 2 (2012): 292.

In order to prevent them, EU Regulation No 1215/2012 provides the EU Member States' courts with a newly established art. 34, establishing a flexible mechanism allowing the courts of the Member States to take into account proceedings pending before the courts of third States. In order to ensure the proper administration of justice, the Member State's court should assess all the circumstances of the case before it, including connections between the facts of the case and the parties and the third State concerned, the stage at which the proceedings in the third State are, and whether or not the court of the third State can be expected to give a judgment within a reasonable time.[95] On the other hand, the US, apart from implementing the *forum non conveniens* doctrine,[96] should rely on the reasonableness test established under § 403 of the Restatement of the Law Third.[97] This provides that, even if complying with one of the titles established by § 402, the exercise of jurisdiction can be considered as unreasonable in light of the overall assessment of the relevant factors, including: the link of the activity to the territory, i.e. the extent to which it takes place within the territory, or has a substantial, direct, and foreseeable effect; the connections based on the defendant's nationality, residence, or economic activity; the character of the activity, the importance of the regulation, the extent to which other States regulate such activities, and the degree of general acceptance of such regulations; the existence of justified expectations; the importance of the regulation to the international political, legal, and economic system; the consistency with the international system; and the extent to which another State may have an interest in regulating the activity.

As domestic remedies and extraterritorial jurisdiction can provide victims of MNCs' human rights and environmental abuses with useful tools to obtain effective and satisfactory response, the implementation of these self-restraint techniques on the part of the US and the EU courts can avoid that new conflicts of jurisdiction between the two radicalize in the future and can help them to strike a balance between State sovereignty, on the one hand, and the protection of the victims' fundamental human rights, including their right to access justice, on the other.

---

95 Regulation No 1215/2012, art. 34 and Recitals 23 and 24.

96 Koebele, *Corporate Responsibility under the Alien Tort Statute*, 323 ff.

97 Restatement of the Law Third, § 403. See M.E. Danforth, 'Corporate Civil Liability under the Alien Tort Statute: Exploring Its Possibility and Jurisdictional Limitations', *Cornell International Law Journal* 44, no. 3 (2011): 685 ff.; K.M. Meessen, 'Conflicts of Jurisdiction under the New Restatement', *Law and Contemporary Problems* 50, no. 3 (1987): 47 ff.

Cases

Connelly v RTZ Corporation Plc, [1997] 3 WLR 373, 24 July 1997.
Corte Provincial de Justicia de Sucumbios, Sala Unica de la Corte Provincial de Justicia de Sucumbios, Juicio No. 2011-0106, 3 January 2012.
Doe v Texaco, Inc., F.Supp.2d, 2006 WL 2053504, N.D. Cal., 2006, 21 July 2006.
Doe v Unocal, 395 F.3d 932, 18 September 2002.
Daimler AG v. Bauman, et al., No. 11–965, 14 January 2014.
Esther Kiobel et al. v Royal Dutch Petroleum Co., Shell Transport and Trading Company Plc., 456 F.Supp.2d 457 (2006), 29 September 2006.
Esther Kiobel et al. v Royal Dutch Petroleum Co., Shell Transport and Trading Company PLC., 06-4800-cv, 06-4876-cv, 17 September 2010.
Esther Kiobel, Esther, et al. v Royal Dutch Petroleum, et al., No. 10–1491, Order in pending case, 5 March 2012.
Esther Kiobel, Individually and on Behalf of Her Late Husband, Dr. Barinem Kiobel, et al., Petitioners v. Royal Dutch Petroleum Co. et al., No. 10–1491, 17 April 2013.
Filartiga v Pena-Irala, 630 F.2d 876 (2d Cir. 1980), 30 June 1980.
In re Estate of Ferdinand Marcos, 25 F.3d 1467 (9th Cir.1994), 16 June 1994.
In Re South African Apartheid Litigation, 346 F.Supp.2d 538, S.D.N.Y., 2004, 29 November 2004.
In re Union Carbide Corp. Gas Plant Disaster at Bhopal, India in December, 1984, 634 F.Supp. 842, S.D.N.Y., 1986, 12 May 1986.
Ken Wiwa et al. v Royal Dutch Petroleum Company and Shell Transport and Trading Company plc., F.Supp.2d, 2002 WL 319887 S.D.N.Y., 28 February 2002.
Khulumani v Barclay National Bank Ltd et al., 05-2141-cv, 05-2326-cv, 12 October 2007.
Lubbe v Cape PLC, [2000] WL 976033, 20 July 2000.
Mario Alberto Tabra Guerrero v Monterrico Metals PLC, Rio Blanco Copper SA, 2009 WL 3171890, 16 October 2009.
Ngcobo v Thor Chemicals Holdings Ltd., 1995 WL 1082070, 9 October 1995.
Oguru, Elfanga, Vereniging Milieudefensie v Shell Petroleum N.V. and The Shell Transport and Trading company Limited, C/09/330891 / HA ZA 09-0579 and C/09/365498 HA ZA 10-1677, 30 January 2013.
Plaintiff 1, Plaintiff 2, Vereniging Milieudefensie, v Royal Dutch Shell Plc, Shell Petroleum Development Company Of Nigeria Ltd., 330891 / HA ZA 09-579, Judgment in motion contesting jurisdiction, 30 December 2009.
Sithole and Others v Thor Chemical Holdings Ltd., 1999 WL 477489, 3 February 1999.
The Presbyterian Church of Sudan et al. v Talisman Energy, Inc. and the Republic of Sudan, 582 F.3d 244, 2 October 2009.
The Presbyterian Church of Sudan et al. v Talisman Energy, Inc. and the Republic of Sudan, 244 F.Supp.2d 289, 19 March 2003.

Bibliography

Alford, R. 'Kiobel Insta-Symposium: Interpreting "Touch and Concern"'. *Opinio Juris* (19 April 2013). At http://opiniojuris.org/2013/04/19/kiobel-insta-symposium-interpreting-touch-and-concern/ (accessed 21 April 2013).

______. 'Human Rights After Kiobel: Choice of Law and the Human Rights After Kiobel: Choice of Law and the Rise of Transnational Tort Litigation', *Emory Law Journal* 63 (2014): 1089–163.

Amnesty International. 'Clouds of Injustice. Bophal Disaster 20 Years On' (29 November 2004): 57–73. At www.amnesty.org (accessed 12 September 2013).

Anderson, K., 'Legally Distinct Corporate Entities and Agency Theory in Bauman v. Daimler AG and Kiobel', *Opinio Juris*. Online. Available HTTP http://opiniojuris.org/2013/10/19/legally-distinct-corporate-entities-agency-theory-bauman-v-daimler-ag-kiobel/ (accessed 25 July 2014).

Backer, Larry Catá. 'Multinational Corporations, Transnational Law: The United Nations' Norms on the Responsibilities of Transnational Corporations as a Harbinger of Corporate Social Responsibility in International Law'. *Columbia Human Rights Law Review* 37, no. 2 (2006): 287–389.

Baude, W., 'Opinion Recap: a Stricter View of General Jurisdiction', *SCOTUSblog* (15 January 2014). Online. Available HTTP: http://www.scotusblog.com/2014/01/opinion-recap-a-stricter-view-of-general-jurisdiction/ (accessed 25 July 2014).

Bonfanti, A. 'Diritti umani e imprese multinazionali dinanzi ai giudici europei: sulla revisione del Regolamento (CE) n. 44/2001'. *Rivista di diritto internazionale privato e processuale* 47 no. 3 (2011): 697–720.

———. *Imprese multinazionali, diritti umani e ambiente. Profili di diritto internazionale pubblico e privato*. Milano: Giuffrè Editore, 2012.

———. 'Kiobel: No Extraterritorial Jurisdiction under the Alien Tort Statute. Which Forum for Disputes on Overseas Corporate Human Rights Violations?' *Diritti umani e diritto internazionale* 7, no. 2 (2013): 379–400.

Boschiero, N. 'Corporate Responsibility in Transnational Human Rights Cases: The U.S. Supreme Court Decision in Kiobel V. Royal Dutch Petroleum'. *Rivista di diritto internazionale privato e processuale* 49, no. 2 (2013): 249–92.

———. 'Il funzionamento del Regolamento Bruxelles I nell'ordinamento internazionale: Note sulle modifiche contenute nella Proposta di rifusione del 2011'. *Diritto del commercio internazionale* 26 (2012): 253–302.

Bradley, C.A. 'Supreme Court Holds That Alien Tort Statute Does Not Apply to Conduct in Foreign Countries'. *ASIL Insights* 17, no. 12 (18 April 2013). At http://www.asil.org/insights/volume/17/issue (accessed 12 September 2013).

Cash, W.C. 'Sosa's Silence: Kiobel and the Fallacy of the Supreme Court's Limitation on Alien Tort Liability'. *Denver Journal of International Law and Policy* 41, no. 1 (2012–13): 101–26.

Cassel, D., 'Suing Americans for Human Rights Torts Overseas: The Supreme Court Leaves the Door Open', *Notre Dame Law Review* 89, (2014): 1773–822.

Childress, Donald. 'A Brave New World of Transnational Human Rights Litigation'. *SCOTUSblog*. Online.

Commission of the European Communities. 'Green Paper on the Review of Council Regulation (EC) No 44/2001 on Jurisdiction and the Recognition and Enforcement of Judgments in Civil and Commercial Matters'. Brussels: Commission of the European Communities, 21 April 2009.

Council of the European Union. 'Proposal for a Regulation of the European Parliament and of the Council on Jurisdiction and the Recognition and Enforcement of Judgments in Civil and Commercial Matters (Recast) – First Reading – General Approach, 10609/12'. Brussels: Council of the European Union, 1 June 2012.

Danforth, M.E. 'Corporate Civil Liability under the Alien Tort Statute: Exploring Its Possibility and Jurisdictional Limitations'. *Cornell International Law Journal* 44, no. 3 (2011): 659–92.

Denniston, L., 'Argument recap: Trying to salvage a lost cause', *SCOTUSblog*. Online. Available HTTP: http://www.scotusblog.com/2013/10/argument-recap-trying-to-salvage-a-lost-cause/ (accessed 25 July 2014).

Enneking, L.F.H. 'Crossing the Atlantic? The Political and Legal Feasibility of European Foreign Direct Liability Cases'. *George Washington International Law Review* 40, no. 4 (2009): 903–38.

Erb, N., and O. Pell. 'Kiobel's New Focus on Extraterritoriality under the Alien Tort Statute Could Put Resolution of the Corporate Liability Issues Indefinitely out of Reach'. *Georgetown Journal of International Law* 43, no. 4 (2012): 1073–76.

European Commission. 'Proposal for a Regulation of the European Parliament and of the Council on Jurisdiction and the Recognition and Enforcement of Judgments in Civil and Commercial Matters'. Brussels: European Commission, 14 December 2010.

European Parliament Committee on Legal Affairs. 'Draft Report on the Proposal for a Regulation of the European Parliament and of the Council on Jurisdiction and the Recognition and Enforcement of Judgments in Civil and Commercial Matters (Recast)'. Brussels: European Parliament, 28 June 2011.

Feder, M. 'Commentary: Why the Court Unanimously Jettisoned Thirty Years of Lower Court Precedent (and What That Can Tell About How to Read Kiobel)'. *SCOTUSblog* (19 April 2013). At www.scotusblog.com (accessed 21 April 2013)

García-Castrillón, C.O. 'International Litigation Trends in Environmental Liability: A European Union – United States Comparative Perspective'. *Journal of Private International Law* 7, no. 3 (2011): 551–81.

Gillies, Lorna. 'Creation of Subsidiary Jurisdiction Rules in the Recast of Brussels I: Back to the Drawing Board?' *Journal of Private International Law* 8, no. 3 (2012): 488–511.

Günter, H. 'The International Labour Office Declaration of Multinational Enterprises and the International Code of Conduct Movement'. *Loyola of Los Angeles International and Comparative Law Review* 4, no. 1 (1981): 1–25.

Hathaway, O. 'Kiobel Commentary. The Door Remains Open to "Foreign Squared" Cases'. *SCOTUSblog* (18 April 2013). At www.scotusblog.com (accessed 12 August 2013).

ILO. 'ILO Tripartite Declaration of Principles Concerning Multinational Enterprises and Social Policy'. 16 November 1977.

Institut de Droit International. 'Multinational Enterprises (Second Commission, Rapporteur: Mr Berthold Goldman)'. The Institute of International Law. At http://www.idi-iil.org/idiE/resolutionsE/1977_oslo_02_en.pdf (accessed 12 September 2013).

International Law Association. 'International Civil Litigation and the Interest of the Public'. Paper presented at the Sofia Conference, Pisa, 18–25 October 2012, 1–8.

Kirshner, J.A. 'Why is the U.S. Abdicating the Policing of Multinational Corporations to Europe?: Extraterritoriality, Sovereignty, and the Alien Tort Statute'. *Berkeley Journal of International Law* 30, no. 2 (2012): 259–302.

Koebele, M. *Corporate Responsibility under the Alien Tort Statute*. Leiden: Nijhoff, 2009.

Lederman, M. 'Kiobel Insta-Symposium: What Remains of the Ats'. *Opinio Juris* (18 April 2013). At http://opiniojuris.org/ (accessed 20 April 2013).

Mares, R., ed. *The UN Guiding Principles on Business and Human Rights: Foundations and Implementation*. Leiden: Nijhoff, 2012.

Meeran, R. 'Tort Litigation against Multinational Corporations for Violation of Human Rights: An Overview of the Position Outside the United States'. *City University of Hong Kong Law Review* 3, no. 1 (2011): 1–41.

Meessen, K.M. 'Conflicts of Jurisdiction under the New Restatement'. *Law and Contemporary Problems* 50, no. 3 (1987): 47–69.

Metlisky, A. 'What's Left of the Alien Tort Statute'. *SCOTUSblog* (18 April 2013). At http://www.scotusblog.com/2013/04/commentary (accessed 20 April 2013).

Meyer, William H., and Boyka Stefanova. 'Human Rights, the UN Global Compact and Global Governance'. *Cornell International Law Journal* 34 (2001): 501–21.

Mooreville, I. 'Kiobel Insta-Symposium: Questions of Personal Jurisdiction Lurk beneath the Surface'. *Opinio Juris* (19 April 2013). At opiniojuris.org (accessed 8 July 2014).

Morgera, Elisa. 'An Environmental Outlook on the Oecd Guidelines for Multinational Enterprises: Comparative Advantage, Legitimacy, and Outstanding Questions in the Lead up to the 2006 Review'. *Georgetown International Environmental Law Review* 18, no. 4 (2006): 751–78.

Morse, C.G.J. 'Not in the Public Interest? Lubbe V. Cape PLC'. *Texas International Law Journal* 37, no. 3 (2002): 541–57.

Muchlinski, P. 'Corporations in International Litigation: Problems of Jurisdiction and the United Kingdom Asbestos Cases'. *International and Comparative Law Quarterly* 50, no. 1 (2001): 1–25.

Nuyts, Arnaud. 'Study on Residual Jurisdiction (Review of the Member States' Rules Concerning the "Residual Jurisdiction" of Their Courts in Civil and Commercial Matters Pursuant to the Brussels I and II Regulations)'. Brussels: European Commission, 3 September 2007.

OECD. *OECD Guidelines for Multinational Enterprises* (OECD, 21 June 1976 (21 May 2011)).

Pocar, F., I. Viarengo, and F.C. Villata, eds. *Recasting Brussels I*. Padova: CEDAM, 2012.

Scovazzi, T. 'Industrial Accidents and the Veil of Transnational Corporations'. In *International Responsibility for Environmental Harm*, edited by F. Francioni and T. Scovazzi. London/Dordrecht/Boston: Graham & Trotman, 1991.

———. 'La sentenza penale sulla catastrofe di Bhopal'. *Rivista Giuridica dell'Ambiente* 26 (2011): 553–59.

Shemberg, A. 'New Global Standards for Business and Human Rights'. *Business Law International* 13, no. 1 (2012): 27–33.

Stanisz, J.M. 'The Expansion of Limited Liability Protection in the Corporate Form: The Aftermath of Kiobel V. Royal Dutch Petroleum Co.'. *Brooklyn Journal of Corporate, Financial and Commercial Law* 5, no. 2 (2011): 573–600.

Theophila, M. '"Moral Monsters" under the Bed: Holding Corporations Accountable for Violations of the Alien Tort Statute after Kiobel V. Royal Dutch Petroleum Co.'. *Fordham Law Review* 79, no. 6 (2011): 2859–908.

UN Human Rights Council. 'Report of the Special Representative of the Secretary-General on the Issue of Human Rights and Transnational Corporations and Other Business Enterprises, John Ruggie: Guiding Principles on Business and Human Rights: Implementing the United Nations "Protect, Respect and Remedy" Framework Guiding Principles'. 9 April 2010, A/HRC/14/27.

UN Sub-Commission for the Promotion and Protection of Human Rights. 'Norms on the Responsibilities of Transnational Corporations and Other Business Enterprises with Regard to Human Rights'. UN Doc. E/CN.4/Sub.2/2003/12/Rev.2, 26 August 2003.

UNCTAD. 'World Investment Report: Transnational Corporations and the Internalization of R&D'. New York and Geneva: United Nations, 2005.

———. 'World Investment Report: Transnational Corporations, Agricultural Production and Development'. New York and Geneva: United Nations, 2009.

———. 'World Investment Report: Transnational Corporations, and the Infrastructure Challenge'. New York and Geneva: United Nations, 2008.

———. 'World Investment Report: Transnational Corporations. Extractive Industries and Development'. New York and Geneva: United Nations, 2007.

United Nations. 'UN Global Compact'. At http://www.unglobalcompact.org/docs/ (accessed 5 March 2014).

Ward, Halina. 'Securing Transnational Corporate Accountability through National Courts: Implications and Policy Options'. *Hastings International and Comparative Law Review* 24, no. 3 (2001): 451–74.

Weissbrodt, D., and M. Kruger. 'Norms on the Responsibility of Transnational Corporations and Other Business Enterprises with Regard to Human Rights'. *American Journal of International Law* 97, no. 4 (2003): 901–22.

Wouters, Jan, and Cedric Ryngaert. 'Litigation for Overseas Corporate Human Rights Abuses in the European Union: The Challenge for Jurisdiction'. *George Washington International Law Review* 40, no. 4 (2009): 939–76.

Chapter 8

The Alien Tort Statute as Access to Justice, Post *Kiobel*: When the International Norm Prohibiting Nonconsensual Human Experimentation is Violated

Bethany J. Spielman

This chapter provides background on the problem of nonconsensual human experimentation; explain why the Alien Tort Statute has been used as a way to provide access to justice for victims of nonconsensual human experimentation; and describe the legal challenge to the Alien Tort Statute in *Kiobel v Royal Dutch Petroleum*. Using three examples of nonconsensual human experimentation abroad, it identifies contextual factors that may play a role in determining how the presumption against territoriality applies.

Background on Nonconsensual Human Experimentation

Geographic Shift

Today there are more than 100,000 clinical trials taking place in more than 170 countries.[1] Western pharmaceutical clinical trials are increasingly being carried out in resource-poor countries. An often-cited study by Glickman[2] shows that one third of phase three trials of the 20 largest United States (US) pharmaceutical companies were being conducted exclusively outside the US and that for those same firms and studies, a majority of study sites (13,521 of 24,206) were outside the US. A study by Tufts University Center for the study of Drug Development showed a steady decline in the percentage of clinical trials in the US and in Western Europe, and a steady increase in the percentage of clinical trials in the rest of the

1 Andrew Buncomb and Nina Lakhana, 'Without Consent: How Drug Companies Exploit Indian Guinea Pigs', *The Independent*, 14 November 2011.

2 Seth W. Glickman et al., 'Ethical and Scientific Implications of the Globalization of Clinical Research', *New England Journal of Medicine* 380 (2009): 813–23.

world during the period from 1997–2007.[3] In India alone, more than 1,500 drug trials involving 150,000 patients have started since 2009.[4]

Justice Questions Raised by the Shift

This shift in the location of clinical trials presents questions about justice. What background injustices create such poor access to affordable medicines that experimental drugs rather than safe and effective drugs seem acceptable? How are the risks and benefits of these experiments distributed? And when an experimental subject is harmed, how can the victim and/or family be compensated, if at all?

I focus on this last question, the compensatory justice issue. There are at least three types of harms that should be compensated: injuries during experimentation, deaths related to experimentation, and the use of research subjects without their consent. My emphasis is on the use of research subjects without their consent, although this is not always entirely separate from injuries and deaths related to experimentation. Often nonconsensual participation is only discovered after journalists learn of the deaths or serious injuries of participants. But I focus particularly on means of compensating the harm of being used in a drug experiment without consent.

Examples

Some of the most notorious nonconsensual human experimentation has been perpetrated by states: Germany, Japan, the former Soviet Union, and of course, the United States, whose list of nonconsensual government-sponsored human experimentation is long. The list includes the malaria penitentiary studies at Joliet's penitentiary, which were cited at Nuremberg as justification by the defence, dermatological experiments on prisoners at the Pennsylvania Holmesburg State Prison in the 1950s, '60s, and '70s, the human radiation experiments of the military and the Atomic Energy Commission, the Tuskegee Syphilis Studies in the US government during the mid-twentieth century, the recently discovered Guatemalan sexually transmitted disease studies led by the US government in the 1940s and '50s, and the twenty-first century's CIA torture experiments on US detainees.

We do not know about all the government and military experiments that are being carried out today. They are secret. But we do know that private, non-government entities conduct a large number of experiments and comprise the largest category of non-secret research. Corporate-sponsored nonconsensual research has been documented by numerous journalists, scholars, advocates, and nonprofit organizations, including, among others, the Dutch Wemos Foundation, *The Times*

3 Kevin O'Reilly, 'Outsourcing Clinical Trials: Is it Ethical to Take Drug Studies Abroad?', *American Medical News* (7 September 2009). Online. Available HTTP: http://www.amednews.com/article/20090907/profession/309079969/4/ (accessed 16 June 2014).

4 Nina Lakhani, 'From Tragedy to Travesty: Drugs Tested on Survivors of Bhopa', *The Independent*, 15 November 2011.

(London), *The Independent*, and in the US *The Washington Post*, *The St. Petersburg Times*, *The Nation* magazine, and the Rebecca Project for Human Rights.

Some recent examples of corporate use of research subjects without their consent, which I briefly describe, are Pfizer's Trovan experiment in Nigeria in 1996; AstraZeneca's Ticagrelor experiments on victims of the Bhopal chemical disaster in India, and GlaxoSmithKline's Synflorix experiments in Argentina in 2007–2008. Of particular importance for this chapter are the geographic locations of the experiments.

Pfizer's Trovan experiment

In March 1996, an epidemic of bacterial meningitis broke out in the state of Kano, Nigeria. Kano was simultaneously dealing with epidemics of measles and cholera. Doctors without Borders (Médecins Sans Frontières, MSF) arrived in Kano shortly after the initial meningitis outbreak to provide medical aid. MSF began to treat the victims at Kano's Infectious Disease Hospital with the intravenous form of Ceftriaxone, the World Health Organization-endorsed generic antibiotic for bacterial meningitis in low-income countries. Within several weeks, Pfizer drew up a plan to test an oral form of an antibiotic, Trovan, on infected children at the Kano clinic. At the time Pfizer was seeking to gain Food and Drug Administration approval for its use on children. Pfizer researchers selected 200 sick children, aged 1 to 13 years, from lines of those awaiting treatment and redirected them to the experiment. Other patients were directed to the MSF area. Pfizer divided the subjects into two groups, treating half with Trovan and half with a lower-than-recommended dose of the standard treatment. Five children who received Trovan and six children to whom Pfizer administered the low dose of Ceftriaxone died. Others suffered blindness, deafness, and paralysis.

In 2000, *The Washington Post* newspaper published 'The Body Hunters', an investigative series including information about the Trovan experiment.[5] The report, which was picked up by Nigerian news media, sparked riots in Nigeria and was a factor contributing to an 11-month-long Nigerian boycott of a polio vaccination campaign in 2004, which had disastrous results in Africa and elsewhere. Parents of the children, aided by human rights lawyers, eventually brought several lawsuits

5 See, Karen DeYoung and Deborah Nelson, 'The Body Hunters: Latin America is Ripe for Trials, and Fraud Frantic Pace could Overwhelm Controls', *The Washington Post*, 21 December 2000; Mary Pat Flaherty, Deborah Nelson, and Joe Stephens, 'The Body Hunters: Testing Tidal Wave Hits Overseas', *The Washington Post*, 18 December 2000; Mary Pat Flaherty and Doug Struck, 'The Body Hunters: Life by Luck of the Draw in Third World Drug Tests, Some Subjects Go Untreated', *The Washington Post*, 22 December 2000; Sharon LaFraniere, Mary Pat Flaherty, and Joe Stephens, 'The Dilemma: Submit or Suffer "Uninformed Consent" is Rising Ethic of Drug Test Boom', *The Washington Post*, 19 December 2000; John Pomfret and Deborah Nelson, 'The Body Hunters: An Isolated Region's Genetic Mother Lode', *The Washington Post*, 20 December 2000; Joe Stephens, 'The Body Hunters: Where Profits and Lives Hang in Balance', *The Washington Post*, 17 September 2000.

under the Alien Tort Statute, claiming, among other violations, that there was no consent. The Nigerian government also brought criminal charges against Pfizer.

AstraZeneca's Ticagrelor experiment

AstraZeneca's Ticagrelor experiment occurred at the Bhopal Memorial Hospital and Research Center, which was set up to treat the victims of the 1984 Bhopal chemical disaster. One of the unwitting subjects of AstraZeneca's experiment was Ramadhar Shrivastave, a 64-year-old survivor of the disaster who was being treated at the hospital for heart disease. He was given two bottles of unlabelled pills and was asked to sign a form that was written in English, and that he did not understand. For about two years, the same doctor phoned each month to remind him to get his pills. Each time Mr Shrivastave signed a form that contained the names and signatures of 10 to 15 other people who apparently were also subjects in the experiment. He was never given any verbal or written details about the trial. After two years he was told he did not need to come back. He learned from a local journalist in 2010 that he had participated in the experiment:

> 'I didn't even know what a clinical trial was until my son explained to me after all this came out,' Mr. Shrivastave said. 'Of course I'm angry. I've been angry ever since I found out. But what can I do? We are poor people. If I had money I would have filed a case against them straight away, but we don't have money. If I'd known it was a drug trial I never would have agreed. How can I ever trust them again? These people should do trials on their own families, not poor people like me. God has saved me twice: first I survived the gas disaster and now this.[6]

GlaxoSmithKline's Synflorix experiment

The Synflorix vaccine experiment of GlaxoSmithKline (GSK) in 2007–2008 used 13,000 Argentine infants, many without the consent of their parents. Babies were selected from poor families that sought medical treatment from public hospitals. Paediatrician Ana Marchese reported the case to the Argentine Federation of Health Professionals and explained to the media how the selection process worked: 'Once a picked patient arrives, it would automatically disappear to be taken somewhere else in order to be treated by those doctors specially recruited by GSK.'[7] According to the paediatrician, 'there already exist very good vaccines for the same diseases, but we all know how laboratories work, they only care for their own business'.[8]

The President of the Argentine Federation of Health Professionals remarked, 'These are people who depend entirely on the state apparatus and who are most

---

6 Lakhani, 'From Tragedy to Travesty: Drugs Tested on Survivors of Bhopa'; IANS, 'Bhopal Gas Victims Allege Unethical Drug Trials', *Deccan Herald*, 24 Febuary 2012.

7 Javiore Cardenal Tajan, 'GSK Fined over Vaccine Trials; 14 Babies Reported Dead', *Buenos Aires Herald*, 22 August 2012; 'Glaxo Smith Kline Fined over Trials on the Babies of Argentinian Poor', *The Telegraph*, 11 January 2012.

8 Tajan, 'GSK Fined over Vaccine Trials; 14 Babies Reported Dead'.

often illiterate. They are vulnerable sections of society. They are unable to read any kind of consent form. GSK's recruitment of these people was absolutely unethical.'[9]

Fourteen babies died following the vaccinations. A great-aunt of one of the babies who died complained, 'A lot of people wanted to leave the protocol but they were not allowed. They forced them to continue under the threat that if they leave they wouldn't get any other vaccines for their children.'[10]

Contributing Factors

How can people be used in experiments without their consent? Four factors contribute heavily to these abuses. First, pharmaceutical companies rush to get their drugs to market. Once a drug is patented (before the experiments begin) the clock starts ticking on the period of patent exclusivity. Time equals money in the clinical trials business, and consent takes time; consent gets in the way of profits. For a pharmaceutical corporation, billions of dollars may be at stake. (For example, Trovan was expected to be a billion-dollar blockbuster drug.) Second, physicians, hospitals, and government administrators who facilitate or mediate the subject's participation have conflicts of interest; they benefit financially from the experiments. (For example, in the Trovan trial in Nigeria, Pfizer gave drugs and equipment to the hospital; in Synflorix vaccine trials in Argentina, local doctors received $350 per research subject.) An exchange takes place between corporations and local officials that depends completely on their access to research subjects but ignores the rights of those subjects. Third, subjects are poor and either illiterate or their first language is not used in the study. And finally, national and international guidelines and regulations that should prevent these abuses are not enforced. The US Alien Tort Statute has thus been seen as a way to provide access to justice for at least some individuals who are used abroad as research subjects without their consent.

The Alien Tort Statute

Alien Tort Statute Basics

The Alien Tort Statute was enacted early in the history of the United States in response to a number of international incidents. Those incidents arose from the fact that legal remedies for foreign citizens were not available in the United States. In 1784, the French Consul General to the United States, François Barbé-Marbois, was assaulted in his residence in Pennsylvania. The incident created an international stir, and the international community demanded a legal remedy. But the US Congress lacked any judicial authority in Pennsylvania. So Congress

9 Tajan, 'Glaxo Smith Kline Fined over Trials on the Babies of Argentinian Poor'.
10 Tajan, 'GSK Fined over Vaccine Trials; 14 Babies Reported Dead'.

drafted a resolution asking the states to allow suits in tort for the violation of the law of nations. However, few states enacted such provisions. It was then that Congress incorporated the Alien Tort Statute in the Judiciary Act of 1789.

The text of the Alien Tort Statute reads, 'The district court shall have original jurisdiction of any civil action by an alien for a tort only committed in violation of the law of nations or a treaty of the United States.'[11]

The Statute is a jurisdictional statute. It is also a hybrid statute: part domestic law and part international law. Its purpose was to ensure that the then very young US could stay out of war by providing access to justice for alien victims of international law violations. The US wanted to prevent retaliation by the victim's home country by showing a commitment to enforcing the law of nations and opening its courts to foreigners who would otherwise be denied justice.

How the Alien Tort Statute Came to be Used by Victims of Nonconsensual Experimentation

For the first 200 years, the Alien Tort Statute was rarely used. From 1789 until 1980, only two courts based jurisdiction on the statute.[12] Since 1980, however, that has changed. There have been over 170 judicial opinions regarding the Alien Tort Statute.[13] And the statute has been regarded as an important human rights tool. Four cases during the last 30 years are of particular importance in understanding how the Alien Tort Statute came to be used by victims of nonconsensual experimentation.

In 1980, the first modern Alien Tort Statute case was decided. The Second Circuit held in *Filártiga v. Peña-Irala* that two Paraguayan citizens could use the Alien Tort Statute to sue another Paraguayan citizen, a former Paraguayan police officer, for torture that occurred in Paraguay.[14] The first case to bring an Alien Tort Statute claim against a corporation rather than a natural person was *Doe v. Unocal* in 1997.[15] Plaintiffs in *Unocal* were Burmese villagers subjected to various human rights violations, including forced labour in the creation of an oil pipeline across their land for the US corporation Unocal.[16] (The corporate violations most often complained of have been aiding and abetting foreign states in human rights violations such as torture, forced labour, and extrajudicial killing.)

The first modern Supreme Court case on the Alien Tort Statute was decided in 2004. A US Drug Enforcement Agency special agent was kidnapped and murdered by a Mexican drug cartel in 1985. After an investigation, the Drug Enforcement

11 Alien Tort Statute, 28 U.S.C. 1350.

12 Gary Clyde Hufbauer and Nicholas K. Mitrokostas, 'International Implications of the Alien Tort Statute', *St. Thomas Law Review* 16 (2003): 607–25.

13 Donald Childress, 'The Alien Tort Statute, Federalism, and the Next Wave of Transnational Litigation', *The Georgetown Law Journal* 100 (2011): 709–57.

14 *Filártiga v Peña-Irala*, 630 F.2d 876 (2d Cir. 1980).

15 *Doe v Unocal*, 248 F 3d 915 (9th Cir. 2001).

16 Ibid.

Agency concluded that Humberto Alvarez-Machain had participated in the murder. A warrant for his arrest was issued by a federal district court. The Drug Enforcement Agency, however, was unable to convince Mexico to extradite Alvarez-Machain, so they hired several Mexican nationals to capture him and bring him back to the United States. The case went to the Supreme Court. In *Sosa v. Alvarez-Machain*, the Supreme Court considered a claim Alvarez-Machain brought under the Alien Tort Statute. Emphasizing the limits of the statute, the Supreme Court noted that, '[a]s enacted in 1789, the Alien Tort Statute gave the district courts "cognizance" of certain causes of action, and the term bespoke a grant of jurisdiction, not power to mold substantive law.'[17] In addition, the Court held that the Alien Tort Statute did not grant federal jurisdiction over all international law violations but only a limited category of offences defined by their high degree of specificity and universal acceptance, and found that Sosa's abduction of Alvarez Machain did not fall within this category.

The first Alien Tort Statute case involving nonconsensual human experimentation was decided in 2009. This was the Trovan case, *Abdullahi v. Pfizer*, in which the Second Circuit Court held that a norm of customary international law prohibiting medical experimentation on nonconsenting human subjects is cognizable under the Alien Tort Statute. On what was that norm based? The *Abdullahi* court relied on the sources of international law outlined in Article 38(1) of the International Court of Justice Statute: international conventions, international custom as evidence of a general practice accepted as law, the general principles of law, and judicial decisions and the teachings of the most highly qualified scholars or jurists.[18]

The *Abdullahi* court recognized four specific sources on which the victim's families had grounded their claim that there exists an international norm prohibiting nonconsensual human experimentation:

1. the Nuremberg Code;[19]
2. the World Medical Association's Declaration of Helsinki;[20]
3. the Guidelines authored by the Council for International Organizations of Medical Services;[21]

---

17 *Sosa v Alvarez-Machain*, 542 U.S. 692 (2004).

18 *Abdullahi v Pfizer, Inc*. 562 F. 3d163 (2nd Cir. 2009).

19 United States v Brandt, 1949 (Trials of War Criminals Before the Nuremberg Military Tribunals Under Control Council Law No. 10, Washington, DC: US Government Printing Office), 2. 181–182. Online. Available HTTP: http://www.hhs.gov/ohrp/archive/nurcode.html (accessed 16 June 2014).

20 World Medical Association, Declaration of Helsinki: Ethical Principles for Medical Research Involving Human Subjects, art. 20, 22, G.A. Res. (adopted 1964, amended 1975, 1983, 1989, 1996, and 2000). Online. Available HTTP: http://www.wma.net/e/policy/pdf/17c.pdf (accessed 20 September 2012).

21 Council for International Organizations of Medical Services, *International Ethical Guidelines for Biomedical Research Involving Human Subjects* (2002), Guideline 4.

4. Article 7 of the International Covenant on Civil and Political Rights.[22]

The majority also considered other sources: a directive passed by the European Parliament and the Council of the European Union; the domestic law of the United States; the domestic law of other nations; and UNESCO's Universal Declaration on Bioethics and Human Rights.[23]

What was the scope of the norm the court recognized? The majority in *Abdullahi* readily concluded that Pfizer's alleged complete failure to disclose the fact that Nigerian children were involved in an experiment fitted within the international prohibition on nonconsensual human experimentation. It noted, however, that less complete failures might not fall within its scope. Disagreement over the best way to secure consent from illiterate or otherwise vulnerable populations would be at the 'fringe' of the norm at issue, as would the failure to disclose the placebo design of a study; 'routine or 'isolated' failures of informed consent might not fall within the norm at all.[24]

Another case involving nonconsensual human experimentation was brought by the Guatemalan victims of the United States' sexually transmitted diseases experiments, which were carried out from 1946–57 but only came to light in 2010. Victims and their families sued US government officials. That claim was dismissed in June 2012 on the bases of sovereign and other types of immunity.[25]

Kiobel and the Future of the Alien Tort Statute

The Kiobel *Challenge*

Some health law scholars have been optimistic about the Alien Tort Statute's potential,[26] just as human rights lawyers and scholars have been optimistic about using the statute to help other victims of other corporate abuses. But the US Supreme Court, for the second time in a decade, considered the Alien Tort Statute in *Kiobel*

---

22 International Covenant on Civil and Political Rights, 1966, art. 7, Dec. 19, 1966, 999 U.N.T.S. 171.

23 *Abdullahi v Pfizer, Inc.* 562 F. 3d163 (2nd Cir. 2009).

24 Ibid.

25 *Garcia et al v Sebelius, et al.*, Civ. Action No. 11–527 (RBW), slip op. (D.D.C. June 13, 2012), mem. op. Online. Available HTTP: http://www.gpo.gov/fdsys/pkg/USCOURTS.pdf (accessed 20 August 2012).

26 George Annas, 'Globalized Clinical Trials and Informed Consent', *New England Journal of Medicine* 360, no. 20 (2009): 2050–53; Stacey Lee, 'Harbinger of Informed Consent Protection Parity?: Abdullahi V. Pfizer and the Alien Torts Statute', *The American Society of Law, Medicine and Ethics, Society Scholars Section* (2010). Online. Available HTTP: http://www.aslme.org/Society_Scholars (accessed 13 February 2014).

v. Royal Dutch Petroleum, and Shell Transport & Trading Co.[27] This is a landmark case about justice and corporate accountability for human rights abuses. The Court's decision will change access to justice for victims of international law violations.

The suit was brought on behalf of the late Dr Barinem Kiobel and other Nigerians from the Ogoni area of the Niger Delta. Royal Dutch Shell partnered with the Nigerian military dictatorship of Sani Abacha to suppress the popular movement of the Ogoni people that opposed Shell's operations and its degradation of their land. In 1994, Dr Barinem Kiobel and other leaders of the Movement for the Survival of the Ogoni People (MOSOP) were detained illegally, held incommunicado in military custody, tortured, and then tried by a special court established by the military government using procedures that were universally condemned as a sham, including bribery of witnesses by Shell. In November 1995, Dr Barinem Kiobel and other leaders were convicted of murder and executed.

The class action suit sought damages and other relief from Royal Dutch Petroleum, which allegedly aided and abetted extrajudicial killing, crimes against humanity, torture, cruel, inhumane and degrading treatment, arbitrary arrest and detention, violation of the rights to life, liberty, security and association, forced exile, and property destruction against the Ogoni people between 1992 and 1995.

On 28 February 2012, the US Supreme Court heard oral arguments on two issues: whether the question of corporate civil liability under the Alien Tort Statute is a merits question or a question of subject-matter jurisdiction; and whether corporations may be sued in the same manner as any other private party defendant under the Alien Tort Statute. A week later, the Court ordered briefing and re-argument on another question: [w]hether and under what circumstances the Alien Tort Statute, 28 U.S.C. §1350, allows courts to recognize a cause of action for violations of the law of nations occurring within the territory of a sovereign other than the United States.[28] On April 17, 2013, the Court decided the case in favour of the defendants on the basis of the last question alone.[29]

Extraterritorial Violations

The question of violations occurring outside the US was present in the facts of *Sosa*, since Alvarez-Machain's abduction took place in Mexico, and both Alvarez-Machain and Sosa were Mexican. In *Sosa*, the Court had also endorsed several cases, including *Filártiga*, in which the plaintiff and the defendant were foreign, and the conduct occurred abroad (sometimes called 'foreign-cubed cases'). But in *Kiobel*, the Court relied heavily on a single canon of statutory interpretation – the presumption against extraterritorial application as interpreted in *Morrison*

27 *Kiobel v Royal Dutch Petroleum Co., et al.*, 621 F.3d 11, order for reargument (US Mar. 5, 2012). Online. Available HTTP: http://www.supremecourt.gov/orders/courtorders/030512zr.pdf (accessed 10 May 2012).

28 Ibid.

29 *Kiobel v Royal Dutch Petroleum Co.*, 133, S.Ct. 1659 (2013), affirmed.

v. National Australian Bank.[30] This presumption provides that, '[w]hen a statute gives no clear indication of an extraterritorial application, it has none.' The Court held that *Morrison* prevented the ATS from reaching conduct occurring abroad. The presumption 'serves to protect against unintended clashes between our laws and those of other nations which could result in international discord.'[31]

Justice Kennedy filed a concurring opinion. Justice Alito also filed a concurring opinion, in which Justice Thomas joined. Justice Breyer, joined by Justices Ginsberg, Sotomayor, and Kagan, reasoned differently from the majority, basing a concurring opinion more squarely on the Court's *Sosa* decision and on foreign relations law. The latter justices would find jurisdiction under the ATS where:

1. the alleged tort occurs on American soil;
2. the defendant is an American national; or
3. the defendant's conduct substantially and adversely affects an important national interest, and that includes a distinct interest in preventing the United States from becoming a safe harbour for a torturer or other common enemy of mankind.

In addition, Justice Breyer's concurrence pointed out that the interest in not being seen as a safe harbour was reflected in *Sosa*, which referred approvingly to *Filártiga*, where the ATS was applied to an extraterritorial violation when the perpetrator fled to the US. Justice Breyer's concurrence also noted that Kiobel had alleged only that the defendants helped others to engage in acts of torture, genocide or the equivalent – not that the defendants directly engaged in those acts themselves.[32]

Narrowing of Access to Justice through the Alien Tort Statute

Of the victims of nonconsensual corporate clinical trials described earlier – Argentine families of the infants used in GlaxoSmithKline's Synflorix experiment, subjects and families of AstraZeneca's Ticagrelor experiment in India, and Nigerian families of subjects of Pfizer's Trovan experiment, only the last group actually brought a claim under the Alien Tort Statute. All three groups might be barred today from bringing such a claim; they would likely not overcome the presumption against territorial application. Although the *Kiobel* court was nonspecific about the conditions under which the presumption could be overcome, it stated that mere corporate presence would not suffice. Claims must touch and concern the territory of the Unites States 'with sufficient force'.

Regarding the Trovan experiment, an analysis of the presumption of extraterritorial application following *Kiobel* could take the following factors into

30 *Morrison v National Australia Bank Ltd.*, 561 U.S (2010).

31 *EEOC v Arabian American Oil Co.*, 449 U.S. 244 (1991).

32 *Kiobel v Royal Dutch Petroleum Co.*, 133 S.Ct. 1659 (2013).

account. Pfizer is headquartered in the US and the trial protocol was developed in the US. Therefore, there is a strong tie to the US. In addition, if the distinction between aiding and abetting and direct conduct to which Justice Breyer's concurring opinion alluded were to make a difference, it would count as a factor toward overcoming the presumption against extraterritorial application. Most corporate Alien Tort Statute cases have involved aiding and abetting; that is, the military or state-hired thugs are the direct killers or torturers and the corporations are the accomplices, as in *Kiobel*. But corporate liability for nonconsensual human experimentation could be different because state actors will probably not be the experimenters. The pharmaceutical corporation or, more likely, the contract research organization, would be the direct experimenter while the state is the indirect actor, or accomplice. This was the situation in *Abdullahi v. Pfizer*, where Pfizer employees were the primary actors. To make things more complicated, though, the private plaintiffs in such direct liability cases may be required to show that the host state was involved jointly with the defendant in a way that meets the standards of 'state action'.[33] In addition, because Pfizer's Nigerian subsidiary was also involved, and perhaps as heavily involved as the parent corporation in the complained-of conduct, and because the relevant conduct took place in Nigeria, the presumption against extraterritoriality could apply.

An analysis of the presumption of extraterritorial application might take the following factors about the Synflorix experiment into account. GlaxoSmithKline is a British multinational corporation with significant US operations, albeit operations that do not appear to have been involved in the experiment. GSK's Synflorix experiments took place in an Argentine public hospital, again raising the issue whether the corporate defendant's involvement would be seen by the court as aiding and abetting the state, or as something more significant, with a higher probability of overcoming the presumption against extraterritorial application.

AstraZeneca's Ticagrelor experiment is tied differently to the US, and analysis of the presumption of extraterritorial application might take the following factors into account. Bhopal Memorial Hospital and Research Center, the site of the experiment, was built for the purpose of treating victims of a chemical disaster created by a US corporation, Union Carbide. The funds for the hospital were part of a compensation agreement with Union Carbide. Quintiles, the multinational contract research organization that AstraZeneca hired to conduct the trials, is headquartered in the US. So there are significant ties to the US. But the ties might not be significant enough to overcome the presumption against extraterritoriality as interpreted in *Kiobel*. This is because the experiment occurred on Indian

33 Bethany Spielman, 'Offshoring Experiments, Outsourcing Public Health: Corporate Accountability and State Responsibility for Violating International Law Prohibiting Nonconsensual Human Experimentation', in *The Globalization of Health Care: Legal and Ethical Challenges*, ed. Glenn Cohen (Oxford: Oxford University Press, 2013), 286–301.

soil, AstraZeneca is headquartered in London, and Quintiles may have used its subsidiary, Quintiles India, to conduct the experiment.

If the concern about providing safe harbour for enemies of mankind were shared by the majority, an issue might arise were an experimenter involved in any of the three experiments to enter the US. It is impossible to know whether there are any circumstances under which a corporation could be viewed as using the US as a safe harbour, thereby touching and concerning the territory of the Unites States 'with sufficient force'. And because the *Kiobel* court did not explicitly decide the issue of corporate liability, there might not be a proper defendant in any case.

There are now significant changes in access to justice under the Alien Tort Statute. The US is no longer a fledgling nation. It is the most powerful corporate empire in the history of the world, and less interested than when the ATS was enacted in preventing retaliatory acts or showing the world that it respects international law.

Kiobel might seem, in some respects, to place victims in the same position as Barbé-Marbois when he was attacked more than 200 years ago: without access to justice. Fortunately for victims of nonconsensual human experimentation abroad, if access to US federal courts is closed in *Kiobel*, it is not necessarily the case that justice will be completely denied them. The Supreme Court decision in *Kiobel* may drive some plaintiffs out of US federal courts, but into other fora. Alien Tort Statute cases have usually included parallel state law claims. For example, the state law claims in Abdullahi were settled after the Second Circuit's decision in *Kiobel*.[34] Scholars have begun to assess the advantages and disadvantages of foreign fora as well. Donald Childress argues that what we may see is 'a brave new world of transnational human rights litigation first in federal courts under state and foreign law, second, in US state courts under state and foreign law, and third, in foreign courts under foreign law.'[35] As Western pharmaceutical corporations increase their use of human subjects abroad, that brave new world may provide access to justice.

Cases

Abdullahi v Pfizer, Inc. 562 F. 3d163 (2nd Cir. 2009).
Alien Tort Statute, 28 U.S.C. 1350.
Doe v Unocal, 248 F 3d 915 (9th Cir. 2001).

---

34 Sue Reisinger, 'Pfizer Settles Lawsuit over Drug Trials on Children in Nigeria', Corporate Counsel (23 February 2011). Online. Available HTTP: http://www.corpcounsel.com/id=1202482854504/Pfizer-Settles-Lawsuits-Over-Drug-Trials-on-Children-in-Nigeria--- (accessed 16 June 2014).

35 Donald Childress, 'Online *Kiobel* Symposium: A Brave New World of Transnational Human Rights Litigation', SCOTUS blog (12 July 2012). Online. Available HTTP: http://www.scotusblog.com/2012/07/online-kiobel-symposium-a-brave-new-world-of-transnational-human-rights-litigation/ (accessed 16 June 2014).

EEOC v Arabian American Oil Co., 449 U.S. 244 (1991).
Filártiga v Peña-Irala, 630 F.2d 876 (2d Cir. 1980).
Garcia et al v Sebelius, et al. Civ. Action No. 11–527 (RBW).
Kiobel v Royal Dutch Petroleum Co., 133 S.Ct. 1659 (2013).
Kiobel v Royal Dutch Petroleum Co., et al., 621 F.3d 11 (U.S. Mar. 5, 2012).
Morrison v National Australia Bank Ltd., 561 U.S. (2010).
Sosa v Alvarez-Machain, 542 U.S. 692 (2004).
United States v Brandt, 1949 (Trials of War Criminals Before the Nuremberg Military Tribunals Under Control Council Law No. 10).

Bibliography

Annas, George. 'Globalized Clinical Trials and Informed Consent'. *New England Journal of Medicine* 360 20 (2009): 2050–53.

Buncomb, Andrew, and Nina Lakhana. 'Without Consent: How Drug Companies Exploit Indian Guinea Pigs'. *The Independent*, 14 November 2011.

Childress, Donald. 'The Alien Tort Statute, Federalism, and the Next Wave of Transnational Litigation'. *The Georgetown Law Journal* 100 (2011): 709–57.

———.'Online *Kiobel* Symposium: A Brave New World of Transnational Human Rights Litigation', *SCOTUS blog* (12 July 2012). At http://www.scotusblog.com/2012/07/online-kiobel-symposium-a-brave-new-world-of-transnational-human-rights-litigation/ (accessed 16 June 2014).

Council for International Organizations of Medical Services. *International Ethical Guidelines for Biomedical Research Involving Human Subjects*. 2002.

DeYoung, Karen, and Deborah Nelson. 'The Body Hunters: Latin America is Ripe for Trials, and Fraud Frantic Pace could Overwhelm Controls'. *The Washington Post*, 21 December 2000.

Flaherty, Mary Pat, and Doug Struck. 'The Body Hunters: Life by Luck of the Draw in Third World Drug Tests, Some Subjects Go Untreated'. *The Washington Post*, 22 December 2000.

Flaherty, Mary Pat, Deborah Nelson, and Joe Stephens. 'The Body Hunters: Testing Tidal Wave Hits Overseas'. *The Washington Post*, 18 December 2000.

Glickman, Seth W., John G. McHutchison, Eric D. Peterson, Charles B. Cairns, Robert A. Harrington, Robert M. Califf, and Kevin A. Schulman. 'Ethical and Scientific Implications of the Globalization of Clinical Research'. *New England Journal of Medicine* 380 (2009): 813–23.

Hufbauer, Gary Clyde, and Nicholas K. Mitrokostas. 'International Implications of the Alien Tort Statute'. *St. Thomas Law Review* 16 (2003): 607–25.

IANS.'Bhopal Gas Victims Allege Unethical Drug Trials'. *Deccan Herald*, 24 Febuary 2012.

LaFraniere, Sharon, Mary Pat Flaherty, and Joe Stephens. 'The Dilemma: Submit or Suffer "Uninformed Consent" is Rising Ethic of Drug Test Boom'. *The Washington Post*, 19 December 2000.

Lakhani, Nina. 'From Tragedy to Travesty: Drugs Tested on Survivors of Bhopa'. *The Independent*, 15 November 2011.

Lee, Stacey. 'Harbinger of Informed Consent Protection Parity?: Abdullahi V. Pfizer and the Alien Torts Statute'. *The American Society of Law, Medicine and Ethics, Society Scholars Section* (2010). At http://www.aslme.org/Society_Scholars (accessed 13 February 2014).

O'Reilly, Kevin. 'Outsourcing Clinical Trials: Is It Ethical to Take Drug Studies Abroad?' *American Medical News* (7 September 2009). At http://www.amednews.com/article/20090907/profession/309079969/4/ (accessed 16 June 2014).

Pomfret, John, and Deborah Nelson. 'The Body Hunters: An Isolated Region's Genetic Mother Lode'. *The Washington Post*, 20 December 2000.

Reisinger, Sue. 'Pfizer Settles Lawsuit over Drug Trials on Children in Nigeria', Corporate Counsel (23 February 2011). At http://www.corpcounsel.com/id=1202482854504/Pfizer-Settles-Lawsuits-Over-Drug-Trials-on-Children-in-Nigeria--- (accessed 16 June 2014).

Spielman, Bethany. 'Offshoring Experiments, Outsourcing Public Health: Corporate Accountability and State Responsibility for Violating International Law Prohibiting Nonconsensual Human Experimentation'. In *The Globalization of Health Care: Legal and Ethical Challenges*, edited by Glenn Cohen. Oxford: Oxford University Press, 2013.

Stephens, Joe. 'The Body Hunters: Where Profits and Lives Hang in Balance'. *The Washington Post*, 17 September 2000.

Tajan Javiore Cardenal. 'Glaxo Smith Kline Fined over Trials on the Babies of Argentinian Poor'. *The Telegraph*, 11 January 2012.

———. 'GSK Fined over Vaccine Trials; 14 Babies Reported Dead'. *Buenos Aires Herald*, 22 August 2012.

Chapter 9
The Role of NGOs and Accountability of Corporations for Human Right Infringements

Genny Ngende

Introduction

The economic power that multinational corporations (MNCs) wield, the political clout they possess, their frequency in aiding and abetting genocide and other core crimes as well as their perceived legal impunity by virtue of their legal persons status have led to a review of what are considered crimes attributable to MNCs, thereby calling for a paradigm shift in the manner in which the law administers punishment and prescribes adherence. As such, multinational corporations are no longer merely connected to white-collar crime, but have graduated to being recognized as the aiders and abettors of mass crimes, as well as violators of human rights. International law has been slow in keeping up with the exponential increase in MNC power and its global reach. Further, the issue of multinational corporations is a contentious one because jurisdictional issues limit the coercive power of international human rights law. Indeed, the onus lies on host countries to ensure corporations abide by domestic laws.

Foreign direct investment has dramatically increased in this age of globalization where Third World countries, in particular, are competing to attract investments. As a result, multinational corporations have replaced official aid avenues as the main source of development finance for Third World countries.[1] Against such a backdrop of MNC proliferation, the influence of MNCs is apparent. The documentation of corporate human rights violations in developing states is unprecedented and indicative of a system unable to control the power and influence of those on which it depends. In a region, such as Africa, where foreign direct investment has exponentially increased, an asymmetrical relationship exists. With corporations as holders of the purse from the onset, such states are legally ill equipped or unwilling to deter corporate human rights violations or provide justice when they do occur, for fear of much-needed investment being withdrawn.

---

1 Susanne Soderberg, 'Taming Corporations or Buttressing Market-led Development? A Critical Assessment of the Global Compact', *Globalizations* 4, no. 4 (2007): 500–513, 502.

Non-governmental organizations (NGOs) are instrumental in bringing public awareness to the existence of abuse. NGOs have a role to set the agenda for government and to identify key human rights issues. Through research, conducted on behalf of intergovernmental organizations (IGOs), governmental bodies or delegations, NGOs help enforce laws as the research conducted enables the state to focus on enforcement. Further, NGOs have the capacity to represent aggrieved parties to obtain remedial redress. The issue of business and human rights is one that has not escaped scrutiny. The remedial gap in Third World states regarding corporate-related human rights abuse has not deterred NGOs from seeking justice. This chapter seeks to examine the role of NGOs in assuring corporate accountability by exposing human rights infringements within under-developed legal systems. South Africa is used as a case study to highlight the role of NGOs in the country and their relevance to the African continent.

The Effect of the Proliferation of MNCs through Globalization

Through globalization information is instantaneously shared and assimilated – an arena in which domestic markets translate into global markets and become increasingly interdependent. The operative word in 'globalization' is 'global': the intention is ultimately to break barriers to trade and enable foreign firms to permeate domestic markets of other states. One of the most effective ways of accomplishing this is through multinational corporations where their production, trade and investment activities, integrates countries into a global market.[2] Globalization results in the figurative collapse of geographical boundaries, enables the transmission of data, and ultimately connects everything and everyone: hence the creation of a 'global village'. Similarly, with multinational corporations, the concept of jurisdiction becomes a fluid term. The proliferation of MNCs has ensured the exponential increase of the 'global firm'. In other words, companies are occupying various jurisdictions while simultaneously evading jurisdiction. As a result, the idea of national jurisdiction within the context of corporate globalization, even with an extended meaning of territoriality, provides difficulties in its application.[3] In a situation whereby violation of human rights law has occurred or a crime has been committed, the claimant/plaintiff in seeking redress for harm suffered in the foreign country often faces a number of difficulties. Indeed, obtaining jurisdiction over a multinational corporation may prove problematic because of the difficulties that come with enforcing local judgment against the multinational where it holds assets. The locally incorporated subsidiary may have

2 Janet Dine, *Companies, International Trade and Human Rights* (Cambridge: Cambridge University Press, 2005), 1–309.

3 P. Rogerson, 'The Common Law Rules of Jurisdiction of the English Courts over Companies' Foreign Activities', in *Globalization and Jurisdiction*, ed. Pieter J. Slot (Leiden: Kluwer International, 2004), 1–324.

insufficient capital to meet the liability and the MNC or the parent company may hide behind the veil of incorporation to avoid liability of the subsidiary debt.[4] Moreover, the local courts may be inadequate to deal with complex tortious and criminal matters. Indeed, greater economic integration suggests more trade and financial openness, and the increase in trade essentially translates into an increase in business activities of MNCs.

Through the figurative removal of borders dividing states, resulting in a homogeneous entity or 'village', the application of sovereignty is viewed as not being afforded the same privilege that it once enjoyed. It is argued by Cohen Edwards that the global economic system is more and more divorced from geography, and gradually less dependent on any particular 'physical territorial location in which to carry out its activities'.[5] Consequently, states are viewed as gradually losing their position as the facilitators or obstacles to the functioning of the global economy, and thus territorial integrity is lost as control over borders is lost.[6] However, an alternative argument is posited on the assertion that state control is very much present and is evident in its endorsement and support of globalization – more specifically its support of multinational corporations.[7] Indeed, most governments of industrialized states explicitly or implicitly acknowledge that one of their key foreign relations priorities is to assist their corporations to 'win contracts in foreign markets and lobby against regulatory and political barriers'.[8] A prime example of this is found in the two billion dollar loan given to Angola by the Chinese government in which the negotiated payment plan consisted of oil deals.[9] This is reflective of a market-led approach in which the lending and borrowing of capital no longer translates into repayment in monetary terms by the borrowing state, but in the exchange of business transactions that benefit the multinational corporation. This approach further buttresses the notion that MNCs are the primary architects and biggest beneficiaries of economic globalization.[10]

The marriage of capitalism and globalization is evident in the same way that economic convergence of world markets is illustrative of neo-liberalism. Through an insatiable quest for economic growth, the ideology of the free market is embraced around the world with great enthusiasm. Economic institutions, such as the World Bank and International Monetary Fund, have aggressively and

4 Ibid., 93.

5 Edward Cohen, 'Globalization and the Boundaries of the State: A Framework for Analyzing the Changing Practice of Sovereignty', *Governance* 14, no. 1 (2001): 75–97.

6 Ibid., 78.

7 Ibid., 79.

8 Robert McCorquodale and P. Simons, 'Responsibility Beyond Borders: State Responsibility for Extraterritorial Violations by Corporations of International Human Rights Law', *Modern Law Review* 70, no. 4 (2007): 598–625.

9 Ian Taylor, 'China's Oil Diplomacy in Africa', *International Affairs* 82, no. 5 (2006): 937–59.

10 Dine, *Companies, International Trade and Human Rights*, 14.

vigorously encouraged Third World governments to relax economic barriers to make markets conducive for foreign capitalists, as well as ensuring low levels of unionization and corporate taxation, lax environmental regulations, legal structures to protect private property, and so forth.[11] This is accomplished through conditional lending practices or structural adjustment policies, which are set as provisos to obtaining loans.[12] As noted by Khan, 'foreign direct investment has increased in this age of globalization', where Third World countries, in particular, are competing to attract investments.[13] As a result, multinational corporations have replaced official aid as the main source of development finance for Third World countries.[14] The common denominator of foreign aid and foreign direct investment is the adoption of a neo-liberal approach. It should be noted that neo-liberalism favours economic globalization. Although Third World countries are politically independent, most are economically dependent on foreign capital. It is stipulated in the New Partnership for Africa's Development (NEPAD) Declaration that, in order for the African continent to achieve the goal of reducing poverty by 5 per cent by 2015, as set forth in the Millennium Development Goal, reliance is to be made on the investments of corporations.[15] An inference drawn here is that these less-developed or developing nations are in fact reliant on both foreign direct investment from multinational corporations and foreign aid from states. Indeed, just as conducive investment climates serve to incentivize corporations in extending their operation to other regions, MNCs are in a predatory search for less restrictive and unsaturated markets. In an era where energy supply is a prized commodity, the search often leads corporations to regions rich in minerals and abundant energy sources, an example of which is the African continent. Conversely, host nations embrace MNCs, as technological advancements and employment creation are seen as consequences of a MNC presence. Indeed, the reaping of benefits by host nations is directly related to enabling domestic policies. However, where domestic legal instruments are void of necessary enforcement measures, an unfettered discretion may be placed on MNCs in the conduct of their operation, as no overarching power exists to quash their influence. In a region, such as Africa, where foreign direct investment equates to a new form of foreign aid, an asymmetrical relationship exists from the onset as corporations are the holders of the purse. Multinational corporations can be considered as global players wielding

11 Soderberg, 'Taming Corporations or Buttressing Market-Led Development? A Critical Assessment of the Global Compact'.

12 Ibid., 503.

13 Md. Azizur Rahman Khan, 'Globalization and the Climate of Foreign Direct Investment: A Case for Bangladesh', *Journal of Money, Investment and Banking* 5 (2008): 98–116.

14 Ibid., 102.

15 Elizabeth Asiedu and Kwabena Gyimah-Brempong, 'The Effect of Liberalization of Investment Policies on Employment and Investment of Multinational Corporations in Africa', *African Development Review* 20, no. 1 (2008): 49–66.

immense power. For example, among the hundred biggest economies in the world, 51 are corporations and only 49 are countries; only 23 nations are bigger than General Motors.[16] Indeed, greater economic integration suggests more trade and financial openness, and the increase in trade essentially translates into an increase in the business activities of multinational corporations.

Various factors have contributed to the rise in power of corporations. The policies pursued by governments during the 1980s and 1990s were intended to produce an international economic system that was generally favourable to multinational corporations. These policies include the 1985 Uruguay Round that resulted in the World Trade Organization, the Single Europe Act, the creation of the North American Free Trade Agreement, and so forth.[17] The business decisions of MNCs are made within a global context, and thus crimes perpetrated and human rights breached have a far-reaching effect. The inability to clearly identify one jurisdiction intensifies anti-corporation sentiments.

The Proliferation of NGOs through Globalization

Non-governmental organizations are not a current phenomenon: they have existed since the anti-slavery movement and have spread across the world to command a global presence. The proliferation of NGOs is a recurring theme; however, it is set apart from its past in that its exponential influence is incomparable. Brown, Khagram et al. pose the question as to whether the increase in power and visibility of NGOs may be attributed to globalization or is merely an incidental occurrence. Second, if there is a causal nexus to globalization, can it expedite the globalization process? Moreover, will NGOs impede the process of globalization by providing ways for those negatively impacted to defend against global trends?[18]

The increase in visibility of NGO initiatives and the increase in numbers is, in part, due to the advancement in technology, communication and production brought by globalization.[19] Indeed, the work of Brown, Khagram et al. seeks to engage in a dialogue and explore the intricacies that have led to the rise of civil society by making reference to the impact of globalization on the relationship between citizens and the state.[20] Exposing the vulnerability of Soviet governments vis-à-vis its citizens upon the demise of the Cold War, and how that dynamic

16 Khan, 'Globalization and the Climate of Foreign Direct Investment: A Case for Bangladesh', 102.

17 Asiedu and Gyimah-Brempong, 'The Effect of Liberalization of Investment Policies on Employment and Investment of Multinational Corporations in Africa', 55.

18 L. David Brown et al., *Globalization, NGOs and Multi-Sectoral Relations Working Paper No. 1* (Boston: The Hauser Center for Non-Profit Organisation and the Kennedy School of Government Harvard University, July 2000).

19 Ibid., 4.

20 Ibid., 5.

altered the state's role as primary provider, highlights the societal metamorphosis. The political system embraced was democracy. The glaring economic equalities brought in by the free market, which undoubtedly enriched some, impoverished others, rendering them vulnerable and at the mercy of economic mismanagement. These sequences of events led to a need for 'greater political and economic equality as well as a broader sense of our economic political and moral interdependence.'[21] The shift in the balance in roles of the state, the market and civil society is attributed to such changes. The political power of states is determined by economic standing; therefore, the market rules over states. While the domestic and foreign policies of the 1980s and 1990s have supported economic globalization, they have, in turn, propelled NGOs to the forefront of international civil polity and the global decision-making processes. This is the case because the inability of states to counter the effect of the market or economic globalization has resulted in movements filling the gap.

The increase of NGO activities is, to a certain extent, also attributed to the abundant resource available for a particular cause.[22] However, due regard is to be given to the current international legal climate. Globalization has facilitated the recognition of universal legal norms. Through the creation of a homogenous culture, or perhaps the process of Westernization, both the political and legal spheres are affected. There lies accord with the political system of democracy and also the universal approach to legal norms. Legal norms dictate that states have a duty to protect and remedy against human rights encroachments. Rights and duties exist to protect citizens from the arbitrary rule of the state. Customary international law and treaties legally binding states exist, and provide a description of the various legal provisions and requirements for adherence. It was noted above that the increase of non-governmental organizations was caused by a need to provide security where state intervention was lacking. Multinational corporations are not legal subjects under international law. Under the Ruggie framework,[23] corporations are deemed to have a responsibility to respect human rights. This responsibility does not impose a legal obligation on corporations. Further, states have been unable to fully protect and provide remedies for corporate human rights abuses. International courts do not have a mandate to hear cases regarding business and human rights. Globalization is multi-faceted in that it affects every aspect of society. One may therefore attribute the growth and importance of NGOs solely to the aspect of globalization that diminishes the role of the state while magnifying the role of civil society. One can further attribute the rise of NGOs to

21 Ibid.

22 Ibid., 12.

23 UN Human Rights Council, 'Report of the Special Representative of the Secretary-General on the Issue of Human Rights and Transnational Corporations and Other Business Enterprises, John Ruggie: Guiding Principles on Business and Human Rights: Implementing the United Nations "Protect, Respect and Remedy" Framework Guiding Principles' (A/HRC/14/27, 9 April 2010).

the globalization of legal norms coupled with the globalization of multinational corporations that have exposed the remedial gap in the legal system that states are unable to fill, and therefore seek alternative means of protecting human rights law through civil society.

NGO Activity and Apartheid South Africa

The 'NGO revolution in Africa', as coined by Welch, was ignited by governmental instability, famine, civil war, systematic exclusion of groups from access to power, and an exponential economic decline that resulted in reliance on non-governmental entities.[24] A further catalyst to the increase of NGOs on the continent was the end of the Cold War that terminated support for some authoritarian states, consequently exposing the fragility of these governments and ultimately moving the focus to how 'society might rescue the state from its own inadequacies.'[25] Africa was plagued with an array of political, economic and societal ailments, which most states were ill-equipped or unwilling to cure. South Africa was under the Apartheid regime; the Democratic Republic of the Congo (DRC) as well as Liberia and Sierra Leone were facing internal instabilities. Indeed, this was a common situation for most African states during the 1970s up until the 1990s, and for some it is a recurring reality. The political landscape in the region was that of turmoil where human rights offences, war crimes, and crimes against humanity were prominent and the perpetrators were often state actors or resistant groups. One of the many prevalent phenomena was the one-party system, where the ruling government was the only political party with no opposition. There were military coups instead of democratic elections; dictators rather than elected officials; and oligarchy as opposed to democracy. Civil society was relegated to fighting primarily the arbitrary rule of the state.

In Apartheid South Africa, direct political activism was prohibited; therefore, NGOs would educate the masses on the Black Consciousness ideology. There were two main groups of NGOs:

1. Those that occupied the medium between the ideological extremes of Afrikaner and African nationalism. The following NGOs fall under this category: Urban Foundation, Black Sash, South African Institute of Race Relations (SAIRR) and the Institute for Democratic Alternatives for South Africa (Idasa).[26]

24 Claude E. Welch Jr, *Protecting Human Rights in Africa Strategies and Roles of Non Governmental Organizations* (Philadelphia: University of Pennsylvania Press, 1995), 1–356.

25 Ibid., 43.

26 Adam Habib and Rupert Taylor, 'South Africa: Anti-Apartheid NGOs in Transition', *Voluntas: International Journal of Voluntary and Non-profit Organizations* 10,

2. Those such as the National Education Crisis Committee, Legal Resource Centre and Trade Union Research Project, who 'openly associated themselves with the African National Congress (ANC) and serviced the mass-base people's organisations of the national liberation movement.'[27]

The Apartheid laws prohibited external monetary funding, and as such anti-Apartheid NGOs concocted ways to mask the source of their funds. Further, publications condemning the ruling government were disallowed, thus alternative means of conveying the Anti-Apartheid movement were also utilized. Once these laws became less restrictive, there was an influx of external funding. It must be noted that, as the racial tension in South Africa was globally condemned, international donors were primarily (if not exclusively) funding non-governmental organizations. Unable to move around the barriers afforded by the state sovereignty and the jurisdiction argument, the United Nations (through the General Assembly) adopted resolutions that were used by NGOs in the battle against Apartheid.[28] The resolutions were directed at citizen activists and encouraged them to challenge the ruling government. Free South Africa is an American-led NGO that was created not only in response to the overwhelming anti-Apartheid movement in South Africa, but in opposition to President Reagan's Southern Africa 'Constructive Engagement' that was viewed as a ploy to preserve Western corporate interests.[29] The formation of this NGO was further premised on the deadlock reached in the General Assembly between Developed States (that presumably had business interests in South Africa) and Developing States, especially African nations. This made the eventual adoption of General Assembly resolutions encouraging activism a poignant moment, perhaps even providing a United Nations' stamp of approval on anti-Apartheid NGOs.

The United Nations/NGO dynamic is best illustrated in the mutual collaboration between NGOs and the UN Special Committee Against Apartheid. A 1987 UN report asserts that NGOs provided 'useful advice' and suggestions for international initiatives.[30] The role of non-governmental organizations within the UN structure prior to this had been met with disdain and was limited. However, the Apartheid case ushered in a paradigm shift in UN/NGO interaction, in which resources and expert advice from NGOs were in demand and indispensable. The word 'Apartheid' became a catchphrase that elicited importance to the extent that the 'power and

---

no. 1 (1999): 73–82.

27 Ibid., 74.

28 Ibrahim J. Gassama, 'Reaffirming Faith and Dignity of Each Human Being: The United Nations, NGOs and Apartheid', *Fordham International Law Journal* 19, no. 4 (1995): 1465–509.

29 Ibid., 1495.

30 UN General Assembly, *Policies of Apartheid of the Government of South Africa: An International Solidarity with the Liberation Struggle in South Africa* (20 November 1987, A/RES/42/23), 2.

prerogative of the Commission on Human Rights were reinforced by taking on specific South African issues'.[31] This foiled the Commission's prior position, as the term 'human rights' (which is the mandate of the Commission) was at the time viewed as 'ineffectual'.[32] An Ad Hoc Working Group of Experts was spawned from this new focus on South African issues, and for the first time an independent group of experts for a human rights violation that was specifically defined by the UN body was used. Further, the remit of the Ad Hoc Group was to gather information from non-governmental sources. The outcome of the Ad Hoc Working Group was a positive achievement for NGOs and human rights issues. The witnesses' oral accounts and statements of the atrocities under the regime translated into public exposure of gross human rights violations occurring in the region.

Indeed, just as external funding sustained NGO activities, the Apartheid regime was also sustained through various financial institutions. South Africa was dependent on international trade and foreign direct investment. The capital flight that ensued after the Sharpeville massacre exposed this dependency. The images of police brutality on unarmed students brought international focus on the racially motivated assaults resulting in a global outcry; these images also raised concerns from civil activists (including NGOs) of external funding sustaining the status quo. It was argued that, without emergency loans from British and American banks, South Africa would have collapsed.[33] A 1976 General Assembly Resolution 'Programme of Action Against Apartheid' called upon member states to terminate diplomatic, economic, cultural and sport relations with South Africa. It further prohibited landing and service facilities for South African aircrafts.[34] Although the General Assembly Resolution does not have the same weight and impact as a Security Council Resolution, it was seen to reflect the moral and political indignation of the international community.[35] It was also reflective of the sentiments shared by NGOs in the United Kingdom, the United States and South Africa. However, economic ambition was the barrier to effective implementation. Crippling the political system by halting economic activity in Apartheid South Africa proved far more difficult when placed against the backdrop of lucrative financial turnovers that, if terminated, translated into industrialized states losing money – in other words, multinational corporations losing money. The role of NGOs was paramount in explaining the nature and subsequent effect of ending economic ties. In a 1980 report on the activities of local anti-Apartheid NGOs in the US, divestment from corporations doing business in South Africa was

31 William Korey, *NGOs and the Universal Declaration of Human Rights: A Curious Grapevine* (New York: Palgrave Macmillan, 2001), 1–656.

32 Ibid., 97.

33 Gay W. Siedman, 'Monitoring Multinationals: Lessons for the Anti-Apartheid Era', *Politics and Society* 31, no. 3 (2003): 381–406.

34 Korey, *NGOs and the Universal Declaration of Human Rights: A Curious Grapevine*, 99.

35 Ibid.

the main objective.[36] Examples of these activities include the American Friends Service Committee and the Federation of Protestant Welfare Agencies in New York divesting its investment portfolio of any stock linked to South Africa.[37] This report highlighted the activism that was occurring at a grassroots level. The momentum from the ground level was intensified: once reached at the national or global level, there was international and UN support. The American Committee on Africa (ACOA), which was relatively small yet an influential NGO, held a consultative status with the Special Committee against Apartheid and indirectly contributed to the shaping of 'an American policy that delivered the decisive blow to the very foundation of Apartheid.'[38] The founder of ACOA, George Houser, had once contacted the leaders of the African National Congress and had been told that he could do publicity work for them. Indeed, the ACOA sought to create awareness through publicity, notably the media.[39]

Non-legal Instruments Taming MNCs: Saviour or Enabler

The corporate social responsibility (CSR) movement has grabbed the attention of the world at large because of the global repercussion attached to the violation of rights.[40] Just as the anti-globalization movement sought to curb the effects of globalization, the CSR movement seeks to curb the effect of multinational corporations.

The Sullivan Principles (hereafter referred to as 'the Principles') were a set of business guidelines that served to guide MNC activity in Apartheid South Africa. The adoption of the Principles was premised on the belief that corporations could use their business influences and resources to change the Apartheid system from within.[41] Under the six principles, corporations were encouraged to adhere to non-discriminatory labour practices with respect to wages, housing, health, transportation and managerial training. Up until 1986, an estimated 150 corporations were signatories to the Principles, which ultimately failed to live up

36 Anita Pfouts and Paul Irish, 'Report of Activities of United States NGOs in Support of Economic Sanctions against South Africa' (report for International NGO Action Conference, Geneva, 30 June–3 July 1980). Online. Available HTTP: http://kora.matrix.msu.edu/files/ (accessed 6 March 2014).

37 Ibid.

38 Ibid., 104.

39 Ibid., 105.

40 Jennifer Zerk, *Multinationals and Corporate Social Responsibility Limitations and Opportunities in International Law* (Cambridge: Cambridge University Press, 2006), 1–368.

41 Helen Keller, 'Corporate Codes of Conduct and Their Implementation: The Question of Legitimacy', in Rüdiger Wolfrum and Volker Röben, eds, *Legitimacy in International Law* (Berlin Heidelberg: Springer, 2008). Online. Available HTTP: http://www.yale.edu/macmillan/Heken_Keller_Paper.pdf (accessed 12 September 2012).

to expectations. Nonetheless, this served as proof to the added value corporations could bring in the fight against Apartheid.[42] However, an alternative argument can be made concerning the eagerness of corporations to become signatories: this served to legitimize MNC presence and maintain the status quo of profit making. As a vast majority of American firms (and perhaps other MNCs) were opposed to sanctions, it served their agenda to be aligned with the Principles. The Principles (just like other business codes of conduct) have been criticized by NGO groups and other stakeholders as lacking legal weight and thus being ineffectual. Indeed, their ineffectiveness was apparent not only in their failure, but in the eventual enactment of the 'Comprehensive Anti-Apartheid Act' that came into fruition as a result of the activism of the ACOA.[43]

It is stressed that the ethical aspect of CSR is done voluntarily, but it is still expected of businesses to abide by an ethical code.[44] This is a paradoxical juxtaposition of two contradictory words, namely 'voluntary' and 'expected', which have the effect not only of bringing uncertainty, but enabling companies to pick and choose which aspect of CSR is more convenient for them, or even opting not be subject to it altogether. This is echoed in the Respect, Protect and Remedy Framework (also known as the Ruggie Framework), as well as all other CSR measures. There is a difference between corporate responsibility and corporate accountability. The former refers to any attempt to get corporations to behave responsibly on a voluntary basis, whereas accountability refers to requiring corporations to behave according to social norms and laws, or else face consequences.[45] However, this does not mean that voluntary undertakings do not play a vital role. Advocates of each approach continue to promote and highlight the efficacy of the respective sides, and thus a voluntary code of conduct is currently favoured by businesses and governments whereas a regulatory approach is being advocated by non-governmental organizations.

Post-Apartheid Struggles: Treatment Action Campaign and CSR

Section 27 (1) (a) of the South African Constitution asserts that everyone has the right to have access to healthcare services, including reproductive care. According to section 27 (3) no one can be denied emergency medical treatment; and section 28 (1) (c) provides for basic healthcare services for children. Further, section 35 (2) (c) posits that adequate medical treatment for detainees and

42 Ibid.

43 Korey, *NGOs and the Universal Declaration of Human Rights: A Curious Grapevine*, 114.

44 Zerk, *Multinationals and Corporate Social Responsibility Limitations and Opportunities in International Law*, 30.

45 Andrew Clapham, *Human Rights Obligations of Non-State Actors* (Oxford: Oxford University Press, 2006), 1–648.

prisoners is at the state's expense.[46] The exponential increase of AIDS-related deaths as well as the number of those infected was not only attributed to a lack of education, but was perceived to be a consequence of the non-fulfilment of the provisions contained in the Bill of Rights. It is against this backdrop that the Treatment Action Campaign (TAC) came into being.[47] The TAC is an NGO with an objective to confront the issue of HIV/AIDS by means of litigation, lobbying, advocacy and all forms of legitimate social mobilization. By making reference to the rights to healthcare, dignity and life, the NGO proceeded to seek legal actions against the government. Indeed, the TAC was forcing government to perform its duties. However, providing antiretroviral medication proved to be a difficult task when faced with the high prices of European and American pharmaceutical companies. The campaign encompassed an array of elements, ranging from the human rights of HIV positive individuals, the positive duties of government, to the patent rights of pharmaceutical companies.

The 1998 campaign demanded that government introduce a national programme in which pregnant HIV positive women would be given a short course of the drug azidothymidine (AZT), which significantly reduces mother-to-child transmission. The government claimed that the high price set by the pharmaceutical company prevented such a programme from materializing. However, Heywood asserts that the 'real' reason was the then administration's AIDS denialism, and plans for a less costly alternative to the AZT drug.[48] Nonetheless, the MNC presence is undeniable. The TAC argued that, since the drug was pivotal and essential to the lives of those infected, the profiteering by GlaxoSmithKline (AZT patent holder) amounted to a breach of the right to life.[49] The TAC further revealed that Pfizer was profiting at the expense of human lives. In purchasing the generic drug from Thailand, the price was 33 cents (US), as opposed to the 15 dollars (US) spent when buying from Pfizer.[50] Both companies are globally known, and wield an enormous amount of power. By framing the campaign as a human rights violation being breached by a corporation, international awareness was raised. The campaign's prominence internationally may not have reached such a level, had it solely been based on the government's inability to fulfil its obligations. The epidemic is not only at a high in South Africa but also in other Southern African countries. However, it is the South

---

46 *Statutes of the Republic of South Africa: Constitution of the Republic of South Africa* (18 December 1996). Online. Available HTTP: http://www.info.gov.za/documents/constitution/1996/96cons2.htm#7 (accessed 6 March 2014).

47 Mark Heywood, 'South Africa's Treatment Action Campaign: Combining Law and Social Mobilization to Realize the Right to Health', *Journal of Human Rights Practice* 1, no. 1 (2009): 14–36.

48 Ibid., 20.

49 Ibid.

50 Mila Pefianco Thomas and Tony Dorono, 'The Treatment Action Campaign: Issue-based Organizing Social Transformation in South Africa', *Social Policy* 35, no. 1 (2004): 52–57.

African issue and the TAC that have garnered international press, thus further buttressing the MNC factor as an element resulting in public outrage. Further, due to the discovery of Pfizer's benefiting from the high price of the drug, coupled with the risk of legal action by the TAC, the pharmaceutical company (in 2002) decided to donate the drug Diflucan to the South African government. The TAC managed to secure a deal that government was unable to do. It was estimated that Pfizer would contribute 50 million dollars' worth of Diflucan.[51] In other words, the TAC saved the government from spending 50 million dollars on HIV/AIDS drugs.

South Africa's 1997 Medicines Act gives the health minister the power to override patent laws in cases of emergency health. This could be done without approval by the patent holder.[52] In the 2001 case of *Treatment Action v the Minister of South Africa*, the Medicines Act and the Bill of Rights were used by the TAC to argue that the state was in no way prohibited from providing essential medication and that unfulfilling its obligations was unconstitutional. The TAC was triumphant in its case against the government, even after the state started proceedings against the organization.

In a reversal of events, 39 pharmaceutical companies brought legal claims against the South African government on the grounds of intellectual property violated by the 1997 Medicines Act. The Clinton Administration supported the pharmaceutical companies' position, while the South African government received support from the TAC and its international social movement.[53] In the 1999 US presidential election, Al Gore received a substantial amount of financial backing from pharmaceutical companies and, as a consequence, served their interests. Consequently, the AIDS Coalition to Unleash Power (ACTUP), allies of TAC, began protesting at campaign events. Subsequently, this had a negative effect on the campaign and led to both Gore and Clinton switching support from the pharmaceutical companies to the Medicines Act. The inference drawn here is that they ultimately began supporting the TAC. In 2001, the Pharmaceutical Manufacture Association dropped their suit.[54]

The Khulumani Group and the US Alien Tort Claims Act

The Khulumani Group is an NGO formed in 1995 that aims to help victims in the following ways:

51 Heywood, 'South Africa's Treatment Action Campaign: Combining Law and Social Mobilization to Realize the Right to Health', 24.

52 Patrick Bond, 'Social Movements and Corporate Social Responsibility', *Development and Change* 39, no. 6 (2008): 1037–52.

53 Thomas and Dorono, 'The Treatment Action Campaign: Issue-based Organizing Social Transformation in South Africa'.

54 Bond, 'Social Movements and Corporate Social Responsibility', 1041.

- to bring survivors and families of victims together to create a collective voice and presence within the community, civil society, the Truth and Reconciliation Commission, and government;
- to assist survivors to engage with the Truth and Reconciliation Commission and its structure;
- to facilitate the access of survivors to appropriate support services, including medical, legal, social and psychological services;
- to assist survivors to rebuild sustainable lives;
- to work for a just reparation policy and to ensure that this policy is fairly and timeously implemented; and
- to develop national and international networks of organizations of survivors.[55]

The Truth and Reconciliation Commission (TRC) was a restorative justice body created after the abolition of Apartheid. Witnesses were given an opportunity to recount the gross human rights violations that occurred under the regime. Perpetrators testified as to their role in such violations and if requested were given amnesty. This served as a platform not only to recount the past, but also to offer closure to the family of victims and to usher in a free democratic South Africa. Public hearings were pivotal in effecting this outcome. Multinational corporations escaped liability and blame. Under the Khulumani Group, victims of corporate related human rights abuse are seeking compensation in American courts.

The US Alien Tort Statute (ATS) is a piece of legislation that has transformed into a powerful tool in which perpetrators of human rights violation are held accountable under tort law. The necessity of the statute is apparent in a globalized world where multinational corporations exert great economic power and political clout over most developing states and, consequently, any domestic court of the host nation may find itself unable or unwilling to exercise legal autonomy.

Defendants find themselves accountable for human rights encroachments before American federal courts due to the structure of US courts, which contains a jury system. Often, monetary compensation amounts to millions of dollars. This accountability mechanism not only has the effect of financially affecting multinational corporations through cost of litigation and operational costs, but also damages their reputation. Where plaintiffs are successful in setting their case, the ATS provides them with a lucrative vehicle to hold MNCs accountable. It does not necessarily have to translate into monetary terms, but the threat of litigation can encourage other MNCs to comply with international human rights law.

The ATS is currently being used to hold various multinational corporations liable for aiding and abetting during Apartheid. The case of *Khulumani et al. v Barclays et al.* encapsulates various issues: notably, the issue of reparations for Apartheid victims; the complicity of corporations in human rights violations;

55 Oupa Makhalemele, 'South Africa Reconciliation Project: Khulumani Case Study' (2004). Online. Available HTTP: http://www.csvr.org.za/docs/reconciliation/.pdf (accessed 6 March 2012).

and the manner in which the state continues to deal with the Apartheid legacy within the context of an economically inclined foreign policy. Khulumani argues that the corporations had exclusive contracts to provide services that created the infrastructure of Apartheid. In the case of IBM, for instance, it is alleged that the computer giant provided the necessary technology to allow the implementation of the Pass Laws. The motor companies are accused of having provided customized vehicles for the security forces to use in townships to stifle resistance.[56] The plaintiffs claim that the defendants 'actively and willingly collaborated with the South African government to maintain a repressive, racially based system.'[57] The Khulumani Group has also played an important role in lobbying the South African government to implement a reparations policy.

Relevance to Africa

The initial price of the ARV medicines, prior to TAC interventions, was 64 dollars (US) per month; and after TAC campaigning it dropped to 42 dollars (US) in 2007. Further, generic versions of the drugs were sold by Brazil and Thailand at much lower prices then offered by the American and European counterparts.[58] How does this benefit Africa? The Treatment Action Campaign (alongside other international NGOs) has done the work of government. By exposing pharmaceutical companies as human rights violators under both South African law and by international standards and by shedding light on financial gains at the expense of human lives, other African states need not fear the withdrawal of foreign direct investment. African states are reliant on investments and some (if not most) are unwilling to defend citizens against corporate abuse, and an NGO that is able to do so, alleviates the pressure on the government.

Indeed, in Africa the epidemic is at a high; thus a cheaper and an alternative market to the US and Europe is embraced. The generic drugs are not only less costly, but are also as effective as the patented drugs. On 15 March 2001, the *Wall Street Journal* reported that Bristol-Myers Squibb was offering to sell its HIV drug, Zerit, to poor African states at a price of 54 dollars (US) per patient per year as opposed to 3,589 dollars (US) per patient per year.[59] Once again in

56 Rebecca Davis, 'General Motors Concedes to Khulumani in Apartheid Reparations Case', *Daily Maverick* (1 March 2012). Online. Available HTTP: http://www.dailymaverick.co.za/article/2012-03-01 (accessed 6 March 2014).

57 Ibid., 223.

58 Heywood, 'South Africa's Treatment Action Campaign: Combining Law and Social Mobilization to Realize the Right to Health', 24.

59 Michael Waldholz and Rachel Zimmerman, 'Bristol-Myers Squibb Offers to Sell Aids Drugs in Africa at Below Cost', *Wall Street Journal*, 15 March 2001. Online. Available HTTP: http://online.wsj.com/article/SB984593017713172966.html (accessed 6 March 2014).

2001, the pharmaceutical company Merck announced that it would slash 45 per cent to 55 per cent of its prices. It should be noted that this was around the time that an Indian company was selling generic drugs at a much lower price.[60] Further, remarks made by Bristol Myers and Merck stating, 'African governments and donor governments in Europe, Japan and the US must join forces with the UN organisations, pharmaceutical companies, NGOs to address this human tragedy',[61] reflects a shift in thinking from business being merely that of shareholder interests to that encompassing the interests of all other stakeholders.

The significance of the case being tried in US courts coupled with the presence of the United Nations further brings exposure and recognition to the NGO and the cause. By removing government from the equation, the NGO is highlighting that the presence of state is not necessary in seeking corporate accountability for the violation of core crimes. How is the Khulumani case relevant to the greater African context? Various other African states have experienced corporate related human rights abuse; notably, Nigeria, Ethiopia, Madagascar, Niger, Somalia, Sudan, and so on. The legal structure of most African states is weak and the human rights accountability of the state vis-à-vis the citizen is often non-existent. The South African experience serves as an example of what civil society is capable of accomplishing. The legacy of globalization is the decrease of state role, the increase of multinational corporations, and the emergence of NGOs as opposition to MNCs and even state authority. Similarly, they can also work together. However, where a governance gap exists, NGOs can play a pivotal role. This proved to be the case in the campaign against Apartheid, in which African states participated. The advocacy led by South African-based NGOs and international NGOs set the agenda at the United Nations, allowing African states to take part in the discussion.

Conclusion

The historical narrative into the role of non-governmental organizations in Africa is best illustrated in its activities in South Africa. The usage of South Africa as a case study enables the examination into the role of NGOs at each stage of the country's political and legal evolution, which in turn parallels the global change in NGO influence. The metamorphosis in global polity further reflects internal changes in South Africa and the continent as a whole.

Unlike other African states, civil society in South Africa influences domestic policies on health, education, welfare, law, and so on. As seen from the TAC and Khulumani Group, the extension of influence of South African NGOs can be global. It has been shown that the work of NGOs in the area of business and human rights affects the future behaviour of corporations in African states. This is especially true in the right to healthcare that led to the decrease in HIV/AIDS

60 Ibid.

61 Ibid.

medication and a cheaper Indian and Thai market for generic drugs. Can one, then, speak of a supranational group? Non-governmental organizations are dependent on donations from government, businesses, individuals and other sources, thus making objectivity an issue. Indeed, other NGOs (such as the TAC) are composed of the individuals experiencing the very cause being fought for. Whether or not NGOs are becoming a supranational group should be explored. However, one thing that can be said is that NGOs have started a movement: one that rethinks the issue of international law and justice.

Bibliography

Asiedu, Elizabeth, and Kwabena Gyimah-Brempong. 'The Effect of Liberalization of Investment Policies on Employment and Investment of Multinational Corporations in Africa', *African Development Review* 20, no. 1 (2008): 49–66.

Bond, Patrick. 'Social Movements and Corporate Social Responsibility', *Development and Change* 39, no. 6 (2008): 1037–52.

Brown, L. David, Sanjeev Khagram, Mark H. Moore and Peter Frumkin. *Globalization, NGOs and Multi-Sectoral Relations Working Paper No. 1*. Boston: The Hauser Center for Non-Profit Organisation and the Kennedy School of Government Harvard University, July 2000.

Clapham, Andrew. *Human Rights Obligations of Non-State Actors*. Oxford: Oxford University Press, 2006.

Cohen, Edward. 'Globalization and the Boundaries of the State: A Framework for Analyzing the Changing Practice of Sovereignty'. *Governance* 14, no. 1 (2001): 75–97.

Davis, Rebecca. 'General Motors Concedes to Khulumani in Apartheid Reparations Case'. *Daily Maverick* (1 March 2012). At http://www.dailymaverick.co.za/article/2012-03-01 (accessed 6 March 2014).

Dine, Janet. *Companies, International Trade and Human Rights*. Cambridge: Cambridge University Press, 2005.

Gassama, Ibrahim J. 'Reaffirming Faith and Dignity of Each Human Being: The United Nations, NGOs and Apartheid'. *Fordham International Law Journal* 19, no. 4 (1995): 1464–541.

Habib, Adam, and Rupert Taylor. 'South Africa: Anti-Apartheid NGOs in Transition'. *Voluntas: International Journal of Voluntary and Non-profit Organizations* 10, no. 1 (1999): 73–82.

Heywood, Mark 'South Africa's Treatment Action Campaign: Combining Law and Social Mobilization to Realize the Right to Health'. *Journal of Human Rights Practice* 1, no. 1 (2009): 14–36.

Keller, Helen. 'Corporate Codes of Conduct and Their Implementation: The Question of Legitimacy'. In *Legitimacy in International Law*, edited by Rüdiger Wolfrum and Volker Röben. Berlin Heidelberg: Springer, 2008. At http://www.yale.edu/macmillan/Heken_Keller_Paper.pdf (accessed 12 September 2012).

Khan, Md. Azizur Rahman. 'Globalization and the Climate of Foreign Direct Investment: A Case for Bangladesh'. *Journal of Money, Investment and Banking* 5 (2008): 98–116.

Korey, William. *NGOs and the Universal Declaration of Human Rights: A Curious Grapevine*. New York: Palgrave Macmillan, 2001.

Makhalemele, Oupa. 'South Africa Reconciliation Project: Khulumani Case Study' (2004). At http://www.csvr.org.za/docs/reconciliation/southernafricareconcilliation.pdf (accessed 6 March 2012).

McCorquodale, Robert, and P. Simons. 'Responsibility Beyond Borders: State Responsibility for Extraterritorial Violations by Corporations of International Human Rights Law'. *Modern Law Review* 70, no. 4 (2007): 598–625.

Pfouts, Anita, and Paul Irish. 'Report of Activities of United States NGOs in Support of Economic Sanctions against South Africa' (report for the International NGO Action Conference, Geneva, 30 June – 3 July 1980). At http://kora.matrix.msu.edu/files/ (accessed 6 March 2014).

Rogerson, P. 'The Common Law Rules of Jurisdiction of the English Courts over Companies' Foreign Activities.' In *Globalization and Jurisdiction*, edited by Pieter J. Slot, 1–324. Leiden: Kluwer International, 2004.

Siedman, Gay W. 'Monitoring Multinationals: Lessons for the Anti-Apartheid Era'. *Politics and Society* 31, no. 3 (2003): 381–406.

Soderberg, Susanne. 'Taming Corporations or Buttressing Market-Led Development? A Critical Assessment of the Global Compact'. *Globalizations* 4, no. 4 (2007): 500–13.

Statutes of the Republic of South Africa: Constitution of the Republic of South Africa (18 December 1996). At http://www.info.gov.za/documents/constitution/1996/96cons2.htm#7 (accessed 6 March 2014).

Taylor, Ian. 'China's Oil Diplomacy in Africa'. *International Affairs* 82, no. 5 (2006): 937–59.

Thomas, Mila Pefianco, and Tony Dorono. 'The Treatment Action Campaign: Issue-Based Organizing Social Transformation in South Africa'. *Social Policy* 35, no. 1 (2004): 52–57.

UN Human Rights Council. 'Report of the Special Representative of the Secretary-General on the Issue of Human Rights and Transnational Corporations and Other Business Enterprises, John Ruggie: Guiding Principles on Business and Human Rights: Implementing the United Nations "Protect, Respect and Remedy" Framework Guiding Principles'. A/HRC/14/27, 9 April 2010.

UN General Assembly. 'Policies of Apartheid of the Government of South Africa: An International Solidarity with the Liberation Struggle in South Africa'. 20 November 1987, A/RES/42/23.

Waldholz, Michael, and Rachel Zimmerman. 'Bristol-Myers Squibb Offers to Sell Aids Drugs in Africa at Below Cost'. *Wall Street Journal* (15 March 2001). At http://online.wsj.com/article/SB984593017713172966.html (accessed 6 March 2014).

Welch Jr, Claude E. *Protecting Human Rights in Africa Strategies and Roles of Non Governmental Organizations*. Philadelphia: University of Pennsylvania Press, 1995.

Zerk, Jennifer. *Multinationals and Corporate Social Responsibility Limitations and Opportunities in International Law*. Cambridge: Cambridge University Press, 2006.

Chapter 10

Non-State Actors and International Climate Justice under Global Climate Governance

Saheed Alabi

Introduction

The pervasive roles of non-state actors are evident in recent environmental governance actions specifically directed to climate change.[1] Since the adoptions of the United Nations Framework Convention on Climate Change[2] and its Kyoto Protocol,[3] these climate treaties have failed to reshape global responses to climate change effectively (in terms of emission reduction, mitigation and adaptation). However, the non-state actors such as the advocacy group have been persistent in putting pressures on various state actors to comply with their commitments to address climate change adequately through activism and litigation.

In 2007, Friends of the Earth (FoE) sued the Canadian government for its failure to meet up with its international emission reduction obligations under the Kyoto Protocol in the federal court of Ottawa.[4] In the lawsuit, Friends of the Earth alleged that such failure amounted to violation of Canadian law.[5] Increasingly, the roles of non-state actors have continued to underpin the development of climate change governance at the domestic and international levels whether on enforcement of obligations or treaty negotiations.

This chapter is divided into three parts. Part I discusses the general concept of non-state actors. Part II explores the role of non-state actors in achieving

1 See, European Environment Agency, 'Global Governance – the Rise of Non-State Actors: A Background Report for the SOER 2010 Assessment of Global Megatrends' (Copenhagen: EEA, 2011).

2 'The United Nations Framework Convention on Climate Change (UNFCCC)', *I.L.M.* 31 (1992). Online. Available HTTP: www.unfccc.int (accessed 20 September 2012). It was completed 9 May 1982 and entered into force 24 March 1994 (hereinafter referred to as 'Climate Convention').

3 'The 1997 Protocol to the U.N. Framework Convention on Climate Change (the Kyoto Protocol)', *I.L.M.* 37 (1998). Online. Available HTTP: http://unfccc.int/resource/docs/convkp/kpeng.pdf (accessed 18 June 2014). Completed on 11 December 1997 and entered into force 16 February 2005.

4 *Friends of the Earth v Canada*, 2008 FC 1183, [2009] 3 F.C.R. 201. Online. Available HTTP: http://reports.fja.gc.ca/eng/2009/2008fc1183.pdf (accessed 20 September 2013).

5 Ibid.

international climate justice. It focuses on the use of litigation by the advocacy groups of non-state actors to reshape global responses to climate change. Part III examines the question of *locus standi* of non-state actors in enforcing climate laws and policies at the domestic and international level. This same part offers various suggestions on how to empower non-state actors in global climate governance. However, the chapter ends with the conclusion that there is a need to strengthen and reform existing national and international structures in global climate governance.

I. The General Concept of Non-State Actors

Invariably at the international level, there are two main actors in promotion and enforcement of international justice – namely, state and non-state actors.[6] This chapter explores and discusses the roles of non-state actors specifically under the global regime for climate change. It is perceived that non-state actors are non-governmental organizations (NGOs) formed to challenge state actors on governance and implementation of policies at domestic and international level.[7] This is not true because non-state actors include individuals, groups or institutions that are not registered as NGOs.[8] Prior to the adoption of climate treaties – namely, the United Nations Framework Convention on Climate Change (UNFCCC) and its Kyoto Protocol – the non-state actors had made concerted efforts to negotiate agreements to reduce greenhouses gases.[9] In fact, during negotiations leading to the Climate Convention, non-state actors participated in official decision making to a certain extent.[10] This contribution gives an insight into how climate justice was promoted.[11] Non-state actors are not accorded voting rights on adoption of the climate treaties, despite their contributions. The power to vote and adopt international agreements is inherent in the sovereign status of state actors.[12] Since non-state actors are not allowed to enforce these agreements before the enforcement branch, a voting right

6 Joyeeta Gupta, *On Behalf of My Delegation,...: A Survival Guide for Developing Country Climate Negotiators* (Washington: Centre for Sustainable Development of the Americas, 2000).

7 Ibid., 27, 28.

8 See, United Nations Environment Programme, 'Major Groups and Stakeholders' (2012). Online. Available HTTP: http://www.unep.org/civil-society/MajorGroups/tabid/2749/Default.aspx (accessed 3 August 2012).

9 See generally the comments of Jessica T. Mathews, 'Power Shift', *Foreign Affairs*, Jan/Feb 1997, 55.

10 Ibid.

11 For detailed discussion on the roles on non-state actors see Chiara Giorgetti, 'The Role of Non-Governmental Organizations in the Climate Change Negotiations', *Colorado Journal of International Environmental Law and Policy* 9 (1998): 115.

12 Non-state actors represented the small island states at the early process of the negotiations, see Gupta, *On Behalf of My Delegation, ...: A Survival Guide for Developing Country Climate Negotiators*.

is not essential. In several environmental treaties, only state actors are competent as parties to settle disputes according to procedures under the agreements.[13] Non-state actors lack legal competence to enforce the climate agreements at the international court or tribunal because they are not regarded as parties.

Non-state actors consist of non-governmental organizations as part of the civil society. Conceptually, non-state actors include academic institutions, religious groups, individuals, and private sectors amongst others,[14] aiming to achieve targeted goals.[15] Such targeted goals encompass enforcement of climate obligations, compensation and settlement resulting from litigation. There are several groups or individuals who are classified as non-state actors. Nine main groups are identified as stakeholders under Agenda 21[16] – namely,

> farmers, women, the scientific and technological community, children and youth, indigenous peoples and their communities, workers and trade unions, business and industry, non-governmental organizations as well as local authorities, as well as other relevant stakeholders.[17]

These non-state actors may be categorized according to their operations. In reference to climate issues, operations of the non-state actors could be divided into social activist or advocacy group, academic or technical or scientific group, and legal activist group. For example, FoE,[18] Greenpeace,[19] the Socio-Economic Rights and Accountability Project (SERAP)[20] and several others, engage in social, academic or legal activism. They organize campaigns and protests, and use litigation to put pressures on state actors and other entities to take actions on climate issues. Such actions include compensations, settlements or damages for indigenous people through the court and other applicable means. Non-state actors such as the Foundation for International Environmental Law and Development

---

13 See, 'The United Nations Framework Convention on Climate Change (UNFCCC)', Article 14.

14 See, United Nations Environment Programme, 'Major Groups and Stakeholders'.

15 See, Independent Media Centre Australia, 'Climate Protest Highlights Environment Funding in the Australian Budget' (2012). Online. Available HTTP: http://indymedia.org.au/2009/05/15/ (accessed 2 September 2012).

16 Ibid.

17 United Nations Environment Programme, 'Major Groups and Stakeholders'.

18 Friends of the Earth International, 'Climate Justice and Energy Explained: The Problem' (August 2012). Online. Available HTTP: http://www.foei.org/en/what-we-do/climate-and-energy/learn-more (accessed 28 August 2012).

19 Greenpeace, 'Ken Saro Wiwa and 8 Ogoni People Executed: Blood on Shell's Hands' (London, 10 November 1995).

20 'Socio-Economic Right Accountability Project'. Online. Available HTTP: http://serap-nigeria.org/ (accessed 10 March 2014).

(FIELD),[21] the Center for International Environmental Law (CIEL), the World Wide Fund for Nature (WWF)[22] and the Climate Action Network (CAN)[23] amongst others, engage largely in academic or technical or scientific research.

Most social, academic or technical or scientific and legal activist groups are regarded as pro-human climate change except the Nongovernmental International Panel on Climate Change (NIPCC).[24] NIPCC does not share the belief that human activity is responsible for climate change. It claims that changes in the climate system are not anthropogenic; as a result they are not catastrophic. Persistently, NIPCC explores areas of scientific findings ignored by the Intergovernmental Panel on Climate Change (IPCC) on scientific evidence of climate change attributed to human activities.[25] It criticizes IPCC's scientific findings for inconsistencies. Whilst the role of NIPCC could be viewed as negating global effort in combating climate change, it has indirectly contributed to international climate justice. This is because its positions have influenced IPCC to publish more convincing scientific reports on anthropogenic climate change. Invariably, NIPCC has criticized the scientific consensus of the IPCC. However, the scientific consensus has increasingly sustained the political drive to combat climate change. Whilst NIPCC has not participated in the activities of the United Nations, other non-state actors have been absorbed into the United Nations Environment Programme (UNEP). In 2004, UNEP created the 'Major Groups and Stakeholder Branch' for 'broad participation in environmental decision-making'.[26] Whilst these groups of non-state actors make significant contributions to the development of the climate regime,[27] this chapter focuses on the ones that have used ligation to promote climate justice.

---

21 'Foundation for International Environmental Law and Development'. Online. Available HTTP: www.field.org.uk (accessed 20 September 2013).

22 'World Wide Fund for Nature'. Online. Available HTTP: http://www.wwf.org.uk (accessed 20 September 2013).

23 'Climate Action Network'. Online. Available HTTP: www.climatenetwork.org (accessed 20 September 2012).

24 'The Nongovernmental International Panel on Climate Change (NIPCC)'. Online. Available HTTP: http://www.nipccreport.org/about/about.html (accessed 20 September 2012).

25 'Intergovernmental Panel on Climate Change'. Online. Available HTTP: www.ipcc.ch (accessed 20 September 2012).

26 United Nations Environment Programme, 'Major Groups and Stakeholders'.

27 See, Dan Tarlock, 'The Role of Non-Government Organizations in the Development of International Environmental Law', *Chicago-Kent Law Review* 68 (1992): 61.

II. International Climate Justice and Non-State Actors

The term justice has philosophical,[28] social[29] and legal[30] conceptualization depending on the context in which it is being applied. Whilst this chapter argues for potential roles of non-state actors in promotion and enforcement of international climate justice, it declines to delve into the discussion of philosophical or ethical concept of justice because it is beyond its scope.

The term 'international climate justice' is of recent coinage. Its concept implies generic meaning under a broader context of environmental justice.[31] There is no generally accepted definition of environmental justice. The concept has not been defined in any multilateral environmental agreement. Nevertheless, domestic environmental frameworks like the United States Environmental Protection Agency (EPA) attempted the definition of environmental justice. EPA defines it as 'the fair treatment and meaningful involvement of all people regardless of race, colour, national origin, or income with respect to the development, implementation, and enforcement of environmental laws, regulations, and policies'.[32] Also, it acknowledges that there are two categories of rights on which environmental justice is underpinned – namely, substantive and procedural environmental rights.[33] Whilst substantive environmental rights entails provisions of rights enshrined in environmental agreements, procedural environmental right focuses on access and participation of these provisions in decision making.[34] The intent inherent

28 See, Richard W. Wright, 'The Principles of Justice', *Notre Dame Law Review* 75, August (2000): 1859; David D. Raphael, *Concepts of Justice* (Oxford: Oxford University Press, 2003).

29 See, Michael Reisch, 'Defining Social Justice in a Socially Unjust World', *Families in Society* 83, no. 4 (2002): 343.

30 See, Herbert L.A. Hart, 'Problems of Philosophy of Law', in *The Encyclopedia of Philosophy*, ed. Paul Edwards (Englewood Cliffs, NJ: Prentice-Hall, 1967), 264, 274–75; Randy E. Barnett, *The Structure of Liberty: Justice and the Rule of Law* (New York: Oxford University Press, 1998).

31 See Hari M. Osofsky, 'Learning from Environmental Justice: A New Model for International Environmental Rights', *Stanford Environmental Law Journal* 24 (2005): 71; Robert R. Kuehn, 'A Taxonomy of Environmental Justice', *Environmental Law Reporter* 30, no. 9 (2000): 10681.

32 See United States Environmental Protection Agency, 'Environmental Justice'. Online. Available HTTP: http://www.epa.gov/environmentaljustice/ (accessed 20 September 2012).

33 For detailed discussion on the emergence and concepts of substantive and procedural environmental rights, see, Ole W. Pedersen, 'European Environmental Human Rights and Environmental Rights: A Long Time Coming?', *Georgetown International Environmental Law Review* 21, no. 1 (2008): 73; Dinah L. Shelton, 'Developing Substantive Environmental Rights', *Journal of Human Rights and the Environment* 1, no. 1 (2010): 89.

34 Pedersen, 'European Environmental Human Rights and Environmental Rights: A Long Time Coming?'; Shelton, 'Developing Substantive Environmental Rights'.

in the concept of environmental justice is protection of human interests (health, good water, availability of food, amongst many others). Some may argue that the environment ought to be the primary intent or focus of environmental justice. In contrast, one could respond that human interest is also inherent in the protection of the environment. This is because, once the environment is healthy, fundamental human rights linking the environment would be enjoyed. At this point, it is imperative to consider the meaning of climate justice. Climate justice has been defined in diverse ways. For example, it means,

> Recognising that the capitalist growth paradigm, which leads to over extraction, over production and over consumption, stands in deep contrast to the biophysical limits of the planet and the struggle for social justice.[35]

Furthermore, the definition provides that climate justice means 'addressing the inequalities that exist between and within countries, and replacing the economic and political systems that uphold them'.[36] However, another definition provides,

> Climate justice is a vision to dissolve and alleviate the unequal burdens created by climate change. As a form of environmental justice, climate justice is the fair treatment of all people and freedom from discrimination with the creation of policies and projects that address climate change and systems that create climate change and perpetuate discrimination.[37]

Robison and Miller argue that, 'climate justice as a concept represents the confluence of different streams of concern with fairness and ethical relations as they relate to people's use of the world's finite carbon resources.'[38] They go further to assert that, 'climate justice is built on the fact that the world's poorest, and those least responsible for the human causes of climate change, are the most vulnerable and exposed to its effects'.[39] A more succinct definition of climate justice is hereby provided: it is the participation of both state and non-state actors in the adoption, implementation and enforcement of climate policies for adequate protection and preservation of all ecosystems. The ecosystem is composed of 'all the living

---

35 See generally, Climate Justice Action, 'What Does Climate Justice Mean in Europe?' Online. Available HTTP: http://www.climate-justice-action.org/resources/documents/what-does-climate-justice-mean-in-europe/ (accessed 18 June 2014).

36 Ibid.

37 See, Climate Institute, 'Climate Justice Movements'. Online. Available HTTP: http://www.climate.org/climatelab/Climate_Justice_Movements (accessed 12 January 2011).

38 Mary Robinson and Alice M. Miller, *Expanding Global Cooperation on Climate Justice* (London: Bretton Woods Project, 2009). Online. Available HTTP: http://www.brettonwoodsproject.org/update/69/bwupdt69_ai.pdf (accessed 20 September 2012).

39 Ibid.

things in an area and the way they affect each other and the environment'.[40] The overarching theme of these definitions is balanced on protection of the environment and human beings. In order to achieve climate justice, the roles of some non-state actors are largely concentrated on humans beings. For example, FoE has suggested that, 'the crucial solution to climate injustice is regarded as *energy sovereignty* which gives right to communities to determine sources of energy, design and healthy consumption patterns'.[41] In this context, climate justice implies human beings and the environment can be protected through community-based right. De Lucia argues that the concept of climate justice is of a 'monetary, distributional, compensatory ideological and universalizing framework' under the United Nations' climate regime.[42] According to De Lucia, many non-state actors supported United Nations' concept of climate justice that he regarded as 'Climate Ethics Consensus' (CEC).[43] He claimed that CEC,

> takes place through processes of dialogical relations that constitute and reproduce what Gramsci called a hegemonic historic bloc: within it, consent is created, shaped and maintained through the acceptance and internalisation of an ensemble of values and world-views that reinforces established power relations.[44]

In spite of the UN concept of climate justice, De Lucia suggested that 'climate justice is necessary for the survival of all the species including the human one'. Whilst aligning with De Lucia's position on doing climate justice to all species, the environment that hosts them must also be protected.

It is relevant, however, to consider diverse roles of non-state actors in promotion and enforcement of climate justice. These roles are discussed according to the sectors with which they are associated.

Participation, Activism and Litigation

The advocacy group of non-state actors uses participation and activism as the dominant social or political tools against poor implementation of laws and

---

40 Cambridge Advanced Learner's Dictionary & Thesaurus, 'Definition of Ecosystem Noun', in *Cambridge Advanced Learner's Dictionary & Thesaurus* (UK: Cambridge University Press, 2008). Online. Available HTTP: http://dictionary.cambridge.org/dictionary/british/ecosystem?q=ecosystem (accessed 18 June 2014).

41 Friends of the Earth International, 'Climate Justice and Energy Explained: The Problem'.

42 Vito De Lucia, 'What Climate Justice? A Critical Analysis', in *Sixth International Conference on Ethics and Environmental Policies: Ethics and Climate Change. Scenarios for Justice and Sustainability* (Padova: International Conference on Ethics and Environmental Policies, 23–25 October 2008), 151.

43 Ibid.

44 Ibid.

policies on climate issues.[45] In this context, participation means involvement in the negotiations and implementation of treaties.[46] Activism takes the forms of campaigns, protests, lobbying or even litigation. Typical examples abound globally where protests, campaigns and petitions are used to force government or private entities to act on their inactions or cease or improve on an action.[47] At the international level, protests, campaigns and lobbying are also used during climate talks such as Copenhagen 2009, Cancun 2010 and Durban 2011 to influence negotiations.[48] These kinds of activities amount to what could be referred to as *participative or activist climate justice* in enforcement of climate obligations. However, non-state actors are frequently arrested and punished for disturbing public peace because they engage in protests, campaigns or any other of forms of civil disobedience against the government actions or inactions.[49] In a pathetic case in Nigeria, nine environmental activists were unjustly executed following their strong opposition to persistent environmental degradation in the Niger Delta of the country.[50]

It appears that protests, campaigns or petition might have contributed to implementation and enforcement of climate obligations globally; litigation as a legal tool has been employed to apply international agreements and policies to climate issues at the domestic level. Litigating has been used as an option to compel state actors to combat climate change adequately. For example, in 2007,

---

45 See the discussions in Paul Wapner, 'Politics Beyond the State: Environmental Activism and World Civic Politics', *World Politics* 47, no. 3 (1995): 311; Lee Kimble, 'The Role of Non-Governmental Organizations in Antarctic Affairs', in *The Antarctica Legal Regime*, ed. Christopher Joyner and Sudhir Chopra (Dordrecht, Netherlands: Martinus Nijhoff, 1988), 33–64.

46 See Principle 10 of the Rio Declaration, which provides that, 'at the national level, each individual shall have appropriate access to information concerning the environment that is held by public authorities, including information on hazardous materials and activities in their communities, and the opportunity to participate in decision-making processes. States shall facilitate and encourage public awareness and participation by making information widely available. Effective access to judicial and administrative proceedings, including redress and remedy, shall be provided.' United Nations General Assembly, 'Report of the United Nations Conference on Environment and Development ("Rio Declaration")' (UN Doc. A/CONF. 151/26/Rev.1 1992), Principle 10.

47 See, Independent Media Centre Australia, 'Climate Protest Highlights Environment Funding in the Australian Budget'.

48 See Heike Schroeder and Heather Love, 'The Role of Non-Nation-State Actors and Side Events in the International Climate Negotiations', *Climate Policy* 12, no. 1 (2012): 23; Pilita Clark and Andrew England, 'Protests over Draft Climate Agreement', *Financial Times*, 9 December 2011.

49 See Louise Gray, 'Copenhagen Climate Conference: 260 Arrested at Protests', *The Telegraph*, 17 December 2009; Emma Reynolds, 'Climate Change Activists Arrested after Scaling Gates of Buckingham Palace and Chaining Themselves to Railing', *The Daily Mail*, 23 June 2012.

50 Greenpeace, 'Ken Saro Wiwa and 8 Ogoni People Executed: Blood on Shell's Hands'; BBC News, 'Nigeria Hangs Human Rights Activists', 10 November 1995.

FoE sued the Canadian government for its failure to meet up with its international emission reduction obligations under the Kyoto Protocol in the federal court of Ottawa.[51] Friends of the Earth alleged in the lawsuit that such failure amounted to violation of Canadian law. FoE made three applications for judicial review of non-compliance with Kyoto obligations on the grounds that,

1. the Minister of the Environment (Minister) failed to comply with the duty imposed upon him under section 5 of the Kyoto Protocol Implementation Act (KPIA) to prepare an initial Climate Change Plan that fulfilled Canada's obligations under Article 3.1 of the Kyoto Protocol;[52]
2. the Governor in Council (GIC) failed to comply with sections 8 and 9 of the KPIA by failing to publish proposed regulations in the Canada Gazette with accompanying statements and by failing to prepare a statement within 120 days setting out the greenhouse gas emission reductions reasonably expected to result from each proposed regulatory change and from other proposed mitigation measures;[53]
3. the application concerned section 7 of the KPIA because the GIC failed in its duty within 180 days to make, amend or repeal regulations necessary to ensure that Canada meet its obligations under Article 3.1 of the Kyoto Protocol.[54]

This case was dismissed on the grounds that FoE had 'no role to play reviewing the reasonableness of the government's response to Canada's Kyoto commitments within the four corners of the KPIA'.[55] A political issue was involved in this case. The Canadian government never supported the passage of the KPIA because it imposed legal responsibilities on the federal government. A private member of parliament initiated the KPIA. It contradicted Canadian governmental policy of the Kyoto Protocol despite the fact that Canadian ratified the treaty. Only the federal government can sponsor a money bill of this nature under Canadian law. As a result, the government was not willing to execute the Act financially. However, this chapter does not explore how the bill managed to become the Act of the parliament. Despite the dismissal of the case, it was first of its kind during the period. This is because domestic legislation was used to enforce international law. FoE litigated against Canada in the domestic court.[56] Eventually, if it had won the case, Canada would have been compelled to comply with Kyoto obligations. The case would have served as a good precedent for international climate litigation.

51 *Friends of the Earth v Canada.*

52 Ibid. See, 'The 1997 Protocol to the U.N. Framework Convention on Climate Change (the Kyoto Protocol)', Article 3(1).

53 *Friends of the Earth v Canada.*

54 Ibid.

55 Ibid.

56 Ibid.

The United States is not a party to the Kyoto Protocol; as a result it has no international obligation to reduce emissions. In order to commit the United States to combat climate change at the federal level, the Inuit Circumpolar Conference, now Inuit Circumpolar Council (the Council), on behalf of Inuit people filed a petition to the Inter-American Commission on Human Rights (IACHR). The Council alleged that continuous emissions by the US violated the rights of Inuit people to benefit from their culture, preservation of health and enjoyment of personal use of property and land.[57] It linked climate change to human and indigenous peoples' rights.[58] Despite the fact that the case was eventually dismissed, it has opened global discourse on potential violation of human rights from emissions. Currently, legal scholarships are emerging addressing climate change from the angle of human rights.[59] Even United Nations Law Commissions[60] and the World Bank[61] financed studies on the relationship between human rights and climate change with a view to addressing how climate change affects the enjoyment of human rights. Despite focused agitations by non-state actors to combat climate change using legal options such as litigation, these moves have been strongly opposed by the defendants who invariably aver that non-state actors do not have standing to bring cases against them.

III. Standing and Enforcement of Climate Treaties and Policies at the Domestic and International Level: Challenges and Prospects

Non-state actors do not have legal obligations to enforce climate treaties because they are not parties to the treaties. No provision of the Climate Convention or

57 Inuit Circumpolar Council (Canada), 'The Climate Change Petition by the Inuit Circumpolar Conference to the Inter-American Commission on Human Rights', Inuit Circumpolar Council. Online. Available HTTP: http://www.inuitcircumpolar.com/index.php?ID=318&Lang=En (accessed 20 September 2012).

58 See, Hari M. Osofsky, 'Inuit Petition as a Bridge? Beyond Dialectics of Climate Change and Indigenous Peoples' Rights', *American Indian Law Review* 31, no. 2 (2006/2007): 675.

59 For detailed discussions on climate change and human rights, see generally Lavanya Rajamani, 'The Increasing Currency and Relevance of Rights-Based Perspectives in the International Negotiations on Climate Change', *Journal of Environmental Law* 22, no. 3 (2010): 391; Daniel Bodansky, 'Climate Change and Human Rights: Unpacking the Issues', *Georgia Journal of International and Comparative Law* 38 no. 3 (2010): 511; John H. Knox, 'Linking Human Rights and Climate Change at the United Nations', *Harvard Environmental Law Review* 33 (2009): 477.

60 OHCHR, 'Report of the Office of the United Nations High Commissioner for Human Rights on the Relationship between Climate Change and Human Rights' (U.N. Doc. A/HRC/ 10/6115 January 2009).

61 Siobhan McInerney-Lankford, Mac Darrow and Lavanya Rajamani, *Human Rights and Climate Change: A Review of the International Legal Dimensions* (Washington: The World Bank Study, 2011).

its Kyoto Protocol empowers them legally to do so at the international level or under the Kyoto enforcement procedures. FoE does not have standing before the Enforcement Branch[62] under the Kyoto Protocol, for instance, to bring a petition that Canada has violated its Kyoto obligations. Legal standing for non-state actors is limited under the climate regime. Nonetheless, hope is not totally lost on the possibilities of non-state actor intervention for enforcement of climate change obligations. National laws may be used to enforce international climate obligations even if it is difficult to do so at the international courts or tribunals. Such cases may succeed in other jurisdictions that are distinct from Canadian legal system. Non-state actors could initiate cases on climate issues to put pressures on government and other private entities to act at the domestic level, since the implementation of climate treaties is to complement or strengthen national reduction of greenhouse gases.

True, *locus standi* or standing or legal competence to institute action may still be a challenge; even at this level, non-state actors can and should mobilize for required changes to legislation on legal competence to overcome technicality. Indeed, in some jurisdictions, it is conceivable that such actions may easily overcome the barrier of legal standing. For example, India has liberal public interest litigation. The question about *locus standi* was raised against FoE to bring up the lawsuit; the court rejected the argument and held that FoE had standing to bring the case based on 'justiciability of the substantive issues it raised'.[63]

In the Philippines, 44 minors (on behalf of themselves and the unborn generation represented by their parents) sued the Secretary of the Department of Environment and Natural Resources in the case of *Oposa v Factoran* – these minors could be regarded as non-state actors.[64] They challenged the grant of licences authorizing the use of forests for economic purposes by the Department of Environment and Natural Resources. 'A timber license is an instrument by which the State regulates the utilization and disposition of forest resources to the end that the public welfare is promoted'.[65] The minors argued that the licences should be revoked because this violated their healthful ecological rights. On appeal, the Supreme Court decided in

62 'The enforcement branch is responsible for determining whether a Party included in Annex I (Annex I Party) is not in compliance with its emissions targets, the methodological and reporting requirements for greenhouse gas inventories, and the eligibility requirements under the mechanisms'. UNFCCC, 'An Introduction to the Kyoto Protocol Compliance Mechanism'. Online. Available HTTP: http://unfccc.int/kyoto_protocol/compliance/items/3024.php (accessed 10 November 2013).

63 'The justiciability of these issues was a matter of statutory interpretation directed at identifying Parliamentary intent: in particular, whether Parliament intended that the statutory duties imposed upon the Minister and upon the GIC by the KPIA be subjected to judicial scrutiny and remediation', *Friends of the Earth v Canada*.

64 *Juan Antonio Oposa et al. v the Honourable Fulgencio S Factoran, Jr, Secretary of the Department of the Environment and Natural Resources et al. (Oposa v Factoran)* (1993), Supreme Court of the Philippines, SCRA 224, 1792; ILM 33, 173.

65 Ibid.

favour of the minors. It revoked the licences that were granted. Like many other cases instituted by non-state actors, *locus standi* becomes an issue for the court to decide.[66] The court ruled in this case that the minors had standing to bring the case on behalf of themselves and the unborn generation. Their claim was underpinned by principles of 'intergenerational responsibility and 'intergenerational justice'.[67] Non-state actors have instituted several cases in many countries, which have contributed directly or indirectly to the promotion of international climate justice. This is because such cases appear to have reduced activities that might have contributed to global emissions.

At the regional level in European countries, the issue of *locus standi* of non-state actors has been put to rest through the Convention on Access to Information, Public Participation in Decision-Making and Access to Justice in Environmental Matters, generally known as the Aarhus Convention.[68] Non-state actors have legal support and obligations to participate in decision making concerning the environment. They have the right to access information concerning the environment held by public authorities and to 'review procedures to challenge public decisions that have been made without respecting the two aforementioned rights or environmental law in general.'[69] This legal instrument has been responsible for the development of procedural environmental justice at the regional level. The non-state actors at the European level have succeeded in applying for European community law on human rights to environmental rights that have elements of climate change.[70] The numbers of non-state actors of the advocacy group are increasing at the international level. They are aiming to combat climate change threats to human beings and the environment by putting more pressures on state actors. They use different avenues of research, media, protests, campaigns, and litigation of climate issues. On this note, the non-state actors should be empowered in promoting and enforcing climate justice in global climate governance.

Empowering Non-State Actors for Climate Justice under International Law

Since non-state actors cannot directly enforce treaties at the international tribunals or court subject to *locus standi* and dispute settlements procedures under such

66 Ibid.

67 Ibid.

68 Aarhus Convention on Access to Information, 'Public Participation in Decision-Making and Access to Justice in Environmental Matters', *I.L.M.* 38 (25 June 1998, entered into force 30 October 2001). Online. Available HTTP: http://www.unece.org/fileadmin/DAM/env/pp/documents/cep43e.pdf (accessed 10 October 2012).

69 European Commission, 'The Aarhus Convention: What Is the Aarhus Convention?' Online. Available HTTP: http://ec.europa.eu/environment/aarhus/ (accessed 8 March 2013).

70 See the decisions of the European Court of Human Rights in the following cases: *Lopez Ostra v Spain* (1994) 20 EHRR 277, 125; *Guerra v Italy* (1998) ECHR 7; *Taskin v Turkey* (2004) ECHR 621; *Moreno Gomez v Spain* (2004) ECHR 633; and *Fadeyeva v Russia* (2005) ECHR 85.

treaties, it is suggested that they should continue to represent prospective litigants of state actors at the international courts or tribunals.[71] Also, since some of the non-state actors have been participating in negotiations leading to climate agreements,[72] they should be deemed as important stakeholders in global climate governance. As a result, they should be considered as having not only moral obligations but legal competence in compliance and enforcement governance.

Dispute settlement procedures are exclusively reserved for state actors to enforce treaty's obligations. It is suggested that non-state actors should be eligible to bring a petition against any country that has not complied with its international climate obligation under a climate protocol that may be adopted after the expiration of the Kyoto Protocol in 2012. Under the Kyoto Protocol, Enforcement Branch has established the power to impose punitive measures on a non-compliant party.[73] Non-state actors may be allowed to bring non-compliance petitions against defaulting state parties. Bringing these kinds of petitions should be to enforce international commitments under the climate change regime and to seek damages for victims of climate change. Although many of the developing and developed countries have made several pledges to reduce emissions,[74] these pledges could not be classified as international legal obligations. They therefore remain mere political pledges that are not enforceable in law. As a result, emission pledges in climate agreements reached in Copenhagen, Cancun, Durban and Doha cannot be used for enforcement of obligations.

Further, a number of other steps may be adopted to strengthen the roles of non-state actors in global climate governance. A treaty modelled after the Aarhus Convention may be adopted under global environmental governance where non-state actors would have access to information, participate in decision making, and

---

71 See, *Friends of the Earth v. Canada*; *Juan Antonio Oposa et al. v. the Honourable Fulgencio S Factoran, Jr, Secretary of the Department of the Environment and Natural Resources et al.*; *Social and Economic Rights Action Center and the Center for Economic and Social Rights v Nigeria*, African Commission on Human and Peoples' Rights, Comm. No. 155/96 (2001).

72 See Giorgetti, 'The Role of Non-Governmental Organizations in the Climate Change Negotiations', 115.

73 UNFCCC, 'Decisions Adopted by the Conference of the Parties Serving as the Meeting of the Parties to the Kyoto Protocol' (FCCC/KP/CMP/2005/8, 30 March 2006). For detailed discussions on non-compliance procedures under the Kyoto Protocol see, René Lefeber and Sebastian Oberthür, 'Key Features of the Kyoto Protocol's Compliance System', in *Promoting Compliance in an Evolving Climate Change Regime*, ed. Jutta Brunnée, Meinhard Doelle and Lavanya Rajamani (Cambridge: Cambridge University Press, 2012), 77–101; Peggy Rodgers Kalas and Alexia Herwig, 'Dispute Resolution under the Kyoto Protocol', *Ecology Law Quarterly* 27 (2000): 53; Meinhard Doelle, 'Compliance and Enforcement in the Climate Change Regime' (2012). Online. Available HTTP: http://ssrn.com/abstract=2070743 (accessed 8 March 2013).

74 UNEP, 'Welcome to the UNEP Climate Pledges Site'. Online. Available HTTP: http://www.unep.org/climatepledges/ (accessed 8 March 2013).

even enforce global regimes linking climate change against any party. Another area to empower non-state actors would be provisions of funds. Since some non-state actors internally generate funds, their operations may be undermined by the unavailability of adequate funding. Therefore, it is suggested that non-state actors operating in the developing countries should be given a small percentage of funds generated from mitigation or adaptation projects under the Kyoto Clean Development Mechanism (CDM) by the developed countries. Currently, a 2 per cent levy is imposed on every project approved for execution in the developing countries under the CDM;[75] the levy may be increased to 4 per cent. Non-state actors operating in the developing countries may access this fund. Forty per cent of the fund realized from the 2 per cent increase in levy should be reserved for registered non-state actors that have been registered as NGOs. They would have to apply for this fund through proposals detailing promotion or enforcement of climate justice. Any competent non-state actor from any developing country may be allowed to apply for funding to finance climate programmes and projects. In addition, the non-state actors active in non-advocacy action such as research activities may attract environmental research projects from the public or private authorities; through this exercise more funding may be generated.

In the developing countries where they are vulnerable to consequences of climate change, non-state actors ought to be remarkably active. Non-state actors in those countries may target American companies operating in the developing countries that have caused environmental harm to the host communities or are responsible for violations of human rights. Since the United States has decided not to accept any international legally binding obligation on emission reduction, mitigation and adaption of climate change, all avenues should be used to frequently make it accountable.[76] Apart from targeting the United States, non-state actors may use litigation at the domestic level to claim damages for victims of climate change given that the question of standing is invariably resolved in their favour.[77]

75 UNFCCC, 'Adaptation Fund'. Online. Available HTTP: http://unfccc.int/cooperation_and_support/financial_mechanism/adaptation_fund/items/3659.php (accessed 8 March 2013).

76 Ch. 20, § 9, 1 Stat. 73 (1789), also called the *Alien Tort Claims Act* (ATCA), see the commentary of Ingrid Wuerth, 'Online Kiobel Symposium: International Law and Alien Tort Statute Litigation', *Scotusblog* (11 July 2012). Online. Available HTTP: http://www.scotusblog.com/2012/07/online-kiobel-symposium-international-law-and-alien-tort-statute-litigation (accessed 20 September 2012). See also critical discussion on the use of ATS, David B. Hunter, 'The Implications of Climate Change Litigation: Litigation for International Environmental Law-Making', in *Adjudicating Climate Change: State, National, and International Approaches*, ed. W.C.G. Burns and H.M. Osofsky (Cambridge: Cambridge University Press, 2009), 357–74.

77 See commentaries and details of settlements using ATS in Ingrid Wuerth, 'Wiwa V. Shell: The $15.5 Million Settlement', *ASIL Insight* 13, no. 14 (2009). Online. Available HTTP: http://www.asil.org/files/insight090909pdf.pdf (accessed 20 September 2012).

Conclusion

The status of non-state actors should be enhanced in terms of eligibility to enforce international agreements against state actors. This is because of their persistent efforts to combat climate change. Currently, only little progress has been achieved in terms of enforcement of climate obligations or award of damages or compensation at the international level. Apart from funding legal competence, non-state actors also experience victimization from governments despite their contributions to global climate governance. However, in order to enhance the status of non-state actors, there is a need to strengthen and reform existing national and international structures in global climate governance.

Cases

Fadeyeva v Russia (2005) ECHR 85.
Friends of the Earth v Canada, 2008 FC 1183, [2009] 3 F.C.R. 201.
Guerra v Italy (1998) ECHR 7.
Juan Antonio Oposa et al. v the Honourable Fulgencio S Factoran, Jr, Secretary of the Department of the Environment and Natural Resources et al. (Oposa v Factoran) (1993), Supreme Court of the Philippines, SCRA 224, 1792; ILM 33.
Lopez Ostra v Spain (1994) 20 EHRR 277.
Moreno Gomez v Spain (2004) ECHR 633.
Social and Economic Rights Action Center and the Center for Economic and Social Rights v Nigeria, African Commission on Human and Peoples' Rights, Comm. No. 155/96 (2001).
Taskin v Turkey (2004) ECHR 621.

Bibliography

'The 1997 Protocol to the U.N. Framework Convention on Climate Change (the Kyoto Protocol)'. *I.L.M.* 37 (1998). At http://unfccc.int/resource/docs/convkp/kpeng.pdf (accessed 18 June 2014).
Aarhus Convention on Access to Information. 'Public Participation in Decision-Making and Access to Justice in Environmental Matters'. *I.L.M.* 38, 517. At http://www.unece.org/fileadmin/DAM/env/pp/documents/cep43e.pdf (accessed 10 October 2012).
Barnett, Randy E. *The Structure of Liberty: Justice and the Rule of Law*. New York: Oxford University Press, 1998.
BBC News. 'Nigeria Hangs Human Rights Activists'. 10 November 1995.
Bodansky, Daniel. 'Climate Change and Human Rights: Unpacking the Issues'. *Georgia Journal of International and Comparative Law* 38, no. 3 (2010): 511.

Cambridge Advanced Learner's Dictionary & Thesaurus. Cambridge: Cambridge University Press, 2008.

Clark, Pilita, and Andrew England. 'Protests over Draft Climate Agreement'. *Financial Times*, 9 December 2011.

'Climate Action Network'. At www.climatenetwork.org (accessed 20 September 2012).

Climate Institute. 'Climate Justice Movements'. At http://www.climate.org/climatelab/Climate_Justice_Movements (accessed 12 January 2011).

Climate Justice Action. 'What Does Climate Justice Mean in Europe?' At http://www.climate-justice-action.org/resources/documents/what-does-climate-justice-mean-in-europe/ (accessed 18 June 2014).

Doelle, Meinhard. 'Compliance and Enforcement in the Climate Change Regime' (2012). At http://ssrn.com/abstract=2070743 (accessed 8 March 2013).

European Commission. 'The Aarhus Convention: What Is the Aarhus Convention?' At http://ec.europa.eu/environment/aarhus/ (accessed 8 March 2013).

European Environment Agency. 'Global Governance – the Rise of Non-State Actors: A Background Report for the SOER 2010 Assessment of Global Megatrends'. Copenhagen: EEA, 2011.

'Foundation for International Environmental Law and Development'. At www.field.org.uk (accessed 20 September 2013).

Friends of the Earth International. 'Climate Justice and Energy Explained: The Problem' (August 2012). At http://www.foei.org/en/what-we-do/climate-and-energy/learn-more (accessed 28 August 2012).

Giorgetti, Chiara. 'The Role of Non-Governmental Organizations in the Climate Change Negotiations'. *Colorado Journal of International Environmental Law and Policy* 9 (1998): 115.

Gray, Louise 'Copenhagen Climate Conference: 260 Arrested at Protests'. *The Telegraph*, 17 December 2009.

Greenpeace. 'Ken Saro Wiwa and 8 Ogoni People Executed: Blood on Shell's Hands'. London, 10 November 1995.

Gupta, Joyeeta. *On Behalf of My Delegation, ...: A Survival Guide for Developing Country Climate Negotiators*. Washington: Centre for Sustainable Development of the Americas, 2000.

Hart, Herbert L.A. 'Problems of Philosophy of Law'. In *The Encyclopedia of Philosophy*, edited by Paul Edwards, 274–75. Englewood Cliffs, NJ: Prentice-Hall, 1967.

Hunter, David B. 'The Implications of Climate Change Litigation: Litigation for International Environmental Law-Making'. In *Adjudicating Climate Change: State, National, and International Approaches*, edited by W.C.G. Burns and H.M. Osofsky, 357–74. Cambridge: Cambridge University Press, 2009.

Independent Media Centre Australia. 'Climate Protest Highlights Environment Funding in the Australian Budget' (2012). At http://indymedia.org.au/2009/05/15/climate-protest-highlights-environment-funding-in-the-australian-budget (accessed 2 September 2012).

'Intergovernmental Panel on Climate Change.' At http://www.ipcc.ch (accessed 20 September 2012).

Inuit Circumpolar Council (Canada). 'The Climate Change Petition by the Inuit Circumpolar Conference to the Inter-American Commission on Human Rights', Inuit Circumpolar Council. At http://www.inuitcircumpolar.com/index.php?ID=318&Lang=En (accessed 20 September 2012).

Kalas, Peggy Rodgers, and Alexia Herwig. 'Dispute Resolution under the Kyoto Protocol'. *Ecology Law Quarterly* 27 (2000): 53.

Kimble, Lee. 'The Role of Non-Governmental Organizations in Antarctic Affairs'. In *The Antarctica Legal Regime*, edited by Christopher Joyner and Sudhir Chopra, 33–64. Dordrecht, Netherlands: Martinus Nijhoff, 1988.

Knox, John H. 'Linking Human Rights and Climate Change at the United Nations'. *Harvard Environmental Law Review* 33 (2009): 477.

Kuehn, Robert R. 'A Taxonomy of Environmental Justice'. *Environmental Law Reporter* 30, no. 9 (2000): 10681.

Lefeber, René, and Sebastian Oberthür. 'Key Features of the Kyoto Protocol's Compliance System'. In *Promoting Compliance in an Evolving Climate Change Regime*, edited by Jutta Brunnée, Meinhard Doelle and Lavanya Rajamani, 77–101. Cambridge: Cambridge University Press, 2012.

Lucia, Vito De. 'What Climate Justice? A Critical Analysis'. In *Sixth International Conference on Ethics and Environmental Policies: Ethics and Climate Change. Scenarios for Justice and Sustainability*. Padova: International Conference on Ethics and Environmental Policies, 23–25 October 2008.

Mathews, Jessica T. 'Power Shift'. *Foreign Affairs*, Jan/Feb 1997.

McInerney-Lankford, Siobhan, Mac Darrow and Lavanya Rajamani. *Human Rights and Climate Change: A Review of the International Legal Dimensions*. Washington: The World Bank Study, 2011.

'The Nongovernmental International Panel on Climate Change (NIPCC)'. At http://www.nipccreport.org/about/about.html (accessed 20 September 2012).

OHCHR. 'Report of the Office of the United Nations High Commissioner for Human Rights on the Relationship between Climate Change and Human Rights'. U.N. Doc. A/HRC/10/61, 15 January 2009.

Osofsky, Hari M. 'Inuit Petition as a Bridge? Beyond Dialectics of Climate Change and Indigenous Peoples' Rights'. *American Indian Law Review* 31, no. 2 (2006/2007): 675.

———. 'Learning from Environmental Justice: A New Model for International Environmental Rights'. *Stanford Environmental Law Journal* 24 (2005): 71.

Pedersen, Ole W. 'European Environmental Human Rights and Environmental Rights: A Long Time Coming?' *Georgetown International Environmental Law Review* 21, no. 1 (2008): 73.

Rajamani, Lavanya. 'The Increasing Currency and Relevance of Rights-Based Perspectives in the International Negotiations on Climate Change'. *Journal of Environmental Law* 22, no. 3 (2010): 391.

Raphael, David D. *Concepts of Justice*. Oxford: Oxford University Press, 2003.

Reisch, Michael. 'Defining Social Justice in a Socially Unjust World'. *Families in Society* 83, no. 4 (2002): 343.

Reynolds, Emma. 'Climate Change Activists Arrested after Scaling Gates of Buckingham Palace and Chaining Themselves to Railing'. *The Daily Mail*, 23 June 2012.

Robinson, Mary and Alice M. Miller. *Expanding Global Cooperation on Climate Justice*. London: Bretton Woods Project, 2009. At http://www.brettonwoodsproject.org/update/69/bwupdt69_ai.pdf (accessed 20 September 2012).

Schroeder, Heike, and Heather Love. 'The Role of Non-Nation-State Actors and Side Events in the International Climate Negotiations'. *Climate Policy* 12, no. 1 (2012): 23.

Shelton, Dinah L. 'Developing Substantive Environmental Rights'. *Journal of Human Rights and the Environment* 1, no. 1 (2010): 89.

'Socio-Economic Right Accountability Project'. At http://serap-nigeria.org/ (accessed 10 March 2014).

Tarlock, Dan. 'The Role of Non-Government Organizations in the Development of International Environmental Law'. *Chicago-Kent Law Review* 68 (1992): 61.

UNEP. 'Welcome to the UNEP Climate Pledges Site'. At http://www.unep.org/climatepledges/ (accessed 8 March 2013).

UNFCCC. 'Adaptation Fund'. At http://unfccc.int/cooperation_and_support/financial_mechanism/adaptation_fund/items/3659.php (accessed 8 March 2013)

———. 'Decisions Adopted by the Conference of the Parties Serving as the Meeting of the Parties to the Kyoto Protocol'. FCCC/KP/CMP/2005/8, 30 March 2006.

———. 'An Introduction to the Kyoto Protocol Compliance Mechanism'. At http://unfccc.int/kyoto_protocol/compliance/items/3024.php (accessed 10 November 2013).

United Nations. 'The United Nations Framework Convention on Climate Change (UNFCCC)'. *I.L.M.* 31 (1992): 849. At www.unfccc.int (accessed 20 September 2012).

United Nations Environment Programme. 'Major Groups and Stakeholders' (2012). At http://www.unep.org/civil-society/MajorGroups/tabid/2749/Default.aspx (accessed 3 August 2012).

United Nations General Assembly. 'Report of the United Nations Conference on Environment and Development ("Rio Declaration")'. UN Doc. A/CONF. 151/26/Rev.1 1992.

United States Environmental Protection Agency. 'Environmental Justice'. At http://www.epa.gov/environmentaljustice/ (accessed 20 September 2012).

Wapner, Paul. 'Politics Beyond the State: Environmental Activism and World Civic Politics'. *World Politics* 47, no. 3 (1995): 311.

'World Wide Fund for Nature'. At http://www.wwf.org.uk (accessed 20 September 2013).

Wright, Richard W. 'The Principles of Justice'. *Notre Dame Law Review* 75, August (2000): 1859.

Wuerth, Ingrid. 'Online Kiobel Symposium: International Law and Alien Tort Statute Litigation', *Scotusblog* (11 July 2012). At http://www.scotusblog.com/2012/07/online-kiobel-symposium-international-law-and-alien-tort-statute-litigation (accessed 20 September 2012).

———. 'Wiwa V. Shell: The $15.5 Million Settlement'. *ASIL Insight* 13, no. 14 (2009). At http://www.asil.org/files/insight090909pdf.pdf (accessed 20 September 2012).

Chapter 11

The Status of Non-State Actors under the International Rule of Law: A Search for Global Justice

Mohammad H. Zarei and Azar Safari

Introduction

In this chapter, we examine the position of non-state actors (NSAs) as new players in international law. NSAs possess significant *de facto* economic, financial and institutional power yet they lack any corresponding legal responsibility. This disproportionateness between power and responsibility needs to be recognized and remedied. Traditional international law norms, mechanisms and arrangements, however, are insufficient to deal with the problems posed by this imbalance. In what follows, we explore some possible measures to address it.

Speaking generally, we propose that non-state actors should be brought within the framework of the international rule of law (IROL). It should be recognized, however, that the idea of the international rule of law has yet to be conclusively defined. The divide between formal and substantive conceptions of the rule of law is as active internationally as it is at the national level. Here, we argue that internationally the formal conception should be preferred to the substantive, which can be read as embracing larger aims such as the achievement of global justice. Within the formal conception, NSAs should be accorded legal personality. They can and should be drawn adequately and effectively to legal account. Despite the existence of the divide between formal and substantive conceptions of the rule of law, however, we argue that both must embrace respect for fundamental human rights enshrined in the major international human rights conventions. Consequently, NSAs should properly be brought to account for any violations of human rights they might commit.

In the first part of this chapter, we examine the legal standing of NSAs. In the second part, we tie their legal standing to the wider idea of the international rule of law.

Concept, Personality and Status of NSAs

It has been some decades since the idea of NSAs made its entrance into the sphere of international law. The idea has been the subject of controversy. According to one definition suggested by Andrew Clapham,

> The concept of non-state actors is generally understood as including any entity that is not actually a state, often used to refer to armed groups, terrorists, civil society, religious groups or corporations.[1]

More broadly, Article 6 of the Cotonou Agreement states:

> The actors of cooperation will include:
> a: State (local, national and regional),
> b: Non-State: – Private Sector; – Economic and social partners, including trade union organizations; – Civil society in all its forms according to national characteristics.[2]

Referring to the dangers that NSAs may pose in the context of war, the UN Security Council has resolved that the states shall be required to refrain from providing any goods, services to, or supporting NSAs that develop, obtain, construct or transfer or use chemical weapons.[3]

NSAs do not possess official or government authorities and powers and do not have institutional and financial relationships with states.[4] As such they have not generally been recognized as traditional objects of international law but, instead, as potentially new subjects of it:

> NSAs are subjects or persons of international law. The conception of NSAs as an object of international law does, however, not sufficiently explain its present day position in the international law … In other words, power and influence of NSAs in many cases goes far beyond that of entities to which international law has traditionally accorded to object-states.[5]

---

1 Andrew Clapham, *Human Rights Obligations of Non-State Actors* (Oxford: Oxford University Press, 2006), 211.

2 Partnership Agreement Between the Members of the African, Caribbean and Pacific Group of States, of the One Part, and the European Community and its Member States, of the Other Part, Signed in Cotonou, Benin on 23 June 2000.

3 United Nations Security Council, 'Non-Proliferation of Weapons of Mass Destruction' (Resolution 1540 (2004), 28 April 2004), 28.

4 There are documents that define these actors directly or draw out their personality implicitly by establishing their responsibilities. This issue will be discussed in the following pages.

5 J.E. Nijman, 'Non-State Actors and the International Rule of Law: Revisiting the "Realist Theory" of International Legal Personality', in *Non-State Actors in International*

Today, the scope of international law is enhanced by issues such as trade, criminal acts, finance, environment and human rights, etc. and by concerns of groups, minorities, non-governmental organizations and particularly, individuals.[6]

In parallel the primary focus of international law has also been changing. As the 2010 report of the Brandeis Institute for International Judges noted,

> The increasingly prominent place of Human Rights in international legal order has brought with it a shift of focus from states to the individual as a subject of international law.[7]

In order to have legal personality, an entity must possess rights as well as obligations within a legal system. If, therefore, we are to regard NSAs as having legal personality, it should come to be recognized that international law confers rights and imposes obligations upon them. There are international instruments that have enumerated various rights and obligations for NSAs, depending on the content and intent of the instrument.[8] International law seems, therefore, to be in the process of recognizing the significance of NSAs. That paves the path for recognizing their formal, legal personality. However, there are debates and worries about the consequences of such recognition of legal personality:

> There is a fear that one 'legitimizes' actors by giving them human rights obligations and implies a power which they may themselves erode, rather than enhancing, human freedom and autonomy.[9]

Law, Politics and Governance Series, ed. Math Noortmann (Amsterdam Center for International Law Research Paper Series, University of Amsterdam, 2010), 2–40, 5.

6 For an analysis of such development in terms of human rights see: John H. Knox, 'Horizontal Human Rights Law', *The American Journal of International Law* 102 (2008): 1–47.

7 Brandeis Institute for International Judges (BIIJ), 'Toward an International Rule of Law' (The International Center for Ethics, Justice, and Public Life, Brandeis University, 2010).

8 For instance: ILO, 'Convention Concerning Forced or Compulsory Labour (Forced Labor Convention) C29' (1930); OECD, 'Convention on Combating Bribery of Foreign Public Officials in International Business Transactions' (1997); United Nations, 'Convention on the Rights of the Child (CRC)' (1989); United Nations Committee on Economic Social and Cultural Rights (CESC), 'The Right to Adequate Food, General Comment No. 12' (E/C.12/1999/5, 1999); 'The Right to Highest Attainable Standard of Health, General Comment No. 14' (E/C.12/2000/4, 2000); 'The Right to Water, General Comment No. 15' (E/C.12/2002/11, 2002); United Nations Committee on the Right of the Child (CRC), 'General Measures of Implementation of Convention on the Right of Child, General Comment No. 5' (CRC/GC/2003/5, 2003); 'International Maritime Organization, 'International Convention on Civil Liability for Oil Pollution Damage' (1969).

9 Clapham, *Human Rights Obligations of Non-State Actors*, 53.

One of the significant reasons for not endowing NSAs with legal personality in traditional state-centred international law is that the states would be reluctant to share their powers and authorities with NSAs. Furthermore, there is a fear of legitimizing the NSAs' unlawful actions by recognizing their legal status and personality. This may in turn lead to the legitimization of their use of violence.[10]

The strength of this argument depends on the nature of the NSA with which one is concerned. For example, one important increasing role of civil society NSAs is their monitoring of human rights treatment by states and government authorities around the world. For instance, in the case of a complaint against the president of Congo, some human rights NSAs applied to the French courts against the president of Congo for committing crimes against humanity. When the case was finally referred to the International Criminal Court (ICC), it was decided by the ICC that the alleged crimes against humanity were not substantiated and thus the request was denied.[11] However, the interesting point was that neither the French courts nor the ICC rejected the request of NSAs based on their standing rules of procedure.

The primary objective of international human rights instruments is the protection of individuals and communities against states. Today, there are a vast number of multi-national corporations (MNCs), non-governmental organizations (NGOs), and other NSAs with economic, financial and institutional powers that can influence political powers, domestically and globally, to alter their institutional behaviour. Such unlimited and unrestricted powers are susceptible to misuse against individuals and groups, and thus must be held accountable in accordance with the terms of international human rights conventions.

Negative Roles of NSAs

In reality NSAs have positive as well as negative functions. The negative role of NSAs can be analysed from different points of view. First, governments, in particular authoritarian regimes, are aware that the legal status of NSAs in international law is not well established and because of that NSAs cannot be held legally responsible for their actions. Furthermore, since states are unwilling for their legitimacy to be questioned in international community, they may seek to co-opt NSAs for use against individuals, opposition groups and minorities.[12] Such states use NSAs as fig leaves to evade international responsibility.

10 Ibid., 46.

11 See Angela M. Banks, 'The Growing Impact of Non-State Actors on the International and European Legal Systems', *Faculty Publications* Paper 132 (2003), 294. Online. Available HTTP: http://scholarship.law.wm.edu/facpubs/132 (accessed 10 October 2013).

12 J. Crawford, 'Human Rights and State Responsibility', in *Twelfth Raymond & Beverly Sackler Distinguished Lecture Series* (Storrs, CT: Thomas J. Dodd Research Center, 2006), 1–15 at 4–5.

These negative relationships between NSAs and violating states take different forms. Sometimes, states directly use NSAs as a means to their ends through contract and agency. In some other form, NSAs are used by states indirectly through guidance and management of their operations. NSA forces and personnel, for example informal militias, have been financed, trained, procured and equipped with weapons by governments. In other circumstances, governments may simply fail to act against human rights violations such as torture, arbitrary arrests, and killings of opposition groups and civil movement activists by NSAs that share the same ideology of states.[13]

In international law, the presumption of innocence of states in such circumstances can hardly be accepted. In fact, the contrary is more accurate, particularly where the government is undemocratic and there has been a previous and constant violation of human rights.[14]

Second, in some cases states may not be at fault or manipulate NSAs in wrongful acts, but NSAs independently may abuse their positions, institutions, personnel and powers against certain groups and individuals. In these circumstances, to prove that states have any direct responsibility for such actions may be difficult. International law in these circumstances may not recognize the direct responsibility of NSAs, notwithstanding that, in several international human rights documents,[15] the obligations of NSAs have been set down. Based on most cases,[16] the states have been addressed as the main responsible bodies. It seems that the only exception

---

13 Nicolas Carrillo Santarelli, 'Non-State Actors Human Rights Obligations and Responsibilities under International Law', *Revista Electronica De Estudios Internacionales* 15 (2008): 1–10.

14 See the following references as examples for establishing direct responsibility of States in those situations: Carsten Hoppe, 'Passing the Buck: State Responsibility for Private Military Companies', *The European Journal of International Law* 19, no. 5 (2008): 989–1014; Ian Brownlie, *Principles of International Law* (Oxford: Clarendon Press, 1998), 452; UN Security Council, 'Resolution 1373 Adopted by the Security Council at its 4385th Meeting, on 28 September 2001' (2001).

15 For instance see: UN Human Rights Committee (HRC), 'CCPR General Comment No. 17: Article 24 (Rights of the Child)' (7 April 1989); 'CCPR General Comment No. 20: Article 7 (Prohibition of Torture, or Other Cruel, Inhuman or Degrading Treatment or Punishment)' (10 March 1992); 'CCPR General Comment No. 18: Non-Discrimination' (10 November 1989); United Nations Committee on the Elimination of Discrimination against Women, 'General Recommendation No. 19 (11th Session) Violence against Women' (1992); United Nations Committee on the Right of the Child (CRC), 'General Measures of Implementation of Convention on the Right of Child, General Comment No. 5'; United Nations Human Rights Committee, 'General Comment 31, Nature of the General Legal Obligation on States Parties to the Covenant', U.N. Doc. CCPR/C/21/Rev.1/Add.13 (2004).

16 For instance see: Inter American Court of Human Rights. Case of Ximenes-Lopes v Brazil. 4 July 2006; ECHR. Lopez Ostra v Spain. Application No. 16798/90. 9 Dec. 1994; Social and Economic Rights Action Center & the Center for Economic and Social Rights v Nigeria. Cited as: Communication No. 155/96. United Nations Committee on The Elimination of Discrimination Against Women; Case of Sahide Goekce v

is in international humanitarian law, where, for example, under the Second Protocol of the Geneva Convention, the direct responsibility of rebels, terrorist and armed opposition groups has been admitted.[17] Hence, since NSAs are not covered completely by international law norms, their acts can become a real threat to national and international security. In addition, because they exist in a wide range of forms and establishments, it is very difficult to determine NSAs' general responsibilities; therefore, it seems that States must bear principal responsibility for preventing their adverse actions given that they possess overarching powers and authorities to criminalize and penalize NSA activities.

Positive Roles of NSAs

In contemporary international relations, NSAs such as human rights advocacy organizations, perform important positive functions ranging from human rights education to the enforcement and monitoring of human rights standards. Perhaps the most significant part of such NSAs is that they have played an effective role in the international norm-making process, like their participation in the preparation of the Draft on the UN Convention on the Rights of Persons with Disabilities.[18]

Sometimes, specialized NSAs in the human rights arena may influence international norm making by participating in consultations on specialist legal matters. They may also act as lobbyists.[19] Another particularly important area of activity is that of international norm making in the international environmental area.[20] Even if not directly participating in processes of norm formation, NSAs may still have an impact through the dissemination of information to the public, which promotes public awareness and transparency.

NSAs also have a significant role in peace-building processes, such as in the Center on Housing Rights and Evictions for the International Protection of Individuals and People of Kosovo.[21]

Austria. Communication Number CN.6/2005.HRC; Case of Herra Rubior v Colombia. Communication no. 161/1983.

17 International Committee of the Red Cross (ICRC), 'Geneva Convention for the Amelioration of the Condition of Wounded, Sick and Shipwrecked Members of Armed Forces at Sea (Second Geneva Convention)', 75 UNTS 85 (12 August 1949).

18 See, unpublished paper, V.J. Bernstorff, 'On the Legality and Legitimacy of NGO Participation in International Law, Non-State Actors in Law Making and in the Shaping of Policy' (2007), 7–21.

19 See C. Ryngaert, 'Imposing International Duties on Non-State Actors and the Legitimacy of International Law', in *Seminar on the FWO Research Community on Non-State Actors in International Law. Leuven* (Leuven: University of Leuven, 2009).

20 K. Raustiala, 'States, NGOs and International Environmental Institutions', *International Studies Quarterly* 41 (1997): 719–40.

21 Khaled Hassine, *Regularizing Property Rights in Kosovo & Elsewhere: Cohre's Impact as Non-State Actor for the International Protection of Housing, Land & Property Rights* (Köln: WiKu-Wissenschaftsverlag, 2010).

Another positive activity of NSAs concerns the enforcement of international law norms and standards. With regard to binding international laws, NSAs and NGOs have had a positive influence on the application of international laws to national legal systems, in particular, where they have already been consulted or taken part in formulating the applied norms and standards.[22] In this way they may reduce the costs of application and enforcement. More significantly, they can minimize the costs of enforcement by engaging in the self-regulation of their activities.

Furthermore, the supervisory function of NSAs cannot be overlooked. This role of NSAs has two aspects: one is their role in supervising the implementation of international norms and standards within their own area, and the other is their role in monitoring states' conduct in the light of international conventions. They may, for example, use the media to reveal the state violation of international legal norms, or they may report abuse of powers to relevant monitoring bodies in the domestic system or to relevant international supervisory bodies such as those in the UN human rights arena.

The International Rule of Law as an Analytical Framework

As explained in the previous section, the status of NSAs in traditional international law is problematic. Their roles, functions and impacts have not yet found their place in a state-centred model of international law. In this section the idea of International Rule of Law (IROL) as a framework for analysis of the NSAs' rights and obligations is examined.

Conceptions of the Rule of Law (ROL)

There are several reasons that justify the need for IROL. First, there are the actions of NSAs that have social, economic, political and legal impacts on individuals, groups and communities nationally and internationally, such as violations of various human rights. These are not directly subject to international law because, in part, there are no legal mechanisms through which to make NSAs accountable. One of the fundamental pillars of the idea of the international rule of law, however, must be that influential actors should act in accordance with the law and, as a consequence, there must be legal responsibility for any breach of the law. Second, as Laurence R. Helfer explained, the international legal system suffers from decentralization and disaggregation:

> In the absence of a centralized, hierarchical authority with the power to coerce behavior, nation states are free to pursue their own interests, with states that

22 Anne Peters, Till Förster and Gretta Fenner Zinkernagel, eds, *Non-State Actors as Standard Setters* (Cambridge: Cambridge University Press, 2009).

> possess more material or financial resources often enjoying a decided advantage in their relations with weaker or poorer countries.[23]

As far as possible, the law's differential treatment of rich and poor states should be minimized. Similarly, the IROL should aim to establish international law and order and thereby overcome the problem of the unequal treatment of influential public and private actors. Third, the idea of the ROL is not just a political or legal ideal. It has also been adopted in international instruments such as the Universal Declaration of Human Rights (UDHR). Mary Ann Glendon, for instance, has argued that the ROL has been enmeshed to the body of the UDHR from the very beginning.[24] She cites the third clause of its preamble, which reads as,

> Whereas it is essential, if man is not to be compelled to have recourse, as a last resort, to rebellion against tyranny and oppression, that human rights should be protected by the ROL.

The ROL has been evolving into a positive condition for the effective application of international law. It constitutes a significant standard of behaviour and decision making in the field of international relations. As such it should apply to states and NSAs equally.

However, the concept of the ROL is a vague and contested idea in domestic public law, international law and political theory. Its definition and demarcation ranges from formal to substantive conceptions. These conceptions cannot be elaborated in detail here. It is, however, sufficient to summarize some of its most important features, and then a suggested amalgamated conception of ROL and its externalization in international law will be analysed.

Formal Conceptions of the ROL

According to the categorization suggested by Brian Z. Tamanaha and Paul P. Craig,[25] theories of the ROL can be divided into two basic categories of formal and substantive conceptions, and each version reflects distinct but contrasting

---

23 L.R. Helfer, 'Constitutional Analogies in the International Legal System', *Loyola of Los Angeles Law Review* 37, no. 2 (2003): 293. Despite this multiplicity, Helfer acknowledges that a degree of an order can be found in a set of treaties, organizations and dispute settlement mechanisms that regulate each subject matter like environment, human rights and trade.

24 Mary Ann Glendon, 'The Rule of Law in the Universal Declaration of Human Rights', *Northwestern Journal of International Human Rights* 2, no. 1 (2004): 67–81.

25 See P.P. Craig, 'Formal and Substantive Conception of the Rule of Law: An Analytical Framework', *Public Law* (1997): 67–87.

perceptions.[26] One concept of the ROL is known as 'Rule by Law'. This notion of the ROL is considered as a means by which the government is authorized to achieve its objectives. In other words, it has an instrumental function to fulfil any kind of political end such as that which occurred during the Third Reich period in Germany or in other authoritarian states. This precept is purely definitional and excludes any substance.[27]

Another variation of the formal conception is known as 'Formal Legality'. It consists of two sets of specifications: first, the legal characteristics of a legal system, and second, institutional/procedural checks on the exercise of powers. It is claimed that these criteria are value free and neutral, and are independent of moral and political values. As a common ground of formal theories, '[they] do not however seek to pass judgment upon the actual content of the law itself.'[28]

The prominent legal philosopher Joseph Raz has argued in response to substantive theorists like Ronald Dworkin that,

> If the rule of law is the Rule of the good law then to explain its nature is to propound a complete social philosophy. But if so the term lacks any useful function … The rule of law is a political ideal which a legal system may lack or possess to a greater or lesser degree. That much is common ground. It is also to be insisted that the rule of law is just one of the virtues by which a legal system may be judged and by which it is to be judged.[29]

With respect to the neutrality of the ROL, Raz acknowledged that,

> A non-democratic legal system, based on the denial of human rights, on extensive poverty, on racial segregation, sexual inequalities, and racial persecution may, in principle, conform to the requirements of the rule of law better than any of the more enlightened Western democracies ….[30]
> The law may … institute slavery without violating the rule of law.[31]

Raz also argues that this account of the ROL aims at establishing law and order and regulating citizens' lives and behaviours. The virtue of the ROL is that it enables citizens to guide their own lives in relation to each other and also in relation to

---

26 B.Z. Tamanaha, *On the Rule of Law: History, Politics, Theory* (Cambridge: Cambridge University Press, 2004).

27 P.M. Nichols, 'Reconceptualizing the Rule of Law as an International Norm' (University of Pennsylvania, 2012).

28 Craig, 'Formal and Substantive Conception of the Rule of Law: An Analytical Framework'.

29 J. Raz, 'The Rule of Law and Its Virtues', in *The Authority of Law: Essays on Law and Morality*, ed. J. Raz (Oxford: Clarendon Press, 1979), 210.

30 Ibid., 211.

31 Ibid., 221.

state authorities. Since this conception is claimed as value free, its objective is not necessarily to curtail abuse of powers by public officials through institutional arrangements like separation of powers or checks and balances.

The virtue of a formal conception of the ROL consists among other things of legal certainty and predictability. Raz categorized its character into two sets of principles: inherent and subordinate.[32] The first set of principles is:

- generality,
- prospectiveness, openness and clarity,
- relative stability.

The second set of principles is necessary for the effective implementation of the first set of principles. The foregoing inherent principles cannot be maintained unless some procedural and institutional guarantees are established. The subordinate principles are:

- independence of the Judiciary,
- principles of procedural justice,
- judicial review power of the courts,
- accessibility to the courts,
- crime preventing agencies that are not corrupted in their functions.[33]

These virtues of the ROL have been more or less agreed by other legal and political philosophers like Dicey, Lon Fuller and Hayek, with a slightly different formulation of the requirements of the ROL.[34] Fuller and Hayek's theories, however, do not necessarily incorporate the element of judicial review and judicial organization into the conception of the ROL.

Individuals and citizens' autonomy and dignity are protected through the above virtues of the legal system; as pursuant to them, they may make their own decisions as to their individual goals and destination. Another advantage is that the political neutrality of the ROL can not only gain support from different right and left wings in politics, but also can incorporate diverging substantive values.

As far as the externalization of the ROL into international law is concerned, Tamanaha points out that,

> This substantively empty quality has been identified by theorists, and by the World Bank and other development agencies, is what renders it amenable to universal application.[35]

---

32 Ibid., 210–23.

33 For an analogy of IROL based on this kind of approach see: Nichols, 'Reconceptualizing the Rule of Law as an International Norm'.

34 See Tamanaha, *On the Rule of Law: History, Politics, Theory*, 93–4.

35 Ibid., 94.

However, Tamanaha criticizes this conception on two grounds: first, although it requires equal application of legal norms to all and prohibits arbitrary differentiation among individuals and organizations, it requires substantive standards to determine what constitutes arbitrariness. Second, the requirement of the ROL, i.e. equality of all before the law, needs to be supplemented by equality in substantive theories like distributive justice.[36] This critique, however, opens the door to the contrary argument made by Raz that substantive standards may open the way to the introduction of an entire social philosophy.[37]

Another aspect of the ROL that cannot be ignored is its preventive function in regulating the exercise of arbitrary powers or the abuse of discretionary powers. This version was well set out in the nineteenth century by A.V. Dicey in his book *An Introduction to the Study of the Law of the Constitution*.[38] He formulated the ROL in three significant facets: first, society should be ruled by law, not by discretionary (arbitrary) powers; second, there should be equality before the law, for private individuals as well as government officials; and third, all persons should be subject to the general jurisdiction of ordinary courts that constitute the best source of legal protection.[39]

Substantive conceptions of the rule of law

The proponents of the substantive conception of the ROL agree on the formal requirements of law, but they go further to incorporate qualitative criteria such as fundamental rights into the conception of the ROL. Ronald Dworkin justifies his arguments for this version of the ROL:

> I shall call the second conception of the rule of law the 'rights' conception … It assumes that citizens have moral rights and duties with respect to one another, and political rights against the state as a whole. It insists that these moral and political rights be recognized in positive law, so that they may be enforced upon the demand of individual citizens through courts or other judicial institutions of the familiar type, so far as this is practicable. The rule of law on this conception is the ideal of rule by an accurate public conception of individual rights. It does not distinguish, as the rule book conception does, between the rule of law and substantive justice; on the contrary it requires, as a part of the ideal of law, that the rules in the rule book capture and enforce moral rights.[40]

---

36 Ibid.

37 See Nichols, 'Reconceptualizing the Rule of Law as an International Norm'.

38 A.V. Dicey, *An Introduction to the Study of the Law of the Constitution* (London: Macmillan, 1885; repr., 2005).

39 See S. Beaulac, 'The Rule of Law in International Law Today', in *Relocating the Rule of Law*, ed. G. Palombella and N. Walker (Oxford: Hart Publishing, 2009), 197–223.

40 R. Dworkin, 'Political Judges and the Rule of Law', *Proceedings of the British Academy* 64 (1978): 262.

Dworkin's rights-based conception of the ROL relies on the existence of underlying community values that underpin the background to positive law. It is the duty of judges in complex and contested cases to deliver their decisions based on moral and political principles that best fit the moral rights of the parties. In hard cases, the duty of the judges is to find the right answer by applying presumptive principles of a moral and political nature.

However, Dworkin's theory is criticized on different grounds: first, communities may be divided on different legal and political principles, in particular with regard to sensitive issues such as abortion, positive discrimination, employment, education, tax, homosexuality, the death penalty, etc. Second, it is too simplistic to believe that law makers and decision makers are always motivated to create laws that reflect communities' values and morality. Third, this theory shifts decision making from elected politicians and gives it to appointed judges, which in turn results in greater judicialization of politics and democratic process.[41]

Another substantive theory of the ROL not only adheres to legal formality and individual rights but also incorporates substantive criteria such as welfare and social rights. The International Commission of Jurists conference held in 1959 declared for instance that,

> The dynamic concept which the Rule of Law became in the formulation of the Declaration of Delhi does indeed safeguard and advance the civil and political rights of the individual in a free society; but it is also concerned with the establishment by the state of social, economic, educational and cultural conditions under which man's legitimate aspirations and dignity may be realized.[42]

Under this rich version of the ROL, states are required, among other things, to take positive actions in order to create a better life for people and ensure a proper standard of distributive justice. However, incorporating social rights into the notion of the ROL complicates the basic concept and invites more controversy to the debate.[43]

Now the question is, what conception of the ROL is amenable to be applied to international law and on what grounds? This chapter argues for a conception that is less contentious among legal and political scholars, lawyers and practitioners, on the one hand, and that bases IROL on the most authoritative international instruments and jurisprudence on the other.

---

41 Tamanaha, *On the Rule of Law: History, Politics, Theory*, 102–4.

42 International Congress of Jurists, 'Declatation of Delhi' (Delhi: International Commission of Jurists, 10 January 1959).

43 Tamanaha, *On the Rule of Law: History, Politics, Theory*, 112–13.

International Rule of Law Considered

In so far as the functions and actions of the NSAs are concerned, and due to the necessity of the establishment of the IROL, as discussed above, it is important to examine how the IROL should be constituted and on what normative basis it should be constituted.

The normative aspect is the most significant aspect of the rule of law but also its weakest form. It seems that most international lawyers and scholars have propounded the idea of IROL in its formal conception, in particular, as formal legality and equality.[44] However, this view does not discount the complexities and problematic nature of the IROL. IROL should still find the means to deal with contemporary issues such as the status of NSAs and societal imperfections such as the problems of inequality, discrimination, poverty, environment, and human rights violations, which traditional international law cannot easily cope with effectively, at least on a general scale.

We propose a formal conception of IROL and therefore need to set out the requirements of this version of the idea. The requirements of formal legality for an IROL can be summarized in the following formulation: first, the existence of a principled legal normativity; second, a norm-making mechanism to create laws that are applicable equally to all subjects, similar to domestic law making; and third, a judicial enforcement mechanism in cases of the breach of international norms or for settlement of disputes with an authoritative and binding character.[45]

Regarding the first requirement, some have argued that international law embraces a body of rules and norms that are capable of application to issues, directly or indirectly through the rules and principles of international law.[46] According to Article 38 (1) of the Statute of International Court of Justice (ICJ), these rules are contained in treaties, customs or non-written sources of international law, and general principles of law that are mostly extracted from domestic legal systems. Furthermore, there are other sources of international normativity, such as the Vienna Convention on the Law of Treaties, which is ratified by more than 108 states. There are also other treaties and international instruments such as the Universal Declaration of Human Rights and the two Covenants on Civil and Political Rights, and Social, Economic and Cultural Rights, and also the European Convention on Human Rights, European and World Trade Organization (WTO) treaties that can control behaviour of states, individuals and NSAs with respect to various trade issues.[47] It is also said that there is a set of rules recognized as *jus cogens* or preventive measures, which function as a set of higher laws from which

44 For instance see: Brandeis Institute for International Judges (BIIJ), 'Toward an International Rule of Law'; Helfer, 'Constitutional Analogies in the International Legal System', 213–14.

45 See Beaulac, 'The Rule of Law in International Law Today'.

46 Ibid., 205.

47 Nichols, 'Reconceptualizing the Rule of Law as an International Norm'.

no deviation is allowed, like unauthorized uses of force and the most serious violations of human rights, such as slavery, genocide, torture, etc.[48]

However, this normative aspect of the contemporary IROL may justifiably be criticized in particular with regard to NSAs. This is because, first, as compared to domestic constitutional law, there is no hierarchical order of norms whereby higher norms legitimize lower norms, whereby constitutional law lays the foundation for domestic legislation. Second, existing international norms have not yet attained universal applicability. Even if there are some effective international instruments such as the Universal Declaration of Human Rights, complete coverage of the conduct and behaviour of states and NSAs has not yet been achieved. In addition, there is often significant controversy as to their interpretation. Third, with respect to NSAs, there are no general rules that address directly their legal status and behaviours. Fourth, the lack of consistency among international instruments needs to be addressed. Every international instrument deals with its particular subject and with its special set of institutions and enforcement mechanisms. As yet there is no legal or procedural solution to the need for the harmonization of the overlapping and contradictory provisions of relevant international norms and rules.

Regarding the second requirement of the IROL, i.e. law-making institutions similar to domestic legislative bodies, it would be beneficial if eventually there were some centralized authority on the international plane to function as a global parliament. Some authors have tried to suggest that the UN Security Council, General Assembly and International Court of Justice act as executive, legislature and judiciary in this way. But their powers and influence are very strictly limited.

It is worth mentioning that, according to formal theorists of the ROL, such as Raz, Dicey, Fuller and Hayek, the existence of a centralized law-making institution and the existence of a rigid model of separation of powers is not a necessary element of the ROL.[49] They have tended to focus on the independence of the judiciary and the presence of judicial review.

Nevertheless, the above analogy seems inaccurate, because the General Assembly is limited to recommendatory powers only. Further, by comparison, there are several international rule-making organizations, such as the WTO, that have more effective rule-making powers with more authority and more powerful enforcement mechanisms.

Regarding normative and institutional hierarchies, Helfer puts the current status of international law in this way:

> The international legal system too contains normative and institutional hierarchies that seem to offer a tool for resolving the difficulties that decentralization and

48 Helfer, 'Constitutional Analogies in the International Legal System', 213–14.

49 For an analogical description of International law and constitutionalism including the idea of international separation of powers see: J.L. Dunoff and J.P. Trachtman, eds, *Ruling the World: International Law, Global Governance and Constitutionalism* (Cambridge and New York: Cambridge University Press, 2009).

> disaggregation may engender. However, these hierarchies do not provide a blueprint for resolving questions of governance in a manner analogous to the hierarchies enshrined in domestic constitutions.[50]

With the emergence of global governance and the emerging power of NSAs in standard setting in fields as diverse as human rights protection, trade, environment, and socio-cultural matters, the need for a broader conception and application of an IROL has become ever more pressing.

The third requirement of an IROL is that there should be a judicial enforcement mechanism to ensure that states and NSAs act in accordance with the principles and rules of international law. Without judicial review to rule on the legality of public and private actions and activities, there is always the possibility that agencies and authorities may abuse their powers. An international judiciary should ensure that the law is implemented in accordance with the legislator's will and that peoples are assured that there will be no arbitrary use of power and no distortion of legislative enactments whether in the public or private spheres.

Some have argued that the ICJ performs as the judicial enforcement apparatus of international law and also may exercise the judicial review power over the other organs of the UN. To provide the ICJ with jurisdiction over disputes arising from UN instruments and over disputes between states is plausible. However, its jurisdiction is limited and it does not yet have a general jurisdiction to review the actions, decisions, or regulations made by organs of the UN such as the Security Council, or to hear and determine complaints from individuals, groups, and NSAs against states or other NSAs.

Although there are no centralized and coordinated international courts or tribunals analogous to domestic courts, there are various international tribunals that possess important and individual jurisdictions. These include the ICJ, the International Criminal Court, the WTO panel for the settlement of disputes, the International Tribunals for the former Yugoslavia and Rwanda, the European Court of Human Rights (ECtHR), the European Court of Justice (ECJ), etc. Some of these courts and tribunals decide on the complaints referred to by both states and NSAs alike, such as the ECtHR, but most of them receive complaints only from states parties to the relevant treaties, like the WTO panel for dispute settlement.[51]

The present system of international courts and tribunals does not yet satisfy the third requirement of the IROL for the following reasons: first, there is no centralized and hierarchical international judiciary; second, these judicial bodies have a very limited scope of jurisdiction; third, individuals and NSAs have no

50 Helfer, 'Constitutional Analogies in the International Legal System', 213.

51 Regarding the enforcement mechanism, Helfer argues that, within the WTO trade dispute settlement system, the crucial compliance force is reciprocity. He asserts, 'This enforcement mechanism is properly used in the trade context. But in cases of Human Rights violations by a state it is not thinkable and morally unjustified.' 'Constitutional Analogies in the International Legal System', 222.

access to most of these courts and tribunals; fourth, those courts and tribunals that do satisfy this requirement lack authoritative enforcement mechanisms. In cases of non-compliance by the defendant party, there is no legal guarantee for the implementation of the relevant decrees and judgments within domestic law and jurisdictions. This latter obstacle is due to the fact that the enabling international treaties are voluntary and consent based.

Although this third element of IROL is problematic, in contrast to the early decades after the Second World War and also the Cold War period, the current status of international courts and tribunals and their roles in resolving disputes, prosecuting crimes and atrocities, and convicting human rights violations, represent a very significant improvement. Generally speaking, these facts show that we are closer to an IROL than at any time previously. According to the BIIJ 2010 report on the IROL,

> Participants also concurred in a general way that there already exists a rule of law at the international level, at least in an emergent form.[52]

It was also reaffirmed that,

> The impacts of international courts and tribunals may include successfully preventing armed conflict, securing a peaceful settlement of boundaries, deterring serious violations of the law, achieving the overall objectives of an international treaty, and obtaining compliance with specific judgments.[53]

Conclusion

Thus far, the IROL has been used in an umbrella sense to encompass certain fundamental values and principles, while at the same time its usage has remained contested. In parallel, however, domestic public law and the traditional model of the ROL have been simultaneously assimilating into the practice of global governance. So, for example, the domestic legal treatment of NSAs, through the medium of good governance and non-state regulatory regimes, is progressively being replicated at international level in the economic, trade, legal and political spheres.

The emergence of participatory regulation and new regulatory regimes shows that national states, in particular market-centred economies, are more and more attuned to and influenced by the participation of NSAs. In a constructive way, the concept of sovereignty is not only diminishing externally through global governance, trade relaxation, and international human rights and humanitarian laws, etc., but also weakening internally, through good governance, privatization

52 Brandeis Institute for International Judges (BIIJ), 'Toward an International Rule of Law'.

53 Ibid., 27.

of economy, participatory democracy, decentralization of government authority, and outsourcing government functions to NSAs.

With respect to the substantive version of the ROL, there have been many attempts to include social justice and welfare rights in the notion of the IROL. However, we believe that this conception is more problematic than the formal version of the ROL. This is because it is contentious not simply from the normative perspective, but also because of the realities of international law and relations. States and international organizations remain much divided as to such matters as global resource allocation, positive governmental obligations to citizens, and the nature of social justice. A formal conception of the rule of law, therefore, is preferable, as its focus is primarily upon the formal and therefore neutral aspects of the law rather than on its substantive and therefore contested bases.

Notwithstanding this, however, there is one element of a substantive conception that we believe should complement the formal one. In the international sphere, the existence of fundamental human rights is sufficiently widely recognized and its content sufficiently certain and defined that human rights standards may now properly be regarded as a crucial constituent of an international rule of law. The reasons are: first, international human rights measures have already been absorbed to the body of positive international laws through international norms such as the Universal Declaration of Human Rights, the International Covenant on Civil and Political Rights, the International Covenant on Social, Economic and Cultural Rights, the European Convention on Human Rights, and the other international human rights conventions. Formal theorists do not now tend to reject the centrality of human rights in favour of the content and operation of the rule of law, and nor should they. Human rights laws and standards are now more than any time previously, addressed, interpreted, judged and enforced at a global level.

As explained in this chapter, NSAs have both negative and positive functions. To benefit from the emergence of NSAs and to avoid their negative impacts, IROL principles should regulate NSA behaviour just as traditional international laws have governed the operation of states.

Cases

Herra Rubior v Colombia. Communication no. 161/1983.

Lopez Ostra v Spain. Application No. 16798/90. 9 Dec. 1994.

Sahide Goekce v Austria. Communication Number CN.6/2005 HRC.

Social and Economic Rights Action Center & the Center for Economic and Social Rights v Nigeria. Communication No. 155/96.

Ximenes-Lopes v Brazil. 4 July 2006, ECHR.

Bibliography

Banks, Angela M. 'The Growing Impact of Non-State Actors on the International and European Legal Systems'. *Faculty Publications* Paper 132 (2003), available at: http://scholarship.law.wm.edu/facpubs/132 (accessed 10 October 2013).

Beaulac, S. 'The Rule of Law in International Law Today'. In *Relocating the Rule of Law*, edited by G. Palombella and N. Walker. Oxford: Hart Publishing, 2009.

Bernstorff, V.J. 'On the Legality and Legitimacy of NGO Participation in International Law, Non-State Actors in Law Making and in the Shaping of Policy'. Unpublished paper, 2007.

Brandeis Institute for International Judges (BIIJ). 'Toward an International Rule of Law'. The International Center for Ethics, Justice, and Public Life, Brandeis University, 2010.

Brownlie, Ian. *Principles of International Law*. Oxford: Clarendon Press, 1998.

Clapham, Andrew. *Human Rights Obligations of Non-State Actors*. Oxford: Oxford University Press, 2006.

Craig, P.P. 'Formal and Substantive Conception of the Rule of Law: An Analytical Framework'. *Public Law* (1997): 467–87.

Crawford, J. 'Human Rights and State Responsibility'. In *Twelfth Raymond & Beverly Sackler Distinguished Lecture Series*. Storrs, CT: Thomas J. Dodd Research Center, 2006.

Dicey, A.V. *An Introduction to the Study of the Law of the Constitution*. London: Macmillan, 1885, 2005.

Dunoff, J.L., and J.P. Trachtman, eds. *Ruling the World: International Law, Global Governance and Constitutionalism*. Cambridge and New York: Cambridge University Press, 2009.

Dworkin, R. 'Political Judges and the Rule of Law'. *Proceedings of the British Academy* 64 (1978).

Glendon, Mary Ann. 'The Rule of Law in the Universal Declaration of Human Rights'. *Northwestern Journal of International Human Rights* 2, no. 1 (2004): 67–81.

Hassine, Khaled. *Regularizing Property Rights in Kosovo & Elsewhere: Cohre's Impact as Non-State Actor for the International Protection of Housing, Land & Property Rights*. Köln: WiKu-Wissenschaftsverlag, 2010.

Helfer, L.R. 'Constitutional Analogies in the International Legal System'. *Loyola of Los Angeles Law Review* 37, no. 2 (2003): 291–95.

Hoppe, Carsten. 'Passing the Buck: State Responsibility for Private Military Companies'. *The European Journal of International Law* 19, no. 5 (2008): 989–1014.

ILO. 'Convention Concerning Forced or Compulsory Labour (Forced Labor Convention) C29', 1930.

International Committee of the Red Cross (ICRC). 'Geneva Convention for the Amelioration of the Condition of Wounded, Sick and Shipwrecked Members of Armed Forces at Sea (Second Geneva Convention)', 75 UNTS 85. 12 August 1949.

International Congress of Jurists. 'Declatation of Delhi'. Delhi: International Commission of Jurists, 10 January 1959.

International Maritime Organization. 'International Convention on Civil Liability for Oil Pollution Damage'. 1969.

Knox, John H., 'Horizontal Human Rights Law', *The American Journal of International Law* 102 (2008): 1–47.

Nijman, J.E. 'Non-State Actors and the International Rule of Law: Revisiting the "Realist Theory" of International Legal Personality'. In *Non-State Actors in International Law, Politics and Governance Series*, edited by Math Noortmann. Amsterdam Center for International Law Research Paper Series, University of Amsterdam, 2010.

OECD. 'Convention on Combating Bribery of Foreign Public Officials in International Business Transactions'. 1997.

Peters, Anne, Till Förster, and Gretta Fenner Zinkernagel, eds. *Non-State Actors as Standard Setters*. Cambridge: Cambridge University Press, 2009.

Raustiala, K. 'States, NGOs and International Environmental Institutions'. *International Studies Quarterly* 41 (1997): 719–40.

Raz, J. 'The Rule of Law and Its Virtues'. In *The Authority of Law: Essays on Law and Morality*, edited by J. Raz. Oxford: Clarendon Press, 1979.

Ryngaert, C. 'Imposing International Duties on Non-State Actors and the Legitimacy of International Law'. In *Seminar on the FWO Research Community on Non-State Actors in International Law. Leuven*. Leuven: University of Leuven, 2009.

Santarelli, Nicolas Carrillo. 'Non-State Actors Human Rights Obligations and Responsibilities under International Law'. *Revista Electronica De Estudios Internacionales* 15 (2008): 1–10.

Tamanaha, B.Z. *On the Rule of Law: History, Politics, Theory*. Cambridge: Cambridge University Press, 2004.

UN Human Rights Committee (HRC). 'CCPR General Comment No. 17: Article 24 (Rights of the Child)'. 7 April 1989

———. 'CCPR General Comment No. 18: Non-Discrimination'. 10 November 1989.

———. 'CCPR General Comment No. 20: Article 7 (Prohibition of Torture, or Other Cruel, Inhuman or Degrading Treatment or Punishment)'. 10 March 1992.

United Nations. 'Convention on the Rights of the Child (CRC)'. 1989

United Nations Committee on Economic Social and Cultural Rights (CESC). 'The Right to Adequate Food, General Comment No. 12'. E/C.12/1999/5, 1999.

———. 'The Right to Highest Attainable Standard of Health, General Comment No. 14'. E/C.12/2000/4, 2000.

———. 'The Right to Water, General Comment No. 15'. E/C.12/2002/11, 2002.

United Nations Committee on the Elimination of Discrimination against Women. 'General Recommendation No. 19 (11th Session) Violence against Women'. 1992.

United Nations Committee on the Right of the Child (CRC). 'General Measures of Implementation of Convention on the Right of Child, General Comment No. 5'. CRC/GC/2003/5, 2003.

United Nations Human Rights Committee. 'General Comment 31, Nature of the General Legal Obligation on States Parties to the Covenant'. U.N. Doc. CCPR/C/21/Rev.1/Add.13 (2004). 2004.

United Nations Security Council. 'Non-Proliferation of Weapons of Mass Destruction'. Resolution 1540 (2004), 28 April 2004.

———. 'Resolution 1373 Adopted by the Security Council at its 4385th Meeting, on 28 September 2001' (2001).

PART III
Rethinking Aspects of International Justice

Chapter 12
The Responsibility to Protect at the United Nations

Spencer Zifcak

The formal recognition of the responsibility to protect (R2P) by the gathering of the world's leaders at the UN World Summit in 2005 was one of the principal achievements of the UN reform process initiated in that year. As is now well known, under heavy pressure to adopt some form of the 'responsibility to protect', diplomatic representatives at the United Nations haggled into the last week before the World Summit in 2005 to try to find the words that might permit a compromise to go to the world's leaders for endorsement.[1] And it was only after frenzied last-minute negotiations that the final text was concluded. While the text was hedged with qualifications and was weaker than that which had been proposed in three reports that recommended its adoption – the report of the International Commission on Intervention and State Sovereignty (ICISS); *A More Secure World*, the Report of the High-Level Panel on Threats, Challenges and Change; and the Secretary General's report *In Larger Freedom* – the consensus adoption of the new responsibility to protect doctrine was, nevertheless, a major achievement.[2] The concluded wording was as follows:

> 138. Each individual State has the responsibility to protect its populations from genocide, war crimes, ethnic cleansing and crimes against humanity. This responsibility entails the prevention of such crimes, including their incitement, through appropriate and necessary means. We accept that responsibility and will act in accordance with it ....
>
> 139. The international community, through the United Nations, also has the responsibility to use appropriate diplomatic, humanitarian and other peaceful means, in accordance with Chapters VI and VII of the Charter, to help protect

1 As to the General Assembly Debate prior to the World Summit see, A. Bellamy, *The Responsibility to Protect* (Cambridge: Polity, 2009), Chapter 3.

2 International Commission on Intervention and State Sovereignty, *The Responsibility to Protect: Report of the International Commission on Intervention and State Sovereignty* (Ottawa: International Development Research Centre, 2001); United Nations, 'High Level Panel on Threats, Challenges and Change, a More Secure World: Our Shared Responsibility', UN Document A/59/565 (2004); Kofi Annan, 'In Larger Freedom: Towards Development, Security and Human Rights for All', UN Doc. A/59/2005 (2005).

> populations from genocide, war crimes, ethnic cleansing and crimes against humanity. In this context, we are prepared to take collective action, in a timely and decisive manner, through the Security Council, in accordance with the Charter, including Chapter VII, on a case-by-case basis and in cooperation with relevant regional organizations as appropriate, should peaceful means be ineffective ....[3]

It is plain from a close reading of the text of the relevant resolution that the doctrine's final form represented a substantial compromise. The textual compromise had the following features, among others:

- The crimes in relation to which a responsibility to protect may arise were limited to genocide, war crimes, ethnic cleansing and crimes against humanity.
- The international community was required to exercise its responsibility by using all appropriate diplomatic, humanitarian and other peaceful means in accordance with the Charter. Collective action would be triggered only when such peaceful means to prevent the commission of international crimes were regarded as having failed.
- The international community, in its Summit embodiment, indicated that it is 'prepared to take collective action'. So, action on the 'responsibility to protect' was to proceed at the instigation of the member states but was not assumed to be an obligation imposed upon them.
- No guidelines or criteria for intervention were specified. Instead, the international community, through the United Nations, would determine on a 'case-by-case' basis whether collective action to defend populations from the commission of international crimes was required. This left open the prospect that the Security Council, as the representative institution of the international community, could make decisions to intervene in a manner more pragmatic than principled.
- The resolution included a non-mandatory recommendation that regional organizations be consulted 'as appropriate' prior to collective action being authorized by the Security Council.
- Collective action under Chapter VII would be considered only where national authorities 'manifestly failed to protect their populations' from the relevant crimes. This was a standard considerably higher than that initially suggested. The original recommendation was that intervention may be countenanced where a state was adjudged to be either 'unable or unwilling' to exercise its own responsibility to protect its peoples.

The fact of this compromise demonstrated clearly that from its very beginning the new doctrine of R2P had been shaped by powerfully contending political

3 UN General Assembly, 'World Summit Outcome: Resolution / Adopted by the General Assembly, 24 October 2005', A/RES/60/1 (2005).

principles and arguments. In this chapter I describe and analyse these arguments through a consideration of the three most significant debates on the responsibility to protect that have taken place in the UN General Assembly.

These debates were, first, the Assembly's discussion prior to the adoption of the World Summit Resolution; secondly, the debate that took place following the tabling of the Secretary-General's report on implementing the responsibility to protect in 2009; then thirdly, the 2012 debate that occurred in the wake of the first major military intervention associated with the R2P in Libya in 2011. The chapter concludes with an assessment of the R2P's standing and influence following from these deliberations.

I. World Summit Disagreements (2005)

Unsurprisingly, given its pivotal role in establishing the ICISS, Canada played a leading role in advocating for the adoption of a resolution encapsulating and underpinning support for the 'responsibility to protect'. It expressed its strong support for the recommendations contained in the ICISS report and, subsequently, in the report of the High-Level Panel. Noting that the responsibility to protect embraced a parallel responsibility to rebuild, Canada shrewdly twinned its argument with one for the successful establishment of a new Peacebuilding Commission. The Commission, it argued, was an essential institutional foundation that would underpin the larger conception. The responsibility to protect, in turn, would in time be 'universally respected as a fundamental component of state sovereignty and independence. There can be no greater goal.'[4]

Outside North America, the most significant support for the adoption of the doctrine came from the nations of Europe. There was little or no dissent here that the nations of the world should recognize their collective responsibility to protect civilian populations that were the subject of genocide, war crimes, ethnic cleansing or crimes against humanity.

Perhaps the most interesting aspect of the pre-Summit discussions, however, was the strong support for the doctrine provided by the nations of Africa.[5] In a sense, this was not surprising. It had been in Africa – perhaps more than in any other region of the world – that mass violations of human rights of the kind sought to be prevented here, had occurred. African nations had first-hand, or near-

4 Allan Rock (Permanent Representative of Canada to the United Nations), 'Statement to the Informal Thematic Consultations of the General Assembly to Discuss the Four Clusters Contained in the Secretary-General's Report "in Larger Freedom", Cluster III: Freedom to Live in Dignity' (20 April 2005).

5 See further, M. Mwanasali, 'Overheating Chapter VII? The Security Council and Africa's Post-Cold War Conflicts', in *From Global Apartheid to Global Village: Africa and the United Nations*, ed. A. Adebajo (Natal: University of KwaZulu-Natal Press, 2009), 239–249.

hand, experience of the atrocities and consequent human suffering with which the doctrine was concerned and an intimate and devastating knowledge of the consequences of both state and international failure. Further, it was no giant step for African countries to embrace the 'responsibility to protect' on the global stage. Authorization for outside intervention to prevent the commission of large-scale human rights abuse had already been incorporated into Article 4(h) of the Constitutive Act of the African Union.[6]

Such arguments, based as they were on the moral responsibility of the nations of the world to prevent the large-scale destruction of their peoples, wherever they may be, appeared, at least in principle, difficult to refute. And yet, there was a significant problem. This was that the United Nations, as the representative institution of the community of nations, must necessarily act within the terms of its Charter. And Article 2(4) of the United Nations Charter appeared to prohibit the international community's undermining of the sovereignty of any nation. This was not a moral principle of a similar order to that invoked when speaking of the 'responsibility to protect'. It was, nevertheless, a constitutional principle that is fundamental to the common understanding and working of the international order. Not unnaturally, therefore, it was upon this principle, and on the supporting provisions of the Charter, that opponents of R2P founded their principal arguments.[7]

India and Pakistan made lucid statements in the Summit debate warning their counterparts of the conceptual and practical dangers attendant upon an uncritical acceptance of the new doctrine. The Permanent Representative from India made clear his country's view that the terms of the Charter should be regarded as paramount. The framers of the Charter, he argued, never intended Article 51, permitting collective action mandated by the Security Council, to cover anything 'beyond its text'. The text was sufficient to cover any presently conceivable danger to peace. Where action was required to deal with situations of gross human rights abuse, it was not the text that stood in its path. Rather, the problem was in garnering the requisite political will to take such action. He warned against conferring legitimacy on a doctrine of humanitarian intervention or turning it into some new ideology of 'military humanism'.[8]

Pakistan, similarly, cautioned against the General Assembly adopting the doctrine of humanitarian intervention, upon which world opinion was very divided, under the semantic cloak of the 'responsibility to protect'. Instead, the international

---

6 B. Kioko, 'The Right of Intervention under the African Union's Constitutive Act: Non-Interference to Non-Intervention', *International Review of the Red Cross* 85 (2003): 807.

7 A. Bannon, 'The Responsibility to Protect: The UN World Summit and the Question of Unilateralism', *Yale Law Journal* 115, no. 5 (2006): 1157.

8 Nirupam Sen (Permanent Representative of India to the United Nations), 'Informal Thematic Consultations of the General Assembly to Discuss the Four Clusters Contained in the Secretary-General's Report, in Larger Freedom, Cluster III: Freedom to Live in Dignity' (20 April 2005).

community should focus its attention upon the right to development. The global community's responsibility with respect to state failure and the consequential commission of human rights abuse must be principally preventive. Countries should be assisted before they collapse. The problems of such 'stressed states' could only be made worse by external interference and regional power plays. Pakistan's ambassador, Munir Akram, acknowledged that, if a state had collapsed, international action may become necessary. But in such a case, he argued, care should be taken not to court the prospect that any such intervention might simply further the strategic interests of the intervening parties. For that reason, no intervention should occur except upon the authorization of the Security Council.[9]

China, which had been joined by Russia, adopted a similarly cautious and conditional position. Focusing upon the complexity of causes that may bear upon state failure and the commission of large-scale abuses of civilian populations, the Chinese delegation urged the Assembly to focus on situations as they arose, on a case-by-case basis. Neither the Security Council nor the General Assembly should adopt vague, general principles invoking some intangible and impractical notion of international intervention in the internal affairs of sovereign states.[10]

This cautious and legally formal opposition was backed by the countries of the Non-Aligned Movement (NAM) and was lent further support by several of the nations of the Middle East including Egypt, Syria and Iran. Egypt characterized the 'responsibility to protect' as a licence for the strong to judge the weak. The adoption of the doctrine, it argued, would serve only to deepen suspicions among civilizations and cultures rather than overcome them.

Despite these significant differences of international opinion, the resolution made its way into the final text. Canada's insistent advocacy, pressure from national capitals, African nations' strong support, and the fear that the entire Summit would break down if last-minute agreements could not be reached, all played their part in the achievement of that remarkable result. Even acknowledging that, however, it was clear first that the resolution embodying the 'responsibility to protect' was one hedged with preconditions; secondly, that it was open to widely differing interpretations: and, thirdly, that the underlying differences among UN member states with respect to the merit of the principle had not dissipated despite the achievement of the formal consensus.

Following the World Summit, R2P was formally recognized by the Security Council. In the context of a debate upon the protection of civilians in armed

---

9 Munir Akram (Permanent Representative of Pakistan to the United Nations), 'Informal Thematic Consultations of the General Assembly to Discuss the Four Clusters Contained in the Secretary-General's Report, in Larger Freedom, Cluster III: Freedom to Live in Dignity' (19 April 2005).

10 Xie Bohua (Counsellor, Permanent Mission of China to the United Nations), 'Informal Thematic Consultations of the General Assembly to Discuss the Four Clusters Contained in the Secretary-General's Report, in Larger Freedom, Freedom to Live in Dignity' (20 April 2005).

conflict, the Security Council approved Resolution 1674 dealing with all aspects of that question, including the promotion of economic growth, poverty eradication, national reconciliation, good governance, democracy, the rule of law and the protection of fundamental human rights.[11] This resolution reaffirmed 'the provisions of paragraphs 138 and 139 of the 2005 World Summit Outcome Document regarding the responsibility to protect populations from genocide, war crimes, ethnic cleansing and crimes against humanity'. Apart from the normative importance of this reaffirmation, the adoption of the resolution marked the first occasion upon which the Security Council acknowledged expressly that its role may extend not just to the prevention of threats to international peace and security but also to the cessation of mass atrocities taking place within state borders.[12]

Soon after, the Security Council invoked the new principle for the first time – in relation to the situation in Darfur. In Resolution 1706, the Council resolved, among other things, to deploy a UN peacekeeping force in Darfur and sought the consent of the Sudanese Government to do so.[13] From that time onwards, the Security Council has referred to R2P consistently in resolutions adopted with respect to conflict situations in which the abuse of human rights has been a prominent component. Recently, for example, in the preamble of Resolution 1973 with respect to the Libyan intervention, the Council reiterated the responsibility of the Libyan authorities to protect the population and reaffirmed that the parties to the conflict bore the primary responsibility for ensuring the protection of civilians.[14] A similar reaffirmation followed in the Council's 2011 resolution on Cote D'Ivoire.[15]

The World Summit resolutions with respect to R2P were highly general in nature. Much work remained to be done at the UN to put flesh on their bones. So, to assist with this task Ban Ki-moon appointed Professor Edward Luck to be his special adviser on the subject. Luck went to work to make the doctrine more comprehensible and concrete. The product was the Secretary-General's report to the General Assembly on the implementation of R2P, which was tabled in January 2009.[16]

---

11 UN Security Council, 'Security Council Resolution 1674 [on Protection of Civilians in Armed Conflict]', S/Res/1674 (28 April 2006).

12 The Security Council recognized and approved the 'responsibility to protect', again in a more recent resolution with respect to the protection of civilians in armed conflict: SC Res. 1894 (November 2009).

13 UN Security Council, 'Security Council Resolution 1704 [on Establishment of the UN Integrated Mission in Timor-Leste (UNMIT)]', S/Res/1704 (25 August 2006).

14 'Security Council Resolution 1973 [on the Situation in the Libyan Arab Jamahiriya]', S/Res/1973 (17 March 2011).

15 'Security Council Resolution 1975 [on Targeted Sanctions against Individuals Meeting the Criteria Set out in Resolution 1572 (2004) on Arms Embargo against Côte D'ivoire]', S/Res/1975 (30 March 2011).

16 See, E. Luck, 'Sovereignty, Choice and the Responsibility to Protect', *Global Responsibility to Protect* 1, no. 1 (2009): 10; UN General Assembly, 'Implementing the Responsibility to Protect: Report of the Secretary-General, 12 January', A/63/677, (2009).

The report was a detailed encapsulation of the new doctrine's principal parameters. It drew heavily on the work of the ICISS and the High-Level Panel, but its cast was much more pragmatic. In elaborating upon R2P, a three-pillar approach to its implementation was proposed. In the first, the nation in which a humanitarian catastrophe is in prospect must assume responsibility for taking timely and appropriate preventative measures. These may include intensive diplomatic steps to mediate impending conflict, the adoption of anti-corruption strategies, the early prosecution of those engaging in violent activity, the promotion of human rights and efforts to establish more effective governance. The second pillar involves a calibrated reaction by the international community. Here, concerted and directed assistance in the form of development aid, foreign investment, technical assistance, economic incentives, rapid police responsiveness and more general capacity building would be crucial. Under pillar three, these measures may be supplemented initially by 'soft' coercion, which could include international fact finding, the deployment of peacekeepers, the imposition of arms embargoes and the application of diplomatic and economic sanctions. Then, when all else has failed, the Security Council might authorize military intervention as the measure of last resort.

The Secretary-General sought to clarify certain issues about which there had been considerable confusion or dissension since the World Summit. He made clear that R2P applied only in relation cases of genocide, war crimes, crimes against humanity and ethnic cleansing. Collective action in the use of force must be undertaken with the authority of the Security Council and in accordance with Chapter VII of the Charter.

The doctrine was to be distinguished from the preceding notion of 'humanitarian intervention'. Humanitarian intervention, the report said, posed a false choice between either standing by in the face of catastrophe or deploying coercive military force to protect populations that were threatened. R2P sought to overcome this binary divide by recasting sovereignty as responsibility and then defining in some detail what the respective duties and obligations of nations, and the international community, to prevent humanitarian disaster should be.

II The General Assembly's 2009 Debate

The World Summit had urged the General Assembly to continuously consider and refine R2P. The Secretary-General therefore urged the Assembly to discuss and endorse his report. After six months of delay, the President of the General Assembly finally agreed to hold an informal interactive dialogue on the Secretary-General's report in late July 2009.

The proceedings began controversially when the Assembly President distributed a concept note to member states prior to the dialogue outlining his reservations with respect to R2P.[17] In this note, the President argued that it had no binding status in international law, that there had been no genuine agreement as to its terms, and that it had not been the absence of such a doctrine that had impeded necessary intervention to prevent humanitarian disaster. Instead, it had been the unrepresentative composition of the Security Council, the inappropriate use of the veto and a lack of political will that had cruelled such interventions. National sovereignty, he concluded, demanded that no external military intervention whatsoever into the exclusively domestic affairs of a state should be either contemplated or permitted.

Soon after this faltering start, however, it became apparent that the President's intervention had been neither appreciated nor influential. To the surprise of most observers, member states expressed substantial concordance with the Secretary-General's report. Ninety-four states took part in the debate and their views were representative of approximately 180 of the Assembly's 192 members. A very clear majority supported the terms of the World Summit resolutions and backed the Secretary-General's three-pillar approach to their implementation.

The significant majority of member states stated unequivocally that the dialogue should not be devoted to a renegotiation of the World Summit Outcome resolutions. They made plain their intention to move forward to a practical understanding of the resolutions rather than to re-open the debate on whether or not the R2P should be recognized or acted upon. The member states' reaffirmation of the resolutions made plain, however, that they regarded them as firmly limited by their terms. All agreed, for instance, that the R2P would apply only in situations that involved the commission of genocide, war crimes, crimes against humanity or ethnic cleansing. Any expansion of the doctrine to cover the consequences of climate change, cyclones, counter-terrorism, external aggression or internal repression was roundly dismissed.

Member states almost without exception welcomed the three-pillar conception outlined in the Secretary-General's report. In this respect, there was assent for the general principle that sovereignty should be defined as responsibility and that the first responsibility of sovereign states should be to protect the rights and interests of their peoples. Pillar 1 encapsulated that understanding. Member states regarded Pillar 2 as the most novel part of the doctrine. The idea that the international community should and would provide early assistance to states at risk of failure was one that was greeted with approval. Unsurprisingly, Pillar 3 was the subject of most contention. Nevertheless, even here there appeared to be agreement that, where one of the four defined crimes was either in prospect or in the course of commission, the international community had a responsibility to intervene, but, in the case of military intervention, only if Security Council authorization had been previously obtained. Further, a sizeable bloc of member

17 Office of the President of the General Assembly, 'Concept Note on the R2P Populations from Genocide, War Crimes, Crimes against Humanity and Ethnic Cleansing' (16 July 2009).

states endorsed the idea that the commission of mass atrocities within a single member state may nevertheless, and depending on the specific circumstances, be regarded as constituting a threat to international peace and security.[18] In such a case, the operation of Chapters VI and VII of the UN Charter could be attracted.

The interaction between state sovereignty and R2P, however, was the subject of continuing disagreement. Some influential states declared that sovereignty was inviolable and that nothing in the new doctrine should be permitted to undermine that inviolability.[19] Even in relation to the four crimes specified, therefore, they argued that international intervention should be countenanced only if requested by the state concerned. At the other end of the spectrum were member states that strongly supported the doctrine and who were willing therefore to countenance some compromise to sovereignty in the interests of avoiding atrocity. None, however, endorsed unilateral intervention and all agreed that military intercession could proceed only if the Security Council authorized it.[20]

Developing nations in particular forcefully expressed their concern that the doctrine may be used selectively and in particular by more powerful states as a means to interfere with the rights and interests of the less powerful. To counter that possibility, many developing countries insisted that decisions as to whether a nation had failed in its R2P its own people had to be taken without fear or favour and with the application of identifiable and identical standards.[21] The Security Council's manifest failure to take action with respect to the Israeli invasion of Gaza in January 2009 was commonly cited as an example of the double standards and selectivity that could occur.

Member states put competing views with respect to the Security Council's recommended role as the arbiter of Pillar 3 interventions. There was agreement that the Council should exercise that role but disagreement about the extent to which, if at all, the General Assembly should also play some part. Many nations, including especially those that aspired to permanent membership of the Council, seemed to condition their support on comprehensive Security Council reform. Still more expressed the view that the P-5 should agree voluntarily to refrain from the use of the veto in situations in which action with respect to genocide, war crimes, crimes against humanity and ethnic cleansing was the subject of Council consideration.

---

18 See, Mr Anders Liden (Permanent Representative of Sweden to the United Nations), 'Statement on Behalf of the European Union at the General Assembly Dialogue on the R2P' (23 July 2009).

19 These states included, for example, China, Cuba, Iran, Nicaragua, Pakistan and Russia.

20 These states included the Netherlands, Austria, Australia, New Zealand, Canada, Denmark and Costa Rica.

21 See for example, the Statement by Ambassador Vanu Gopala Menon (Permanent Representative of Singapore), 'Statement at the General Assembly Dialogue on the R2P' (24 July 2009).

Many states expressed uncertainty as to the circumstances in which international aid, assistance or intervention should be triggered. The World Summit resolutions stated, for example, that the international community was committed to helping states build capacity to protect their populations from the commission of mass atrocities, as necessary and appropriate. At what stage, then, and under what circumstances would the criteria of necessity and appropriateness properly be engaged?

Several nations observed that the World Summit resolutions referred to mass atrocities consequent upon state failure. Nothing there appeared referable, however, to crises that had been caused by the actions of *non-state actors*. In what circumstances the international community might intervene to prevent atrocities at the hands of such actors, therefore, was a matter placed on the table for further deliberation.

Finally, and interestingly, member states seemed quite unclear as to the standing of R2P in international law. In line with the opinions expressed by the High-Level Panel and the former Secretary-General in his report to the World Summit, some member states were sufficiently confident to declare the doctrine either as a norm of international law or at least as a principle that was in the process of maturing into such a norm. Others, however, regarded the doctrine not as legal but as political. It represented a political commitment by most nations to take steps to prevent mass atrocities but brought with it no specific legal content or obligation. Still others maintained that R2P could more than adequately be contained within and elaborated from within the existing law of the United Nations Charter. Those opposed to the advance of the doctrine made clear their view that it had no legal standing whatever.

Perhaps the most considered view expressed was that R2P was a doctrine primarily of a political rather than legal character. The Brazilian position was illustrative:

> In Brazil's view, (R2P) is not a principle proper, much less a novel legal prescription. Rather it is a powerful political call for all States to abide by legal obligations already set forth in the Charter, in relevant human rights conventions and international humanitarian law ....[22]

Subsequent Secretary-General's Reports

The UN Secretary-General presented three further reports on R2P from 2010–2012. The first of these focused on early warnings of possible genocide, crimes against humanity, war crimes and ethnic cleansing.[23] It outlined a series of institutional innovations that would assist in the primary tasks of detection and prevention.

---

22 Statement by Ambassador Maria Luiza Ribiero Viotti (Permanent Representative of Brazil), 'Statement at the General Assembly Informal Dialogue on the R2P' (23 July 2009).

23 UN General Assembly, 'Early Warning, Assessment and the Responsibility to Protect: Report of the Secretary-General', A/64/864 (14 July 2010).

Within the UN the key innovation was the establishment of a joint office for special advisers on genocide and the responsibility to protect. The report recommended that regional organizations and civil society should create similar advisory offices directed towards the monitoring and evaluation of potential conflict situations.

The second report focused more specifically on the role of regional inter-governmental organizations in implementing the responsibility to protect.[24] The Secretary-General proposed a global–regional partnership in the implementation of all three pillars of the responsibility to protect. He committed the United Nations to collaboration with all major regional organizations, including the African Union, the Economic Community of West African States (ECOWAS), the Organization of American States (OAS), the Association of Southeast Asian Nations (ASEAN) and the Arab League in the development of the doctrine's conceptual framework and in its practical implementation.

The most important of these reports was the third in 2012 on 'timely and decisive response'.[25] This report was significant because it was the first in the UN system to be directed at illuminating the parameters and practice of coercive intervention. It was also the first in which the Secretary-General could address disagreements that had emerged in the course of the UN-sanctioned NATO intervention in Libya in 2011.

The report set down five key lessons that had been learnt from the experience of the doctrine's implementation to that time:

1. While each instance of its application had been distinct, the doctrine's principles could and should be applied uniformly. Its mechanisms and methods, however, had necessarily to be shaped by circumstances on the ground.
2. The Security Council had become more engaged than previously when responding to gross human rights violations.
3. A more integrated and nuanced understanding of how the three pillars related to one another was required. None of the pillars was likely to stand on its own. The purpose of Pillar 3 intervention, for example, was directed primarily to enabling national authorities to resume their responsibility to protect their own peoples in conformity with the legal obligations inherent in Pillar 1.
4. Any effective and integrated strategy was likely to involve elements of response and prevention. Capacity building, through the establishment of independent commissions of inquiry, for example, embraces elements of both.

24 UN Security Council, 'The Role of Regional and Subregional Arrangements in Implementing the Responsibility to Protect: Report of the Secretary-General', A/65/877–S/2011/393 (28 June 2011).

25 'Responsibility to Protect: Timely and Decisive Response', UN Doc. A66/874–S/2012/578 (5 September 2012).

5. Finally, the value of partners, in particular regional inter-governmental organizations, had been invaluable. Every effort should be made to strengthen the ties between the two in the joint battle to prevent mass atrocities.

Treading onto the more uncertain territory of coercive intervention, the Secretary-General's report was at pains to point out that Pillar 3 interventions did not necessitate the application of military force. A comprehensive range of less-intensive measures was available, including sanctions, the restriction of scientific and technical co-operation, the constraint or severance of diplomatic ties, and the control of the availability of high-value commodities or weapons. Even under s.42 of the UN Charter, military intervention could be left as a last resort in favour of the establishment of security and no-fly zones.

As for the NATO intervention in Libya, the Secretary-General explained diplomatically that,

> the Security Council decided to authorize the use of force after most of its members had come to the conclusion that a series of peaceful measures had proven inadequate. Some member states, however, have contended that non-coercive measures were not given sufficient time to demonstrate results ... Others have expressed the view that those charged with implementing Council resolution 1973 exceeded the mandate they were given by the Council. Whatever the specific merits of the arguments, it is important that the international community learn from these experiences and that concerns expressed by member states are taken into account in the future.[26]

This third report, like that in 2009, was valuable for its illumination of key theoretical and practical issues that had emerged since the responsibility to protect's introduction. At the same time, the report implicitly acknowledged that the Libyan intervention had acted to disrupt the doctrine's steady and incremental evolution and acceptance.

III. The General Assembly Debate on Pillar 3 Coercive Intervention

After a steady period of consolidation, the General Assembly's debate on the Secretary-General's 2012 report on R2P revealed again that significant differences of opinion among member states remained regarding core aspects of R2P's implementation.[27] These arose sharply in the wake of the NATO campaign to protect Libyan civilians from widespread violence unleashed by the Gaddafi regime against rebel forces in the east of the country.

---

26 'Responsibility to Protect: Timely and Decisive Response', para. 54.

27 Ibid.

Some member states, particularly those from the global North, saw the intervention as a success. They argued that the Libyan intervention, unlike many of its predecessors, had proceeded with the authorization of the UN Security Council. This was not a unilateral intervention by Western forces such as that which had created such enormous legal controversy in Kosovo. The Libyan intervention fell squarely within the terms of the UN Charter. Further, the Security Council had acted following preceding, strong action by the Human Rights Council. It had condemned outright the human rights abuses being committed in Libya and, still in the early days of the conflict, recommended that the General Assembly expel Libya from the Council.[28]

The role of regional organizations had also been significant.[29] The Arab League, in particular, took firm action against Libya, condemning the government's attitudes and actions and expelling the country from its membership. Buttressed by the support of these regional bodies, and following the League's recommendation that a no-fly zone be imposed as one means of staunching the bloodshed, the Security Council was in a far stronger position to act without courting the criticism of selectivity.

Remarkably, success in Libya came without the imposition of 'boots on the ground'. Resolution 1973 had explicitly excluded the deployment of forces of occupation. That exclusion had been critical to its adoption.

Despite these positives, the intervention had also seemed to reveal significant problems with R2P's implementation. The sceptics and opponents of R2P, particularly from the global South, took advantage of contentious aspects of the Libyan campaign to ramp up their criticisms of the intervention in general and R2P in particular.

The most severe criticism of the Libyan case related to 'mission creep'.[30] Those members of the Security Council who abstained from the vote on resolution 1973 attacked forcefully what they saw as the abuse of the Council's mandate. In their view there was no way in which the Security Council resolution could have permitted the transformation of the mission from the protection of civilians, to the objective of regime change. Russia, China, India and Brazil also objected strongly to the alteration of NATO's military stance from the relative neutrality of civilian protection to evident partiality in taking the rebel side.[31, 32]

---

28 UN Human Rights Council, 'Report of the Human Rights Council on its Fifteenth Special Session', Res S–15/1, UN GA, UN Doc A/HRC/Res/S–15/1 (25 February 2011).

29 UN Security Council, 'Res 1973 Adopted by the Security Council at its 6498th Meeting', UN Doc S/Res/1973 (17 March 2011), 5.

30 James Pattison, 'The Ethics of Humanitarian Intervention in Libya', *Ethics and International Affairs* 23 (2011): 273.

31 For example, Mr Churkin (Russian Federation) & Mr Baodong (China), UN Security Council, '6528th Meeting', S/PV.6528 (4 May 2011).

32 See further Gareth Evans, 'Keynote Address: R2P and RWP after Libya and Syria', in *The Responsibility while Protecting: What Next?* (Rio De Janeiro: Global Centre for the Responsibility to Protect and the Stanley Foundation, 2012).

Many member states expressed deep reservations as to the legality of the military campaign. Here, the argument was that resolution 1973 could not be stretched to cover actions such as intervention in a civil war, the assassination of a government's leadership and the overthrow of the regime.[33] Security Council endorsement was critical to underpin the legality of the intervention, particularly as it took place without Libyan consent. But it was argued that the actions of the coalition forces appeared to take the intervention well beyond the resolution's terms and, therefore, beyond what the UN Charter could be interpreted to allow.

Next, the nature of the military campaign raised starkly the question of whether it could have taken a different form and still have been as effective. If so, then in accordance with the three-pillar approach to R2P, prevention and pacific response should have been tried first. Even if a Pillar 3 intervention had become necessary, it should have been more targeted and limited. These general disagreements about the conduct of the Libyan campaign overflowed into the General Assembly's consideration of the Secretary-General's 2012 report on 'timely and decisive response'.

Against this background, the first positive aspect of the debate was that there was no dissent from the proposition that when genocide, crimes against humanity, war crimes or ethnic cleansing were threatened or being committed, the international community could not and should not stand idle. The delegation from Rwanda, a nation ravaged by genocide, put the matter tellingly:

> We have to face the reality that there are times when prevention and lesser measures fail. The best course of action, in our view, is to prepare for collective action under the UN Charter as the lack of a multilateral option under the Charter will only encourage unilateral interventions, weakening UN credibility and respect for international law. Where these principles have been applied, they have largely worked. Where states and international organizations have hesitated or been frozen by division, wounds have festered and conflicts escalated.[34]

The EU declared that, while a careful assessment needed to be made of the nature and progression of any conflict and the crimes that might have been committed during its course, non-action in the face of international criminality was not an option.[35] Even so, the member states participating in the dialogue were agreed that R2P should not be extended beyond the four crimes identified. There was also a general consensus

33 Mr Mashabane (South Africa), UN Security Council, '6566th Meeting: Libya', UN Doc S/PV.6566 (27 June 2011).

34 Ambassador Eugene-Richard Gasana, the Permanent Representative of Rwanda to the United Nations, UN General Assembly, 'Responsibility to Protect: Timely and Decisive Response', UN Doc. A66/874/ – S/2012/578. UN GA, Informal Dialogue on the Responsibility to Protect, 5 September 2012.

35 Ambassador Ioannis Vrailas, Deputy Head of Delegation, Delegation of the European Union to the United Nations, ibid.

that the UN's response to conflicts should be determined on a case-by-case basis rather than being restricted by the application of any pre-determined prudential criteria. This was so even if the absence of criteria might encourage selectivity in the choice of conflicts to which the Security Council may respond.

In this context, it was also interesting that the order to be applied to the Secretary-General's three-pillar formulation of R2P, while seemingly technical, became a significant source of contention. In his report, Ban Ki-moon proposed that these three pillars ought not to be regarded as sequential. Instead, they should be regarded as interconnected. He argued that the nature of the international community's response to a potential or present conflict must of necessity be dictated by circumstances of the ground and by an informed judgment of the likely consequences of preventive or interventionist action. It may make no sense, for example, to embark upon prevention if thousands of lives were already at risk.

In debate, France argued that to insist upon chronological sequencing in the implementation of international action could act as a pretext for inaction.[36] Germany said the question was not one of sequencing but of determining how best the objective of protecting those who might be the targets of atrocities could be achieved. Measures under Chapter VII of the Charter did not require the prior futile use of other less coercive means.[37] Brazil proposed that the implementation of the three pillars should be logical but flexible.[38] Israel said simply that no template for intervention could be dictated in advance.[39]

In contrast, Malaysia insisted that the pillars must be actioned chronologically and it was not until the prior had been exhausted that the next should be enacted: 'My delegation cannot stress enough the need for chronological sequencing in the application of the three pillars. It is only with this can we ensure that the use of force is truly the last resort'.[40] India argued similarly that resort to Chapter VII measures could only be justified after serious and genuine measures at peaceful settlement of a conflict had failed.[41] Russia stated that in every case priority should be given to strengthening preventive mechanisms that might allow states and the international community to detect problematic situations and prevent mass atrocities.[42] This disagreement reflected directly the concern among several

36 Statement delivered on behalf of the Permanent Mission of France to the United Nations, ibid.

37 Ambassador Miguel Berger, Deputy Permanent Representative of Germany, ibid.

38 Ambassador M.L.R Viotti, Permanent Representative of Brazil to the United Nations, ibid.

39 Ambassador Ron Prosor, Permanent Representative of Israel to the United Nations, ibid.

40 Ambassador Hussein Haniff, Permanent Representative of Malaysia to the United Nations, ibid.

41 Ambassador H.S. Puri, Permanent Representative of India to the United Nations, ibid.

42 Statement delivered on behalf of the Permanent Mission of Russia to the United Nations, ibid.

influential South states with respect to the Security Council's decision to authorize the use of force in Libya before any meaningful steps towards pacific settlement of the conflict had been taken.

There was general agreement among the member states that, wherever possible, regional organizations should be involved in decision-making about Pillar 3 interventions in their locale. Where a decision was taken by the Security Council to intervene, it would also be desirable that regional forces take part in peacekeeping or other forms of military action. Nigeria and South Africa proposed that regional and sub-regional organizations such as the AU, the Arab League, ECOWAS and others should support the development of regional capability to fashion and ensure appropriate regional and national responses to the commission of mass atrocities.[43]

There were spirited interventions, in particular by the S-5 countries, with respect to the exercise of the veto in cases where mass atrocities were being committed or appeared to be in contemplation. In several preceding papers put before the General Assembly, the S-5 nations – Singapore, Costa Rica, Lichtenstein, Jordan and Switzerland – had argued that the veto-wielding members of the Security Council should voluntarily deny themselves the use of the veto when the Security Council considered its response to any conflict in which genocide and similar crimes were alleged to be taking place.[44] In debate Singapore made the point forcefully:

> The P5 refused to agree that their veto power should not be used to block action in impending R2P situations. They wanted to reserve *their* right to use *their* veto power, even if there was compelling evidence of impending mass atrocity crimes. And this position was shared by *all* the P5 members. Even those P5 countries who are fervent supporters of R2P … are the same ones who adamantly reject any limitations on the use of the veto.[45]

Unsurprisingly, no member of the P-5 chose to comment on this during the course of the Assembly Dialogue.

Singapore also provided a refreshingly honest assessment of character and import of R2P in general. It pointed out that there was no dissent among UN member states as to the preventive character and desirability of pillars 1 and 2. The content of these pillars did not differ from existing international obligations that were derived from human rights conventions, state responsibilities and

---

43 Ambassador U. Joy Ogwa, Permanent Representative of Nigeria to the United Nations, ibid.

44 See for example, UN General Assembly, 'Enhancing the Accountability, Transparency and Effectiveness of the Security Council', A/66/L.42/Rev.1 (15 May 2012), Annex, para. 20.

45 Ambassador Albert Chua, Permanent Representative of Singapore to the United Nations, 'Responsibility to Protect: Timely and Decisive Response', UN Doc. A66/874–S/2012/578.

essential prerequisites for national development. For this reason, it asserted that they were no more than 'window-dressing'. The crux of R2P was Pillar 3. If, then, R2P were to become an enduring facet of the work of the UN in ensuring international peace and security, member states needed to accept the reality that coercive interventions may be necessary and to focus upon defining the terms in accordance with which such interventions might be justified. The self-interest of P-5 nations, the Singapore statement concluded, could only serve to harm the prospects for R2P's effective implementation.[46]

As the debate wore on, it became increasingly apparent that much of this prior argumentation was mere shadow-boxing. The main event was the disagreement between states as to the primacy, or contingency, of state sovereignty. The Nigerian delegation put the matter succinctly:

> The concept of R2P and its three pillars not only derives its global legitimacy from international humanitarian and human rights law, as well as from the World Summit of 2005. It also represents a global conceptual and policy shift from the notion of sovereignty and security, to a new emphasis on human security rather than state security … Nigeria believes that the raison d'être of the state revolves around the R2P and its essence is that while the ruled must be obedient to constituted authority, the State must in turn act responsibly and accountably.[47]

China, in contrast, was immoveable on the primacy and centrality of sovereignty.[48] In the General Assembly it reaffirmed the principle that individual states bore the principal responsibility for the protection of their citizens. The role of the international community was secondary. It consisted only of a responsibility to provide constructive assistance. In doing so the international community must adhere closely to the purposes and principles of the United Nations Charter and, in particular to the principles of sovereignty, territorial integrity and non-interference in the domestic affairs of states. Further, any acts of assistance must first obtain a mandate from the Security Council within the broader Charter framework. China observed that R2P was a complex matter. Absent a consensus upon its core elements, the UN should be very careful about the promotion and implementation of the doctrine.

Russia agreed.[49] Controversially it cast doubt as to the degree to which UN member states were at one as on the adoption of R2P. The doctrine, it opined, had not yet attained sufficient clarity and maturity to be implemented without

46 Ibid.

47 Ambassador U. Joy Ogwa, the Permanent Representative of Nigeria to the United Nations, ibid.

48 Ambassador Wang Min, Deputy Permanent Representative of China to the United Nations, ibid.

49 Statement delivered on behalf of the Permanent Mission of Russia to the United Nations, ibid.

disagreement and dissent. There were insufficient protections against its abuse. Only a clear consensus would provide the UN with the requisite mandate to make the doctrine operational. Moreover, coercive action should be taken only as a last resort and its primary aim should be to prompt the responsible state to implement its international obligations rather than to supplant them. Cuba, Venezuela and Tunisia joined Russia in questioning the existence of a consensus as to R2P, but, aside from questions of implementation, this remained very much the minority view.

Norway countered by arguing that there is never a situation in which states do not have a responsibility to protect their populations from mass atrocities. The same duty may be extrapolated to the international community.[50] The question then is not whether R2P should apply to a situation of state-sponsored criminality but rather how best the doctrine might be applied in any given circumstance. The United Kingdom emphasized again that the international community must learn the lessons of Rwanda and Srebrenica. If, therefore, prevention fails, the UN as the representative institution of the global community must be able and willing to authorize coercive action quickly and decisively.[51] The United States remarked that difficult judgments will always need to be made about options, actions and consequences. What the global community cannot do is condone inaction in the face of atrocity or mass violence. It cited Libya as one example of a situation in which a timely military intervention had saved countless lives.[52]

The Libyan case, however, was one that provoked sharp disagreements among member states participating in the debate as to how R2P should be executed. So, while Northern nations generally reflected positively on the Libyan intervention, the nations of the South were united in their criticism. Argentina encapsulated the Southern position in this way:

> The concerns risen by the coercive action in Libya include resorting to the use of force without trying other measures first, regime change, the adequacy of air strikes to protect civilians, the need for the Security Council to do a follow up of the authorized measures and accountability of those authorized to use military force. These reservations and concerns must be addressed to ensure that action by the United Nations does not cause more victims than civilians protected, that it does not concur in legitimizing political objectives beyond those of the UN and, in the end, to ensure the legitimacy of collective action by the UN.[53]

---

50 Ambassador Geir Otto Pedersen, Permanent Representative of Norway to the United Nations, ibid.

51 Ambassador Michael Tatham, Permanent Mission of the UK to the United Nations, ibid.

52 Ambassador Elizabeth Cousens, U.S. Permanent Mission to the United Nations, ibid.

53 Ambassador Mateo Estreme, Charge D'Affaires of the Permanent Mission of Argentina to the United Nations, ibid.

India joined the fray with a typically robust intervention.[54] It asserted that almost every important provision of resolution 1973 relating to Libya, including a ceasefire, arms embargo and no-fly zone, were violated. This, it said, was not to protect citizens because the Libyan regime had long before lost its capacity to fight. The objective was to change the regime. That objective took the intervention far beyond what was permissible under the Security Council's mandate.

This transition from civilian protection to regime change caused many nations, not least the BRICS countries – Brazil, Russia, India, China and South Africa – to review their positions on Pillar 3 interventions. South Africa, for example, urged the Security Council to ensure that the self-interest of nations that participate in a coercive intervention should not determine the manner in which an intervention is undertaken. It was the Security Council's resolutions that must set the framework and limits of any international incursion. R2P must proceed within the confines of the UN Charter and international law.[55]

Those involved in the Libyan campaign took a quite different view. The UK declared that NATO's actions in Libya were 'necessary, legal and morally right'.[56] France believed that the Security Council had been kept more than adequately informed by the forces on the ground concerning the character and progress of the Libyan campaign.[57] The Netherlands regretted that some countries appeared still to favour an absolutist conception of sovereignty over the idea of sovereignty as responsibility.[58] The USA believed that the international community's intervention in Libya following the passage of resolutions 1970 and 1973 had prevented imminent, mass slaughter.

By the conclusion of the debate, it was clear that the Libyan intervention had acted as the catalyst for a wide gap to open between member states concerning the proper authorization and conduct of R2P Pillar 3 interventions. The immediate casualty was Security Council action on Syria. With Russia and China vetoing three successive resolutions condemning the Assad regime and calling for a comprehensive political solution and the BRICS countries pulling back their support for any significant sanction including the forcible opening of humanitarian corridors, the Council was paralysed. Singapore aptly summarized the stalemate:

---

54 Ambassador H.S. Puri, Permanent Representative of India to the United Nations, ibid.

55 Statement Delivered on behalf of the Permanent Mission of South Africa to the United Nations, ibid.

56 Ambassador Michael Tatham, Permanent Mission of the UK to the United Nations, ibid.

57 Statement delivered on behalf of the Permanent Mission of France to the United Nations, ibid.

58 Ambassador Herman Schaper, Permanent Representative of the Netherlands to the United Nations, ibid.

> Though many have hailed the intervention in Libya as a vindication of R2P, the reality is far more complex. There remain deep concerns over how Libya was handled. Some would say that there was 'buyer's regret' amongst those Security Council members who had supported Council action in Libya. How R2P was invoked in Libya has cast a long shadow, resulting in the current impasse in Syria. Arguably what happened with Libya has not only not helped the long-term development of R2P but may have done it damage.[59]

The Responsibility while Protecting?

The 2012 debate left the General Assembly in a quandary. While support for the essential principles of R2P remained strong, the Libyan intervention had left it with serious disagreements concerning the conduct of Security Council-mandated coercive interventions in response to potential or actual mass atrocities. In November 2012, the Brazilian delegation to the UN introduced what it hoped might be a circuit breaker. In a letter to the Secretary-General, the Brazilian ambassador presented an annexed paper entitled, 'Responsibility while Protecting: elements for the development a promotion of a concept'.[60] This paper set down a series of guidelines that Brazil believed might complement R2P and, in doing so, finesse some of the disputation that had emerged.

The Brazilian paper proposed a series of guidelines for the conduct of R2P operations. It proposed that the three pillars of R2P should be sequenced chronologically. All available diplomatic means should be used to prevent or restrain the commission of crimes prior to coercive intervention being considered. Coercive intervention should be contemplated only where it is clear that the situation dealt with constitutes a threat to international peace and security. Prior to force being employed the Security Council should carefully consider the consequences of military action on a case-by-case basis. Judicious evaluation was critical in order to avoid historically recognizable adverse consequences of military action. These had included an increase in the vulnerability of civilian populations, the generation of new cycles of violence and the advent of terrorist activity.

Once the Security Council has sanctioned a coercive intervention, the international community must observe a 'responsibility while protecting'. Interventions should proceed according to an agreed set of fundamental principles, parameters and procedures. So, for example, military action should be strictly constrained by the terms of the Security Council mandate in accordance with which it is authorized. It should be implemented in conformity with international humanitarian and human rights law. The use of force should be 'judicious,

---

59 Ambassador Albert Chua, Permanent Representative of Singapore to the United Nations, ibid.

60 Annex to letter, 'Letter Dated 9 November 2011 from the Permanent Representative of Brazil to the United Nations Addressed to the Secretary-General', A/66/551–S/2011/701 (11 November 2011).

proportionate and limited to the Security Council's objectives'. The Security Council should strengthen its monitoring procedures so that it may continuously assess the manner in which its resolutions are being translated into military practice on the ground. It should draw its authorized military forces to account for the manner in which force is deployed.

More than half the member states participating in the 2012 Assembly debate referred to the Brazilian initiative. Almost all responded positively to it. It was difficult not to. The guidelines proposed were pitched at such a level of generality that all may easily be agreed to in theory but very little concrete meaning can be attributed to them in practice.

When the practical realities of the conduct of military campaigns on the ground are considered, it can readily be appreciated that the realization of this implementation related responsibility may become very difficult indeed.[61] So, for example, Security Council members are highly unlikely to take to the judicious consideration of possible interventions if that means, as the Brazilian Ambassador has suggested, that they should evaluate the possibility of intervention according to fixed, 'just war' criteria. The Council does not presently possess either the methods or resources necessary effectively to monitor and determine whether actions in the field match the terms of its resolutions. It is difficult to imagine what procedures and measures the Council could adopt to draw military commanders to account in the midst of battle. Military commanders themselves are unlikely to be impressed by a somewhat abstract imperative that their objectives, strategies and actions should conform to pre-determined steps and take place within pre-determined parameters. Coercive interventions are likely to be hamstrung rather than facilitated if micro-managed by Security Council members having political but no military experience. As with R2P itself, the responsibility while protecting is far easier to accept in theory than it is to effect in reality. Here, both the Security Council and the General Assembly have much more work to do to inject practicality and detail into the responsibility while protecting's overarching generalities.

Conclusion

Thirteen years after its conceptualization and eight years after its adoption by the World Summit in 2005, it is apparent that R2P rests on somewhat fragile ground. Despite its strong moral foundation, the UN community remains considerably divided as to how the doctrine might best be fashioned to meet its undoubtedly imperative and laudable objectives. No one wishes to abandon it. But powerful states still agitate to limit its reach and application. While drawing all these threads together is a problematic exercise, I think it may be said with modest confidence

61 See, Global Governance Institute, 'The Responsibility to Protect and the Responsibility While Protecting: Friends or Foes?', *GGI Analysis* Paper 6 (September 2012).

that the general propositions listed below as to R2P's political standing and practical implementation now prevail.

Following the Libyan campaign:

- The intervention in Libya established the central role of the Security Council in providing authorization, on behalf of the international community, for military intervention to take place in response to the commission of crimes against humanity. Such authorization lends essential political legitimacy and legal force to any intervention that may be contemplated pursuant to R2P.
- The intervention also established the crucial role that recognized regional organizations can play in determining whether an intervention may be appropriate and if so, what form it might best take. Without the backing of a relevant regional organization, it is far less likely that the Security Council will be moved to endorse a Pillar 3 incursion upon the sovereignty of a state, not least so as to avoid the charge of selectivity.
- Security Council approval for a coercive intervention is unlikely unless intensive diplomatic means for the settlement of a conflict have first been tried and then proven to have failed.
- The Libyan intervention demonstrated that much work remains to be done in determining the nature and limits applicable to coercive interventions. In this context, the Security Council is likely to frame its resolutions more precisely and define the objectives and parameters of any intervention more clearly than in the Libyan case.
- It seems clear, following the mission creep that occurred in Libya, and the subsequent paralysis over Syria, that it is highly unlikely that the Security Council will agree to endorse a Pillar 3 intervention whose declared objective is a change in regime.

Following the General Assembly debates:

- The adoption by the Security Council of 'just war' criteria to guide its decision-making with respect to the authorization of coercive interventions is highly unlikely.
- While the debate as to the chronological sequencing of the three-pillar approach to R2P remains a live issue, practicality is likely eventually to dictate that it give way to one that favours the adoption of an individual combination of R2P-related measures according to the specific circumstances of the particular case.
- The application of R2P will be strictly confined to cases in which there is clear evidence of the potential or actual commission of genocide, crimes against humanity, war crimes or ethnic cleansing.

- The P-5 will not give up their right to exercise the veto in cases where a coercive intervention is contemplated to protect the citizens of a country from the commission of these crimes.
- Powerful nations more generally are disinclined to accept the argument that state sovereignty should be trumped, even in limited circumstances, by reference to the moral contention that the protection of human security is paramount. So long as this is the case, progress with the international acceptance of the R2P doctrine is likely to follow an uncertain and rocky road.
- The central idea behind the 'responsibility while protecting', that the Security Council should exercise greater responsibility for monitoring the conduct of coercive interventions and drawing those involved to account for their actions, is likely to be accepted abstractly. Whether or not it can be realistically realized, however, remains an open question.

Bibliography

Akram, Munir (Permanent Representative of Pakistan to the United Nations). 'Informal Thematic Consultations of the General Assembly to Discuss the Four Clusters Contained in the Secretary-General's Report, in Larger Freedom, Cluster III: Freedom to Live in Dignity'. 19 April 2005.

Annan, Kofi. 'In Larger Freedom: Towards Development, Security and Human Rights for All'. UN Doc. A/59/2005. 2005.

Bannon, A. 'The Responsibility to Protect: The UN World Summit and the Question of Unilateralism'. *Yale Law Journal* 115, no. 5 (2006): 1157.

Bellamy, A. *The Responsibility to Protect*. Cambridge: Polity, 2009.

Bohua, Xie (Counsellor, Permanent Mission of China to the United Nations). 'Informal Thematic Consultations of the General Assembly to Discuss the Four Clusters Contained in the Secretary-General's Report, in Larger Freedom, Freedom to Live in Dignity'. 20 April 2005.

Evans, Gareth. 'Keynote Address: R2P and RWP after Libya and Syria'. In *The Responsibility while Protecting: What Next?* Rio De Janeiro: Global Centre for the Responsibility to Protect and the Stanley Foundation, 2012.

Global Governance Institute. 'The Responsibility to Protect and the Responsibility While Protecting: Friends or Foes?' *GGI Analysis* Paper 6 (September 2012).

International Commission on Intervention and State Sovereignty. *The Responsibility to Protect: Report of the International Commission on Intervention and State Sovereignty*. Ottawa: International Development Research Centre, 2001.

Kioko, B. 'The Right of Intervention under the African Union's Constitutive Act: Non-Interference to Non-Intervention'. *International Review of the Red Cross* 85 (2003): 807.

Liden, Anders (Permanent Representative of Sweden to the United Nations). 'Statement on Behalf of the European Union at the General Assembly Dialogue on the R2P'. 23 July 2009.

Luck, E. 'Sovereignty, Choice and the Responsibility to Protect'. *Global Responsibility to Protect* 1, no. 1 (2009): 10.

Menon, Vanu Gopala (Permanent Representative of Singapore). 'Statement at the General Assembly Dialogue on the R2P'. 24 July 2009

Mwanasali, M. 'Overheating Chapter VII? The Security Council and Africa's Post-Cold War Conflicts'. In *From Global Apartheid to Global Village: Africa and the United Nations*, edited by A. Adebajo. Natal: University of KwaZulu-Natal Press, 2009.

Office of the President of the General Assembly. 'Concept Note on the R2P Populations from Genocide, War Crimes, Crimes against Humanity and Ethnic Cleansing'. 16 July 2009.

Pattison, James. 'The Ethics of Humanitarian Intervention in Libya'. *Ethics and International Affairs* 23 (2011): 271.

'Responsibility to Protect: Timely and Decisive Response'. UN Doc. A66/874/ – S/2012/578. 5 September 2012.

Rock, Allan (Permanent Representative of Canada to the United Nations). 'Statement to the Informal Thematic Consultations of the General Assembly to Discuss the Four Clusters Contained in the Secretary-General's Report "in Larger Freedom", Cluster III: Freedom to Live in Dignity'. 20 April 2005.

Sen, Nirupam (Permanent Representative of India to the United Nations). 'Informal Thematic Consultations of the General Assembly to Discuss the Four Clusters Contained in the Secretary-General's Report, in Larger Freedom, Cluster III: Freedom to Live in Dignity'. 20 April 2005.

UN General Assembly. 'Early Warning, Assessment and the Responsibility to Protect: Report of the Secretary-General'. A/64/864. 14 July 2010.

———. 'Enhancing the Accountability, Transparency and Effectiveness of the Security Council'. A/66/L.42/Rev.1. 15 May 2012.

———. 'Implementing the Responsibility to Protect: Report of the Secretary-General, 12 January'. A/63/677. 2009.

———. 'Letter Dated 9 November 2011 from the Permanent Representative of Brazil to the United Nations Addressed to the Secretary-General'. A/66/551–S/2011/701. 11 November 2011.

———. 'World Summit Outcome: Resolution / Adopted by the General Assembly, 24 October 2005'. A/RES/60/1. 2005.

UN Human Rights Council. 'Report of the Human Rights Council on its Fifteenth Special Session'. Res S–15/1, UN GA, UN Doc A/HRC/Res/S–15/1. 25 February 2011.

UN Security Council. '6528th Meeting'. S/PV.6528. 4 May 2011.

———. '6566th Meeting: Libya'. UN Doc S/PV.6566. 27 June 2011.

———. 'Res 1973 Adopted by the Security Council at Its 6498th Meeting'. UN Doc S/Res/1973, 17 March 2011.

———. 'The Role of Regional and Subregional Arrangements in Implementing the Responsibility to Protect: Report of the Secretary-General'. A/65/877–S/2011/393. 28 June 2011.
———. 'Security Council Resolution 1674 [on Protection of Civilians in Armed Conflict]'. S/Res/1674. 28 April 2006.
———. 'Security Council Resolution 1704 [on Establishment of the UN Integrated Mission in Timor-Leste (UNMIT)]'. S/Res/1704. 25 August 2006.
———. 'Security Council Resolution 1973 [on the Situation in the Libyan Arab Jamahiriya]'. S/Res/1973. 17 March 2011.
———. 'Security Council Resolution 1975 [on Targeted Sanctions against Individuals Meeting the Criteria Set out in Resolution 1572 (2004) on Arms Embargo against Côte D'ivoire]'. S/Res/1975. 30 March 2011.
United Nations. 'High Level Panel on Threats, Challenges and Change, a More Secure World: Our Shared Responsibility'. UN Document A/59/565. 2004.
Viotti, Maria Luiza Ribiero (Permanent Representative of Brazil). 'Statement at the General Assembly Informal Dialogue on the R2P'. 23 July 2009.

Chapter 13
Is Justice the First Virtue of International Institutions?

Charles Sampford

Introduction

One of Rawls's most memorable and famous lines was the claim that 'justice is the first virtue of social institutions.' In posing a question that reflects that claim, this chapter might be imagined to be a paean to this most important of late twentieth-century American political philosophers. To dispel this impression, it might be appropriate to commence with a variation of the words Shakespeare put into Mark Antony's mouth:[1] 'I have come to bury Rawls not to praise him'. But I shall not say that either. Rawls effectively buried himself as a serious philosopher of international relations with his famous 'law of peoples'.[2] In *A Theory of Justice*,[3] Rawls had imagined a group of people who are ignorant of their own circumstances (the pre-contractual 'original position'), sitting down to discuss the principles on which their created society would be based. He argued that these negotiators would came up with three principles counted (which he counted) as two and in which the second and then third only came into operation when the higher ones were as fully operationalized as possible – they were, in his terms, 'lexically ordered'.[4]

Rawls's first principle was one of individual civil and political rights. The second was one of equality of opportunity. The third was the in-egalitarian distributions of social and economic benefits that would be justified if it benefited the least well off.[5]

Rawls sought to revive social contract theory by merging it with Kantian deontology. For some it might seem remarkable that he generated a set of principles that was very close to mainstream liberal opinion in New England. These are the kind of principles that you might imagine a group of very bright liberal American academics sitting down in their Harvard common room might

1 W. Shakespeare, *Julius Caesar* (London: Cambridge University Press, 1968).

2 John Rawls, *The Law of Peoples* (Cambridge, MA: Harvard University Press, 1999).

3 *A Theory of Justice* (Cambridge, MA: Belknap Press of Harvard University Press, 1971).

4 Ibid., 42.

5 My first serious piece of writing was my honours thesis for politics and philosophy in 1975, discussing Rawls's then recently published masterwork.

come up with (except that they would not agree!). Rawls's radical suggestion is that people who did not know their views, position in society or the nature of the society that was being created would come up with the same principles. But this is not really so remarkable. There is a near-universal tendency for social contract theorists[6] to argue that people in a pre-societal state of nature will come up with a sophisticated version of a political view common at the time that they happen to hold. For those who cannot persuade others to their point of view, it is much easier to create a group of compliant contractors in an imagined state of nature with whom they can do business. Social contract theory may constitute a neat way to order your pre-existing ideas and possibly develop them. But it is not a way of validating those ideas – something that Rawls effectively admitted later. He demonstrated this technique very effectively in the 'Law of Peoples',[7] which employed a different process to generate a moderately principled version of American liberal internationalism complete with a semi-respectful recognition of other countries as 'liberal societies' (such as the US), decent societies (societies with different conceptions of justice), 'outlaw states' and 'burdened states'.

It is remarkable that the philosopher with an unremittingly individualistic and rights-based social contract within polities could produce a collectivist and power-based social contract in international affairs. Pogge[8] helps to explain this by pointing out the radical difference between the methodology by which Rawls derived his domestic principles of justice and that by which he derived his 'law of peoples':

> 1. Rational deliberators in the respective original positions *peoples* not *individuals* in the original position.
> 2. Representation is only granted selectively, to those societies which pass either the 'liberal' or 'decent' society test.
> 3. The veil of ignorance is *thinner*, allowing peoples to tell whether they are liberal or merely decent, with two separate deliberations involving greater knowledge.
> 4. Parties to the international original position are not, as one might have expected, charged with agreeing on a public criterion for the assessment, design, and reform of the global institutional order, but charged with

---

6 Consider the works of Thomas Hobbes, *Leviathan* (Oxford: Clarendon Press, 1909 (1651)); John Locke, *Second Treatise of Government* (Indianapolis, IN: Bobbs-Merrill Educational, 1980 (1689)); Jean-Jacques Rousseau, The Social Contract & Discourses (London: Dent, c1913). Online. Available HTTP: http://oll.libertyfund.org/?option=com (accessed 3 March 2013); David Gauthier, *Morals by Agreement* (Oxford: Clarendon Press, 1986).

7 Rawls, *The Law of Peoples*.

8 Thomas Pogge, 'Do Rawls's Two Theories of Justice Fit Together?', in *Rawls's Law of Peoples: A Realistic Utopia?*, ed. R. Martin and D. Reidy (Oxford: Blackwell, 2006).

> agreeing on a set of rules of good conduct that cooperating peoples should (expect one another to) obey.[9]

By this time, it must be obvious that I do not have a great deal of sympathy for social contract theory. I have long dismissed all social contract theory with the unimpeachable fact that human beings are social beings descended from social primates without interruption. This continuity of social life denies the historical space in which a contract could have been forged. It also denies the intellectual possibility of social contract theory because the minds who come to make the social contract have already been socialized into ways of thinking about their society.

It is not unimportant that social contract theory emerged after markets had been institutionalized and growing in importance for 200 years. The idea that contract might be the basis of a social order only emerged after the social order had developed in directions where contracting was common and generally legitimate. But these were contracts within a society that valued contracts rather than a contract about a society. Unless you lived in such a society, you would not imagine that contracts could fulfil such important purposes. If you did not live in such a society, you would not imagine social contract theory. But that only demonstrates that society comes first and contracting second, and it cannot be the other way around.

This argument reflects a kind of category mistake[10] made by social contract theory. You cannot go into the marketplace of ideas and choose which kind of polity you would like in the same way you can go to a market and decide whether you want bananas or mangoes. The polity is like the market itself in which you find the choices limited or non-existent. Social contract theorists failed to realize that contracts occur within polities that institutionalize them rather than about polities.

For the purposes of Rawls's distinction between domestic and international institutions, it is particularly noteworthy that the distinction itself is so historically dependent on the rise of sovereign states and the emergence of an international order in the seventeenth century – something I shall touch on in the next section.

It is a dangerous delusion that politics can be side-stepped by rigging pre-societal debate. The real social contract (or maybe social compact) is between the state and its citizens and, in particular, between those who have and those who have not – that those who have less accept the rules that allocate them less. It is for real debate, discussion and democratic decision.

Social contract theorists are important contributors to ideas about the virtues of institutions, or, as I would prefer to argue, the values that our institutions should deliver. The results of their thought processes are much more interesting than the thought processes themselves. It is in this light that I look at Rawls's idea that justice is the first virtue of institutions. I shall consider the values and virtues of state institutions and international institutions as they have developed over the last 350 years. In both cases, justice was far from the first virtue to be asserted and

9 Ibid., 207.

10 Gilbert Ryle, *The Concept of Mind* (London: Penguin, 1963).

it was a long time before justice could even seriously be considered as the first virtue. However, various elements of justice became increasingly critical within the domestic and international orders. For both domestic and international orders, I argue that justice is not, but can be, and should be, the first virtue of institutions.

Domestic Polities and the First Virtues of their Institutions

Stability

Sovereign states emerged in Europe in the seventeenth century. The Treaty of Westphalia in 1648 is a convenient event and date to crystallize what had been happening for 150 years and continued thereafter. For Hobbes,[11] stability was paramount. Men would contract with each other to subject themselves to a sovereign to avoid a state of nature, a 'state of warre' of all against all, in which the life of man would be 'nasty brutish and short'. This dismal prospect did not seem so farfetched when he was writing the Leviathan. Germany seemed to have fallen into that abyss in the Thirty Years' War (1618–48) and England had stared over the edge during its Civil War. Avoidance of that state of nature was the first virtue of state institutions in time and in precedence (Rawls's sense of 'first virtue').

Legitimacy

At the foundation of the modern state, the other contestant for the first virtue was legitimacy. The concept of 'legitimacy' has a long history in the law and politics within sovereign states and the relations between them. It started when sovereign states were seen in terms of individual sovereigns – individuals that were not so much the head of state but the state itself. Legitimacy was the key to dynastic succession in the same way as it was in the inheritance of titles and property – based on those born in wedlock (with complex rules for each when the sovereign or property holder did not have a direct male heir).[12] This does not mean that sovereign power was always transferred according to the faithful application of those rules. The availability, and application of, force was always relevant. However, even when a palace coup was staged, the usurpers had to claim lineage and if they could not do so, they exercised power as a regent, strongman or 'kingmaker'. As it was domestically, so it was internationally. Invasions were generally based on purportedly superior claims to being the legitimate heir (from

---

11 Hobbes, *Leviathan*.

12 This is related to two Oxford English Dictionary (OED) definitions. The OED defines legitimacy of a child as 'born of parents lawfully married to each other', and legitimacy of a sovereign as 'having a title based on strict hereditary right'. Online. Available HTTP: http://www.oxforddictionaries.com/definition/english/legitimate (accessed 3 March 2014).

the Hundred Years' War between England and France to Spanish and Austrian wars of succession in the late seventeenth and eighteenth centuries).

In Christian Europe, this concept of legitimacy was linked with divine authority – first that he blessed the royal household with a son and secondly that the successor was deemed to be anointed by God, something that his earthly bishops confirmed in coronation ceremonies. Links to divine authority were found in other polities – from the claims that pharaohs, kings or emperors were gods (for example, Egypt), to claims that they were descended from Gods (for example, Japanese), became Gods on death (for example, Rome), or held the highest religious office (for example, the Caliph). The Chinese deduced a mandate of heaven based on the very fact that power had been successfully seized or retained.

As modern states developed into complex entities in which power was divided among a number of officials, few, if any, of them attained office through birth alone. Sovereign legitimacy in domestic and international law was based upon the effective control of territory by what Austin called an 'independent political community'.[13] The test was not the genetic material of the king but whether or not the regime in which those officials worked was in effective control of a territory (what Kelsen called 'by and large efficacious',[14] and what I referred to as the 'prior successful use of force'[15]).

The democratic revolutions from the eighteenth century onwards generated a different concept of sovereignty – initially based on acquiescence,[16] then consent, then the active choice of the governed. That active choice of the governed (according to constitutional rules about how that choice is exercised) is now the basis for legitimacy in the domestic polities of the majority of states (including a majority in numbers, residents and GDP). Active choice has also come to be the basis of legitimacy of international agencies, which are established by treaty and which, with very few exceptions, only apply to those who have signed those treaties. However, it is not the basis for the recognition and legitimacy of states within the international system – where the 'prior successful use of force' remains the criterion.[17]

---

13 John Austin, *The Province of Jurisprudence Determined* (London: John Murray, 1832).

14 H. Kelsen, *General Theory of Law and State*, trans. A Wedberg (Cambridge, MA: Harvard University Press, 1945); *Pure Theory of Law*, trans. Max Knight (Gloucester, MA: Peter Smith, 1989).

15 The 'prior successful use of force' in C.J. Sampford and M. Palmer, 'The Theory of Collective Response', in *Protecting Democracy: International Response*, ed. Morton H Halperin and Mirna Galic (Lanham, MD: Lexington Books, 2005).

16 Demonstrated through the non-exercise of the right to depose sovereigns who had breached a Lockean social contract.

17 See C. Sampford, 'Sovereignty and Intervention', in *Human Rights in Theory and Practice*, ed. T. Campbell and B.M. Leiser (Aldershot: Ashgate, 2001). I discuss the causes of this disconnect, the potential resolutions of it, and the consequences of its elimination including: liability for sovereign debt; the inefficacy of rigged elections; the convergence

I have previously argued that this change reflected the 'great leap forward' in Western political philosophy.[18] It involved a Feuerbachian inversion in the relationship between states and individuals.[19] For centuries subjects had had to justify their conduct on the basis of their loyalty and service to the sovereign. The enlightenment philosophers said that it was the other way around: states had to justify themselves to their citizens. In the majority of countries that are, more or less, functioning democracies, it would now be outrageous to suggest that control of territory is sufficient for a claim to sovereign legitimacy and a right to rule. However, this reversal has not occurred in international systems and only the faintest hint of it has emerged so far. When treason prospers, the treasonous get the keys to their country's embassies, their country's seat at the United Nations, and they are afforded the capacity to borrow against sovereign credit to oppress the people who will have to repay this toxic debt if and when they overwhelm their oppressors.[20]

Legitimacy was not unrelated to stability because the general belief in the legitimacy of the sovereign was more likely to promote stability (though this advantage could be outweighed when the genetic lottery might throw up someone incapable of doing so), and arguments about legitimacy provided readymade reasons for conflict. Legitimacy was also partly related to justice, but the justice was in who exercised sovereign power, rather than how that power was exercised. Indeed, the greater the perceived legitimacy of the regime, the greater the difficulty in asserting the injustice of its actions.

Group Virtues

For many states, representing group identity and pursuing group interests was seen as the first virtue. For some, it is the reason for having states at all. Indeed, many nation states were based on the concept of a nation that demanded a state (though this could equally have been seen as a way of seeking the status and privileges that a state-based international system gave to sovereign states). The Second World War both tarnished and reinforced these virtues. While the Nazi and Fascist views of ethnically based states in competition for their racial destiny formally died,

---

of 'Public Law' and 'Public International Law' and the influence of the former on the latter; international legal personality; the unification of sovereignty and human rights; and, most particularly in this case, the legitimation of what is now seen as 'intervention' to protect civilian populations from governmental authorities that are not accountable to them.

18 'A Tale of Two Norms', in *The Laws of Protection: Protection of Civilians and the Responsibility to Protect*, ed. Charles Sampford, et al. (Geneva: United Nations University, 2012).

19 Ibid., 104.

20 See ibid. for the tension between sovereign legitimacy at the domestic level and the international level and the resulting emergence of a norm of humanitarian intervention and the responsibility to protect civilian populations.

European states became much more ethnically pure after that war, and the duty of states to protect and project national identity is a common feature of more than merely neo-fascist groupings.

A more benign and 'respectable' virtue is that of 'solidarity' – the sense that members of organizations should support each other. Even less controversial is the ideal of 'community' – though there is always the danger that these may be used to stifle individual human rights to express views that are different from, or supposedly undermining of, solidarity or community.

Enlightenment Governance Values

Not long after Hobbes outlined the case for stability as the first virtue of the sovereign,[21] other philosophers started to suggest other virtues for the emerging modern state. Locke's conception of the state of nature[22] was much less violent and influenced more by images of settlers in empty North American landscapes than civilians in states wracked by civil war. In that environment, individuals had rights and they contracted with the sovereign to protect them and those rights. For Locke, the first virtue might be seen as fidelity to the social contract, but that involved recognition of some human rights. The philosophers and revolutionaries of the 'North Atlantic enlightenment'[23] suggested a number of values that would civilize the strong sovereign states that had emerged during the seventeenth century – liberty, equality, fraternity (citizenship), the rule of law, human rights and democracy (which also formed the basis for their approach to legitimacy). These became the key virtues of domestic institutions and the basis on which they should be judged. Where domestic institutions did not live up to these values, men had a right to revolt against their sovereigns, however legitimate under existing theory. After that overthrow, those men (converted from subjects to citizens) continued to have input into who led them and what those leaders should do to advance those values. However, concerns about stability continued and it was more common to prefer the greater recognition of those values within stable regimes to the overthrow of stable regimes in the hope and expectation of a fuller realization of those values. These values might be aggregated into 'justice'.

It could be argued that liberty, equality, fraternity, democracy, human rights, rule of law and the environment encapsulate all related governance values. It could be that we see them as elements of justice and that a concept of 'justice' does or should bring them all together. Alternatively, justice could be seen as a different concept that overlaps them but calls for judgment between and within various governance values. I would argue that we need to pursue both dialogues rather than attempting to subsume one with the other.

21 Hobbes, *Leviathan*.

22 Locke, *Second Treatise of Government*.

23 Sampford, 'Sovereignty and Intervention'.

We should also be aware that debate and discourse over justice recognized a number of forms of justice that were, while generally mutually reinforcing, distinct, discrete and capable of conflicting with each other. These forms of justice were collectively more extensive than Rawls's conception of justice and each was important in its own way. More importantly, some of them incorporate elements of stability and legitimacy and, for the purposes of this chapter, all of them have potential parallels in international affairs.

Formal justice

Formal justice involves the application of law through formal processes themselves set down by law or long-held traditions but is silent on the content of laws other than laws that set out those processes. As such, it forms a part of the rule of law.

Procedural justice

Procedural justice is similar to formal justice but it does reflect values about the formal processes – including principles of natural justice such as the right to know about any allegations in advance, the right to see the case against them, and the right to be heard by an unbiased judge. This is, again, a key part of the rule of law.

Substantive and distributive justice related to the content of laws and the outcomes produced by government agencies

Advocates of various theories of conceptions of justice will argue for the inclusion of a range of values. Prominent among these are human rights (though there will be arguments about the prominence given to various generations of rights), civil and political rights (first generation of negative rights), socio-economic rights (second-generation and positive rights), and cultural and environmental rights (third-generation rights). Some philosophers and politicians downplay or even reject some rights and generations of rights, but most give them different priorities. While Rawls rejects the extreme position that ignores second-generation rights, Rawls is extreme in giving lexical superiority to first-generation rights.[24] However, it is important to recognize that human rights is not the only relevant discourse in considering issues of substantive justice. There are different ways of entering into this 'normative space'. Ideals of welfare can be expressed in terms of socio-economic rights but not always without remainder. In the last two decades, two different ideals have been expressed. Human security in general and its various forms (economic security, food security, health security, environmental security, personal security, community security, political security) were set out in the 1994 Human Development Report and further developed by the Human Security Commission led by Professor Amartya Sen and Madame Sadako Ogata.[25] These rights do not conflict with human rights but package them in different ways.

24 Rawls, *A Theory of Justice*.

25 United Nations Development Programme, 'Human Development Report 1994: New Dimensions of Human Security' (New York: UNDP, 1994); Commission on

Similarly, the 2000 Millennium Development Goals (MDGs) were approved at the 2000 UN Millennium Summit and emphasized particular practical goals that could be seen as furthering human rights and human security but that were, again, packaged in a different way and emphasized the least well off.[26] As the successors to those 2000 goals for the period after 2015, there is ample opportunity for discussing and comparing these congruent ideas that look at the same normative space.

Retributive Justice

For much of human history, this was the primary form of justice that the state was expected to further. For some proponents of 'law and order' it appears to be the most important. This approach may reflect a utilitarian mechanism for making those who would deny justice to others think twice. Or else, it may appeal to victim's rights or the legitimacy of anger towards law breakers. For some, it is a matter of vengeance or a felt need that sinners should not go unpunished. For others, it is an expression of community values and community outrage at certain forms of behaviour. Some of us are uncomfortable about giving these ideas too much sway, but it is an important form of justice in the minds of many.

Criminal Justice

This concept can include elements of retributive justice but might be better seen in terms of formal and procedural justice applied to those accused of crime as well as the appropriate response to those found guilty of breaching the law on the basis of rehabilitation, deterrence and community protection (a mixture of motives that can easily be confused and compromised).

Access to Justice

This aspect emphasizes the ability of those to whom injustices are done to seek redress through the legal system. Access to justice is a critical part of the rule of law and one that is often denied through the cost of access.

Restorative Justice

This form of justice concentrates on the harm done to victims of crime and, more generally, victims of injustice. This form of justice is both longstanding (where compensatory justice through the payment of families for the wrongful death or injury to family members was a way of dealing with wrongdoing and preventing

Human Security, 'Human Security Now: Protecting and Empowering People' (New York: Commission on Human Security, 2003).

26 United Nations General Assembly, 'United Nations Millennium Declaration' (A/RES/55/218, September 2000).

feuds) and contemporary (where perpetrators are encouraged to make their peace with those they harmed and do something to, at least partly, compensate for their actions).

International Systems

There has been a variety of international systems and a range of virtues ascribed to such systems and the international organizations that were created.

State of Nature

For some, the world of states might seem to be a state of nature of another kind. In the absence of an overriding authority, states are seeking their self-interest and are totally unconstrained in the means they pursue. For subjects drafted to fight in the wars that result, their lives may be just as short as in Hobbes's state of nature. But their capacity to continue drafting them means that the life of nations is nasty, brutish and *long*. In such systems, there were no international institutions and no virtues of the international system as such.

Division between 'civilized' and others

There were a number of attempts to limit the nature and extent of conflict between feudal lords – through warrior codes (chivalry in mediaeval Europe and Bushido in Japan) or through the recognition of religious leaders whose status could sometimes settle disputes, sometimes delegitimize one side (for example, when Pope Alexander II excommunicated King Harold II), or develop a theory of 'just war' or justifications for war. Where a 'state system' was based on one religion or culture more or less shared between groups of states, it was common to regard limitations on warfare as only applying within that group. This was found in Islam, which distinguished between *Dar al-Islam* and *Dar al-Harb*.[27] When those they regarded as infidels became stronger, the compliment was returned with European states considering the restraints on war making (limited though they were) as only applying between them. Neither those limitations nor the recognition as states, applied to those outside the 'civilized world'. In such systems, international organizations were likely to be very limited. In Islam, it was the administration of the holy sites and the haj.[28] In Europe, it was limited to the Catholic Church and some of its branches – including the Papacy itself and the martial orders. Their virtue was in helping to maintain some unity among the faithful and reduce conflict between the faithful – in considerable part to expend more efforts fighting states

27 The house of Islam and the house of war.

28 For an overview of the historical development of Islam see Ira M. Lapidus, 'Between Universalism and Particularism: The Historical Bases of Muslim Communal, National, and Global Identities', *Global Networks* 1, no. 1 (2001): 37–55.

outside their system. In the case of the Catholic Church, the Papacy confirmed legitimacy of, and could mediate between, princes. The perceived virtues of international institutions might have been seen as the confirmation of legitimacy on sovereign members and the reduction in conflict between 'civilized states'. In Westphalian Europe, international organizations were slow to emerge. The most important from 1648 to 1920 were conferences in which diplomats negotiated treaties and other agreements. The virtues of these institutions were seen as reducing conflict and achieving stability. Justice was not relevant.

Empire

In some areas, one group (be it based on a city, an ethnic group or a leader) conquered so much of the world known to them that they did not face any comparable group. Both Howe and Doyle offer useful insights into what constitutes Empire, broadly defined as relating to domination by a central political entity and subordination of peripheries, usually through conquest.[29] What had once been independent groups (based similarly on city, group or leader), were under the control of that Empire. Those outside were of a different character, culture and economy – in the case of Chinese, Indian, Middle Eastern (successively Babylonian, Assyrian, Persian and Greek) and Roman empires, the others were the nomadic and semi-nomadic tribes of the Steppes. The empires themselves rarely touched. Indeed, the only two that did so on a regular basis were those based on the central Mediterranean and those based on the 'fertile crescent'. The virtue of empires was, again, stability, especially protection from outsiders.

Middle Kingdom

While China has been, with few exceptions, a series of empires internally, its relationship with other kingdoms involved a different kind of 'states' system. China did not directly rule neighbouring territories. However, the rulers of those territories had to show deference to the 'Middle Kingdom' in a number of ways.[30] These included the provision of tribute (symbolic or otherwise) to indicate inferior status in an asymmetric relationship.[31] But the element that I would highlight is that the neighbouring territories would avoid acting against the Middle Kingdom's interests and wishes. This kind of arrangement is found in other states systems, even when they are nominally equal. A relatively weak form was the role of the

---

29 Michael W. Doyle, *Empires* (Ithaca, NY: Cornell University Press, 1986); S. Howe, *Empire: A Very Short Introduction* (Oxford: Oxford University Press, 2002).

30 See generally, Christopher A Ford, *The Mind of Empire: China's History and Modern Foreign Relations* (Lexington, KY: University Press of Kentucky, 2010).

31 Morris Rossabi, 'Introduction', in *China among Equals: The Middle Kingdom and Its Neighbors, 10th–14th Centuries*, ed. Morris Rossabi (Berkeley, CA: University of California Press, 1983), 3–4.

United States in the west during the Cold War and globally during the 1990s. A much stronger form was found in the Warsaw Pact. The virtues of this kind of state system are stability and predictability but not justice.

The Concert of Europe

From 1814 to 1848, European monarchies sought to maintain the peace between themselves (as monarchies) but to protect each other from republican revolution. For them the virtues of the system were the protection of a particular kind of internal governance and the maintenance of the balance of power between them – the two were seen to be related because the greatest threat to both had come from the French revolutionary wars. The Warsaw Pact[32] could be seen in the same light, dedicated to the protection of communist rule as well as collectively strengthening members against NATO[33] militarily, politically and economically. Another version is to be found in the African Union, to which member states concede the right to intervene in the case of coups d'état.[34] In making that point, I do not seek to suggest equivalence. Indeed, I have argued that there is a justification for the difference.[35] As indicated above, governments have long claimed to represent the people within the territories they control, even if they have secured that control and international recognition through the 'prior successful use of force'. Such claims are trumped by subsequent successful uses of force. However, once a government is chosen by its people through democratic means, it is very difficult for a government that overthrows such democratically elected government to claim greater legitimacy. Force trumps force, but it does not trump choice. It is very difficult to argue that a regime that has ousted those whom the people have chosen represents those same people. Accordingly, a concert of democracies does not suffer the same objections as a concert of Europe or a Warsaw Pact.

The perceived virtues of all such systems are the preservation of a particular form of governance – a virtue that is more important than non-intervention – and the avoidance of conflict.

32 'Treaty of Friendship, Co-Operation and Mutual Assistance between the People's Republic of Albania, the People's Republic of Bulgaria, the Hungarian's People's Republic, the German Democratic Republic, the Polish People's Republic, the Romanian People's Republic, the Union of Soviet Socialist Republics and the Czechoslovak Republic' (I-2962 14/05/1955).

33 North Atlantic Treaty Organization.

34 African Union, 'Constitutive Act of the African Union' (11 July 2000). See article 4 (h) and (j) concerning the right of the Union, in cases of war crimes, genocide and crimes against humanity, to intervene in a member state and for the right of a member state to request intervention.

35 Sampford and Palmer, 'The Theory of Collective Response'.

International Arbitration

In Europe, the Pope was occasionally asked to determine issues between states – most famously in demarcating the interests of Spain and Portugal in the Treaty of Tordesillas.[36] Starting with the Jay Commission of 1794,[37] Western states started appointing commissions to determine matters between themselves on an ad hoc basis. This method was formalized into the Permanent Court of Arbitration by the Hague Convention in 1899,[38] to which states could jointly and voluntarily submit disputes. The Permanent Court of International Justice, established by the League of Nations, and later the International Court of Justice, offer further examples of institutions based on international arbitration submitted to voluntarily by states.[39] The first virtues of these institutions were the resolution of disputes, the reduction of conflict, and increased confidence in international trade and intercourse. While formal and procedural justice was accorded by the court, the voluntary nature of participation and compliance meant that even those limited forms of justice were at the discretion of the parties.

The League of Nations

The intended virtue of the League of Nations[40] and its agencies was stability in the form of the avoidance of war between member states. As those member states involved large colonial empires whose treatment of their own peoples was not an issue that could be effectively raised, justice was not a virtue for the League.

The United Nations

The United Nations (UN) was the first international organization to openly proclaim elements of justice as part of its core business. But while the Charter of the United Nations ('the Charter') aimed to further human rights, stability and

36 'Treaty of Tordesillas' (1494) – highlighting the use of the papal support of Alexander VI to demarcate new territorial claims, namely between the interests of Spain and Portugal.

37 'Treaty of Amity, Commerce, and Navigation (Jay Treaty)'. Online. Available HTTP: http://avalon.law.yale.edu/18th_century/jay.asp (accessed 3 March 2014) – established commissions of arbitration to determine disputes between Britain and the United States relating to boundaries and war debts.

38 The Convention for the Pacific Settlement of International Disputes established the Permanent Court of Arbitration.

39 The establishment of the PCIJ was detailed in the Covenant of the League of Nations, with the Statute of the Permanent Court of International Justice passed in 1920 and its first matter heard before the court in 1922. The International Court of Justice heard its first matter in 1946, replacing the PCIJ.

40 Established by the 'Treaty of Versailles (Treaty of Peace between the Allied and Associate Powers and Germany)' (1919).

the avoidance of conflict (international peace and security) were listed first and overriding.[41] Thus member states were encouraged, but not required, to respect human rights. Neither the UN nor member states could force other states to respect human rights.[42] The only circumstances where the UN Security Council (UNSC) could take action to protect human rights was if the breach threatened international peace and security – further underlining the priority. This is not surprising. The impetus was another thirty years' war (1914–45), starting in Europe and spreading to the rest of the world. So, once again, stability was the first virtue of the UN. As Cabot Lodge said, '[t]his organization is created to prevent you from going to hell. It isn't created to take you to heaven',[43] echoed by Dag Hammarskjöld to underline the main role of the UN and the 'attitude of mind that we should bring to its support': 'the United Nations was not created in order to bring us to heaven, but in order to save us from hell'.[44]

As the UN developed, various aspects of what is broadly called 'justice' have become more prominent. Partly, this has been through the discourse of the United Nations – promoting discussion and awareness of human rights and, more recently, the rule of law and democracy. The UN has also assisted in the development of new ways of expressing and bringing together those values – particularly in the development and articulation of the ideals of human security and the Millennium Development Goals as practical means to further them (mentioned above).

The UN's attempts to prevent hell on earth are surprisingly good. The three scourges of 'war, famine and pestilence'[45] have not been totally eliminated, but all three have been drastically reduced in extent and effect over the last seven decades. While it has not managed to prevent all war, it has limited the number and generally the extent of wars through the UNSC and the Department of Peacekeeping Operations (DPKO), and has assisted the victims of conflict through the office of the United Nations High Commissioner for Refugees (UNHCR), aid programmes, and UNSC-authorized action for the Protection of Civilians (POC). While the UNSC has been largely re-active on the first scourge, the Food and Agriculture Organization (FAO) and the World Health Organization (WHO) have been able to be far more proactive on the second two scourges, while international aid agencies have become expert in famine relief, generally with the leadership

---

41 United Nations, 'Charter of the United Nations' (1945), Art. 1. Online. Available HTTP: https://www.un.org/en/documents/charter/ (accessed 3 March 2014).

42 Ibid., Art. 2.

43 Henry Cabot Lodge Jr, 'New York Times 28 January 1954', in *The New Penguin Dictionary of Modern Quotations*, ed. Robert Andrews (London and New York: Penguin Books, 2000).

44 Dag Hammarskjöld, 'Address at the University of California Convocation, Berkeley California 13 May 1954', in *Public Papers of the Secretaries-General of the United Nations Volume II Dag Hammarskjöld 1953–1956*, ed. Andrew W. Cordier and Wilder Foote (New York: Columbia University Press, 1972), 301.

45 Note the concept of the Four Horsemen of the Apocalypse in the New Testament, 6:1–8: war, famine, disease and death.

and co-ordination of the UN World Food Programme. Overall, these efforts have enabled the UN to take a lead in putting a floor under human misery. This is actually very much in keeping with John Rawls's 'maximin' principle in which welfare was directed to the needs of the least well-off individuals.[46] While UNESCO, UNDP and the World Bank have been less successful in overall development to assist the least well-off nations, there is recognition that this is now the core business of the UN and the international community. The MDGs (recognized in 2000) and post-2015 Sustainable Development Goals (SDGs) are part of that recognition.

International NGOs

The work of the UN has been aided, gingered and occasionally led by a variety of international NGOs who are clearly committed to one or more of the forms of justice outlined above. For them, justice is the first virtue of their institutions. This started with the International Committee of the Red Cross (ICRC) in 1863[47] and the Carnegie Endowment for International Peace in 1910,[48] and it has continued with Amnesty International[49] (1961), Human Rights Watch,[50] and a host of NGOs concerned with medical and humanitarian emergencies (for example, Médecins Sans Frontières (MSF)), famine relief (Care), development and, more recently governance (Transparency International, Integrity Action and Global Integrity). One feature of this development has been the establishment by the professions of NGOs or programmes to assist victims of injustice (International Bar Association and MSF) or to assist the human development of the least well off (for example, Engineers Without Borders).

46 Rawls, *A Theory of Justice*.

47 Established as 'an impartial, neutral and independent organization whose exclusively humanitarian mission is to protect the lives and dignity of victims of armed conflict and other situations of violence and to provide them with assistance.' 'International Committee of the Red Cross'. Online. Available HTTP: http://www.icrc.org/eng/who-we-are/mandate/index.jsp (accessed 28 February 2014).

48 This is 'a private, nonprofit organization dedicated to advancing cooperation between nations and promoting active international engagement by the United States.' 'Carnegie Endowment for International Peace'. Online. Available HTTP: http://carnegieendowment.org/about/ (accessed 28 February 2014).

49 Established in 1961 to 'undertake research and action focused on preventing and ending grave abuses of [human] rights.' Amnesty International, 'Statute of Amnesty International' (As amended by the 30th International Council, meeting in Noordwijkerhout, the Netherlands, 14 to 19 August 2011). Online. Available HTTP: http://www.amnesty.org.au/about/comments/21692 (accessed 28 February 2014).

50 Founded in 1978 to protect the 'human rights of people around the world', Human Rights Watch aims to 'prevent discrimination, to uphold political freedom, to protect people from inhumane conduct in wartime, and to bring offenders to justice'. Human Rights Watch. Online. Available HTTP: http://www.hrw.org/about (accessed 28 February 2014).

Varieties of International Justice Virtue in the Current International System

While this indicates the growing importance of justice in UN agencies and other international institutions, it is worthwhile taking an overview of the extent to which justice in the various senses is a virtue for international organizations. As we shall see, there is much progress to be made.

Formal Justice

While all states are formally equal and have the right to an equal vote in the UN General Assembly, in most ways that matter, there is no formal equality. The five permanent members of the UNSC are not only more than equal, they can override the views of all other countries. While international tribunals have strong traditions of formal justice, this is only accorded to states when other states agree to be bound by the court's decisions. Individuals generally have no rights against states or each other in international tribunals. Individuals can be prosecuted for war crimes, but whether or not they are prosecuted depended, initially, on whether they were on the winning or losing side. More recently, it depends on their government's accession to the Rome Statute or the political decision of the UNSC to establish a tribunal or refer a matter to the ICC. There are legitimate concerns about ad hoc tribunals such as the International Criminal Tribunal for the Former Yugoslavia (ICTFY) that are established to pursue a particular group of offenders after the offences are committed, that are funded by a group of countries and that do not investigate allegations of war crimes by the armed forces of those countries.[51]

European regional courts do much better, as do European Union (EU) institutions generally. However, their operation is confined to Europe, and the EU could be seen as much as a partially federated union as a new set of international institutions.

Procedural Justice

International tribunals generally accord natural justice in the few cases that come before them. However, the limited number, and selectivity, of those cases means that the international system as a whole sees little of this. Indeed, while the rule of law in international affairs was endorsed by all members of the UNGA in 2005,[52] there appears little practice of this aspect in international institutions.

---

51 See discussion in C. Sampford, 'Legality and Legitimacy: A Dozen Years after Goldstone', in *Responsibility to Protect and Sovereignty*, eds Charles Sampford and Ramesh Thakur (Farnham: Ashgate, 2013), 143–70.

52 United Nations, 'World Summit Outcome: Resolution Adopted by the General Assembly' (New York: United Nations, UN Doc A/RES/60, 24 October 2005).

Substantive and Distributive Justice

Human rights and human security are promoted by the UN and international agencies, including traditional civil and political rights as well as socio-economic rights. Civil and political rights are sometimes secured by pressure from UN agencies and, especially, NGOs such as Amnesty International. It could be argued that UN agencies generally do more to secure socio-economic rights through the FAO, WHO and United Nations Development Programme (UNDP). Application of this form of justice is seen as a major goal and is certainly a virtue promoted by the UN and its agencies. On a global scale, their success is very limited, certainly compared to the much greater success in developed countries.

Compensatory Justice

Compensatory justice was once a major goal of international activity, with winners extracting 'indemnities' or 'reparations' from those who lost to them in wars. This form of justice is at least as old as the Punic Wars[53] and was notorious in the nineteenth century when the Western powers imposed indemnities on China after the wars they started.[54] While Germany complained of the reparations imposed on it after the First World War, the country had demanded reparations after the Franco-Prussian War[55] and left soldiers in France until it was paid in full and had imposed reparations on Russia the year before Versailles. One of the most outrageous impositions of reparations was by Russia on Finland, despite the fact that Russia had invaded first.[56]

One of the problems with traditional reparations was that the losses had often been borne by individuals while the reparations were secured by the state, which rarely used these funds to compensate the individual victims. The reparations imposed on Iraq after the 1991 Gulf War were the first to be specifically directed to individual victims.[57]

Retributive and Criminal Justice

Retribution was once an explicit goal of many states engaged in international affairs. Punitive measures were deliberately taken against defeated armies and

53 264–146 BC.

54 Dong Wang, *China's Unequal Treaties: Narrating National History* (Lanham, MD: Lexington Books, 2005); Immanuel C.Y. Hsu, *The Rise of Modern China* (New York, Oxford: Oxford University Press, 1995), for example, see 188–93.

55 Treaty of Frankfurt, 1871.

56 For an overview see John H. Wuorinen, 'The Finnish Treaty', *Annals of the American Academy of Political and Social Science* 257 (1948).

57 Andrea Gattini, 'The UN Compensation Commission: Old Rules, New Procedures on War Reparations', *European Journal of International Law* 13, no. 1 (2002).

civilian populations. The move to criminal justice through the Nuremberg trials was an important development. The lead prosecutor set out a central virtue of criminal (as well as formal) justice: 'Let me make clear that while this law is first applied against German aggressors, the law includes, and if it is to serve a useful purpose it must condemn aggression by any other nations, including those which sit here now in judgment.'[58]

That ideal is now repudiated by this country and the noble experiment of the ICC has yet to blossom because that form of justice, like others, gives way to other values and to the self-interest of major states. However, it must also compete with the values of peace and stability. It is frequently argued that it is better not to pursue prosecutions because this will deflect, stall or prevent an effective peace process. The general and understandable willingness to let a tyrant flee with immunity to stop wider suffering indicates that justice is not the first virtue of international institutions.

Access to Justice

Access to justice is a critical part of the rule of law. It is limited in national institutions and even more limited in international institutions. Restorative justice is new enough in national affairs and is not generally discussed in international affairs.

Overall

Stepping back from the varieties of justice propounded in national and international affairs, the distribution of benefits and burdens is even less just in the latter than in the former. Again, justice is trumped by stability. For example, the Global Financial Crisis was caused by First World banks, but the burdens have been borne by the poor in poorer nations. The 'Global Carbon Crisis' was caused by the consumption of high-carbon products and services by the middle classes of affluent countries. But the greatest consequences will be borne by the poorest. The most commonly advocated response is to give property rights to emit carbon with the lion's share to those who have caused most of the problem.[59]

Ultimately, it is not just a matter of sharing the burdens but of sharing the opportunities created by human civilizations, that is now emerging as a global human civilization. This view goes beyond human security to human development to being a full part of a human community, gaining both from the contribution to and the benefits of human life. As I suggested earlier, we are

58 Robert Jackson, Chief US Prosecutor, Opening Address at Nuremberg, The International Military Tribunal, *Trial of the Major War Criminals before the International Military Tribunal (Blue Series) 14 November 1945–1 October 1946*, vol. 2 (Nuremberg, Germany; 1947, reprinted in 1995: Hein, 1947), 154.

59 C. Sampford, 'Trust, Governance and the Good Life', in *Fiduciary Duty and the Atmospheric Trust*, eds K. Coghill, C. Sampford and T. Smith (Farnham: Ashgate, 2012).

social beings descended from social primates. The essence of being a social being is that two-way participation. The essence of the enlightenment is that it must be for the benefit of the individual as well as the group. The terms on which we contribute and benefit are a matter of justice. Even when we have worked out the principles, we still need to work out the institutions that will deliver them – a mixture of global, national, sub-national, corporate, religious and professional groupings.

Conclusion

Justice was not the first virtue of domestic institutions of the sovereign state. For a long time, such a statement would have seemed like dangerous radical nonsense that justified vigorous repression. The enlightenment got us thinking about governance values and other institutional virtues. Stability was no longer sufficient; democracy was critical.

International institutions have been following behind – in some cases, a long way behind. The virtues of stability and peace generally outweigh the virtue of justice, placing justice a poor second or third. The UN and international institutions have already contributed to the debate and the delivery of human rights though encouragement and suasion, not by enforcement (except though R2P in extreme cases).

Justice can become the first virtue of international institutions, if we debate it and then make it happen. Optimism in thought is just happy musing in the absence of action. Optimism in action is what makes a difference. This is not a call to arms but a call to argue about the ends of international institutions and to laws and institutions at all levels to secure those ends. The new social contract needs to be between the citizens of the world, not imaginary negotiators or constructs that bear such a remarkable likeness to the person who constructs or creates them. Just as social contract must give way to democratic debate within the societies of states, so it must do so in international society.

If there seems little room for optimism, we must remember that history is a long game extending beyond my life and yours. But you have to play to have a chance to win; and the goal is less remote than it would have been to the philosophers who proposed that national institutions be subject to the values of *liberté, égalité, fraternité*, the rule of law, human rights and democracy.

For Rawls, justice is not the first virtue of international institutions.

I agree that it is not.

I assert that it should be and can be.

Bibliography

African Union. 'Constitutive Act of the African Union'. 11 July 2000.

Amnesty International. 'Statute of Amnesty International'. (As amended by the 30th International Council, meeting in Noordwijkerhout, the Netherlands, 14 to 19 August 2011). At http://www.amnesty.org.au/about/comments/21692 (accessed 28 February 2014).

Austin, John. *The Province of Jurisprudence Determined.* London: John Murray, 1832.

Cabot Lodge Jr, Henry. 'New York Times 28 January 1954'. In *The New Penguin Dictionary of Modern Quotations*, edited by Robert Andrews. London and New York: Penguin Books, 2000.

'Carnegie Endowment for International Peace'. At http://carnegieendowment.org/about/ (accessed 28 February 2014).

Commission on Human Security. 'Human Security Now: Protecting and Empowering People'. New York: Commission on Human Security, 2003.

Doyle, Michael W. *Empires*. Ithaca, NY: Cornell University Press, 1986.

Ford, Christopher A. *The Mind of Empire: China's History and Modern Foreign Relations*. Lexington, KY: University Press of Kentucky, 2010.

Gattini, Andrea. 'The UN Compensation Commission: Old Rules, New Procedures on War Reparations'. *European Journal of International Law* 13, no. 1 (1 February 2002): 161–81.

Gauthier, David. *Morals by Agreement*. Oxford: Clarendon Press, 1986.

Hammarskjöld, Dag. 'Address at the University of California Convocation, Berkeley California 13 May 1954'. In *Public Chapters of the Secretaries-General of the United Nations Volume II Dag Hammarskjöld 1953–1956*, edited by Andrew W. Cordier and Wilder Foote. New York: Columbia University Press, 1972.

Hobbes, Thomas. *Leviathan*. Oxford: Clarendon Press, 1909 (1651).

Howe, S. *Empire: A Very Short Introduction*. Oxford: Oxford University Press, 2002.

Hsu, Immanuel C.Y. *The Rise of Modern China*. New York, Oxford: Oxford University Press, 1995.

Human Rights Watch. At http://www.hrw.org/about (accessed 28 February 2014).

'International Committee of the Red Cross'. At http://www.icrc.org/eng/who-we-are/mandate/index.jsp (accessed 28 February 2014).

Kelsen, H. *General Theory of Law and State*. Translated by A. Wedberg. Cambridge, MA: Harvard University Press, 1945.

———. *Pure Theory of Law*. Translated by Max Knight. Gloucester, MA: Peter Smith, 1989.

Lapidus, Ira M. 'Between Universalism and Particularism: The Historical Bases of Muslim Communal, National, and Global Identities'. *Global Networks* 1, no. 1 (2001): 37–55.

Locke, John. *Second Treatise of Government*. Indianapolis, IN: Bobbs-Merrill Educational, 1980 (1689).

Pogge,Thomas. 'Do Rawls's Two Theories of Justice Fit Together?' In *Rawls's Law of Peoples: A Realistic Utopia?*, edited by R. Martin and D. Reidy, 206–25. Oxford: Blackwell, 2006.

Rawls, John. *The Law of Peoples*. Cambridge, MA: Harvard University Press, 1999.

———. *A Theory of Justice*. Cambridge, MA: Belknap Press of Harvard University Press, 1971.

Rossabi, Morris. 'Introduction'. In *China among Equals: The Middle Kingdom and Its Neighbors, 10th–14th Centuries*, edited by Morris Rossabi, 1–13. Berkeley, CA: University of California Press, 1983.

Rousseau, Jean-Jacques. *The Social Contract & Discourses*. London: Dent, c1913. At http://oll.libertyfund.org/?option (accessed 3 March 2013).

Ryle, Gilbert. *The Concept of Mind*. London: Penguin, 1963.

Sampford, C. 'Legality and Legitimacy: A Dozen Years after Goldstone'. In *Responsibility to Protect and Sovereignty*, edited by Charles Sampford and Ramesh Thakur, 143–70. Farnham: Ashgate, 2013.

———. 'Sovereignty and Intervention'. In *Human Rights in Theory and Practice*, edited by T. Campbell and B.M. Leiser, 335–91. Aldershot: Ashgate, 2001.

———. 'A Tale of Two Norms'. In *The Laws of Protection: Protection of Civilians and the Responsibility to Protect*, edited by Charles Sampford, Angus Francis, Vesselin Popovski and Ramesh Thakur, 98–116. Geneva: United Nations University, 2012.

———. 'Trust, Governance and the Good Life'. In *Fiduciary Duty and the Atmospheric Trust*, edited by K. Coghill, C. Sampford and T. Smith, 43–68. Farnham: Ashgate, 2012.

———, and M. Palmer. 'The Theory of Collective Response'. In *Protecting Democracy: International Response*, edited by Morton H. Halperin and Mirna Galic, 101–26. Lanham, MD: Lexington Books, 2005.

Shakespeare, W. *Julius Caesar*. London: Cambridge University Press, 1968.

The International Military Tribunal. *Trial of the Major War Criminals before the International Military Tribunal (Blue Series) 14 November 1945–1 October 1946*. Vol. 2, Nuremberg, Germany; 1947. Reprinted in 1995.: Hein, 1947.

'Treaty of Amity, Commerce, and Navigation (Jay Treaty)'. At http://avalon.law.yale.edu/18th_century/jay.asp (accessed 3 March 2014).

'Treaty of Friendship, Co-Operation and Mutual Assistance between the People's Republic of Albania, the People's Republic of Bulgaria, the Hungarian's People's Republic, the German Democratic Republic, the Polish People's Republic, the Romanian People's Republic, the Union of Soviet Socialist Republics and the Czechoslovak Republic'. I-2962 14/05/1955.

'Treaty of Tordesillas'. 1494.

'Treaty of Versailles (Treaty of Peace between the Allied and Associate Powers and Germany)'. 1919.

United Nations. 'Charter of the United Nations' (1945). At https://www.un.org/en/documents/charter/ (accessed 3 March 2014).

———. 'World Summit Outcome: Resolution Adopted by the General Assembly'. New York: United Nations, UN Doc A/RES/60, 24 October 2005.

United Nations Development Programme. 'Human Development Report 1994: New Dimensions of Human Security'. New York: UNDP, 1994.

United Nations General Assembly. 'United Nations Millennium Declaration'. A/RES/55/2, 18 September 2000.

Wang, Dong. *China's Unequal Treaties: Narrating National History*. Lanham, MD: Lexington Books, 2005.

Wuorinen, John H. 'The Finnish Treaty'. *Annals of the American Academy of Political and Social Science* 257 (1948): 87–96.

Chapter 14
Is it Justice or Justice(s)? The Concept of Justice in Western and Islamic Natural Law Traditions

Ahmet Ulvi Türkbağ

God Commands Justice (adl) and fair dealing (ihsan)

Nahl (16:90)

You can't go to heaven if you don't believe in God (Allah cc) and you can't believe in God (Allah cc) if you don't love each other.[1]

Müslim, Îmân, Hadith: 9; Tirmizî, Et'ıme 45

The Argument

This chapter tries to clearly and briefly discuss a much-debated argument that can be stated in two steps. Despite the long and historically apparent examples on a local and global scale as evidenced by today's disappointing picture, the first step deals in historical sequence with three main religious systems – that is, Judaism, Christianity and Islam, which have both the same grounds and more common elements than popularly thought. The second and logical conclusion of the first point is that, apart from the huge extent of discussion about the universality or the universal validity of ethical concepts, Western (Judaeo-Christian) and Islamic concepts of justice are very similar concepts in their ethical origins. The two steps merge into one argument because they are inherently and logically connected with each other. Furthermore, in order to support and strengthen its argument, being very different from earlier works, this chapter uses an approach or method that is completely Western in style. It takes on religious matters as if they are only philosophical and sociological matters so as not to deny or to diminish their

1 Ahmed Şemsüddin (1998) *Dâru'l-Kütübi'l-İlmiyye*, Beyrut; Muhammed Sıdki Muhammed Cemil (1994) *Dâru'l-Fikr*, Beyrut. The translation from Turkish to English is mine; one of most the beautiful expressions of Islamic justice and its relation to Allah is Goethe's West-Eastern Divan: 'Justice (adl) is apportioned to each one('s) wills(will) who is the just alone. Name his hundred names, and then be this name lauded high! Amen.' Wolfgang Von Goethe (1914) *The West-Eastern Divan, I. Book of The Singer*, Trans. Edward Dowden, J.M. Dent and Sons, p. 5, brackets are mine.

ecumenical principles or rituals but to keep their objectiveness, as far as can be possible, in order to support a meaningful argument.

It should be stated that *the method* that is used to demonstrate the argument is a 'unique' one despite being inspired by H.L.A. Hart and G. Gurvitch, because firstly it deals with intercultural justice problems via a new approach that shows not only popular 'mis-preconceptions' regarding the differences between Western and Islamic concepts of justice, but also many similarities that are generally unrecognized. Secondly, it presents a new outlook, which can be useful in philosophy and sociology of law in order to clarify the formation process of norms and therefore deserves a brief elaboration to clarify the inner connection of the argument.

The Method

The method is a hybrid one and is composed of two levels of argumentation and one assumption. In the first level it uses Hart's 'descriptive sociology', and in the second level Gurvitch's 'normative fact'; it accepts the assumption that in a society or in a group a norm-formation process is very similar to a word-formation process. That is, the process by which a word becomes an accepted and known word in language is very similar to the process by which a social practice becomes a norm in a society or group, in that both spring from a normative element – an idea, a belief, a confirmation of 'ought' – regardless of their original source.

Introduction

Justices?! The title of this chapter seems mistaken – unless, of course, it refers to US Supreme Court judges, who are often referred to as 'Justices'. Perhaps this is an opportunity to explore the true character of justice; as English speakers talk about justice in the singular, English knows justice is an uncountable word! But the title includes the word 'Justice(s)'. How can it be 'justices' in the plural?

The Matter

This paradoxical word use can be clarified following a logical approach. Instead of discussing meanings of justice in the West and in the East, it is preferable to follow different methods to put the argument and clarify a common ground of justice. At this point, let us refer to H.L.A. Hart's well-known book *The Concept of Law*.[2] Here he declares that this book 'may also be regarded as an essay in descriptive sociology'. What is *descriptive sociology*? It is a method that uses language in order to clarify some ethical or legal concepts. It accepts that ordinary (daily) uses

2 H.L.A. Hart, *The Concept of Law* (Oxford: Oxford University Press, 1961), Preface, vi.

give us a true clue to explore the exact meaning of a word. Therefore, this chapter can launch a descriptive sociological analysis with the grammatical structure of the word, Justice. So what does descriptive sociological analysis say about why the word 'justice' is singular in English? This chapter argues, that this immediate thought has been inspired by Hart's approach that justice is uncountable because there can be only one solution or way to satisfy the criteria of justice. Indeed, Hart's approach of 'descriptive sociology' seems open to critics, but at the same time it has important potential to help us understand clichés that unconsciously guide our daily thoughts and gestures. Furthermore, a Freudian or Jungian (and Durkheimian) analysis of personal or collective subconscious can be found in descriptive sociology. An additional discovery is that it relies on an implied assumption that in a language every word is an outcome of a consensus (maybe because of being on a widely shared cultural basis): that is, people who speak this language share the same or similar feelings and attitudes towards the word and the experience of life that the word represents. If this were not so, the word would be forgotten and would not survive. Apart from some of the technical or technological words that become settled quickly after invention, a word always needs this underground consensus. It can even be said that all a word needs to survive is the gradual process that at the end reaches a consensus. The roots of this process are not a clear and defined discussion period but rather are found in the patterns of a vague and indefinite time that is impossible to determine in daily life. But this kind of study goes beyond descriptive sociology.[3]

This collective acceptance, which is also a *sine qua non* for a word, includes a normative component: an idea about right and wrong. It has an ethical basis in the broadest sense. The accepted form of a word is characterized as 'true' not only grammatically but also, sometimes, normatively. In the area of sociology of law (and philosophy of law too), there is a fierce debate and a 'mystery' about how a pattern of behaviour becomes a norm. On the one hand, there is the famous objection or criticism of Hume about fact and norm; on the other hand, there is a long history, from W. Graham Sumner to Durkheim and Georges Gurvitch, that gives explanations about how and by which stages a social practice can gain a normative element, a popular belief about its necessity, become a moral imperative and in the end a norm. These kinds of explanations, to put it concisely, show the stages and the process in which repeated behaviour becomes the norm. For example, according to Sumner these stages are Usages, Manners, Customs, Mores, and Morals.[4] There is a similar but more complex process in Durkheim,

3 See these two major works and their followers: Michel Foucault, *The Archaeology of Knowledge*, trans. A.M.S. Smith (London: Routledge, 2002); Friedrich Nietzsche, *On the Genealogy of Morals*, trans. C. Diethe (Cambridge: Cambridge University Press, 1994).

4 Matheu Deflem, *Sociology of Law* (Cambridge: Cambridge University Press, 2008), 31. Only the title of Sumner's book gives sufficient idea of the stages: William G. Sumner, *Folkways: A Study of Sociological Importance of Usages, Manners, Customs, Mores, and Morals* (Boston: Ginn and Company, 1906).

from the source of mechanical solidarity to criminal law and from the source of organic solidarity to civil law.[5]

The most interesting and seminal idea is the concept of 'normative fact' in Gurvitch that seems to give clues about the transformation or transition process from a fact into a norm, in philosophical terms from 'to be' to 'ought to be', or from ontology to axiology. Gurvitch writes in his Sociology of Law:

> Now every form of sociality is capable of becoming, under certain conditions, the basis of a guarantee of this kind, consequently the birth place of law, protected or not by constraints which are imposed by the unity of the group. We can also express these observations in the following statements. Having designated as 'normative fact' each manifestation of social reality capable of engendering law, i.e., to be its primary or material source … we can conclude: the normative facts of the all-inclusive societies possess in the jural life primacy over the normative facts of particular groups; and the latter possess primacy over the normative facts of forms of sociality. But this does not at all hinder each form of sociality from giving birth to its own peculiar kind of law; the forms of sociality play, beside and inside groups and all-inclusive societies, in which they are integrated, the role of primary sources of law, and this role is a very important and decisive one; for it is impossible to understand the jural life of groups and inclusive societies without referring to the jural life of forms of sociality.[6]

The core function and crucial point of 'normative fact' can easily be seen in its contradictory name: normativity belongs to area of 'ought to' as opposed to 'a fact', which always belongs to the area of 'to be'; it is an observable thing and its nature is completely different from a normative one (being). Everybody knows that the statement 'there is a glass of milk on the table' is very different from the statement 'there should be a glass of milk on the table'. So the 'normative' as an adjective is contradictory with a 'fact' as a name. According to the basic rules of logic, no one thing can be both 'normative' and 'a fact' at the same time. Despite this, in the sociological area of social reality, it is not only a possibility but also an ordinary thing that a fact, a repeated observable behaviour or an act in the course of time, becomes a norm. So 'normative fact' is a unique clue to explore the nature of normativity. It needs 'certain conditions', according to Gurvitch:

> The first condition is the capacity of these social facts to embody positive values by their very existence; this capacity … is certified by the collective acts of intuitive recognition, acts in which the participants yield to a social fact realizing

5 Emile Durkheim, *The Division of Labor in Society*, trans. G. Simpson (New York: Martino Fine Books, 2012).

6 Georges Gurvitch, *Sociology of Law* (London: Kegan Paul, 1947), 158.

> one of the multiple aspects of the idea of Justice. The second condition is that in these facts prevails the active element, a task to be accomplished.[7]

Combining 'descriptive sociology' as a method, and 'normative fact' as an 'atom' or 'foetus' of a norm, the conclusion can be reached that the acceptance of a word, especially in the broadest sense, that is related to justice necessarily includes an ethical content, as was stated above. Therefore, according to descriptive sociological analysis, which gives a basis for the assertion that English-speaking people believe in the long history of their experiences, there can be only one justice; one way or solution that is just or fair, as Gurvitch wrote in the above passage.

The same descriptive sociological outlook can be used to find justice in the Islamic world. In the Arabic language, justice is '*adl*' or '*adalah*' (and '*kst*'), and the Turkish form is '*adalet*'.[8] What does it mean, and is it completely different from Western concepts? It means to put something in its *right place*, according equal treatment to others and reaching *a state of equilibrium* in transaction with them.[9] 'Putting in the right place' or 'putting in a state of equilibrium', are the literal meanings of justice. If anyone wonders where the meanings comes from, he or she would find an interesting story, an etymological story about the origin.[10] It is a well-known fact that in many cultures a camel is an important animal because of its crucial functions in desert life. You can carry everything needed in the desert in bags that are carried on the back of your camel. These bags are tied to each other with a bond; let us call it a packsaddle. So if two bags on each side of your camel are in equilibrium, you would carry your essential items and valuables safely. First, your camel would not get tired as quickly. Second, and more importantly, your necessities, for instance water and bread, can be carried safely. Therefore, if you make a mistake – that is, if you carry things in an unbalanced condition – you risk losing some of them or your camel would get tired more quickly. Your life would depend upon the equilibrium of the burden on the back of your camel. That is the origin of the Arabic verb '*adl*', equilibrium of life! And maybe it is surprising that one form of '*adl*', which means justice, is uncountable in its English counterpart! In Arabic there is a word, '*udul*' as a plural form of 'adl', but it can only be used

7 Ibid.

8 Abdurrahman Elmalı, 'Kur'an-ı Kerim'de Adâlet (Adl) Kavramı', *Harran Üniversitesi İlahiyat Fakültesi Dergisi* III (1997): 283. The writer informs us, in order to show the importance of '*adl*' (justice) in Islamic theology, that '*adl*' and its grammatical forms are used in the Quran 28 times, and '*kst*' and its grammatical forms are used in the Quran 27 times. See, Adnan Koşum, 'Hukukun İşlevleri Arasında Zıtlık Ve Adaletin Üstünlüğü Bakımından İslam Hukuku', *AÜİFD* 47 no. 1 (2006): 64–65.

9 Mohammad H. Kamali, *Freedom, Equality and Justice in Islam* (Cambridge: The Islamic Text Society, 2002), 103.

10 The source of the story is unclear, and the story is not widely known. I heard the story from Professor Hüseyin Hatemi, who is an eminent professor of civil and Islamic law, but this interpretation is mine.

to refer to a person or people. For example, '*Es-sahabetü külluhum udulun*': 'All friends of the Prophet were fair people'.

I shall try to differentiate between the fundamental differences separating the West and the East. There have been a lot of historical clashes and debates between the two civilizations, their cultural outlooks and their understandings of what is a good life. But apart from the misty cloud of history, is there truly a fundamental difference between the two religious concepts of justice? It is often assumed that there are many differences between the two major religious systems and therefore their concepts of justice must be very different. This chapter takes exception to the assumption that there are two discretely separate forms of justice(s).

The relationship between the major religious systems is much debated, but my point is that the main religions not only chronologically follow each other but also share some fundamental bases. For example, Abraham is a holy ancestor for each religion. His name is a mix of Hebrew and Arabic language; and you cannot reject completely and consistently one of them, while accepting the other logically. You can do this only theologically; that is, you would accept the axiomatic truths of one religion and from these bases only you can reject the others.

Christianity is suitable as a good example. To be a Christian involves a person's accepting to some extent and according to his or her interpretation the New Testament and other canonical texts. He or she, at the same time, can accept precepts of the Old Testament only if they do not contradict the New Testament. Additionally, he or she does not believe Islamic texts are religiously binding on them (though they can seek inspiration from them, as they can the works of one religion they respect). However, these and other religious judgments or precepts cannot be based epistemologically – they have only a religious basis that is reduced from religious axioms, as stated before. Despite the fact that the concept of God can be different in three religions and even in chapters of holy books, the epistemological structure of the main religions and their ethical outlooks are inherently connected.

In order to show the relation between Western and Islamic Natural Law traditions, I have chosen two key thinkers – one of them is St Thomas Aquinas and the other one is Al-Ghazali. Essentially, according to Aquinas there are four types of law: the eternal, the divine, the natural and the human. Eternal Law is God's law and is not knowable by human beings. It is in the mind of God. We know eternal Law through two ways: Divine Law and Natural Law. Holy books and other holy texts include Divine Law. Natural Law can only be grasped via the use of reason:

> The light of natural reason, whereby we discern what is good and what is evil, which is the function of natural law, is nothing else than an imprint on us of the Divine Light. It is therefore evident that the natural law is nothing else than the rational creature's participation of the Eternal law.[11]

11 Aquinas, 'Treatise on Law', *Summa Theologiae* [1272], 15–16. Online. Available HTTP: http://www.basilica.org/pages/ebooks/St.%20Thomas%20Aquinas-Summa%20Theologica.pdf (accessed 10 July 2014).

So Aquinas's point of view is that God is the source of all order, not only physical but also social. We can reach God's law in one way from the Divine Law of revelation or the Natural Law of reason, which is indirect because it comes not directly from God but from the God-giving reason.

When we turn to the East, to Al-Ghazali, we see the concept of 'Maslaha', which in English means 'to evaluate'. 'Ghazali used the term of maslaha to fuse fact and value in nature, and thereby grant reason ontological authority in the sharia. He asserts that fusing fact and value is possible because of divine grace.'[12] Maslaha is closely connected to God. According to him,

> Fulfilling maslaha is the goal of the divine legislator (God that is Allah el shaira) and is required for the wellbeing and fulfilment (zaruret el halk) of all of God's creations.
>
> Reason evaluates (the maslaha) and judges whether or not there is express law. No law can be without maslaha, according to those who speak of good and the bad as rational matters. We do not deny the power of rational capacities to indicate the beneficial and the corrupt, and their ability to warn.[13]

It is easy to see that Aquinas and Ghazali both define Natural Law as reason. Reason is the common base of both of these thinkers who represent their religion and culture. But what is reason, and how does it work to find Natural Law? The most important difference between Aquinas and Ghazali is reason's role or function in finding true law or just solution. Their concept of reason is different. I do not intend to debate this problem in detail, but I wish to state only one crucial point.

There is a historical reality, an institution of law that created the Islamic law: *ijtihad*. *Ijtihad* is a judgment, a legal decision that solves a legal problem or is a resolution of a dispute. But *ijtihad* generally is not a demonstrative process that is only to state the logical steps of a given or available solution. Rather, it is a creative endeavour to find a new solution or to develop a new way to go. *Ijtihad* consists of not only divine revelation but also human reason. So when we talk about the *ijtihad*, the different concepts of reason that Ghazali and Aquinas have are actually very close to each other.

Conclusion

> And the Lord said, Behold, the people are one.
> So the Lord scattered them abroad from thence
> upon the face of all the earth … Therefore is the
> name of it called Babel; because the Lord did

12 Anver M. Emon, *Islamic Natural Law Theories* (Oxford: Oxford University Press, 2010), 132.

13 Ibid.

> there confound the language of all the earth: and
> from thence did the LORD scatter them abroad
> upon the face of all the earth.
>
> *Genesis 11* (6–9)

> O mankind … We have … made you peoples and tribes
> that you may know one another ….[14]
>
> *Hujurat* (49:13)

> And mankind was not but one community but they differed ….
>
> *Yunus* (10:19)

> And We have revealed to you, [O Muhammad], the Book in
> truth, confirming that which preceded it of the Scripture
>
> *Ma'idah* (5:48)

Current tendencies and conditions support, and even may exaggerate, the role of *Islamic justice*, which is popularly thought to play a key role in the new world order, especially after 9/11 and then the Arab Spring. Globalization, again and again, leads Third World peoples to confront huge shortfalls in their expectations that seem to indicate problems of distributive justice between themselves and the developed part of the world. All around the world there appears to be bedlam. There is a confusion of concepts and conceptions that flies in the air. The crucial point over and above the confusing portrait of the current world is the polarization of religious systems and civilizations. Popular images that use current technological advancement show the sharp differences between every aspect of the opposing of life.

Is this true? Does it really represent our world? The images that show these differences originally belong to Judaism, Christianity and Islam. *What about the Enlightenment or even the Reformation?* Current images, maybe, are more representative not of Christianity but of the Enlightenment, which is deeply rooted in secular philosophy. The Islamic world faces another challenging problem because it is not only being divided into many inconsistent parts but also because of deep theological contrasts, as evidenced by the current sectarian violence between Sunni and Shiite Muslims. Its images, therefore, have only a partial quality of representation.

If anybody wishes to reach the authentic truth, he or she should look to the origins of religious systems, especially the psycho-social conditions and geographical location of their origination. Furthermore, consider the situation and conditions of ancient Egypt at the time of Exodus or of Judaea at the time of Pontius Pilate as the Prefect of the Roman Empire, or of the Arabic peninsula at the time of Jahiliyyah – the age of ignorance that was epitomized by the killing of girls who were born before boys. The common element of these times was

14 These translations are available at http://quran.com/10 (accessed 22 January 2014).

extremely unjust conditions that almost completely denied the minimum basis of existence for some groups of people or were deeply against the basic features of human nature.

The attractiveness of justice comes from its relation between these basic human interests as stated above and life itself. In the final analysis, justice is reminiscent of survival; to have or being capable of having the conditions that are crucially needed to survive. This was the basis of every dimension of life according to the Greek understanding of nature,[15] and Islamic tradition, which was deeply influenced by that understanding, shares this same basis – as the second caliph of Rashidun caliphates Umar ibn al-Khattab implied, justice is the fundament of all dimensions of existence: the nature, the society and the state.[16]

It is not wrong to say that every religious system emerged for justice and the core shared by all of them is the concept of justice but not justices! All of them were good remedies, cures, hopes of life, in their times unthinkable conditions. Therefore, justice is a minimum, necessary and sufficient condition of life that all religious systems must uphold.

References

Aquinas, 'Treatise on Law', *Summa Theologiae* [1272]. At http://www.basilica.org/pages/ebooks/St.%20Thomas%20Aquinas-Summa%20Theologica.pdf (accessed 10 July 2014).

Deflem, Matheu. *Sociology of Law*. Cambridge: Cambridge University Press, 2008.

Douzinas, Costas. *The End of Human Rights*. Oxford: Hart, 2000.

Durkheim, Emile. *The Division of Labor in Society*. Translated by G. Simpson. New York: Martino Fine Books, 2012.

Elmalı, Abdurrahman. 'Kur'an-ı Kerim'de Adâlet (Adl) Kavramı'. *Harran Üniversitesi İlahiyat Fakültesi Dergisi* III (1997): 283–328.

Emon, Anver M. *Islamic Natural Law Theories*. Oxford: Oxford University Press, 2010.

Foucault, Michel. *The Archaeology of Knowledge*. Translated by A.M.S. Smith. London: Routledge, 2002.

Goethe, Wolfgang von. *The West-Eastern Divan, I. Book of the Singer*. Translated by Edward Dowden. London: J.M. Dent and Sons, 1914.

Gurvitch, Georges. *Sociology of Law*. London: Kegan Paul, 1947.

Hart, H.L.A. *The Concept of Law*. Oxford: Oxford University Press, 1961.

---

15 The ancient Greek view of nature was very different from today's Enlightenment-based understanding. It was a pyramidal, hierarchical understanding of nature: see Costas Douzinas, *The End of Human Rights* (Oxford: Hart, 2000), 19–20, 28–29.

16 The Rashidun caliphates are, in historical sequence, Abu Bakr (Ebubekir), Umar (Omer), Uthman (Osman) and Ali. They are the first four caliphates after the prophet and the period of Rashidun caliphates is between c. 632 and 661.

Kamali, Mohammad H. *Freedom, Equality and Justice in Islam*. Cambridge: The Islamic Text Society, 2002.
Koşum, Adnan. 'Hukukun İşlevleri Arasında Zıtlık Ve Adaletin Üstünlüğü Bakımından İslam Hukuku'. *AÜİFD* 47 no. 1 (2006): 55–66.
Nietzsche, Friedrich. *On the Genealogy of Morals*. Translated by C. Diethe. Cambridge: Cambridge University Press, 1994.
Şemsüddin, Ahmed. *Dâru'l-Kütübi'l-İlmiyye*. Beyrut 1998.
Sıdki, Muhammed, and Muhammed Cemil. *Dâru'l-Fikr*. Beyrut 1994.
Sumner, William G. *Folkways: A Study of Sociological Importance of Usages, Manners, Customs, Mores, and Morals*. Boston: Ginn and Company, 1906.

Chapter 15
General Principles of Law and International Law-Making

Gábor Sulyok

Introduction

General principles of law are frequently ranked among the most controversial categories of international law. Nearly each and every important parameter of these principles has induced prolonged and intense academic debates ever since the advisory committee of distinguished jurists entrusted with the preparation of a report on the Statute of the Permanent Court of International Justice decided nine decades ago to include 'the general principles of law recognized by civilized nations' in the catalogue of sources that would be applied by the future judicial organ.[1] In the spirit of expediency and positive experiences, a quarter-century later the drafters of the Statute of the International Court of Justice took over from the preceding document the provision on applicable sources in an identical shape, save for a minor specifying addendum.[2] Nevertheless, it remains a matter of debate whether general principles of law form part of positive law or natural law, originate from domestic law or international law, carry a distinctively private law or public law content, possess a subsidiary or supreme character, qualify as an independent source of international law, and occupy a separate, if any, position in the international legal order. Finally, the methods and conditions of their international applicability likewise yield much disagreement in the scholarly community.[3]

This chapter merely seeks to examine whether general principles of law constitute a source of international law, and by what legislative means they might achieve that status. The following investigation is based on the assumption that general principles – this complex set of private and public, substantive and procedural rules, such as the principle of equity, the prohibition of abuse of rights, the prohibition of unjust enrichment, the protection of acquired rights, the principle of reparation, *res iudicata, audiatur et altera pars* or *pacta sunt servanda* – belong to the domain of positive law and originate from domestic law. Hence these rules should not be deemed equivalent to the so-called 'principles of international law',

1 Statute of the Permanent Court of International Justice, Article 38, paragraph 3.

2 Statute of the International Court of Justice, Article 38, paragraph 1, sub-paragraph (c).

3 B. Cheng, *General Principles of Law, as Applied by International Courts and Tribunals*. Reprint (Cambridge: Cambridge University Press, 1994), 2–5.

such as the sovereign equality of states, the prohibition of threat or use of force, the prohibition of intervention, the peaceful settlement of international disputes and the right to self-determination of peoples. Nor should they be seen as totally synonymous with the 'general principles of international law', 'principles of international organizations', 'principles of transnational law' and 'principles of supranational law'. Though these latter categories may occasionally overlap with general principles of law, it is but a terminological anomaly that does not have any significance here.[4]

International lawyers have been divided over the questions in the focus of our investigation from the outset. The negative position typically holds that general principles originating from domestic law cannot be categorized as a source of international law, as they were not created by the concurrent wills of two or more states to govern their international relations. Their international application is based on a special rule of customary law that authorizes international judicial organs, with a view to avoid *non liquet*, to resort, by way of analogy, to principles borrowed from the technically more advanced national legal systems in the settlement of disputes, where gaps in the system of international law would otherwise render a decision impossible. That rule of authorization was codified in Article 38, paragraph 3, of the Statute of the Permanent Court of International Justice and Article 38, paragraph 1, sub-paragraph c) of the Statute of the International Court of Justice.[5]

Incontestably, the abstract and general principles at issue spring from the legislative will of a single state, derive from a multitude of specific interconnected legal norms, permeate the entirety or segments of the legal system, and are meant to regulate domestic social relations, and to provide guidelines for national law-making and law enforcement. These features obviously do not match those of the sources of international law. However, it would lead to premature and tenuous results, if we ceased our investigation here, relying on a brief and superficial analysis of the problem. In order to answer the question concerning their nature as a source of international law, we must disregard the peculiar formation and characteristics of general principles. Instead, it should be thoroughly examined whether there has been any legislative act in the international level after the domestic consolidation of these principles, which made them an independent source of international law.

---

4 For more details, see, G. Sulyok, 'General Principles of Law as a Source of International Law', in *International Law – A Quiet Strength (Miscellanea in memoriam Géza Herczegh)*, ed. P. Kovács (Budapest: Pázmány Press, 2011), 166–68.

5 G. Herczegh, *General Principles of Law and the International Legal Order* (Budapest: Akadémiai Kiadó, 1969), 97–100. See also, H. Bokor-Szegő, 'Les principes généraux du droit', in *Droit international: bilan et perspectives*, vol. 1, ed. M. Bedjaoui (Paris: A. Pedone – UNESCO, 1991), 228–29; H. Kelsen, *The Law of the United Nations: A Critical Analysis of Its Fundamental Problems, with Supplement* (London: Stevens & Sons Ltd, 1951), 533.

Reception of General Principles of Law

Erstwhile literature suggests that the necessity to apply domestic legal rules, as a separate source of law, to the international conduct of states had already surfaced in the period of traditional international law. In the nineteenth century these rules had been supplied by internationally relevant municipal laws and regulations of selected states,[6] but at the beginning of the twentieth century their place was taken over, for various theoretical and practical reasons, by 'the general principles of law recognized by civilized nations'.[7] Thus the development of international law has and does not terminate the need for assistance by the technically more advanced national legal systems. The explanation lies in the paradoxical effects of progress: while the growth of conventional and customary law decreases the number of gaps and the value of domestic legal solutions, the expansion of legal regulation to new fields generates new gaps, and maintains the demand for provisions originating from domestic law.

If the picture canvassed by scholars of traditional international law broadly corresponds to past realities, the elevation of certain rules of national legal systems, including general principles of law, to the international level primarily served to more comprehensively govern the international conduct of states in fields inadequately regulated by other sources of law rather than to facilitate the settlement of disputes submitted to international judicial organs by the prevention of

6 See, for example, J.C. Bluntschli, *Das moderne Völkerrecht der civilisirten Staten als Rechtsbuch dargestellt* (Nördlingen: C.H. Beck'schen, 1868), 58–59; C. Calvo, *Le droit international théorique et pratique, précédé d'un exposé historique des progrès de la science du droit des gens*, 4th edn, vol. 1 (Paris – Berlin: Guillaumin et Cie – Puttkammer et Mühlbrecht, 1887), 161–62; P. Fiore, *Nouveau droit international public, suivant les besoins de la civilisation moderne*, 2nd edn, vol. 1 (Paris: G. Pedone-Lauriel, 1885), 158–59; F. von Holzendorff and A. Rivier, *Introduction au droit des gens: recherches philosophiques, historiques et bibliographiques* (Hamburg: Verlagsanstalt und Druckerei AG, 1889), 83; T.J. Lawrence, *The Principles of International Law* (Boston: D.C. Heath and Co, 1895), 105–06; F.F. Martens, *Traité de droit international* (Paris: A. Chevalier-Marescq, 1883), 252–53; P.L.E. Pradier-Fodéré, *Traité de droit international public européen & américain, suivant les progrès de la science et de la pratique contemporaines*, vol. 1 (Paris: G. Pedone-Lauriel, 1885), 88–89; H. Wheaton, *Elements of International Law, with a Sketch of the History of the Science* (Philadelphia: Carey, Lea and Blanchard, 1836), 49.

7 See, for example, E.M. Borchard, 'The Theory and Sources of International Law', in *Recueil d'études sur les sources du droit en l'honneur de François Gény*, vol. 3 (Paris: Sirey, 1934), 354–56; L. Le Fur, 'La coutume et les principes généraux du droit comme sources du droit international public', *ibid.*, 366–72; A. Verdross, 'Les principes généraux du droit comme source du droit des gens', *ibid.*, 383–86; C. de Visscher, 'Contribution à l'étude des sources du droit international', *ibid.*, 395–98. See also, H. Lauterpacht, *Private Law Sources and Analogies of International Law, with Special Reference to International Arbitration* (London: Longmans, Green, and Co, 1927), 69–71; J.B. Scott, ed., *The Proceedings of the Hague Peace Conferences: The Conference of 1907*, vol. 1 (New York: Oxford University Press, 1920), 351.

non liquet.[8] That presupposes international law-making, even if its exact course and date can hardly be ascertained from the distance of approximately one and a half centuries. Its occurrence is confirmed by its results only: the disturbingly chaotic literary reflections and the vague remarks made by international judicial organs.

However, it causes little difficulty to outline the hypothesis of a law-making process culminating in the international recognition of general principles of law. This process is arguably based on an automatism, the beginning of which is marked by the emergence of a customary rule of reception. Accordingly, states accept, without exhaustive enumeration or further measures, principles originating from domestic law as an integral part and unwritten source of international law, if they are generally recognized and suitable to govern international relations. Following the emergence of the rule of reception, the incorporation of general principles takes place automatically, provided that the two conjunctive conditions are met. The fulfilment of these conditions is continuously 'verified' by the rule of reception, as it will be displayed later with regard to the question of termination. (It may be inferred by exclusion of other possibilities that the rule of reception forms part of universal customary law. Simply put, it could not have come into existence in any other way.[9])

The requirement of general recognition does not imply that a principle has to exist in the domestic law of every state in the world. Notwithstanding that the reference to 'civilized nations' in the Statute of the International Court of Justice is utterly obsolete and rightly criticized,[10] it seems sufficient, if the dominant legal systems of principal families of law accept a provision with identical or similar content.[11] Notably, this allegation may prove implausible for extreme positivists, who have been reluctant to regard general principles of law as a source of law, unless they are recognized by every state, claiming 'those are the rules of international

8 'The general principles of law, therefore, permanently rectify a more primitive law in the spirit of a more advanced and progressive law.' J. Csiky, *Az általános jogelvek, mint a nemzetközi jog forrása [General Principles of Law as a Source of International Law]* (Szeged: Szeged Városi Nyomda és Könyvkiadó, 1934), 43. (Emphasis omitted.)

9 In the past, a less-known scholar also traced back the legal nature of general principles of law to customary law, but he did not hypothesize the existence of a rule of reception. Instead, he suggested that customary law behaved as 'a source of law, which designates another source of law'. Csiky, *Az általános jogelvek, mint a nemzetközi jog forrása [General Principles of Law as a Source of International Law]*, 21–22.

10 *North Sea Continental Shelf Cases (Federal Republic of Germany/Denmark) (Federal Republic of Germany/Netherlands)*, Judgment of 20 February 1969, ICJ Reports 1969, Separate Opinion of Judge Fouad Ammoun, 132–34. Cf. *Reparation for Injuries Suffered in the Service of the United Nations*, Advisory Opinion of 11 April 1949, ICJ Reports 1949, Dissenting Opinion by Judge Krylov, 219.

11 Distant similarities can be revealed in this respect between general principles of law and ancient Roman *ius gentium*. Gaius, *Institutionum commentarii quattuor*, I.1; *Digest*, 1.1.9.

law only, to which states in some way consent'.[12] Yet such an interpretation of general recognition is dubious, as it looks for the intentions of states in the wrong place, and erroneously confounds their domestic and international legislative wills. The international legislative will that manifests itself in the rule of reception and elevates general principles to the international level is not an aggregate or a reflection of domestic legislative wills that originally establish the principles concerned. These wills prevail in different realms, pursue different objectives, and carry different contents. Hence the internationally relevant manifestation of legislative intention and engagement should be sought not in domestic law, but in the rule of reception, which does not demand recognition by every state for the elevation of a principle to the international level. Indications are that it is enough, if the dominant legal systems of principal families of law accept it with identical or similar content. The verification of general recognition calls for the application of the comparative method,[13] but in the procedure of the International Court of Justice, a consensus among judges representing the main forms of civilization and the principal legal systems of the world might as well suffice.[14]

The requirement of suitability to govern international relations must likewise be interpreted in a flexible manner. This condition merely implies that a domestic provision, which is to be reckoned as a general principle, must be capable of producing effects on the international plane in view of the similarities between the typical behaviour of private persons and states. Once these conditions are met, a principle is elevated to the international level, albeit its content is at this point

12 Csiky, *Az általános jogelvek, mint a nemzetközi jog forrása [General Principles of Law as a Source of International Law]*, 15. (Emphasis omitted.)

13 It has been submitted that this process consists of two operations. The vertical move involves the abstraction of legal principles from domestic rules; the horizontal move involves the verification of general recognition of principles thus obtained. F.O. Raimondo, *General Principles of Law in the Decisions of International Criminal Courts and Tribunals* (Leiden – Boston: Martinus Nijhoff, 2008), 45 *et seq.* The process has also been described as a threefold test comprising the verification of general character, recognition by civilized nations and capability of being incorporated into international law. M. Bos, *A Methodology of International Law* (Amsterdam – New York – Oxford: North-Holland, 1984), 262. See also, M.C. Bassiouni, 'A Functional Approach to "General Principles of International Law"', *Michigan Journal of International Law* 11, no. 3 (1990): 809–16; B. Conforti, *International Law and the Role of Domestic Legal Systems* (Dordrecht: Martinus Nijhoff, 1993), 64–65. It is essential to prevent imbalances caused by the dominance of world languages, especially English and French, in the course of the process. C. Tomuschat, 'International Law: Ensuring the Survival of Mankind on the Eve of a New Century. General Course on Public International Law', *Recueil des Cours* vol. 281 (1999): 339.

14 Statute of the International Court of Justice, Article 9. Cf. *Anglo-Iranian Oil Co. Case (United Kingdom v Iran)*, Preliminary Objection, Judgment of 22 July 1952, ICJ Reports 1952, Dissenting Opinion of Judge Levi Carneiro, 161.

still extremely abstract and raw. It is primarily the task of the judiciary to disclose, specify and elaborate on that content.[15]

Even though the process under deliberation rests on a rule of customary law, it does not yield as an outcome new customary norms, for it is not a convergence of general practice and *opinio iuris* of states that creates the domestic provisions elevated to the international level. In fact, states endeavoured by the establishment of the rule of reception to fill the gaps of conventional and customary law by generally recognized domestic principles capable of governing international relations. Consequently, on account of its gap-filling function and the differences of various law-making processes, the rule of reception incorporates general principles of law into the system of international law as an independent source of law rather than as customary law. This surely does not preclude a subsequent conventional or customary reaffirmation of certain principles,[16] but it will affect neither their nature as general principles of law nor the independence of this unique source of law. Similar intertwinements regularly occur between conventional and customary international law without any bearing on their respective self-identities.[17]

Due to the exceptionally high degree of abstraction of general principles, their effects can barely be perceived in everyday life: upon the examination of the conduct of members of the international community, we much earlier and more

---

15 Cf. 'International law has recruited and continues to recruit many of its rules and institutions from private systems of law. [...] The way in which international law borrows from this source is not by means of importing private law institutions "lock, stock and barrel", ready-made and fully equipped with a set of rules. It would be difficult to reconcile such a process with the application of "the general principles of law". In my opinion, the true view of the duty of international tribunals in this matter is to regard any features or terminology which are reminiscent of the rules and institutions of private law as an indication of policy and principles rather than as directly importing these rules and institutions'. *International Status of South-West Africa*, Advisory Opinion of 11 July 1950, ICJ Reports 1950, Separate Opinion by Sir Arnold McNair, 148.

16 G. Gaja, 'General Principles of Law', in *The Max Planck Encyclopedia of Public International Law*, vol. 4, ed. R. Wolfrum (Oxford: Oxford University Press, 2012), 375. It is often regarded as a fundamental function of general principles of law to facilitate the development of international law. Cheng, *General Principles of Law, as Applied by International Courts and Tribunals*, 39; Herczegh, *General Principles of Law and the International Legal Order*, 116; P. Kovács, *A nemzetközi jog fejlesztésének lehetőségei és korlátai a nemzetközi bíróságok joggyakorlatában [The Perspectives and Obstacles of the Development of International Law in the Practice of International Courts]* (Budapest: Pázmány Péter Katolikus Egyetem Jog- és Államtudományi Kar, 2010), 85–88; Raimondo, *General Principles of Law in the Decisions of International Criminal Courts and Tribunals*, 50. See also, M. Bartoš, 'Transformation des principes généraux en règles positives du droit international', in *Mélanges offerts à Juraj Andrassy*, ed. V. Ibler (La Haye: Martinus Nijhoff, 1968), 1–12; W. Friedmann, 'The Uses of "General Principles" in the Development of International Law', *American Journal of International Law* 57, no. 2 (1963): 279–99.

17 *Military and Paramilitary Activities in and against Nicaragua (Nicaragua v United States of America)*, Merits, Judgment of 27 June 1986, ICJ Reports 1986, 93–96.

easily come across a relevant conventional or customary norm, than a general principle of law, as the former relates to the latter as *lex specialis* relates to *lex generalis*. Therefore, these provisions mostly surface in judicial proceedings, when judges encounter gaps in the law during the peaceful settlement of international disputes. It is no coincidence that the literature of general principles of law focuses on the practice of international judicial organs, as their existence, contents and effects are best observable in that field. Otherwise, these provisions are not a particularly effective source of international law.[18]

It should be added that the customary rule of reception is not identical to the rule of authorization, as codified in Article 38, paragraph 3, of the Statute of the Permanent Court of International Justice and Article 38, paragraph 1, sub-paragraph c) of the Statute of the International Court of Justice, which permits international judicial organs to resort to general principles of law by way of analogy. The rule of reception precedes the rule of authorization in terms of both the time of formation and the logic of functioning. That leads to two further conclusions. First, the rule of authorization sanctions the application of international law rather than domestic law. Second, it was not the cited statutes that established the general principles of law – these documents only rendered them applicable in the procedure of the two courts.

Let us recall at this point a remark made by the Permanent Court of International Justice that portrayed municipal laws as mere facts from the standpoint of international law.[19] If we project this statement to Article 38, paragraph 3, of the Statute of that court, it becomes evident that 'the general principles of law recognized by civilized nations', considered by several prominent drafters of the document as provisions originating from national legal systems, could be important for the judicial settlement of international disputes insofar as they were applied in their international rather than domestic legal capacity. Article 38, paragraph 1, of the Statute of the International Court of Justice explicitly confirms this assessment by virtue of the sole amendment to the text of the former provision, as a result of which the sentence introducing the catalogue of applicable sources, including general principles of law, now reads as follows: 'The Court, whose function is to decide *in accordance with international law* such disputes as are submitted to it, shall apply [...].'[20] (It reaffirms the disparity of the rule of reception and the rule of authorization, as well.)

The significance of the highlighted reference to international law has at times been rejected on the basis that it does not prove that general principles of law truly constitute a source of international law.[21] This approach obviously contradicts the

18 G.J.H. van Hoof, *Rethinking the Sources of International Law* (Deventer: Kluwer, 1983), 146–48.

19 *German Interests in Polish Upper Silezia (Germany v Poland)*, Judgment No. 7, 25 May 1926, PCIJ Series A, No. 7, 19.

20 Statute of the International Court of Justice, Article 38, paragraph 1. (Emphasis added.)

21 Cf. Herczegh, *General Principles of Law and the International Legal Order*, 18–19.

basic rules of treaty interpretation, and may lead to other misconceptions.[22] These misconceptions include, for example, the parallel treatment of the application of general principles and the choice of law method, claiming that both point towards a foreign legal system as seen from the perspective of the forum applying the law. This parallel has far-reaching consequences. It amounts to a denial of general principles of law as a source of law to regard their application as a special manifestation of the choice of law method, for that method does not entail the incorporation of foreign legal rules into the law of the forum.[23] However, it requires little effort to explore the fundamental differences in the respective bases, techniques and normative backgrounds of the application of general principles and foreign legal rules, and in the contents and characteristics of the provisions invoked. Therefore, no matter how appealing this parallel may appear, it can be challenged along several dimensions, and has to be deemed unsubstantiated.

Finally, we need to counter a negative position, which maintains that, in spite of the identical wording, the sub-paragraph of the Statute of the International Court of Justice concerning general principles of law has a meaning different from that of the Statute of the Permanent Court of International Justice due to the divergent historical circumstances prevailing at the time of adoption of the two documents.[24] Though historical interpretation is a universally accepted supplementary means of interpretation of international treaties,[25] the *travaux préparatoires* of the statutes do not support this allegation. Nor can a fundamental change of circumstances explain the alleged modification of the original content of the provision, because the wording, as already mentioned, was deliberately left unaltered in light of positive experiences.

Beyond the introductory sentence of Article 38, paragraph 1, of the Statute of the International Court of Justice, miscellaneous other pieces of indirect evidence too attest that general principles of law constitute an independent source of international law. These pieces of evidence include the law of the European Union, a legal order distinct from both international law and the national legal systems of member states, where the development of law and the strengthening of integration necessitated the recognition of general principles of law as a source of law. The European Court of Justice has played an instrumental role in the process. Notwithstanding that the founding treaties do not expressly authorize the application of general principles, there is widespread agreement that the legal basis of this practice can be derived from Article 19, paragraph 1, of the Treaty

22 Vienna Convention on the Law of Treaties, Vienna, 23 May 1969, Article 31, paragraphs 1 and 4.

23 Cf. Herczegh, *General Principles of Law and the International Legal Order*, 99.

24 G.I. Tunkin, *A nemzetközi jog elméletének kérdései [Questions of the Theory of International Law]* (Budapest: Közgazdasági és Jogi Könyvkiadó, 1963), 154.

25 Vienna Convention on the Law of Treaties, Vienna, 23 May 1969, Article 32.

on European Union, and Articles 263 and 340, paragraph 2, of the Treaty on the Functioning of the European Union.[26]

The European Court of Justice has taken into account the domestic laws of member states, the law of the European Community, and later the law of the European Union, and international law, especially the European regime of human rights protection, for the determination and application of general principles of law. Several groups of principles have so crystallized, but a consensus on their exact boundaries has not been reached yet. Nevertheless, the extensive case law of the body indicates that general principles of law that have been incorporated into the law of the European Union include, for example, the respect for fundamental rights,[27] the prohibition of discrimination,[28] the protection of legitimate expectation,[29] the requirement of effective judicial control,[30] the prohibition of retroactive effect,[31] *ne bis in idem*[32] *and pacta sunt servanda.*[33] The founding treaties, on the other hand, scarcely contain explicit references to general principles. Such references can be found in Article 6, paragraph 3, of the Treaty on European Union, concerning the protection of fundamental rights, and Article 340, paragraphs 2 and 3, of the Treaty on the Functioning of the European Union, concerning the obligation to make good any damage caused by the institutions or their servants in the performance of their duties.[34]

General principles of law undoubtedly rank among the primary sources of the law of the European Union, and possess a 'constitutional status'.[35] Knowing that the development of the law of the European Union has been greatly inspired

26 O.J. C 326, 26.10.2012, 27, 162–63, 193.

27 C-29/69, *Erich Stauder v City of Ulm, Sozialamt* [1969] ECR 419; C-11/70, *Internationale Handelsgesellschaft mbH v Einfuhr- und Vorratsstelle für Getreide und Futtermittel* [1970] ECR 1125; C-4/73, *J. Nold, Kohlen- und Baustoffgroßhandlung v Commission of the European Communities* [1974] ECR 491.

28 C-20/71, *Luisa Sabbatini, née Bertoni v European Parliament* [1972] ECR 345; C-149/77, *Gabrielle Defrenne v Société anonyme belge de navigation aérienne Sabena* [1978] ECR 1365.

29 C-112/77, *August Töpfer & Co. GmbH v Commission of the European Communities* [1978] ECR 1019.

30 C-222/84, *Marguerite Johnston v Chief Constable of the Royal Ulster Constabulary* [1986] ECR 1651.

31 C-63/83, *Regina v Kent Kirk* [1984] ECR 2689.

32 C-14/68, *Walt Wilhelm and Others v Bundeskartellamt* [1969] ECR 1.

33 C-162/96, *A. Racke GmbH & Co. v Hauptzollamt Mainz* [1998] ECR I-3655.

34 O.J. C 326, 26.10.2012, 19, 193.

35 Opinion of Advocate General Trstenjak, delivered on 30 June 2009, C-101/08, *Audiolux SA e.a. v Groupe Bruxelles Lambert SA (GBL) and Others and Bertelsmann AG and Others* [2009] ECR I-9823, para. 70. See also, C-101/08, *Audiolux SA e.a. v Groupe Bruxelles Lambert SA (GBL) and Others and Bertelsmann AG and Others* [2009] ECR I-9823, para. 63. For more details, see, T. Tridimas, *The General Principles of EU Law*, 2nd edn (Oxford – New York: Oxford University Press, 2006).

by international law, the recognition as a source of law of general principles partly derived from the national legal systems of member states should not be underestimated regardless of the particular circumstances. If this process came to pass in a short period of time in the European legal order, it could also have easily happened in the considerably older and in many ways standard-setting international law. The special features of the law of the European Union do not undermine the validity of this assumption. Thus it seems permissible to draw a parallel between international law and the law of the European Union as regards their attitude towards the general principles of law.

Elements of the practice of international organizations and institutions and states likewise indirectly prove that general principles of law constitute a source of international law. For example, the Secretary-General of the United Nations described them as one of the principal sources of law in an early memorandum on the codification of international law.[36] The World Trade Organization has adopted a similar approach, and general principles now play an important role in its dispute settlement mechanism.[37] Furthermore, selected principles originating from domestic law have gained special emphasis in international criminal law, where different international and hybrid, *ad hoc* and permanent judicial organs have resorted to them on many occasions since the end of World War II.[38] (International human rights instruments too tend to recall general principles with respect to criminal procedure.[39])

National legal systems treat general principles of law as a source of international law, as well. It is true that the diverse constitutional clauses on the relationship of international law and domestic law typically reaffirm the generally recognized principles and/or rules of international law, and omit express references to general principles of law, but they are habitually interpreted in a manner so as to embrace these principles.[40] However, the constitutional clauses on international law are not

---

36 Survey of International Law in Relation to the Work of Codification of the International Law Commission: Preparatory Work within the Purview of Article 18, Paragraph 1, of the Statute of the International Law Commission. Memorandum submitted by the Secretary-General, 10 February 1949, UN Doc. A/CN.4/1/Rev.1, 22.

37 J. Cameron and K.R. Gray, 'Principles of International Law in the WTO Dispute Settlement Body', *International and Comparative Law Quarterly* 50, no. 2 (2001): 248–98.

38 Raimondo, *General Principles of Law in the Decisions of International Criminal Courts and Tribunals*, 73 *et seq.* See, for example, United States of America v Wilhelm List *et al.*, Judgment of 19 February 1948, Nürnberg Military Tribunal, vol. 11, 1235.

39 See, International Covenant on Civil and Political Rights, New York, 16 December 1966, Article 15, paragraph 2; Convention for the Protection of Human Rights and Fundamental Freedoms (European Convention on Human Rights), Rome, 4 November 1950, Article 7, paragraph 2. See also, N.K. Hevener and S.A. Mosher, 'General Principles of Law and the UN Covenant on Civil and Political Rights', *International and Comparative Law Quarterly* 27, no. 3 (1978): 596–613.

40 For a European overview, see, V.S. Vereshchetin, 'New Constitutions and the Old Problem of the Relationship between International Law and National Law', *European*

the only domestic provisions that need to be taken into account. General principles of law also appear in fundamental rights catalogues of constitutions or other laws and regulations in connection with the guarantees of criminal procedure, often indicating the influence of international human rights instruments.[41]

Modification and Termination of General Principles of Law

If we accept that general principles of law constitute a source of international law, we inevitably face the questions of modification and termination. It has to be stated at the outset that modification, in this context, does not designate the indispensable process by which the inherently abstract and raw content of principles originating from domestic law is disclosed and specified by the judiciary. Nor does it amount to modification, if various judicial organs interpret the same principle, within their margin of discretion, with negligible differences. Modification here denotes any alteration of the content of a general principle, which occurs after its reception into international law, and substantially transforms its nature in line with the intentions of states.

Since general principles of law originate from domestic law, the question of modification must be examined in the realms of both international law and domestic law. We may draw a surprising conclusion at the very beginning of our investigation: general principles cannot be directly modified by international law-making, for it is incompatible with the peculiar way of their creation. These principles are automatically incorporated into international law by a customary rule of reception, if they are generally recognized and suitable to govern international relations. Apart from the establishment of the continuously functioning rule of reception, no other legislative act has taken place in the international level. Hence states could make an attempt to modify the content of a general principle by conventional or customary law-making only.[42] Still neither of these processes can

---

Journal of International Law 7, no. 1 (1996): 29–41; L. Wildhaber and S. Breitenmoser, 'The Relationship between Customary International Law and Municipal Law in Western European Countries', *Zeitschrift für ausländisches öffentliches Recht und Völkerrecht* 48, no. 2 (1988): 163–207.

41 See, for example, Canada, Constitution Act 1982, Part I, Article 11, paragraph g); Constitution of the Democratic Socialist Republic of Sri Lanka, 1978, Article 13, paragraph 6; Hong Kong Bill of Rights Ordinance, 1991, Part II, Article 12, paragraph 2.

42 The question of modification has already been raised in the practice of the International Court of Justice. The relevant separate opinion did not rule out that an international treaty may provide further rights in addition to those that spring from a general principle of law, but the interpretation of treaty stipulations led the judge to doubt that it had actually happened in the present case. Despite that the wording leaves room for different interpretations, the structure of reasoning suggests that the granting of further rights would have taken place within the framework of the treaty, and would not have modified the principle itself: 'That general principle of law concerning the rights or status

perform the expected adjustment. They would instead produce a new conventional or customary rule with a content different from the general principle concerned that, in turn, would remain unaltered and preserve its independent existence. The explanation is simple: different law-making processes necessarily yield different sources of law.[43] Given that the general principle would retain its original content and independence regardless of the modifying conventional or customary rule, a dual regime would emerge, in which potential conflicts would have to be resolved by rules of legal logic, such as *lex specialis derogat legi generali* and *lex posterior derogat legi priori*. That is why conventional or customary rules cannot formally modify, only derogate from general principles that have become undesirable by reason of their contents.

General principles of law can be modified exclusively through the medium of domestic law. Remarkably, this process may be attributed not only to national, but also to international legal factors. However, in the latter case the conventional or customary rules of international law cannot and do not directly modify the general principles, as this possibility has just been ruled out – international law merely induces the modification of these principles through the medium of domestic law. In order to comprehend this process, we need to reach back to the relationship of international law and domestic law. It is commonly known that states incorporate the rules of international law into their national legal systems either by the monistic technique of adoption or the dualistic technique of transformation, and, at the same time, they must ensure harmony between international law and domestic law.[44] Naturally, the techniques of adoption and transformation too incorporate into domestic law the conventional or customary rules that have been created by states with a view to derogate from the content of a general principle of law. Having been incorporated into domestic law, these conventional or customary rules may induce a change in the content of the domestic legal principle from which the general principle originates, in conformity with the requirement to ensure harmony between international law and domestic law. If this process

of shareholders, which underlies not only Italian Company law but also the company law of some other civil law countries, may not be altered by any treaty aimed at the protection of investments unless that treaty contains some express provision to that end. […] Yet there is no reason to interpret the [treaty] *as having granted* […] *any further rights in addition to those* to which the same shareholders would have been entitled under Italian law as well as under the general principles of company law.' *Elettronica Sicula S.p.A. (ELSI) (United States of America v Italy)*, Judgment of 20 July 1989, ICJ Reports 1989, Separate Opinion of Judge Oda, 86, 88–89. (Insertion and emphasis added.)

43 With the establishment of the rule of reception, an automatic mechanism emerged in customary international law, the products of which – that is, the general principles of law – cannot be directly influenced or modified by other customary rules due to the differences of various law-making processes.

44 See, for example, I. Seidl-Hohenveldern, 'Transformation or Adoption of International Law into Municipal Law', *International and Comparative Law Quarterly* 12, no. 1 (1963): 88–124.

uniformly takes place throughout the dominant legal systems of principal families of law, the customary rule of reception will elevate the domestic legal principle to the international level with its new content, and overwrite the general principle of law, from which states previously strove to derogate by conventional or customary law-making. (Evidently, this process presupposes general international treaties or universal customary rules.)

Domestic legal factors may change the content of a domestic legal principle, as well. If the new content becomes generally recognized and continuously allows the international application of the provision, the content of the corresponding general principle of law will automatically and accordingly change in international law by virtue of the rule of reception.[45] Normally, this is a subtle and lengthy evolution that can be perceived from a distance of decades or centuries only. Fast and radical changes, on the other hand, may also occur, and reveal an odd phenomenon. Similarly to the conventional and customary rules of international law, general principles of law are incorporated by states into their national legal systems. These provisions travel an intriguing road: they depart from domestic law, gain reception into international law, then return to domestic law as rules of international law. Hence selected principles exist in national legal systems in two forms: as general principles of law and as principles of domestic law. In spite of expectations to the contrary, a change of the latter does not immediately modify the former. It should not be forgotten that such modification takes place only if a change becomes generally recognized in the dominant legal systems of the principal families of law. In other words, a change in the content of a domestic legal principle is followed by a change of the corresponding general principle of law with a delay. Until the general recognition of the new content of a domestic legal principle and the resulting modification of the general principle of law, the principle concerned exists in the national legal system not only in two forms, but also with two different contents. If a change is modest and tolerable, practical problems are unlikely. But in extreme cases, the requirement of harmony between international law and domestic law may slow or delay the modification of a domestic legal principle, and secure the preservation of the minimum standards of the rule of law.

The termination of general principles of law must also be examined in the realms of both international law and domestic law. Yet it would be a grave mistake to automatically adopt the conclusions drawn with regard to modification to the question of termination, and to presume that the only feasible way of termination is through the medium of domestic law. The situation is quite different. In the international level, it is equally possible to terminate the entire category of general principles of law, and to terminate individual principles. The total elimination of general principles of law as a source of law requires the termination of the customary rule of reception, or the substantial modification of its purpose and

45 Cf. Csiky, *Az általános jogelvek, mint a nemzetközi jog forrása [General Principles of Law as a Source of International Law]*, 43.

functioning. Conversely and understandably, it is impossible to directly terminate individual principles by persistent objection[46] or international law-making.[47] There is but one scenario that involves the termination of a general principle on account of circumstances in the international level: if the provision is rendered unable to govern international relations by changes in the international environment. Let there be no misunderstanding: it is not the mere fact of alteration of international relations that terminates the general principle, but the rule of reception that reacts to this alteration automatically, in absence of further measures by states. Since international applicability is an essential condition of their recognition as a source of law, objectively inapplicable general principles cannot exist in the system of international law. If a general principle is no longer able to govern international relations due to changes in the international environment, and as such, one of the features required for its elevation to the international level fades away, then it will become invisible to the rule of reception, and ultimately disappear from international law. (Theoretically speaking, nothing precludes the 'revival' of principles that have so been terminated by subsequent changes in the international environment.)

The termination of individual general principles can also be achieved through the medium of domestic law. All it takes to realize that is to breach the requirement of general recognition by removing the principle from a large number of national legal systems, or to widely modify its domestic legal content in a manner that it becomes unable to govern international relations in the future. Such a generally unrecognized principle may nevertheless continue to exist in national legal systems, but it will remain invisible to the rule of reception and ineligible for elevation to the international level, for failing to meet the required conjunctive conditions.

It should be stressed that the question of modification or termination is mainly of academic importance. The practical probability of these measures is negligible. The overwhelming majority of general principles of law came into existence several centuries ago, and have become inseparable from the normal functioning of law. Substantial alterations of any kind thus seem unnecessary and futile. Moreover, it is always far more convenient for states to derogate from an undesirable general

46 In light of that the customary rule of reception was established more than a century ago, a detailed examination of persistent objection may be dispensed with. Suffice it to note that persistent objection would have thwarted the elevation of general principles to the international level *in toto* (as such, it would have been ineffective against individual principles), and it would have had an effect on those states only that had rejected the rule of reception in the course of its formation. (On the recognition of general principles of law by newly independent states, see, S.P. Sinha, 'Perspective of the Newly Independent States on the Binding Quality of International Law', *International and Comparative Law Quarterly* 14, no. 1 (1965): 124.)

47 Since states are not at all defenceless against the flow of principles towards international law, and have numerous ways to dispose of undesirable provisions, this statement is not irreconcilable with the postulation that international law does not bind sovereign states against their will. *S.S. Lotus (France/Turkey)*, Judgment No. 9, 7 September 1927, PCIJ Series A, No. 10, 18.

principle by conventional or customary law-making. Derogation, of course, would not bring about the modification or termination of the principle, but at least it offers a chance to evade its application with the help of rules of legal logic, such as *lex specialis derogat legi generali* and *lex posterior derogat legi priori*.

Conclusion

In sum, it may be stated that general principles of law constitute an independent source of international law, created and maintained by a customary rule of reception. Due to their unwritten character, gap-filling function and insignificant influence on the everyday life of the international community, the existence, contents and effects of these principles mainly become palpable in the practice of international judicial organs. Hence they are frequently described as being subsidiary or auxiliary in nature, though it should not be taken as if they actually occupied a subordinate or inferior position in the international legal order. In absence of a hierarchy between the various sources of international law, general principles of law are of equal rank with their more 'robust' counterparts, including international treaties and customary international law. For that reason, the catalogue contained in Article 38, paragraph 1, of the Statute of the International Court of Justice reflects the logical train of thought of a judge in search of rules applicable to a particular case, not a hierarchy of sources.[48] Clearly, general principles of law may be labelled as a source of law in a formal sense only. In a material sense, the source of law is the community of states that established the customary rule of reception, or alternatively, the circumstances that necessitated this legislative act. General principles of law themselves can at best be deemed a material source of law in the context of the development of international law; even so, it is most doubtful whether rules are capable of serving as a means of laying down new rules.[49] But it is exactly how this ethereal source of law attracts the attention of generations of international lawyers: every question answered leads to even more.

Cases

A. Racke GmbH & Co. v Hauptzollamt Mainz [1998] ECR I-3655, C-162/96.

Anglo-Iranian Oil Co. Case (United Kingdom v Iran), Preliminary Objection, Judgment of 22 July 1952, ICJ Reports 1952, 93.

Audiolux SA e.a. v Groupe Bruxelles Lambert SA (GBL) and Others and Bertelsmann AG and Others [2009] ECR I-9823, C-101/08.

48 Cheng, *General Principles of Law, as Applied by International Courts and Tribunals*, 22; Gaja, 'General Principles of Law', 375.

49 M. Virally, 'The Sources of International Law', in *Manual of Public International Law*, ed. M. Sørensen (London – New York: Macmillan – St. Martin's, 1968), 147.

August Töpfer & Co. GmbH v Commission of the European Communities [1978] ECR 1019, C-112/77.

Elettronica Sicula S.p.A. (ELSI) (United States of America v Italy), Judgment of 20 July 1989, ICJ Reports 1989, 15.

Erich Stauder v City of Ulm, Sozialamt [1969] ECR 419, C-29/69.

Gabrielle Defrenne v Société anonyme belge de navigation aérienne Sabena [1978] ECR 1365, C-149/77.

German Interests in Polish Upper Silezia (Germany v Poland), Judgment No. 7, 25 May 1926, PCIJ Series A, No. 7, 4.

International Status of South-West Africa, Advisory Opinion of 11 July 1950, ICJ Reports 1950, 128.

Internationale Handelsgesellschaft mbH v Einfuhr- und Vorratsstelle für Getreide und Futtermittel [1970] ECR 1125, C-11/70.

J. Nold, Kohlen- und Baustoffgroßhandlung v Commission of the European Communities [1974] ECR 491, C-4/73.

Luisa Sabbatini, née Bertoni v European Parliament [1972] ECR 345, C-20/71.

Marguerite Johnston v Chief Constable of the Royal Ulster Constabulary [1986] ECR 1651, C-222/84.

Military and Paramilitary Activities in and against Nicaragua (Nicaragua v United States of America), Merits, Judgment of 27 June 1986, ICJ Reports 1986, 14.

North Sea Continental Shelf Cases (Federal Republic of Germany/Denmark) (Federal Republic of Germany/Netherlands), Judgment of 20 February 1969, ICJ Reports 1969, 3.

Regina v Kent Kirk [1984] ECR 2689, C-63/83.

Reparation for Injuries Suffered in the Service of the United Nations, Advisory Opinion of 11 April 1949, ICJ Reports 1949, 174.

S.S. Lotus (France/Turkey), Judgment No. 9, 7 September 1927, PCIJ Series A, No. 10, 4.

Walt Wilhelm and Others v Bundeskartellamt [1969] ECR 1, C-14/68.

References

Bartoš, M. 'Transformation des principes généraux en règles positives du droit international'. In *Mélanges offerts à Juraj Andrassy*, ed. V. Ibler, 1–12. La Haye: Martinus Nijhoff, 1968.

Bassiouni, M.C. 'A Functional Approach to "General Principles of International Law"'. *Michigan Journal of International Law* 11, no. 3 (1990): 768–818.

Bluntschli, J.C. *Das moderne Völkerrecht der civilisirten Staten als Rechtsbuch dargestellt*. Nördlingen: C.H. Beck'schen, 1868.

Bokor-Szegő, H. 'Les principes généraux du droit'. In *Droit international: bilan et perspectives*, vol. 1, ed. M. Bedjaoui, 223–30. Paris: A. Pedone – UNESCO, 1991.

Borchard, E.M. 'The Theory and Sources of International Law'. In *Recueil d'études sur les sources du droit en l'honneur de François Gény*, vol. 3, 328–61. Paris: Sirey, 1934.

Bos, M. *A Methodology of International Law*. Amsterdam – New York – Oxford: North-Holland, 1984.

Calvo, C. *Le droit international théorique et pratique, précédé d'un exposé historique des progrès de la science du droit des gens*, 4th edn, vol. 1. Paris – Berlin: Guillaumin et Cie – Puttkammer et Mühlbrecht, 1887.

Cameron, J. and Gray, K.R. 'Principles of International Law in the WTO Dispute Settlement Body'. *International and Comparative Law Quarterly* 50, no. 2 (2001): 248–98.

Cheng, B. *General Principles of Law, as Applied by International Courts and Tribunals*. Reprint. Cambridge: Cambridge University Press, 1994.

Conforti, B. *International Law and the Role of Domestic Legal Systems*. Dordrecht: Martinus Nijhoff, 1993.

Csiky, J. *Az általános jogelvek, mint a nemzetközi jog forrása [General Principles of Law as a Source of International Law]*. Szeged: Szeged Városi Nyomda és Könyvkiadó, 1934.

Fiore, P. *Nouveau droit international public, suivant les besoins de la civilisation moderne*, 2nd edn, vol. 1. Paris: G. Pedone-Lauriel, 1885.

Friedmann, W. 'The Uses of "General Principles" in the Development of International Law'. *American Journal of International Law* 57, no. 2 (1963): 279–99.

Gaja, G. 'General Principles of Law'. In *The Max Planck Encyclopedia of Public International Law*, vol. 4, ed. R. Wolfrum, 370–78. Oxford: Oxford University Press, 2012.

Herczegh, G. *General Principles of Law and the International Legal Order*. Budapest: Akadémiai Kiadó, 1969.

Hevener, N.K. and Mosher, S.A. 'General Principles of Law and the UN Covenant on Civil and Political Rights'. *International and Comparative Law Quarterly* 27, no. 3 (1978): 596–613.

Holzendorff, F. von and Rivier, A. *Introduction au droit des gens: recherches philosophiques, historiques et bibliographiques*. Hamburg: Verlagsanstalt und Druckerei AG, 1889.

Kelsen, H. *The Law of the United Nations: A Critical Analysis of Its Fundamental Problems, with Supplement*. London: Stevens & Sons Ltd, 1951.

Kovács, P. *A nemzetközi jog fejlesztésének lehetőségei és korlátai a nemzetközi bíróságok joggyakorlatában [The Perspectives and Obstacles of the Development of International Law in the Practice of International Courts]*. Budapest: Pázmány Péter Katolikus Egyetem Jog- és Államtudományi Kar, 2010.

Lauterpacht, H. *Private Law Sources and Analogies of International Law, with Special Reference to International Arbitration*. London: Longmans, Green, and Co, 1927.

Lawrence, T.J. *The Principles of International Law*. Boston: D.C. Heath and Co, 1895.

Le Fur, L. 'La coutume et les principes généraux du droit comme sources du droit international public'. In *Recueil d'études sur les sources du droit en l'honneur de François Gény*, vol. 3, 362–74. Paris: Sirey, 1934.

Martens, F.F. *Traité de droit international*. Paris: A. Chevalier-Marescq, 1883.

Pradier-Fodéré, P.L.E. *Traité de droit international public européen & américain, suivant les progrès de la science et de la pratique contemporaines*, vol. 1. Paris: G. Pedone-Lauriel, 1885.

Raimondo, F.O. *General Principles of Law in the Decisions of International Criminal Courts and Tribunals*. Leiden – Boston: Martinus Nijhoff, 2008.

Scott, J.B., ed. *The Proceedings of the Hague Peace Conferences: The Conference of 1907*, vol. 1. New York: Oxford University Press, 1920.

Seidl-Hohenveldern, I. 'Transformation or Adoption of International Law into Municipal Law'. *International and Comparative Law Quarterly* 12, no. 1 (1963): 88–124.

Sinha, S.P. 'Perspective of the Newly Independent States on the Binding Quality of International Law'. *International and Comparative Law Quarterly* 14, no. 1 (1965): 121–31.

Sulyok, G. 'General Principles of Law as a Source of International Law'. In *International Law – A Quiet Strength (Miscellanea in memoriam Géza Herczegh)*, ed. P. Kovács, 151–86. Budapest: Pázmány Press, 2011.

Tomuschat, C. 'International Law: Ensuring the Survival of Mankind on the Eve of a New Century. General Course on Public International Law'. *Recueil des Cours* vol. 281 (1999): 9–438.

Tridimas, T. *The General Principles of EU Law*, 2nd edn. Oxford – New York: Oxford University Press, 2006.

Tunkin, G.I. *A nemzetközi jog elméletének kérdései [Questions of the Theory of International Law]*. Budapest: Közgazdasági és Jogi Könyvkiadó, 1963.

Van Hoof, G.J.H. *Rethinking the Sources of International Law*. Deventer: Kluwer, 1983.

Verdross, A. 'Les principes généraux du droit comme source du droit des gens'. In *Recueil d'études sur les sources du droit en l'honneur de François Gény*, vol. 3, 383–88. Paris: Sirey, 1934.

Vereshchetin, V.S. 'New Constitutions and the Old Problem of the Relationship between International Law and National Law'. *European Journal of International Law* 7, no. 1 (1996): 29–41.

Virally, M. 'The Sources of International Law'. In *Manual of Public International Law*, ed. M. Sørensen, 116–74. London – New York: Macmillan – St. Martin's, 1968.

Visscher, C. de. 'Contribution à l'étude des sources du droit international'. In *Recueil d'études sur les sources du droit en l'honneur de François Gény*, vol. 3, 389–99. Paris: Sirey, 1934.

Wheaton, H. *Elements of International Law, with a Sketch of the History of the Science*. Philadelphia: Carey, Lea and Blanchard, 1836.

Wildhaber, L. and Breitenmoser, S. 'The Relationship between Customary International Law and Municipal Law in Western European Countries'. *Zeitschrift für ausländisches öffentliches Recht und Völkerrecht* 48, no. 2 (1988): 163–207.

Index

Aarhus Convention 225
Abdullahi v Pfizer, Inc. 181–2, 183, 185–6, 189
access to justice 289, 298
accountability *see* multinational corporations (MNCs)
Additional Protocols (1977) 66
Africa *see also* South Africa
  ARV medicines 207–8
  NGO activity 199–200
AIDS Coalition to Unleash Power (ACTUP) 205
Al Bashir, Omar 119, 120
Al-Adsani v UK (2001) 116–17
Al-Bassiouni case 69–70
alien occupation 53–4
Alien Tort Statute (ATS) (US) 8, 163–7
  applicability of extraterritorial jurisdiction 170–71
  challenges to 186–7
  Daimler AG v Bauman et al 168–70
  extraterritorial violations 187–8
  Kano trovafloxacin trial litigation 185–6
  Kiobel v Royal Dutch Petroleum Co (2013) 186–7
  multinational corporations (MNCs) 156–9
  overview 183–4
  Sosa v Alvarez-Machain 184–5
  use by victims of human experimentation 184–6, 188–9
  use post-Apartheid 206–7
Alvarez-Machain, Humberto 185
Ananyev and Others v Russia 96
Anglo-Iranian Oil case 130–31, 140
Apartheid
  funding by MNCs 201–2
  and NGO activity 199–202
  Sharpeville massacre 201
  the Sullivan Principles 202–3
Argentina
  GlaxoSmithKline Synflorix experiment 182–3, 188
armed forces
  belligerent's privilege 49–50, 52–3
Arrest Warrant case 114–17
ARV medicines
  HIV/AIDS Treatment Action Campaign (TAC) 207–8
AstraZeneca
  Ticagrelor experiment 182
aut dedere aut judicare 103–6
Ayala, Balthazar 28

Basic Principles and Guidelines on the Right to a Remedy and Reparation (UN) 84–5
belligerent's privilege
  armed forces 49–50
  combatant immunity 23–4, 29, 34
  and the dualistic axiom law of war 30–31
  early modern Europe 30–34
  under the Geneva Conventions
    armed forces 49–50
    levée en masse 53
    occupied regimes 53–4
    partisans 51–2
    and prisoner of war status 54–5
    racist regimes 53–4
    summary 55–6
    unrecognized armed forces 52–3
  irregular forces 44–6
  medieval warfare 24–9
  overview 23
  prisoner of war status 24
  reciprocal agreements 31–3
  twentieth century 48–9
Bhopal gas tragedy 157, 181, 182, 189–90

bilateral investment treaty (BIT) 135–6, 141
Brazil
responsibility to protect (R2P) guidelines 274–5
Broniowski v Poland (2004) 95
Brussels Declaration 42, 44–6
belligerent's privilege criteria
irregular forces 44–6
levée en masse 46–9

Canada
Kyoto Protocol violations 213, 220–21
Peacebuilding Commission 257
Cape PLC 158
Case Concerning the Arrest Warrant (2000) 114–17
Center for International Environmental Law (CIEL) 216
Charter of the United Nations (UN) 81
Christianity 304
civil protection 3–5
in the Gaza Strip 70–72
international humanitarian law (IHL) 3–4, 65–7
civilians
guerrilla warfare 35
levée en masse
Brussels Declaration 46–9
European approach 34, 36–8
US approach 34
scope of non-combatant immunity 27–8
Climate Action Network (CAN) 216
climate change *see* environmental protection
Climate Ethics Consensus (CEC) (UN) 219
'climate justice' *see* international climate justice
clinical trials *see* nonconsensual human experimentation
colonization
and belligerent's privilege 32, 53–4
combatants *see also* non-combatants
immunity 23–4, 29, 34 *see also* belligerent's privilege
Lieber Code (US) 39–41
compensatory justice
Apartheid victims 206–7
nonconsensual human experimentation 180
war reparations 297
Concert of Europe 292
Conference on Trade and Development (UNCTAD) 151
Congo
human rights abuses 236
Convention against Torture (UNCAT) 103–5, 121
Convention for the Protection of Human Rights and Fundamental Freedoms (ECHR) 83
corporate accountability *see* multinational corporations (MNCs)
corporate social responsibility (CSR) 201–2
see also multinational corporations (MNCs)
Respect, Protect and Remedy Framework 203
the Sullivan Principles 202–3
corporate veil 159, 195
corps francs 38
corruption 154–5
Cotonou Agreement 234
Council of Europe
Convention for the Protection of Human Rights and Fundamental Freedoms (ECHR) 83
Statute 81
councils of war (US) 39
criminal justice 289, 297–8
Criminal Justice Act (1988) (UK) 105
customary international law
prohibition of torture 97
State immunity 106–8
ratione materiae 111–17
ratione personae 102, 108–11, 121

Daimler AG v Bauman et al 168–70
Daimler Financial Services v Argentine Republic 136, 140
Declaration on Fundamental Principles and Rights at work (ILO) 154
democracy 285–6

'descriptive sociology' 304–5
dispute resolution 293 *see also* investment treaty arbitration
distributive justice 288–9, 297
divine authority 285
Doe v Chevron Texaco 156–7
Doe v Unocal (1997) 156, 184
Droop, H.R. 42–4
dualism 87
dualistic axiom 30–31, 32

early modern Europe 30–34
EC Regulation No 44/2001 158, 159
EDFI v Argentina case 131–2
effective interpretation principle 138–44
ejusdem generis rule 134–6, 143, 144
Empire 291
employment rights 154, 158
Environment Programme (UNEP) (UN) 216
environmental protection
  activism 219–22
  corporate accountability 152–3, 156–7
  Framework Convention on Climate Change (UN) 213, 214
  Global Carbon Crisis 298
  Guidelines on Multinational Enterprises (OECD) 153
  and human rights 222
  international climate justice
    definition 217–19
    legal enforcement 222–7
  Kyoto Protocol 213, 214, 220–21, 222, 225
  legal enforcement
    non-state actors 222–7
    state actors 224–5
  litigation 156–7, 220–21
  role of non-state actors 214–16, 219–22
  United Nations Framework Convention on Climate Change 213, 214
Environmental Protection Agency (EPA) (US) 217
ethics
  concept of justice 303–9
  corporate social responsibility (CSR) 202–3
  social contract theory 281–4
EU Regulation No 1215/2012. 158, 159
Europe
  Concert of Europe 291–2
European Convention on Human Rights
  obligations of contracted parties 89–91
European Court of Human Rights
  caseload 91–2
  rules of procedure
    effective and available remedies 93
    exhaustion rule 83–5
    pending claims 93
    pilot-judgement procedure 92–3, 95–7
    repetitive case applications *see* pilot-judgement procedure
    unilateral declaration 93–4
European Union
  applicability of extraterritorial jurisdiction 170–71
  corporate accountability
    case law 156–9
    EC Regulation No 44/2001 158, 159–63
    EU Regulation No 1215/2012. 158, 159–63
    extraterritorial jurisdiction 161–3
European warfare 30–34
  irregular militias 36–8
exhaustion rule 83–4
extraterritoriality
  Alien Tort Statute (ATS) (US) 187–90
  EU regulations 161–3
  interpretation under US and EU law 170–71
  Kiobel v Royal Dutch Petroleum Co (2013) 163–7

Fact Finding Mission on the Gaza Conflict (UN) 72–3
Filártiga v Peña-Irala 165–6
Filártiga v Peña-Irala (1980) 165, 167, 184, 187
foreign direct investment 193, 195–6
formal justice 288, 296
formal legality 241, 245–8
forum non conveniens 170–71

Foundation for International Environmental Law and Development 215–16
France
  corps francs 38
  Franco-Mexican War (1861–67) 37–8
  Franco-Prussian War (1870–71) 38
  levée en masse 34, 36–7, 38
  Napoleonic Wars (1803–15) 36–7
Franco-Mexican War (1861–67) 37–8
Franco-Prussian War (1870–71) 38
francs-tireurs 38
Friends of the Earth (FoE) 213, 215, 219
functional immunity 102

Gaza Strip
  civil protection, legal framework 70–72
  human rights violations 68–70, 72–4
  Israeli blockade 69–70
  Operation Cast Lead (2008–09) 68, 72–3
General Orders 100 *see* Lieber Code (US)
Geneva Conventions 3–5, 49–56, 66–7
GlaxoSmithKline
  Synflorix experiment 182–3, 188
Global Carbon Crisis 298
Global Compact (UN) 153, 154–5
Global Financial Crisis 298
globalization
  foreign direct investment 195–6
  impact 194–7
  and proliferation of NGOs 197–9
Goldstone report 72–3
Greenpeace 215
guerrilla warfare
guerrillas 35, 36, 41
  Peninsular War (1807–14) 36–7
Guidelines on Multinational Enterprises (OECD) 152, 153, 155
Guiding Principles on Business and Human Rights (UNSRSG) 7, 153, 154, 155–6

Habré, Hissène 104
Hague Convention (1899) 293
Hague Convention 1899
  Martens Clause 48
Hague Conventions 42
Hague Regulations (1907) 66
health care
  HIV/AIDS Treatment Action Campaign (TAC) 204–5
heinous offense 28
High-Level Panel on Threats, Challenges and Change (UN) 1
HIV/AIDS Treatment Action Campaign (TAC) 207–8
Hobbes 286–7
Holmesburg prison experiments 180
human experimentation *see* nonconsensual human experimentation
human radiation experiments 180
human rights 64
  civil protection 3–5, 65–7
  corporate accountability 152, 157
    Daimler AG v Bauman et al 168–70
    Guiding Principles on Business and Human Rights (UNSRSG) 153, 154, 155–6
    role of NGOs 194
  and environmental protection 222
  Guidelines on Multinational Enterprises (OECD) 153–4
  human experimentation *see* nonconsensual human experimentation
  International Rule of Law (IROL)
    concept overview 239–40
    formal conceptions 240–43
  Kiobel v Royal Dutch Petroleum Co (2013) 186–7
  labour rights 154, 158
    case law (US and EU) 156
  NGO activity 199–202
  nonconsensual human experimentation
    AstraZeneca Ticagrelor experiment 182
    compensatory justice 180
    contributing factors 183
    examples 180–81
    GlaxoSmithKline Synflorix experiment 182–3
    Kano trovafloxacin trial litigation 181–2, 183, 189
    use of Alien Tort Statute (ATS) (US) 184–6

non-state actors (NSAs) role 238–9
South Africa
Khulumani Group 205–7
Treatment Action Campaign (TAC) 204–5
Truth and Reconciliation Commission (TRC) 205–7
and substantive justice 288–9
Human Rights Committee 65
Human Rights Committee (UN) 82–3
human rights law (HRL)
codification 63–5
Convention for the Protection of Human Rights and Fundamental Freedoms (ECHR) 83
domestic jurisdiction 82–6
Ananyev and Others v Russia 96
Broniowski v Poland (2004) 95–6
Pinto Act (Italy) 94–5
European Convention on Human Rights
obligations of contracted parties 89–91
European Court of Human Rights 93
procedures 92–4
unilateral declaration 93–4
intergovernmental treaties 81–2
International Covenant on Civil and Political Rights (CCPR) 82–3
obligations of contracted parties 87–9
Rule of Prior Exhaustion of Local Remedies 83–4
state application of international norms 86–91
universal jurisdiction 76

Iberian Peninsula 36–7
immunity *see* State immunity
Impregilo v Argentina tribunal 141–2
impunity 117–18
In re Estate of Ferdinand Marcos 165–6
In Re South African Apartheid 156
India
AstraZeneca Ticagrelor experiment 182
Bhopal gas tragedy 157, 181, 182, 189–90
Institut de Droit International 108
insurrection
and *jus militare* 28
Inter-American Commission on Human Rights (IACHR) 222
international aid 195–6
International Bill of Human Rights 64
international climate justice
definition 217–19
legal enforcement
non-state actors 222–7
state actors 224–5
International Commission on Intervention and State Sovereignty (ICISS) 255–7
responsibility to protect (R2P) 9, 255–7
global support and opposition 257–61
International Court of Justice (ICJ)
Anglo-Iranian Oil case 130–31, 140
International Covenant on Civil and Political Rights (CCPR) 64, 65, 82–3
obligations of contracted parties 87–9
International Covenant on Economic, Social and Cultural Rights (ICESCR) 64
International Criminal Court (ICC)
Palestinian civilian access 74–5
Rome Statute 103, 119–20
International Criminal Tribunal for the Ex-Yugoslavia (ICTY) 71, 118
International Criminal Tribunals of Rwanda 4, 118
international humanitarian law (IHL)
civil protection 3–5, 65–7
enforcement 70–72
universal jurisdiction 76
international institutions
justice, virtue of 296–9
arbitration 293
'civilised' and 'uncivilised' 290–91
Concert of Europe 292
Empire 291
Middle Kingdom 291–2
non-governmental or 295
United Nations 293–5
International Labour Organisation (ILO)

Declaration on Fundamental Principles and Rights at Work 154
Tripartite Declaration 153, 154
international law 303–9
civil protection 3–5
non-state actors 6–7
non-state actors role 6–7
principles
overview 313–14
International Law Commission (ILC), Anglo-Iranian Oil case 131
International Rule of Law (IROL) 239–43
concept of justice 288–9
concept overview 239–40
formal conceptions
formal legality 241
preventative function 243
Rule by Law 241
formal legality
requirements 245–8
non-state actors (NSAs) role and obligations
substantive conceptions 243–4
Inuit Circumpolar Council 222
investment treaty arbitration
ejusdem generis rule 134–6, 143, 144
most-favoured-nation (MFN) clauses
Anglo-Iranian Oil case 130–31, 140
applicability 128–30, 132–3
breaches in provision 130–31
Daimler Financial Services v Argentine Republic 136, 140
EDFI v Argentina case 131–2
effective interpretation principle 138–44
ejusdem generis rule 134–6
function 127–8
grounds for claim 130–32
Impregilo v Argentina tribunal 141–2
interpretative rules 137–8
multilateralism/bilateralism 135–6
umbrella clauses 131–2
Wintershall Aktiengesellschaft v Argentine Republic 137–8
irregular forces
belligerent's privilege criteria 44–6
European approach 34, 36–8, 42
guerrillas 35, 36, 41
levée en masse 34–8
Mosby's Raiders (US) 40–41
Ordenanza 36
partisans 40–41
prisoner of war status 42–4
US approach 34, 38–42
Islam 304
Italy
Pinto Act 93–4

Jay Commission (1794) 293
Jones and Others v UK 116
Judaism 304
jus ad bellum 30–31, 34
jus cogens 101, 103, 106
jus gentium 30–31
jus in bello 30–31, 35, 42, 54, 56
jus militare see also Just War Theory
belligerent's privilege
combatant immunity 23–4, 29, 34
criteria 29
overview 23
prisoner of war status 24
and insurrection 28
and non-Christian conflicts 28
non-combatants 27–8
overview 24
for the 'privileged' classes 24–7
right authority 24, 26–7, 29, 34, 35
Just War Theory 24–6, 290–91
dualistic axiom 30–31, 32
jus ad bellum 30–31, 34
jus gentium 30–31
jus in bello 30–31, 35, 42, 54, 56
temperamenta belli 31, 35

Kano trovafloxacin trial litigation 181–2, 183, 188–9
Khulumani Group 205–7, 208
Kiobel v Royal Dutch Petroleum Co (2013) 163–7, 186–7
Kyoto Clean Development Mechanism (CDM) 226
Kyoto Protocol 213, 214, 220–22, 225

labour rights 154, 156

Lama, Col. Kumar 105
Landsturm edict (1813) 37
Landwehr 37
Law of Armed Conflict *see* international humanitarian law (IHL)
'law of peoples' 282–3
law of war *see also* international humanitarian law (IHL); Just War Theory; responsibility to protect (R2P)
belligerent's privilege
combatant immunity 23–4
criteria 29
dualistic axiom 30–31
overview 23
prisoner of war status 24
Brussels Declaration 42
codification of *levée en masse* 44
dualistic axiom 30–31, 32
Hague Conventions 42
irregular militias
European approach 36–8
jus militare
and insurrection 28
and non-Christian conflicts 28
non-combatants 27–8
overview 24
for the 'privileged' classes 24–7
reciprocal agreements 31–3
right authority 24, 26–7, 29, 34
Just War theory 290–91
Lieber Code (General Orders 100) 39–42
monetary claims 24, 26
League of Nations 293
legal formalism 241
lèse majesté 27, 29
levée en masse 34, 44
levée en masse
belligerent's privilege 53
liberal constitutions 86–7
Liberia
Charles Taylor case 118
Libya
NATO intervention 266–8
NATO intervention in Libya 276
Lieber Code (US) 39–42
guerrillas 41
levée en masse 41
partisans 40–41
prisoner of war status 39–41
Lubanga, Thomas 118

Martens Clause 48
medieval law of war 24–9
Mexican–American War (1846–48) 39
Mexico
irregular militias 37–8, 39
Middle Kingdom 291–2
Milieudefensie 157
Millennium Development Goals (MDGs) (UN) 2–3, 289
Millennium Project (UN) 2–3
'mission creep'. 267
moderation in war *see temperamenta belli*
monism 87
Mosby's Raiders 40–41
most-favoured-nation (MFN) clauses
Anglo-Iranian Oil case 130–31, 140
applicability
conditions 132–3
substantive v procedural obligations 128–30
breaches in provision 130–31
Daimler Financial Services v Argentine Republic 136, 140
EDFI v Argentina case 131–2
ejusdem generis rule 134–6, 143, 144
function 127–8
Impregilo v Argentina tribunal 141–2
interpretative rules 137–8
effective interpretation principle 138–44
limitations
ejusdem generis rule 134–6
multilateralism/bilateralism 135–6
umbrella clauses 131–2
most-favoured-nation (MFN) clauses
Wintershall Aktiengesellschaft v Argentine Republic 137–8
multinational corporations (MNCs)
accountability 152
addressing corruption 154–5
case law (US and EU) 156–9
environmental protection 152–3, 156–7

Guidelines on Multinational Enterprises (OECD) 152–3
Guiding Principles on Business and Human Rights (UNSRSG) 153, 154, 155–6
human rights 153–4, 156, 156–7, 168–70 *see also* nonconsensual human experimentation
labour rights 154, 156
Norms on the Responsibilities of Transnational Corporations (UN) 153
role of NGOs 194
the Sullivan Principles 202–3
Tripartite Declaration (ILO) 153
UN Global Compact 153, 154–5
Alien Tort Statute (ATS) (US) 156–9
corporate social responsibility (CSR) 202–3
corporate veil 159, 195
definition 151–2
EU regulations 158, 159–63
financing the Apartheid regime 201–2
foreign direct investment 193, 195–6
impact of globalization 194–7
legal structure 151–2
pharmaceutical industry 179–90, 204–5, 207–8
power and influence 193, 197
role 194
Treatment Action Campaign (TAC) 204–5

Napoleonic Wars (1803–15) 36–7
Nepal
Col. Kumar Lama 105
criminal justice system 105–6
Netherlands
approach to *levée en masse* 34
New Partnership for Africa's Development (NEPAD) Declaration 196
Nicaragua v The United States of America (1986) 114
Nigeria
Kano trovafloxacin trial litigation 181–2, 183, 185–6, 189
Kiobel v Royal Dutch Petroleum Co (2013) 186–7
Non-Aligned Movement (NAM) 259
non-combatants
immunity 35
nonconsensual human experimentation 170–71
Alien Tort Statute (ATS) (US) 184–6, 188–9
AstraZeneca Ticagrelor experiment 182
clinical trials 179–80
contributing factors 183
Filártiga v Peña-Irala (1980) 187
GlaxoSmithKline Synflorix experiment 182–3, 188
Kano trovafloxacin trial litigation 181–2
Nongovernmental International Panel on Climate Change (NIPCC) 216
non-governmental organizations (NGOs)
activity in Apartheid South Africa 199–200
Khulumani Group 205–7
proliferation through globalization 197–9
pursuit of justice 295
role 194
Treatment Action Campaign (TAC) 204–5
non-state actors (NSAs) *see also* multinational corporations (MNCs); non-governmental organizations (NGOs)
abuse of position 7, 237–8
advocacy role 238
categories 215
climate justice enforcement 222–7
definition 234
environmental protection role 214–16, 219–22
human rights protection role 6–7, 236
law enforcement role 238
legal status 233–5
peace-building role 238
positive roles 238–9
relations with violating states 236–7
rights and obligations 235–6
as subjects of international law 234
supervisory function 239

'normative fact' 304
Norms on the Responsibilities of Transnational Corporations (UN) 153, 155
Nuremberg Trials 117

occupation
and belligerent's privilege 53–4
Operation Cast Lead (2008–09) 68
Optional Protocol (UNCAT) 104
Ordenanza 36
Organisation for Economic Co-operation and Development (OECD)
Guidelines on Multinational Enterprises 152, 153, 155

partisans 40–41
belligerent's privilege 51–2
Peninsular War (1807–14) 36–7
Permanent Court of Arbitration 293
Pfizer
Kano trovafloxacin trial litigation 181–2, 183, 185–6, 189
pharmaceutical industry 182
clinical trials
AstraZeneca Ticagrelor experiment 182
contributing factors 183
geographic location 179–80
GlaxoSmithKline Synflorix experiment 182–3
Kano trovafloxacin trial litigation 181–2, 183, 185–6, 189
HIV/AIDS drugs 204–5, 207–8
pilot-judgement procedure 92–3, 97
Broniowski v Poland (2004) 95–6
Pinochet No.3 judgement (1999) 102, 111–14
Pinto Act (Italy) 94–5
Poland
human rights law (HRL) 94–5
Presbyterian Church v Talisman Energy 156
pressure groups *see* non-state actors (NSAs)
prisoner of war status
and belligerent's privilege 23, 24
irregular militias 42–4
Lieber Code (US) 39–41
privileged combatants *see* belligerent's privilege
procedural justice 288, 296
Prosecutor v Thomas Lubanga Dyilo 106, 118
protected persons 67
Prussia
Franco-Prussian War (1870–71) 38
levée en masse 34, 37, 38

Questions Concerning the Obligation to Prosecute or Extradite (Belgium v Senegal) 104–5

racist regimes
and belligerent's privilege 53–4
ransom 27
ratione materiae 102, 107, 111–17
ratione personae 102, 108–11, 121
Rawls, John 281–4
reciprocal agreements 31–3
religion
and concepts of justice 303–4
repetitive case applications *see* pilot-judgement procedure
Respect, Protect and Remedy Framework 203
responsibility to protect (R2P) 9, 255–7
coercive intervention 266–74
detection and prevention 264–6
General Assembly 2009 Debate 261–5
global support and opposition 257–61
NATO intervention in Libya 266–8
to three-pillar approach 269–74
global–regional partnership 265
intervention parameters 265–6
invocation 260
NATO intervention in Libya 266–8, 276
three-pillar approach 261, 262–4
restorative justice 289–90
retributive justice 289, 297–8
right authority 24, 26–7, 29, 34, 35, 56–7
right conduct in war *see jus in bello*
right to go to war *see jus ad bellum*
Roberts, Sir Adam 49
Rome Statute 103, 119–20

Royal Dutch Shell 157, 163–7
Ruggie Framework 203
Rule by Law 241
Rule of Law (ROL) *see* International Rule of Law (IROL)
Rule of Prior Exhaustion of Local Remedies 83–4
Russia
  human rights law (HRL) 96
Rwanda
  International Criminal Tribunals 4, 5, 118

Saro-Wiwa, Ken 157
Scott, General Winfield 39
secessionist movements 43
Senegal
  Questions Concerning the Obligation to Prosecute or Extradite (Belgium v Senegal) 104–5
Sharpeville massacre 201
social contract theory 281–4
Socio-Economic Rights and Accountability Project (SERAP) 215
Sosa v Alvarez-Machain 185, 187
South Africa
  NGO activity
    categories of NGO 199–200
    HIV/AIDS campaign 204–5
    Khulumani Group 205–7, 208
  Sharpeville massacre 201
  Truth and Reconciliation Commission (TRC) 206
sovereign authorization *see* right authority
sovereign states *see* states system
sovereignty 33
Spain
  Peninsular War (1807–14) 36–7
Special Committee Against Apartheid (UN) 200–201
Special Court for Sierra Leone (SCSL) 118
spoils of war *see jus militare*
State immunity 101–2, 106–8
  Al-Adsani v UK (2001) 116–17
  Arrest Warrant case 114–17
  Charles Taylor case 118
  and individual criminal responsibility 117–18
  International Criminal Tribunals of Rwanda 118
  International Criminal Tribunals of Yugoslavia 118
  Jones and Others v UK 116
  Nicaragua v The United States of America (1986) 114
  Nuremberg trials 117
  Omar Al Bashir case 118, 120
  overview 101–2
  Pinochet No.3 judgement (1999) 111–14
  Prosecutor v Thomas Lubanga Dyilo 106, 118
  ratione materiae 111–17, 121
  ratione personae 102, 108–11, 121
  Tokyo Trials 117
State Immunity Act (1978) (UK) 108
state of nature 287, 290
states system
  'civilised' and 'uncivilised' 290–91
  Concert of Europe 291–2
  and Empire 291
  governance values 287–8
  international arbitration 293
  justice, virtue of 288–90
  legitimacy 284–6
  Middle Kingdom 291–2
  solidarity/community virtues 286–7
  stability 284
  state of nature 287, 290
Stateville Penitentiary malaria Study 180
Statute of the Council of Europe (CoE) 81
substantive justice 288, 297
  human rights 288–9
Sudan 119
Sullivan Principles 202–3
Synflorix clinical trial 182–3, 188

Taylor, Charles 118
temperamenta belli 31, 35
terrorism 8–9
Third Geneva Convention 1949 (GPW) 24, 47
Thor Chemicals 158
Ticagrelor clinical trial 182
Tokyo War Crimes Tribunal 117
torture

official State use 103–6
prohibition 101
State immunity from prosecution 101–2, 106–8
test cases 104–5
and universal jurisdiction 103–6
Trafigura case 158
Treatment Action Campaign (TAC) 204–5
treaty arbitration *see* investment treaty arbitration
Treaty of Westphalia (1648) 284
Tripartite Declaration (ILO) 153, 154
Truth and Reconciliation Commission (TRC) 206
Tuskegee Syphilis Studies 180

unification movements 43
unilateral declaration 93–4
Union Carbide 157, 189
United Kingdom
Criminal Justice Act (1988) 105
State Immunity Act (1978) 108
United Nations
Basic Principles and Guidelines on the Right to a Remedy and Reparation for Victims of Gross Violations 84–5
Charter 9, 81
Climate Ethics Consensus (CEC) 219
Conference on Trade and Development (UNCTAD) 151
Convention against Torture (UNCAT) 103–5, 121
Environment Programme (UNEP) 216
Fact Finding Mission on the Gaza Conflict 72–3
Framework Convention on Climate Change 213, 214
Global Compact 153, 154–5
Guiding Principles on Business and Human Rights 7
Guiding Principles on Business and Human Rights (UNSRSG) 153, 154, 155–6
High-Level Panel on Threats, Challenges and Change (UN) 1–2
Human Rights Committee 82–3
inequality between member states 296
Kyoto Protocol 213, 214, 220–21
Millennium Development Goals (MDGs) 2–3, 289
Millennium Project 2–3
Norms on the Responsibilities of Transnational Corporations (UN) 153, 155
responsibility to protect (R2P) 9, 257–61
coercive intervention 266–74
conduct guidelines 274–5
detection and prevention 264–6
General Assembly 2009 Debate 261–5
global–regional partnership 265
intervention parameters 265–6
invocation 260
NATO intervention in Libya 266–8, 276
Secretary-General reports (2010–12) 262–4
three-pillar approach 261, 262–4, 269–74
role and functions 293–5
Special Committee Against Apartheid (UN) 200–201
World Summit (2005) 255–7
United States
Alien Tort Statute (ATS)
challenges to 186–7
Daimler AG v Bauman et al 168–70
Filártiga v Peña-Irala (1980) 165, 167, 184, 187
Kano trovafloxacin trial litigation 185–6
Kiobel v Royal Dutch Petroleum Co. 163–7, 186–7
multinational corporations (MNCs) 156–9
overview 183–4
Sosa v Alvarez-Machain 184–5
use by victims of human experimentation 184–6, 188–9
use post-Apartheid 206–7
approach to *levée en masse* 34
corporate accountability
case law 156–9

Daimler AG v Bauman et al 168–70
extraterritorial jurisdiction 163–7
councils of war 39
environmental abuse 222
Environmental Protection Agency (EPA) 217
irregular militia treatment 38–42
Lieber Code (General Orders 100) 39–42
Mexican–American War (1846–48) 39
Mosby's Raiders 40–41
United States v Alvarez-Machain 184–5
Universal Declaration of Human Rights 64
universal jurisdiction 5–6, 76, 101
and torture 103–6
unprivileged belligerent *see also* belligerent's privilege
under the Geneva Conventions 54–5
protections 24
reciprocal agreements 31–3

veil of incorporation 159, 195
Vienna Convention on Diplomatic Relations 108
Vienna Convention on the Law of Treaties 136
volunteer corps 44–6

Wintershall Aktiengesellschaft v Argentine Republic 137–8
Wiwa v Royal Dutch Shell 157
World Summit (UN) (2005) 255–7
World Wars I & II 49
World Wide Fund for Nature (WWF) 216

Yugoslavia
International Criminal Tribunals 4–5, 71, 118

Zardad, Faryadi 105

For Product Safety Concerns and Information please contact our
EU representative GPSR@taylorandfrancis.com Taylor & Francis
Verlag GmbH, Kaufingerstraße 24, 80331 München, Germany